DONALD MUNRO, CHAMBERLAIN OF THE LEWS (LEFT), IN STRIKING POSE WITH ONE
CAPTAIN SINCLAIR OF THE MILITIA STATIONED AT THE MANOR FARM, STORNOWAY
used by kind permission of Sheriff Colin Scott MacKenzie DL

None Dare Oppose

None Dare Oppose

The Laird, the Beast and the People of Lewis

John MacLeod

BIRLINN

First published in 2010 by
Birlinn Limited
West Newington House
10 Newington Road
Edinburgh
EH9 1QS

www.birlinn.co.uk

ISBN: 978 1 84158 909 1

British Library Cataloguing-in-Publication Data
A catalogue record for this book is available from the British Library

Typeset by Iolaire Typesetting, Newtonmore
Printed and bound by MPG Books Limited, Bodmin

for
Peter Cunningham
Jordanhill boy and Highland gentleman

Contents

Preface

The name of Donald Munro – a fourth-rate provincial solicitor from Tain who, by craft and cunning, attained, and abused, untrammelled power over the Isle of Lewis for almost a quarter of a century – is still execrated in the West Highlands.

But the story of this evil man, and how he was finally brought down by the brave and disciplined men of one small Lewis corner, deserves a wider audience. And it has to be understood, too, within the general context of Lewis history and the wider picture of a new and malignant Highland land-lordism which had such infamous consequence generally in the nineteenth century. There has only been one previous attempt – by James Shaw Grant, in 1992 – to explore the career and atrocities of Donald Munro and, unfortunately, though a very important source, it is far from Grant's best book and has never been widely read.

I am grateful to Hugh Andrew, Andrew Simmons and all at Birlinn Ltd, Edinburgh, for the opportunity to write this study. I owe much besides to many previous writers over the decades, whom I have acknowledged in a comprehensive bibliography; to Mrs Mary Ferguson and all staff of Storno-way Public Library; and to Mr Malcolm MacDonald of the Stornoway Historical Society. I am most grateful to staff of Museum nan Eilean, Stornoway, for furnishing images, and to the family of the late Norman Morrison of Shawbost, *Tormod an t-Seoldair*, for gladly assenting to the use of his warm, dignified photograph of one island family. A casual chat at a local barbecue with Mr Alasdair MacLeod and Mr William MacKay cast a new light on the modern affairs of Jardine Matheson. And I have a particular debt to that great lady, Mrs Mor MacLeod of Brue, folklorist and tradition-bearer; born in 1914, Mrs MacLeod personally remembers many who witnessed these events, and in conversations over the years has done much to bring them to vivid life.

Dr Robert Dickie and Mr Bill Heaney patiently looked over this work in draft and made many useful and helpful comments. I am indebted to Lawrence Osborn for his editorial services in personally difficult circumstances. And

I appreciate besides the ongoing friendship of Mr Duncan MacLean, Mr Ruairidh Moir, Mr Tearlach Quinnell and Mr David Torrance; and the diverting messages from Mr Daniel Murray in the final days of toil.

John MacLeod,
Marybank, Isle of Lewis,
November 2010
jm.macleod@btinternet.com

1

Judgement: A doctor is called . . .

August 12, 1890; and late, late this night on this silent Stornoway street, and a thick black night it was for the time of year, with summer fast ebbing and an unease and chill in the wind, and dark fowl flying, and something still heavier and unspoken in the air – late, when Anna, a shawl draped over her nightgown, answered the insistent knocking at the door.

Anna was maid to Dr Charles MacRae, and she was young, and she was from Bernera in Uig, and it was by no means uncommon – considering his profession – for urgent word to the household at any hour of the night, to call forth her master and his skills.

And, of course, she knew the old man concerned – this Donald Munro, that disgraced one, that dethroned chamberlain, now gurgling his last a little up the road; knew his name; knew it as a byword for evil and oppression – and especially as a daughter of Bernera; had often passed him in his last broken years, limping through Stornoway in threadbare garb and with the heels of him coming through his shoes, and the urchins of town skipping about him, mimicking, mocking, 'Cuiridh mi às an fhearann thu! Cuiridh mi às an fhearann thu! I'll have the land from you! I'll have the land from you!'

And sometimes he would wheel, and snarl, and wave his stick, and if authority and terror had long forsaken him, the darkness in the man – now baleful, raging, fit to spit in the eye of Jehovah – was more ghastly than ever. She had known he was not well. She had not known, until just now, that it was unto death, and Anna could not – though it did disturb her – quite suppress something of fierce relief in her. And she wondered now, tripping up the stairs to rouse her master, if it were for the soul of Donald Munro this night that the ravens flew.

Her master was already up, half-dressed, fumbling with cufflinks. He was the son of the late *Maighstir Uilleam*, the Reverend William MacRae, sometime parish minister of Barvas; and in that trade – Anna knew – *Tearlach a' Maighstir Uilleam* had intended himself to follow. And he had applied, and had trained, and the day came for Charles MacRae to be licensed to preach the Gospel, and the Presbytery assembled; and at a critical moment – when any present with an objection to the life or doctrine of Mr Charles MacRae was now invited to make themselves known – a man had risen, and declared – amidst gasps and whispering – 'As long as my right arm is in my sleeve, this man will never be a minister of the Gospel.' And when ground was demanded, he announced, 'There is a girl with child' – naming her – 'and he is the father.' And the Moderator turned and asked the young man, 'What have you to say?' and he said, white-faced, 'I have nothing to say in answer to that.' And not a sermon, then, did he ever preach; but Charles MacRae took a steamer back to the mainland and went by gig and rail to the city, and trained anew for the cure of bodies.

He was in a class taught by James Young Simpson, the pioneer of chloroform in anaesthesia, and in his final year Charles walked away with the class medal, and changed his first name to Doctor. He could have made a name, a reputation, a fortune in the city. But – and we cannot now know why; and we can barely imagine the courage it took in the circumstances – he returned to his native island, and to the looks and nods and murmuring, and where fees (which many could not pay at all) were as apt to be rendered in chickens as in silver; and Dr Charles MacRae would serve it, selflessly, for 55 dogged, thoughtful years as a wise, determined physician – for many of them one of only two on all Lewis.

And Anna knew besides that once, years afterwards, in a certain district, Dr MacRae had looked sharply at a lass by the road, and ordered his coachman to stop the gig, and called the girl over, and said, 'Co leis thu? Whose are your people?' And she said, 'They say that I am the daughter of Tearlach mac Mhaighstir Uilleam, Charles the son of the Reverend William.' And the doctor said no more, and told her nothing, and asked her nothing, but instead gave her money, and as far as Anna knew or anyone knows to this day, he never laid eyes on his daughter again, but grew in girth, and in stature, and in esteem, as a loved, respected island institution.

But something hardened in that expression when Anna told him the present duty, and he grabbed what he needed, and she helped him with his frock-coat, and he donned his tall hat, and stepped out into the blustery gloom, and his authoritative steps faded up the street.

Anna knew the drill of those occasions: that Dr MacRae might be gone a good while; that she had things to do. She set and lit a fire, and she made for the kitchen to be sure there was enough for an unexpected cold collation – bread, butter, beef, ham, pickles; and all in readiness for some tea, and perhaps a glass of what was not tea.

Dr MacRae was not away long.

She answered the door for him, and he strode in. There was something set about his face and a look that was terrible in his eyes.

'What will you have, sir?' said Anna, after moments of strain and silence.

Dr Charles MacRae gazed at her, and with eyes that did not quite see her; for he was thinking on a day in court, and a wild-eyed mother, and a terrorised father, neither of whom saw their fiftieth birthday, and he thought, especially, of their tiny twins, who had never attained their first.

And Anna still remembered those words some 40 years later, as Mor, hearing them then, recalls them in solemn relish a further 80 years later in this July of 2010, and to the very syllable. 'Please give me a basin,' rasped Dr MacRae, in Gaelic, 'with warm water, Lysol and soap. I need to wash my hands, because I have been handling the body of the Beast.'

Donald Munro was a minor provincial solicitor who, on 5 November 1841, newly arrived on the Isle of Lewis, was admitted to practise in Stornoway Sheriff Court and 'having taken the oaths to government and *de fideli administrione officio*', the faithful execution of his office, was appointed procurator fiscal for all Lewis.

The post – roughly equivalent to that of a district attorney in America – put Munro in charge of all local law enforcement, criminal investigation and the prosecution of offenders; power, in the circumstances of any rural community in early Victorian Scotland, which might have turned the head of any fellow. Unfortunately, Donald Munro was not any fellow. He was an officious, vindictive, highly dangerous man; in many respects echoing the sort of humourless jobsworth – still with us today – who will fully exploit any position, however minor, in a sort of bleak spite. Worse, Munro was a wicked man, who – to this day – is remembered on Lewis as a byword for absolute power coupled with petty, malignant and vainglorious evil.

Today such men seldom attain significant authority and in any event are constrained by all sorts of checks and balances: democratically elected councillors, a free and probing press, an articulate and confident public. There were no such restraints on Donald Munro, who began at once to amass as much power as he could, either into his immediate hands or those of people he could effortlessly dominate – people related to him; people who worked for him. In 1844, all Lewis was bought by a new landlord, James Matheson, and in 1851 this laird gave Donald Munro the break of his life, appointing him his factor for the entire estate. As 'Chamberlain of the Lews' – the grandiloquent title reflected the terrifying power this office afforded – the office was self-evidently incompatible with the post of procurator fiscal, which not only granted Munro might over criminal law but enormous, distorting influence over the due process of civil cases. But no one did anything about it. The irregularity would never have been tolerated down south but it was all right for the Outer Hebrides.

And the gross conflict of interest did not end there. Munro seized, annexed, wheedled or cheated his way to grabbing one post of influence after another. At the height of his reign – which lasted almost 25 years – he would hold nearly 30 public offices.

As factor, he was in absolute control of estate employment and, critically, crofting rents and tenancies, at a time when Highland smallholders enjoyed all the rights and security of a pub pianist. As procurator fiscal, he could direct criminal prosecutions, baffle any civil action against the Lewis Estate or himself: all the more easily when he was one of only two solicitors on the island, and the other, William Ross, was both his cousin and his business partner, and when Munro besides was a Justice of the Peace and a 'baron baillie' – able on any occasion to appear at Stornoway Sheriff Court under a variety of hats, and send forth the local police as his own private army. In any event, he commanded a real one, for Munro quickly made himself commanding officer of the local 'Volunteer Force', or militia, and could (and did) threaten to turn out its part-time troops on the rare occasions things became sticky.

Donald Munro also made himself chairman of each of the four Parish School Boards on Lewis – which, among other useful powers, gave him untrammelled appointment of many island teachers. He chaired besides the four Parochial Boards, which administered the new 'poor law' and its scanty benefits on Lewis, and exercised various other functions of local government. He made sure he was also the retained legal adviser to these boards. From its 1864 inception, he crowned himself vice-chairman of the Stornoway Harbour Trust (the laird, Sir James Matheson, was chairman, but happy to leave control of all local shipping and port revenues in the hands of his familiar, and seldom bothered to attend meetings); chief magistrate of Stornoway; deputy chairman of the Road Trust; a director of the Stornoway Gas Company (bankrolled by Matheson) and of the Stornoway Water Company (also bankrolled by Matheson).

Donald Munro became besides a Commissioner of Supply; a Commissioner under the Income Tax; and the island's only notary-public (alone qualified, in Scots law, to administer oaths). He was already a Freemason – which, however one might dismiss the more paranoid notions surrounding the Craft and its supposed nefarious reach today, was in the nineteenth century a considerable force in Scottish public life and is to this day no mean force in Stornoway – and even, laughably, and to cap everything, won himself the captaincy of the Matheson Cricket Club, though it is most unlikely this chilly fellow took any joy in the sport, or joy in anything much beyond the exercise of total power.

For, of course, he bent every one of those offices to the furtherance of his authority and reach as factor. By the mid 1850s, the power of the Chamberlain of the Lews was absolute. By 1865 – all the more abetted by an unquestioning, doting proprietor who, on several fronts and in other appointments, proved a woeful judge of character – Munro ran all Lewis with untrammelled despotism. He is recalled with loathing, of course, because he did very many vile things to poor, defenceless people. But he is hated still more – to this day – on other grounds.

For one, Munro himself was a Highlander (as, indeed, was his boss), son of a general merchant and reared in Tain, Easter Ross; not an English satrap or even one of the Gael's true and historic foes, a Lowland Scot. And he was a Gaelic speaker: oddly enough, the execrable character of that East Highland Gaelic (of flawed grammar, toiling vocabulary and unpleasant accent) is still darkly remembered on this island. For another, he was at once spiteful and capricious. There was no safe way under such a man, who could change his mind on a whim and lash out a talon regardless of any tenant's care, watchfulness or obedience. It was not merely enough to avoid offending the chamberlain. You could do nothing – nothing at all; not any improvement to your holding, nor betterment of your house, nor furtherance of your income – that might in the least way attract his attention. And, for still another, there was something irrational and inhuman about the chamberlain's lust for dictatorship. Munro made not the least effort to enrich himself. He seems never to have tried to build any sort of personal fortune. He lived modestly and in an unremarkable Stornoway town-house. He would leave nothing when he died, and for some reason that bewildered and angered the thousands who loathed him as much as anything else. Lucre and fraud and the heaping of much ill-gotten gold any Lewisman could understand, if not admire. Wintry, sterile and absolute malice he could not.

And avoiding the eye of this tyrant grew all the more difficult as the years passed, and Donald Munro piled ever more rules and regulations on the Lewis Estate, enforced them with full rigour, and demanded – on pain of eviction – entire and unquestioning obedience. 'The Commandments of our Great Master are only ten in number,' one crofter would in time lament, even years after Munro's fall, 'and a reward is offered if we keep them; but those of our well-meaning and easy insular tyrants are impossible of being observed; and all we can expect is to live as slaves and die as beggars.'

The chamberlain – locals at length referred to him despairingly as the 'Shah', or, still more darkly, the 'Beast' – would at last be overthrown by the concerted and desperate action of a people, driven at last to make a stand against him, shoulder to shoulder and whatever the consequences, in the drama of 1874 still remembered as the 'Bernera Riot' – though it was nothing of the kind.

Yet what was the first effective battle of what is now known as the 'Crofters' War' is oddly overlooked in most narratives of that people's struggle, which usually focuses on events in Skye almost a decade later. That is partly because Skyemen wrote much of the history and, no doubt, because a remarkable Skye woman – Mary MacPherson, *Màiri Mhòr nan Oran* wrote the best songs. It is partly because the Battle of the Braes, in 1882, and the dramatics ensuing, forced action from the Liberal administration of William Gladstone: whereby a Commission, under Lord Napier, made thorough investigation of Highland conditions. Though the administration fell before much could be done, a subsequent election in 1885, on a greatly enlarged franchise, returned the Liberals and Gladstone to power and besides saw the sensational election of four 'Crofters' Party' MPs. In short order the Crofters Holdings (Scotland) Act of 1886 at last granted absolute and enduring rights to Highland tenants.

But the men of Lewis had drawn first serious blood in the overthrow of Donald Munro. And it may be plain anti-Lewis spite, an abiding factor in wider Highland and even ecclesiastical sentiment to this day, that has largely brushed their achievement from wider awareness.

Lewis remains an oddly resented community, atypical in various Hebridean respects. No part of Gaeldom – or anywhere else in Scotland, save Shetland – has been more moulded by Norse influence, for a over a millennium ago it was thoroughly colonised by dozens, then hundreds, of young Viking men, who in turn were Gaelicised by local women. The Norse influence is evident to this day, in construction, in agricultural implements, in a distinctive Gaelic vocabulary, in the blond, blue-eyed and Scandic appearance of many Lewis people, and in topography. Lewis is so dominated by Norse place-names that any village dubbed in Gaelic, like Achmore or Ballantrushal or Tolsta Chaolais, is invariably of very modern creation; all coastal features (for the Vikings were quintessentially mariners) have Norse names; and, especially in the north of the island, even lochs and mounds and summer camps far inland are dubbed in Norse too. The contrast between the flat-voweled tones of the typical *Leodhasach* and the classically Highland, Gaelic lilt of someone from Harris (the southern part of the same landmass, but separated by a mountain range and with a wholly distinct history) is very striking to the visitor.

As this, essentially, is a tale about a lawyer gone wrong and a rule of law gone bad, we might look at one lingering legacy of Norse rule – the authority of the Brieves, who dispensed rough, ready, decisive and indeed hereditary justice. For the Brieve was the person of the given chief of Clan Morrison, in the north of Lewis: and their ancient seat was Dun Eisdean, more of a rock-stack than an island, a mile or so south of the Butt on the Minch coast. In later centuries the Brieve lived in a home, which still survives, as a grassed heap of stones, on the

Habost machair. These Morrisons, by the way – *Na Moireasdanaich* – are a clean different clan from the Morrisons of Harris, whose seat was on Pabbay (as a bardic cast to Clan MacLeod) and whose Gaelic patronymic is *Mac Ghille-Mhoire.* Some Lewis descendants indeed, until very recently, tried to preserve the distinction with the affected spelling of 'Morison'.

And, long after their legal office had gone, the house of the Brieves continued to produce gifted natural leaders: the most eminent Protestant ministers in Lewis, in the first centuries after the Reformation, were Morrisons of this line, and as recently as 1999 another, Alasdair Morrison, was elected the first Member of the Scottish Parliament for the Western Isles.

'The Brieve is a kind of judge among the islanders,' Sir Robert Gordon recorded sententiously, 'who hath an absolute judicatory, unto whose authority and censure they willingly submit themselves, when he determineth any debateable question between party and party.' So the Morrison chief presided over both civil and criminal cases, and his role was at once judicial and inquisitorial. It is doubtful – as Dr Donald MacDonald of Gisla sensibly warned – that the office was quite as ancient as some recent Celtic Twilight romantics have suggested; it may just have reached back to the first Christian millennium. And it is most unlikely, especially when we consider the Morrisons' impressive collection of local enemies, that their authority ran much beyond the modern parish of Barvas, which is all rural Lewis north of the Shawbost river on the west and Tolsta on the east. The *Deemster* on the Isle of Man, in historic times, was perhaps its nearest (and also, of course, Viking-begotten) equivalent: an acknowledged authority who pronounced not just on guilt or innocence, but also the appropriate 'doom', or punishment.

But, writes Dr MacDonald, the Brieve certainly 'was judge in cases of life and death, as well; as in the most trifling contentions. His presence, whether in house or field, on horseback or on foot, constituted a court; his decisions were guided either by what he could remember of like cases, or by his sense of justice, and this *lex non scripta* was called "breast law". On assuming office he swore he would administer justice between man and man as evenly as the backbone of the herring lies between the two sides of the fish . . .' It is highly doubtful that any Brieve ever spoke English, or needed to, though most were probably literate in Gaelic and there is evidence of some sort of basic, battered text carried about by successive executives of Morrisons and local justice. In an age, too, of daily subsistence and scrabble, when being fed and watered in prison would have been thought quite an attractive way of life, punishment was usually brutal. Most districts in northern Lewis have a *Beinn na Croiche* – a 'gallows hill'.

And the savagery with which the Morrisons fought their most bitter foe – the MacAulays of Uig – still lingers in local lore. There were vicious battles (usually about cows). A rock a little north of the Habost cemetery is still known as Clach na Fola or 'stone of blood', where the more respectable prisoners-of-war were beheaded, and not far away, close to the modern Butt of Lewis lighthouse, the less lucky MacAulays were shoved precipitously to eternity over the edge of Creag an Uigich, 'the Uigman's cliff'. Certainly, the folk memory of such all-encompassing office, still real to a late Habost grand-uncle of my own, Angus Thomson, would have been very vivid indeed even in early Victorian times and might well explain why men from Uig finally led the revolt against Donald Munro while those of Barvas and Ness failed to take any initiative until the chamberlain was fatally damaged.

Its engrained Norse legacy aside, Lewis is of Hebridean note in another respect. Whatever grievances have since been cultivated – it is much grander to assert that one's great-grand pappy was 'cleared' from Uig to Shawbost than to say that he was kicked out because he was up to his neck in arrears of rent – the island largely escaped the wholesale evictions and forced emigration for which the Hebrides and West Highlands two centuries ago became infamous. Certainly, especially in the early decades of the nineteenth century, people in certain districts were forced out, against their will, from their own lands to other parts of the island. Certainly – especially, as we shall see, early in the Matheson regime – there were programmes of assisted emigration overseas. But the 'Lewis Clearances', as Bill Lawson demonstrated in a controversial but incontestable paper some years ago, are almost wholly a myth. Lewis was never emptied as, for instance, Mull or Sutherland were emptied – reduced for the most part to human desert – nor as upended, with people being decanted back and forth and hither and yon at the whims of laird and factor, as the likes of Raasay, Harris or South Uist (which endured the cruellest Clearances of all, executed with shocking brutality).

As a result, granted besides certain commercial advantages and resources, and a clever and industrious and good-humoured people, the Isle of Lewis has maintained – into the twenty-first century – a considerable native population, if much reduced from its peak in 1911 of 29,603; it is much more imbalanced today in favour of the elderly, to the point where ongoing school provision is a matter of real crisis. She is the last corner of Scotland where Gaelic is still largely spoken and where Evangelical religion is still a respected (and hated) defining social force. Rural Lewis also boasts dozens of villages of remarkable human continuity. Nowhere in Harris will you find people on the holdings their forebears tilled 200 years ago. North of the border, in the likes of Carloway and Shawbost, Bragar and Arnol and the villages of Ness by the very Butt, families still reside in communities their forebears have occupied for a thousand years, as rooted and part of the very rock and soil themselves as any agrarian corner of the United Kingdom.

These are a decent, disciplined folk of quiet pride. And still another reason why the Munro decades are recalled so bitterly is how, under the indolent complacency of a new landlord, the folk of Lewis were systematically humiliated, forced to a grovelling, cap-tugging deference under a chamberlain of unmitigated wickedness and the bland condescension of his nouveau riche employers – gentry, but in many respects, their moral and spiritual inferiors.

Herewith a tale. Around 1850, as part of a wider programme of 'rationalisation' we shall examine in detail, Matheson decided to abandon plans to reclaim deep moorland for settlement and instead created new crofts on the 'skinned land' backing a few coastal villages, where peat had long since been cleared for fuel or where significant ground had been apportioned for a 'tack', or rented farm. One such tack was Pairc Shiabost – Park Shawbost – on the west side of Lewis; much of the neat dry-stone wall that surrounded the old holding still stands. It was now broken up into crofts, and local families in need of land (and many more from townships Matheson had cleared in Uig) were allotted them. Without additional aid or resources, they had to erect houses and break the ground. Much of the Park – the Estate grandly christened it 'New Shawbost' – is inordinately wet and boggy. The first months – years – were hard, as crofters and their families toiled to dig ditches and field drains, and bear creel upon creel – by the thousand – of seaweed and shell-sand from the shore, a good tramp away, to try and turn this indifferent, boulder-packed swamp into reasonable arable ground.

About 1855, Lady Matheson herself decided to sally forth from the new, stately Lews Castle to have a look. Even by one of her husband's new roads, it was no light excursion by horse-drawn carriage to Carloway and then up the West Side. At least she was under cover, which was just as well, for the day was inordinately wet. When the little party reached Pairc Shiabost to inspect the latest feat of Matheson beneficence, it was practically deserted. There was only one person to be seen, a middle-aged woman, labouring in her waterlogged field. (The burden of the croftwork fell much on women in what, like most of coastal Lewis, was essentially a fishing community; Angus MacLean, of 4 New Shawbost, was out as usual chasing ling by long-line with his crew, and to his wife Catherine fell most of the daily grind of winning the fruits of the soil.)

Lady Matheson was naturally gratified to see someone, and sent her coachman at once to fetch the peasant over. She padded humbly to the carriage, wiping earth and filth from her hands. She could not look Her Ladyship in the eye. And, of course, Catherine had scarcely any English; Lady Matheson had not then, and never would, make any effort to learn Gaelic. The coachman was pressed to service as an interpreter. Were the MacLean family happy here? Yes, indeed, thank you, Your Ladyship. Was the land good? Yes, Your Ladyship. Were they not glad to have their own land? Indeed, Your Ladyship. Was there many of a family? Yes, thank you kindly, Your Ladyship, the Lord had blessed them with six sons and two daughters. Were they not obliged to their gracious landlord? Indeed, Your Ladyship, they were very grateful indeed.

Lady Matheson felt very tickled by this encounter, and such humility and charm. She had so enjoyed meeting Mrs MacLean, she said. Well, I am most honoured to meet Your Ladyship. Would Mrs MacLean like to get a bolt of new cloth for a dress? I could not possibly be putting Your Ladyship to such trouble. But she insisted. Well, if it would please Your Ladyship. And what colour of stuff might Mrs MacLean like? I could not presume to advise Your Ladyship – whatever colour Your Ladyship saw fit. Well, fine cloth would be on its way, declared Lady Matheson, and bade farewell, and instructed her coachman to proceed back to town, highly delighted with the day's ploy.

Days later, family lore records, a bolt of beautiful red fabric – highly sought after and expensive – was delivered to that island black-house. But the ordeal my great-great-grandmother endured through those long, tense minutes – when one false word, a single mis-step before a great and august personage, could cost them home and land – still clutches today. Catherine, after all, was daughter of a blinded hero of the wars against Napoleon, happy wife to an industrious and literate man who, 30 years earlier, had been one of the very first in Shawbost to learn to read, and who had precented – as a young boy and in a little brown kilt – at great open-air services for that remarkable Highland evangelist, Finlay Munro. Indeed, Angus MacLean himself, the great-grandson of a chiefly MacLean of Coll who had fled to Lewis in 1689 after fighting for his king at Killiecrankie, was a descendant of princes, of the early Stewarts and The Bruce himself. He was, by blood and heritage, arguably of nobler stock than James Matheson. And Angus's wife, skilled and hardy and resourceful as she herself was, was in every important respect save riches and standing more than Lady Bountiful's equal. But all this good Lewis woman knew was anxiety and terror and self-doubt; and the protracted humiliation of their encounter rings down through the decades to her descendants like a slap across the face. And the vice of Donald Munro had only just begun to squeeze, and the meaningful rule of law to collapse.

The Long Island of Lewis and Harris is the largest of Great Britain's offshore islands – bigger than Skye, or Mull, or Islay, or Man, or Wight; but Harris has a very distinct geography and a quite independent history, and has little part in our story. Sir Donald Monro, Archdeacon of the Isles just before the Reformation, toured his territory in 1549 and afterwards, in an important account, wrote up his impressions; he recorded of Harris – in evident surprise and as an important selling-point – that 'there are no wolves there'. Over a century later, in 1654, preparing a rather impressive *Atlas Novus* and the first modern map of the Hebrides, Joannis Blaeu – a Dutch cartographer – laboriously recorded 'Lewis and Herray of the number of the Western Yles, which two although they ioyne be a necke of land ar accounted dyvers ylands.'

In fact, the boundary is some miles and a formidable mountain bulwark beyond the Tarbert isthmus. And the southern part of Lewis is relatively hilly, most notably in the Park and Uig districts and generally south of a geological fault running from Shawbost in the west to Laxay in the east. Lewis, as Roger Hutchinson neatly paints her, is the 'largest and most populous of all the Hebrides', and encompasses

the placid and picturesque lochside villages in the shadow of the mountains which separated them from Harris, the urban centre of Stornoway and the northerly windswept fishing parish of Ness. It ran from fertile machair soil on the north-eastern seaboards to rocky, cliff-bound inlets on the distant south-western shore. A vast, brooding, uninhabited moor of peatbog and low hills dominated its northern inlands, and to the south a kaleidoscope of miniature lochs shone under a flat and shifting sky. These no-man's-lands were deceptive in scale and proportion. While entirely visible from north to south and – mostly – negotiable on foot in a day, they were hostile, uncharted territory to any stranger. From the beginning of recorded time the stern heart of his island had offered refuge to the Lewisman, sanctuary from the incursions of violent invaders or officers of lowland law.

It was and would remain a proud and foreign place. Its size and variety of landscape meant that, almost uniquely within the Hebrides, Lewis was largely self-supporting. It had been able to survive, if not prosper, far from and free from the compromises of the British mainland. Its Gaelic language was . . . intact. Its faith was unitary. Its sons and daughters were far-flung, but their belief in themselves as Leodhasaich was strong. Even their accent, in Gaelic and English, was starkly different from that of any other Hebridean island. It was an intelligent, curious, obstinate voice, fully aware of and wholly indifferent to its insistent inflection.

This is an austere environment. The Long Island rests on 'Lewisian gneiss', a hard, impermeable, crystalline rock said to be the oldest in the world, and which flatly refuses to break down into good soil; what little it does yield is very acidic. The glaciers of the Ice Age scoured and crushed this terrain and draped it in no less impermeable boulder-clay. In early historic times the climate was much warmer and dryer than it is now; it has been reliably asserted that, at the time the Callanish Stones were built – probably 2200 to 1800 BC – the local weather resembled that of modern, southern France. Good arable ground had been built or won near the coast – slaked by blown, lime-rich shell-sand and fattened with seaware – and there was much low, shrub-like woodland. By the time the Viking incursions began in the last centuries of the first Christian millennium, the weather was changing. It grew rapidly much wetter and cooler, and the struggle of Lewis tree-cover to survive was not helped by the importation of grazing stock in unprecedented quantities, the felling of timber for new settlements – the distinctive Norse 'long-house' survived as the Lewis black-house far into the twentieth century, with some still being erected even after the First World War – and the slash-and-burn depredation of Magnus Bareleg, King of Norway, whose determined eleventh-century assault on renegade realms in the Hebrides is gleefully recorded in the sagas of, for instance, Bjorn Cripplehand, and included the deliberate firing of island forest.

But the new chill, soggy weather did the real damage; and the combination of acidic rock, cold conditions, a poor evaporation cycle and minimal drainage did to Lewis what it does generally: instead of decaying naturally into good earth, timber and vegetation dissolved into the black, carbon-packed colloid of peat. A blanket of the stuff – 10 feet deep in places – swathes Lewis to this day. Peat proved (and remains) a welcome source of fuel, free to anyone prepared to put in the hours and toil to win it; but it is largely resistant to agriculture, save for mile upon mile of what is effectively summer grazing, and indifferent at that. The Lewis economy became, and remains, emphatically coastal, save for the annual *airighean*, the 'shielings', when women and children early each summer moved for some weeks into the moor with their livestock, leaving the men to rethatch their homes and the arable crops to grow on the good 'by-land' unmolested by cattle. This ancient form of transhumance – among its last manifestations in Europe – would endure until after the Great War; the famous 'Point drove' – when crofters from the Eye Peninsula would merrily drive prodigious quantities of sheep through a seething, grid-locked Stornoway, late each spring, to grazings west of the town lasted into the 1970s, and some older islanders still regularly take a break in moorland summer-huts.

It was essentially a pastoral economy, centred not on the growing of crops (save for winter fodder and basic subsistence) but the tending of cattle; whatever the disadvantages of wet, mild West Highland weather, it is ideal for the growing of grass. 'Crofting', as we know it today – each family tied to a given strip of land, divided as fairly as possible between the rich, the indifferent and the appalling, and with rights besides in the common grazing of their township – is actually a most modern invention, scarcely 30 years old when Donald Munro's boots first hit Lewis. Indeed the word 'croft' is not Gaelic or even Scottish, but Dutch, and in daily conversation an islander refers to his 'holding' or 'lot'.

But Lewis was not, until around 1811, the modern landscape of straggling villages, houses facing each other across a road with each holding stretching behind like the tail of a tadpole. It was a place of huddled little settlements or 'clachans' by the shore, houses cheek-by-jowl, and working all the land, in communal rotation, by a system called 'run-rig'. Granted the safety valve of emigration, some support from seasonal employment on the mainland or at sea, and unmolested, unfettered access to available land, it supported a reasonable standard of living and a rich community life. And it went wrong, as part of a wider Highland problem, as de-cultured clan chiefs and lairds grew remote from their people and began to experiment in 'improvement' geared not to the good of their tenants but to their own enrichment.

The modern system of crofting was devised as a deliberate scheme to the benefit of landlords, at a time when the Napoleonic Wars made the import of chemicals essential for the manufacture of glass, soap and munitions very costly and the rich seaweed of the Hebrides and West Highlands – gathered as 'kelp' and burned to slag and a good source of potash and so on – for a brief period very, very lucrative. The land-holding class deliberately engineered a change in the law to price Atlantic emigration beyond the reach of the ordinary Highlander (to conserve its biddable labour-force) and likewise engineered a change in agriculture, to the crofting pattern, to ensure no household had quite enough land to live on and had to seek immediate means in the chill, drenching work of cutting seaweed – and on grossly exploitative terms.

Such engineering, in a day when homage to the supposedly equitable free market is all but de rigueur among British politicians, is a sobering reminder that through history it has been readily fixed to the advantage of the rich and powerful. The quiet oppression of the new order was all the more readily accomplished as the inept and ill-thought reforms to the Highland order of the 1745 Rising saw, in the succeeding decades, the wholesale emigration of the 'tacksman' class – the basically educated and generally sensible men in Hebridean communities who afforded their natural leadership. When the war against Napoleon ended, and the value of kelp collapsed, it brought economic and human catastrophe as lairds up and down the western seaboard struggled to maintain the cash-hungry lifestyles to which they had become quickly accustomed – or went bankrupt, letting their estates and affairs fall into the administration of 'trustees' who were invariably hard, distant lawyers and largely in Edinburgh, men who cared not for people but for balance sheets.

Lewis, as we shall see, escaped neither the kelp boom (though she survived its ultimate crash better than most of the Hebrides) nor the imposition of the crofting order. Her size and relative remoteness – and the fact that she had remarkably few proprietors – served to protect her in large part from the human disaster visited elsewhere. But she was nevertheless part of Gaeldom, that culture and heritage rapidly alienated from the Scottish court and national life from the early decades of the second millennium, despised, mocked and even feared in certain corners of our national establishment to this very day.

Anti-Highland prejudice is venerable; it can readily be traced back through the Battle of Harlaw (when the last seriously powerful Lord of the Isles bade, unsuccessfully, to win the Earldom of Ross for Clan Donald) to the rapid Anglicisation of the Scottish court from the reign of Malcolm Canmore and his bigoted, Romanising, Saxon queen. And the lies, even by early in the seventeenth century, were distinctly barnacled. But they were nevertheless potent, especially when allied to the fevered greed of the wisest fool in Christendom.

King James VI – chafing in the wings as he awaited further promotion to King James I of England – had persuaded himself by 1597 that this near-fabulous Lewis – this distant, heath-clad part of his realm – was a veritable El Dorado of wealth – 'inrychit with ane incredibill fertilitie of cornis and store of fischeings and utheris necessaries, surpassing far the plenty of any pairt of the inland'. It was such a pity about the people. King James made no secret of his view of them and, in the last years of the sixteenth century, it was endorsed not only by the Parliament of Scotland but, to their lasting shame, even by some leaders of the newly Reformed Kirk, which would prove so disgracefully slow in the evangelism of the Highlands and would take, incredibly, till 1801 to produce a complete translation of the Bible in Scottish Gaelic.

The folk of Lewis, declared the Scottish Executive of its day and its allies in prayer, were 'voyd of any knowledge of God or His religoun'; no more than a depraved peasantry 'gavin thameselfis over to all kind of barbaritie and inhumanitie'. In 1600, Scotland's Privy Council eagerly chorused in like sentiment, asserting that the distant islanders rejoiced in 'blude, murthour and all kind of barbarous and beastlie crueltie'. The latest Bishop of the Isles, Andrew Knox, was responsible before God and men for every soul in the Hebrides; that did not prevent his astonishing description of his flock as a 'falss generation' and a 'pestiferous' people, wholly dedicated to the pursuit of 'barbaritie and wickedness'.

There was only one way to claim the riches of Lewis for the better sort of Scot: by an early sort of venture capitalism and an initial essay in the 'plantation' policy King James would later export, far more successfully and with still bloodier and abiding consequence, to northern Ireland. The expedition history remembers as the 'Fife Adventurers' was given a respectable veneer of Protestant evangelism: an early, earnest star of the Kirk, Robert Durie, accompanied the party. But he was there not as a missionary, but as a padre to the bandits – led by the king's own cousin, the Duke of Lennox – and an accomplice to a policy shamelessly declared. It was a programme of genocide, of 'ruiting out the barbarous inhabitantis' by such 'slauchter, mutilation, fyre-raising or utheris inconvenieties . . . not by agreement with the country people bot by extirpation of thame'. Should any of the Lewis folk be thoughtless enough to survive their sovereign's kindly attentions, their economic prospects were bleak, for henceforth no land was to be 'disponit in feu, tak or utterways bot to Lowland men . . .' As James Hunter, in 1992, rightly observed, as far as King James and his councillors were concerned the people of the Hebrides 'were no more part of civil society than were the Cheyenne or the Sioux'.

In the event, the mission of the Fife Adventurers was a bloody, humiliating failure, a sustained, glorious, car-crash of an enterprise still of high satisfaction to anyone of Lewis descent. Fred Silver has written a good, detailed account in his 2009 study of Stornoway, and we need only summarise. The assorted colonials, robbers and mercenaries were ill-equipped, complacent and at the end of dangerously long, thin, supply lines. The MacLeods and the people of Lewis rose against them with desperate courage. Ships were captured in the open Minch; Stornoway Castle, initially taken by the Lowlanders, was seized once, then seized again – and held; and at last the entire murderous garrison was overwhelmed and put to the sword in a protracted and incredibly involved struggle and counter-struggle between assorted Lowland hopefuls and dubiously allied MacLeods who were not, as occasion suited, above betraying one another.

The scheming of the Edinburgh court coincided neatly with mounting crises among the MacLeods of Lewis and opportunistic manoeuvres by the Mac-Kenzies of Kintail, who coveted the lands (especially the hunting grounds and the fighting men by which a Highland chief's glory most counted) and were already ambitious allies of the Stuart monarchy. The MacLeods of Lewis, *Siol Torcuil* – 'Torquil's Seed', distinguishing them from the senior line of Harris and Dunvegan, *Siol Tormod* – would, just, beat off, with surprising success, the long and increasingly hopeless campaign of the Fife Adventurers. But while frustrating King James, they failed to beat the MacKenzies, and paid for it with their final dispossession and ruin. 'The Clan Torkil in Lewis were the stoutest and prettiest men,' wrote a clerical scholar, the Reverend James Fraser, in 1699, 'but a wicked, bloody crew whom, neither law nor reason could guide or model, destroying one another, till in end they were expelled that country, and the McKenzies now possess it.'

For the central problems were three. First, the MacLeod succession was in serious dispute after the final, lingering demise of the old chief, Roderick X, an illiterate dotard who could not even sign his own name, but who had managed in his 95 indolent years to beget an impressive variety of sons by a scarcely less impressive succession of wives and concubines. Second, one of those lads, Torquil MacLeod – *An Conanach*, or the man from Conon – was the son of an ill-judged third marriage by the old fool to Janet MacKenzie of Kintail; moreover, it was generally known on Lewis that his father was not Roderick X at all (whose conjugal capacities were by that point in well-deserved doubt) but a bastard of John Morrison, thirteenth and last of the brieves. This Torquil was silly enough to join the MacKenzie intrigue, and prudent enough around 1597 – a year or two after the death of Roderick X – to sign over the 'barony of Lewis' to them, rather than trying himself to seize it. Third – at a most critical period, when they were surrounded by enemies and with the state itself toiling to destroy them – the MacLeods persisted stubbornly in fighting each other, even as control of their island ebbed remorselessly away.

The king's expedition had been in conception since at least 1595. It would not be finally abandoned until 1613 and, when MacLeods were not busy killing Lowland nobles, or indeed other MacLeods, they had old foes closer at hand to make this an excessively interesting time in island history: notably their two ancient rivals, the MacAulays of Uig and those Morrisons of Ness. In just one detail from a saga so involved and bloody that one interesting Lewis historian, Donald MacDonald, in 1978 granted it several close-typed pages, Neil MacLeod – *Niall Odhar* – betrayed his own brother Murdo to the Crown and actually accompanied him south for trial and execution; moreover, toting it casually along as if it were his lunch, Neil carried the heads of 12 slain Morrisons in a sack. (And, this Cain and Abel of the Lews apart, there was the still bigger problem of Torquil Conanach and the MacKenzies.)

It was all sadly typical of a protracted, brutal period in Highland history, fruits of an ongoing anarchy the Scottish monarchy had itself created: barely a century before, the king's great-grandfather, James IV (our last sovereign who could speak Gaelic), had deliberately broken the last Lord of the Isles, annexed the title to his heir (it remains among the subsidiary handles of the Prince of Wales) and smashed what had been a strong, policing principality on the western seaboard without erecting any effective authority in its place. Perhaps the oddest aspect of the obdurate loyalty, to the last, of many noble Highlanders to the House of Stuart is why they persisted in such blind obedience to a dynasty whose policy in Gaeldom had been almost uniformly bad.

MacKenzie of Kintail – then really rather a minor clan in Highland affairs – lost their chief, Kenneth, in 1611, when the lately ennobled Lord MacKenzie of Kintail carelessly died; the new chief, Colin, was only a boy, and the final triumph in Lewis would be executed by his uncle and effective regent, or 'Tutor' – *Ruairidh Mor*, 'Big Roderick'.

Ruairidh Mor was as savage, when he deemed it necessary, as any godless Highland warrior of his day; he is unusual because of his robust honour – at no point, as he could readily have done, did he incarcerate or bump off his nephew and claim the great prize himself – and still more unusual, in this bloody era of West Highland history, because he was exceptionally smart.

By charm and hard argument the Tutor of Kintail had no difficulty reviving his late brother's mandate from the Privy Council – as 'His Majesty's Justice and Commissioner' for Lewis, to sail thereon 'and their with fire and sword and all kind of hostility, to search, seik, hunt, follow and persew, the said Neill his complices, assistaris and pertakers by sea and land, quairever they may be apprehendit' – and with an additional sweetener: entire immunity from prosecution, whatever means were deployed. Like the Campbells of Argyll, the Mackenzies had deftly positioned themselves in support of the Crown when the Lordship of the Isles was in its sights. By all this late calculation they had by 1600 won a precious thing – written title to their Ross-shire lands; in a few short years, by Ruairidh Mor's tireless endeavour, their domain would run from the northern Outer Hebrides to all Ross-shire and the Black Isle.

Niall Odhar was finally cornered on Dun Berisay in Loch Roag, tried to bargain with Edinburgh when he managed to capture a passing English pirate (whom, characteristically, he had taken care to befriend first), thought better of it, fled to Harris and was turned over to the Crown by Rory, his kinsman and the Harris chief. Niall Odhar was brought to trial in March 1613 for 'fire-raising, burning, murder, theft and piracy'. Proceedings were perfunctory. The verdict, of course, was a foregone conclusion. The last effective chief of the MacLeods of Lewis was beheaded at the Mercat Cross, Edinburgh, where we are assured he died 'verie Christianlie' – though one scrap of Lewis lore asserts that when, on the very scaffold, a young official told him rudely and in mongrel-Gaelic to hurry up, the tough old fellow laid him out with a single punch. Assorted minor MacLeods, despite a determined little pogrom – it would be very many years before it was safe to be known, on Lewis, as a near kinsman of the chiefly house – caused occasional trouble into the 1620s.

Sympathy should be limited; the MacLeods of Lewis had themselves won Lewis in disgraceful fashion from the Nicolsons, and subsequently hunted all conceivable Nicolson claimants to extinction with no less impressive industry.

But Ruairidh Mor – that sharp and selfless uncle – was now on Lewis, and a man whose ruthlessness would be bitterly remembered on the island, according to Donald MacDonald of Tolsta: there was for long a proverb that the three worst evils which could afflict a tenant were 'May frost, July mist, and the Tutor of Kintail'.

Though not much more vicious than the MacLeods, he was far cleverer. Shrewdly, though Ruairidh Mor soon seized Stornoway Castle – which survives today only as a pile of rocks beneath what is now the town's 'No. 1 Pier', and should not be confused with the Lews Castle of Matheson's erection – the Tutor for some time established MacKenzie headquarters not at Stornoway, which is almost an island between Broad Bay, the Eye Peninsula and the Minch and could readily be assaulted and besieged by enraged locals, but well to the south, by Seaforth Head at the inland extremity of the eponymous sea-loch.

Apart from the easier escape by sea to Skye and the mainland, and the much greater difficulty of gathering and leading a hostile force such a distance over grim cragged ground against the MacKenzies, the rich game of Park – the South Lochs peninsula – was a big attraction. The MacKenzies of Kintail had, even by the standards of Gaeldom, an unusual lust for field sports and a veneration of the deer that was all but occult. The heraldic crest of the MacKenzie chief was a stag's head, and his patronymic, *Caberfeidh* – literally, 'the rafters of the deer' – is a poetic reference to a great, triumphant hall crowned with antler trophies. (Today, it is best known in Lewis as the name of an expensive, decidedly mid-Atlantic Stornoway hotel, with just enough MacKenzie tartan and mounted horns to give the joint atmosphere.) The Tutor was not long in charge before a dyke had been built – good lengths of it still survive – between Loch Erisort and Loch Seaforth at the Park isthmus, setting it apart as a private playground.

It is noted to this day for fleet deer and fine trout; in odd anticipation of later events the Tutor henceforth forbade the people of Uig to shiel there in the summer, as they had done since time immemorial. Meanwhile, a great many MacKenzie tacksmen were now set up with lands here and there on Lewis, both as folk owed favours and a useful, supportive colonial class; two native clans – the MacIvers and the Morrisons – were readily brought on board as allies.

As if he had known a new age was coming, and had not the least desire to be part of it, the last Brieve, John Morrison, had already met a sticky end. More criminal than law-man, his name was already MacLeod mud after the widely known dalliance with the old chief's Kintail wife. Later, John had pirated a

Dutch ship, lured his hereditary enemy – Donald Cam MacAulay – aboard, got him thoroughly drunk, and lashed him to the mast. A watery end was planned when Domhnall Cam managed to escape, still with a great weight chained to his ankle; in the spirit of the day, he kept this triumphantly as a souvenir.

The boozy, womanising, violent antics of the final Brieve of Lewis soon ran out of road, about 1600. On a mainland jaunt to Assynt, he immersed himself – unnecessarily – in an exceptionally violent brawl, at Inverkirkaig, and was battered and hacked to death. His worthy henchmen were determined to take home the remains, but the weather was against them, and as a storm blew and blew they huddled grimly with the corpse 'on a little island off Lochinver', James Shaw Grant writes, 'still known as the Brieve's Island.' It was a long wait and it was warm weather. The brieve's body began to smell. Soon, it smelled very bad indeed, and – being practical Lewismen – they simply gutted him. John Morrison, thirteenth in his line and the end of his great if robust office, is largely buried in Ness, but his bowels lie in Sutherland. 'The last of the Brieves was clearly the representative of a society and polity in disarray,' Grant concludes, and adds rightly, 'which makes a nonsense of the popular belief that the watershed for the Gaelic-speaking Highlanders came at Culloden.'

In 1628 the MacKenzies, thoroughly enjoying their summer playground of Park, rubbed in their new island authority further with a detailed charter for the preservation of game and the punishment of poachers – and in this same year the grim old Tutor died, having completed a MacKenzie empire of such impact on Lewis that, to this day, more features and street-names in Stornoway honour a MacKenzie than any MacLeod (though the latter remains the commonest Lewis surname).

Colin, his nephew and the chief, was now a grown man. Handsome and popular – the beautiful Princess Elizabeth, daughter of King James and from whose Hanoverian grandson our present monarch's throne was inherited, used to coo over 'my Highlander' – young Colin had been cleverly sent off to court, partly to gain royal favour and partly to keep him out of the way.

And when, in 1623, King James decided to raise the pet and gentrified Teuchter still higher, the youthful chief of Clan MacKenzie – no doubt by his uncle's shrewd council – had chosen a title all the better to rub in the notable Lewis triumph. The Earl of Seaforth he duly became, processing regularly between his seats of power – 'Chanonry', or modern Fortrose; Brahan; and Stornoway. This House of Seaforth would last just long enough, in its westerly island dominion, for the arrival of Donald Munro.

2

Princes: The Seaforths; a curse; and Charles Edward Stuart

In 1613, a doughty MacKenzie uncle had cannily massed his fighting force at Seaforth Head, by the vitals of Lewis and with the Harris hills at his back. On 4 May 1746, at almost the same spot and in far less force, a brave, younger and rather less shrewd soldier pitched up on the shore in a much more hapless position. This was no MacKenzie, claiming at last estates wrung by law and guile from a Stuart monarch and now to be seized for real and by force. This was a Stuart, a great-great-grandson of that same king, and on the run for his life.

It was not three weeks after the debacle of Culloden. Charles Edward Stuart, titular Regent, Jacobite claimant to the throne, and son of the lugubrious, charisma-free zone that was 'King James VIII and III,' was still but 25 years old. He was a much more interesting fellow, and a lot tougher, than the impression given in surviving, oddly effeminate portraits. For a start, he was clever. By adulthood, the hope of the Jacobites was fluent in French, Spanish and Italian, as well as his native English – though born and raised in Rome and, by strict parentage, half-Polish, half-Italian. His English had a marked Irish accent and, by the end of his famous British adventure, Charles Edward had a good command of Gaelic.

He was very tall and, by the standards of his time, very handsome. He was tough, a good horseman, deft with a sword, and a crack shot: in those desperate weeks, his ability to bring down dinner on the wing, time after time and with a single shot, astonished the grubby little band of Irish and Highlanders who were now his only court. The prince enjoyed tennis and badminton, took a keen interest in art and music and science, and had but three weaknesses.

For one, Charles Edward could not swim a stroke. For another – and it was evident even in his teens – he had an undue taste for alcohol. And – third – he struggled with the truth, with honest appraisal of reality and in honest appraisal of others. There was besides a fourth problem. He hated his father (who in turn viewed him with loathing and envy). After 1744, though the Old Pretender lived another 22 years, they never met again, and the prince's transferred distrust of all older, senior, bossy figures did much to undo the '45 itself.

Self-discipline, and a buoyant optimism, had kept him in fine fettle until, at Derby, his officers finally revolted, tired of waiting for the flocking of untold English Jacobites to their colours and the arrival, in vast quantities, of French troops and French gold, as their prince had repeatedly promised them. (In fact, meaningful opposition on the road to London – where king and court were already on the brink of flight – was non-existent; the French were already moving but the clan chiefs and Charles Edward knew none of this, and at a critical moment a man, a Hanoverian spy called Bradstreet, was admitted to this council of war to relate a pack of lies.) The prince was implacably overruled and, in distant London, as word came that the terrible Highlanders had inexplicably turned tail and begun marching back to Scotland, the vital psychological advantage was lost. As that feline diarist Horace Walpole crowed joyfully in his journal, 'No one is afraid of a rebellion that runs away.'

Charles Edward cannot be blamed for the gutless loss of nerve by his commander, Lord George Murray (there are still those in the Highlands convinced that he, too, was a double agent on government pay, though it seems improbable) and his oversight of a central military principle: concentration of force. As Lord George seems to have had little clear idea what to do next, save to head north, and further north, and still further north, he must shoulder most of the blame for, by April 1746, luring a vengeful, frightened British army into the heart of the Highlands. And a useless Irish adjutant, John William O'Sullivan – placed in fateful charge of commissariat and logistics, on the basis of his greatly exaggerated competence – ensured only that, by Drumossie Moor, Charles Edward's army was malnourished and starving. (Lord George was still more angry about O'Sullivan's failure to move on cue and in strength at the Battle of Falkirk, which the Jacobites had won and, properly exploited, could have turned about the whole campaign.)

But Charles Edward – whose habits and character had deteriorated steadily after Derby, sleeping late and shaving erratically and drinking murderously – must take responsibility for Culloden. It was the one battle of the '45 he personally directed – from choice of the ground to tactics on the field – and the only battle of the entire Rising the Jacobites lost. But it was bloody, epochal – and terminal.

That was not least the prince's own choice, for there was a great pitched rally afterwards at Ruthven, south of Inverness, and an action could well have continued that might at least have diverted Hanoverian troops from their abundantly documented atrocities. But the prince sent only an imperious note to Ruthven. He had panicked, not least after evidence, before his very eyes, that his Highlanders were not in fact invincible. All must now make shift for themselves. He was flying to France and would return in short order with considerable force.

That was not lightly accomplished, through straths and glens, hills and Hebrides soon crawling with government patrols and girt by seas seething with the Royal Navy. It would be fully autumn before Charles Edward Stuart, with a fortune of £30,000 on his head and only a few desperate men for company and succour, was safe away to the Continent. His first venture at escape, after a frantic scuttle across country to the Moidart coast, was to the Outer Hebrides, making landfall on Rossinish, Benbecula, by a whisper – for the boat was leaking – and then cooking a crude dinner with great difficulty, in a pot with a hole in it. Word came from the local MacDonald chief, old Clanranald, imploring the prince to stay and fight – the clansman was shrewd enough to grasp the consequences for the Highland order if the government triumphed now – but word followed hard on that of a Hanoverian pincer-movement: Fort Augustus had fallen to the Duke of Cumberland, and the Earl of Loudon had arrived in some might at Arisaig from Skye. No campaign from the west could be renewed now. The prince abandoned brief dalliance with renewed endeavour, and determined to reach France. That meant securing a sizeable, seaworthy boat. And his best hope of obtaining one was the port of Stornoway.

It proved a fraught business, and the prince's ordeal, skulking about the western seaboard like a stalked deer, had latterly a nightmarish element, as this or that retainer and supporter came and went: Irishmen, Highlanders, a priest or two. They were not familiar with the coast of the Outer Hebrides, the glens of Skye or the mountains of Knoydart. The weather was less than co-operative and the craft they had about as seaworthy as a colander. Such locals as they encountered in Benbecula, though determined not to betray the prince, were equally determined not to help him in any way that could invite serious trouble. He kept recruiting oarsmen – the craft needed four – but these kept slinking off home, for fieldwork or family concerns or natural fear, whenever left unsupervised. Few who have done any serious camping or tramping in the West Highlands, or tried to explore uninhabited corners of the Hebrides by small boat, will not feel a sympathetic shudder for this ill-fated prince. Showers of rain, even in summer, can be horizontal, frequent and drenching. In late April and May, there can be violent hail. By June – and we have many notes of the prince's suffering in this regard – you have besides, in still and balmy conditions, to contend with midges. The wind is always capricious, and even an athletic young man will tumble, frequently and painfully, as he leaps ashore on steep, hard rocks vaguely discernible under slimy sea-wrack.

That first Benbecula dinner was of milk begged only with difficulty and beef shot and butchered without permission. Worse, there had been a breach of security: by great mischance, Clanranald's visitors on their arrival included the Reverend John MacAulay, young minister of South Uist and whose formidable father, the Reverend Aulay, was minister of Harris and a fervent supporter of the government. John lost no time dashing off a note to Daddy, who in turn sent word to still another minister – the Reverend Colin MacKenzie of Lochs – and meanwhile got up a little posse, mindful of the Protestant succession and no less mindful of £30,000. This frightful old man (who had blithely stolen the congregational library at his previous charge of Coll and Tiree) would take care to leave in his will a sum for the Harris beadle, to show future visitors where the great Mr MacAulay was buried. One Jacobite, Duncan Cameron, would leave more bitter memorial – 'a devil of a minister who did us a' the mischief in his power'.

Charles Edward and his party were, for now, blithely unaware; and his boozing was starting to cause comment. Weeks later, when they had been forced back to Uist, Neil MacEachen would recall that the prince 'took care to warm his stomach every morning with a hearty bumper of brandy, of which he always drank a vast deal, for he seemed to drink a whole bottle a day without being in the least concerned . . .' At a later, roisterous party, 'his Royal Highness was the only one able to take care of the rest, in heaping them with plaids and at the same time merrily sang the *De Profundis* for the rest of their souls.' Hugh MacDonald, another occasional good companion, saw the prince matched glass for glass with MacDonald of Boisdale, and although that minor chieftain 'was, I dare say, as able a bowlsman as any in Scotland', the heir *de jure* to the thrones of Great Britain, France and Ireland drank him under the table.

On the evening of 29 April they set heroically to sea, concocting a convincing story for the quays and howffs of Stornoway. They were all Orcadians. They had been shipwrecked – on Tiree. They would really like to charter a boat. While they were at it, they were rather keen, too, to buy a cargo of meal. The prince was 'Mr Sinclair, junior', and O'Sullivan his portly old father. But the weather was vile and a strong sou'-westerly wind precluded the risky voyage past East Loch Tarbert. The prince and his party were forced ashore at Scalpay. Scalpay was not then the bustling, faintly rapacious community that would be created – indeed, grossly overcrowded – as a by-product of the Harris Clearances, but (coupled with Maraig, a green inlet on the Harris side of Loch Seaforth) a tack, occupied only by Donald Campbell and his family. Mr Campbell was from a well-known and enterprising Harris family, with one of the most ancient lineages on the Long Island and who still prosper to this day. It is doubtful if Campbell hearts sang for joy as they grasped the identity of their guest. His good lady was a 'rigid Loyalist' of Jacobite sympathy, notes Eric Linklater; Campbell himself was a Whig and a dogged, though unenergetic, government supporter. But their hospitality is undoubted. The Campbells immediately laid and lit a great peat fire for the soaked, chill visitors, and the tenant then 'entertained the Prince royally in his farmhouse', writes Frank McLynn. 'There were eggs, milk and butter to eat. There was also a bed and clean sheets. But it is significant of the Prince's deep fear of betrayal that he insisted on sleeping with his clothes on.'

The prince was restless indeed: strained and frightened, eager for company and distraction. MacDonald of Baleshare, another witness to this period, later wrote Bishop Duncan Forbes for *The Lyon In Mourning*,

> He'd be on foot every morning before man or woman stirred in the hous, would go to the landlady's closet and ask what he'd have fore brakefast the day. Once this was told, he'd then ask what was for his neighbours. Be what it will, he was still pleased. One morning as he got up he goes in to the kitchin, where in a cask of seeds he found a cuple of new laid eggs, with which he coms to the landlady's closet, and begg'd the favour she'd allow him the eggs, which was done and prepared for brakefast. After brakefast he and one Kenneth Campbell, a young boy, the landlord's son, goes a fishing. The Prince catches a small coad, which he pouch'd and immediately went hom, stood by as it was dresst for supper . . . But now, as the boy and the fisher were returning home, there meets them a cow of Mr Campbell's bogg'd. The boy attempted to drive her out, but would not do for him. The fisher seeing this threw off his upper coat, into the ditch with Kenneth Campbell he gets and trails the cow out of the bog; got his britches and white stockiness all dirtied . . .

Donald MacLeod, a doughty 68-year-old Skyeman from Galtrigill in Duirinish, slipped ahead to Stornoway on 1 May. (It is one of the cruelties of history, as James Shaw Grant pointed out in 1977, that this brave old man – who accompanied Charles Edward at untold peril for two months, has been quite eclipsed by Flora MacDonald, who put up with the prince for all of two days and collared most of the publicity.) But MacLeod was nevertheless most anxious and frightened, and he was not the first man, and certainly not the last, to broach Stornoway on a fraught errand and fortify himself with a little Dutch courage.

As Donald MacLeod tippled, and talked in a succession of Stornoway hostelries, the prince had a serious fright: on 3 May, 'militiamen' – bored agents of MacAulay the local minister – landed on Scalpay. It was pure mischance. They had no idea Charles Edward was anywhere on Harris. He lay low and Campbell managed, under great strain, to steer the volunteers out of any notion of visiting his home. He seems flatly to have refused to lie: the prince was there, he was his guest, the party was armed and if the visitors wanted now to grab this prize clutch of Jacobites and the very 'Young Pretender', they would have to fight them – and him – and, indeed, Campbell himself. The prince, though, was now determined to run, and had the excuse once word came from Donald MacLeod in the distant town that he had managed to charter a brig. Their fragile boat was once again readied, the brandy immediately broached and – at Charles Edward's insistence – all took a celebratory dram before setting forth on voyage – not round by the broken, lonely, exposed coast of Lochs, in full sight of Navy patrols, but up the long, grey-green fjord that is Loch Seaforth.

It is possible the prince had no realistic idea of the terrain between Seaforth Head and Stornoway – in what would remain, for another century, a largely roadless island – and still less of the distance; even now, by a good paved highway, the walk would take a man a day. It was not far from dusk when their boat ground into the mud and wrack of Seaforth Head, and the nightmare that followed is well described by McLynn as Charles Edward, his little party and an unknown local guide tramped heroically to distant town. Linklater mentions one report that, wandering and weaving, they walked a full 38 miles; another says, in all, they took 18 wretched hours, for, as Frank McLynn describes:

> Only then did they realise the dreadful nature of the country through which they were passing. This part of Lewis was a maze of hills and small lochs. The desolate hills rose abruptly from sea-level to 2,500 feet. Many tiny lochs lay in open moorland, surrounded by soft, black bogs. It was a wet and stormy night, and there would be no moon until half past two in the morning.
>
> In such conditions, even the local guide lost his way. Predictably, the prince thought this was a deliberate attempt to betray him. They floundered through the boggy country, skirting the dozens of lochs, all night long. In the morning, after walking in semicircles for some eighteen hours, they found themselves at Arnish, two miles from Stornoway.

But if the prince thought his ordeal had earned him the right to a respite, he was soon disabused. For Stornoway, it now transpired, was up in arms against him.

It was not entirely Donald MacLeod's fault. Stornoway was then a very small place – a busy port, yes, but with almost as many pubs as houses, and, thanks to Mr MacAulay, the town had already been put on the alert by the local ministers. Besides, the ageing Skyeman had let his tongue rattle too much amidst assorted flowing bowls. A subsequent sworn statement by one Captain Alexander MacDonald – who had later to do some fast talking to government agents, mindful of his own tender neck – asserts that MacLeod and he did quickly strike a deal for the charter of a 40-ton brig, for £100. But the master of the ship had then become suspicious, and tried to back out. MacLeod then unwisely offered to buy the whole tub – for £300. The astute Lewisman rolled tongue in cheek and said he would consider £500. When MacLeod unhesitatingly agreed to that outrage, the seaman grasped entirely whom the Skyeman served. According to Felix O'Neil – who, as McLynn warns, is not entirely reliable – MacLeod, well in his cups, obligingly confessed it anyway. Dr Alasdair MacLean writes then that, all but exploding, the 'captain told him that "if he should load the ship with gold he would not employ her for that purpose".' The mariner then lost no time scurrying about town telling everyone what was going on, and Donald MacLeod had to flee.

Around eleven o'clock in the morning, with Stornoway in sight, the prince sent their embarrassed guide on in search of the Skyeman, and besides for bread and cheese and (still more importantly) a bottle of brandy: after their little overnight hike, after all, as MacLeod himself dryly admitted long afterwards, 'they stood much in need of a little refreshment.' He himself, tired and embarrassed, was soon reunited with the party near Arnish, and had now to confess entire failure.

Charles Edward, so near to escape – and so far – was soaked, exhausted and now furious. But he refused quite to abandon hope. No one lives at Arnish now – save for the present residents of the long-automated lighthouse – and the sight today is dominated by a rather ghastly offshore-fabrication yard; but in 1746 it was the demesne of the widow of Colin MacKenzie of Kildun, who, like other close kin, had won a pleasant holding on Lewis. (Some accounts place him at Aignish, but this is no doubt confusion between two very similar place-names.)

These MacKenzies of Kildun were (or had become) ardent Roman Catholics, and the late Colin of Kildun had waged determined war with an earlier Stornoway minister (once sending armed men to bring him in for what would probably have been a most physical conversation) and been spectacularly humiliated by the family tutor, a young and somewhat giddy priest of Rome who had not only fallen in love with a Kildun daughter but got her in an interesting condition. ('Kildin's daughter Jean is wt child,' crowed the Lewis-born minister of Contin, another offspring of the brieve Morrisons, 'and as the report goes she has declair'd to some friends, priest Conn is the man ha ha.') The enraged Kildun not only had the wretched cleric seized and bound, and incarcerated first on soggy little Fladda in Loch Roag and then – when the authorities began to take an interest – on distant, sea-girt North Rona, where it seems poor Father Conn was finally rescued by a passing ship – only in turn to be flung, for a time, into the depths of Edinburgh Castle. He later converted to

Protestantism, though it is not clear whether that was new, profound theo-logical insight or merely the discovery of women.

The villainous old Colin himself had died some years before; but Donald MacLeod took his prince to the cosy, if modest, manor and the widow Kildun gave them all a most gracious welcome. Another mighty fire was lit; whisky, eggs and milk, tea and biscuits were shortly on the table, and the prince's wringing shirt was thoughtfully dried. There was not much that could be done about his blisters, though a clean new shirt and a fresh pair of shoes were sacrificed for him. Despite the emergency, he was exhausted, all-in, and for a few fraught hours they had all to wait on tenterhooks as Charles Edward snatched a few hours of desperately needed sleep. Donald MacLeod, who seems still to have hoped he might just wrangle the brig – if not her captain and crew – padded back towards town. He was aghast – and astonished – to find two or three hundred men, literally up in arms, marshalled and with dirks, swords and pistols in nervous hands. MacLeod kept his head; one wrong word could have cost him (and his hunted little party) their lives. He spoke quietly. It became evident that this, too, was the work of the Reverend Aulay MacAulay; it was not just that the folk of Stornoway now knew the prince lurked close at hand, but they genuinely believed he commanded a force of some 500 men.

But, protested the Skyeman – accurately, and in good Gaelic – Charles Edward had but two men, 'and when I am there I make up the third. And let me tell you farther, gentlemen, if Seaforth himself were here, by God he durst not put a hand to the Prince's breast.' MacLeod knew there was much mixed feeling among the frightened men before him, and, certainly, as Linklater relates, 'there was no animosity to the Prince himself, no intention of doing him the smallest hurt, but devoutly they wished to get rid of him, and would do nothing to help him.' The Skyeman might just have bought the crewless brig for much gold – the prince and his party had a healthy hoard with them – but he knew nothing of the safest part of the mainland coast for a landing, and dared not venture on the crossing without adequate crew or a pilot. It was fast evident there was no hope of either, though Peter Cunningham rightly asserts that 'the behaviour of the townspeople throughout this episode, garrisoned as they were by government troops, was beyond all praise. W. C. Mackenzie in his account states that it would be difficult to find a parallel for such chivalrous loyalty to a lost cause.'

So he trudged back to the house of Kildun – probably through what are now the great woods of the Lews Castle Grounds – and there they all lingered for one sad night more, as twilight crept and the lights of Stornoway, friendly, implacable, twinkled over on the other side of Glumaig, winking from homes and taverns where, though none would betray, none would help.

That night, the prince's party killed a cow, and with great difficulty persuaded the lady of Kildun to take money for the beef; she assented at length, but then pressed on them butter, bread, meal and brandy and sugar, and even a wooden trencher for kneading some sort of loaf. On the morning of 6 May they sailed south for Scalpay, until forced ashore (on a tiny, deserted island called Iubhard, in the mouth of Loch Shell in Park) by the glimpse of government frigates. They spent four dull days and nights sheltering in a squalid hut, eating salt ling and haddock and cod left hanging for wind-cure by local fishermen, making crude alcoholic punch and baking still cruder bannocks. They made Scalpay on 10 May, and could not linger – for Campbell himself was briefly on the run – and, off Finsbay in South Harris, they were sighted and chased by HMS *Furness*, eluding her only by deft turn into the shoals of the Sound of Harris, where she could not follow.

Charles Edward Stuart would not return to the Long Island and, after his final voyage from Arisaig for France on 19 September, would never again see Scotland, though he did make at least one very quiet visit to London, years on and when all hopes were dust. His life and purpose had, really, died at Derby, and later decades brought only futility, a squalid marriage of convenience, obesity and infirmity and the relentless advance of alcoholism. In his final years, cared for by his bright, somewhat put-upon illegitimate daughter, visitors were warned on no account to talk to him of Highlanders, so distressed and incoherent would the old man become.

The prince had looked to Stornoway for succour because, stubbornly adhering to the policy that had made them, the Seaforths stuck long in steadfast loyalty to the Stuarts – and, unlike others, such as Clan Campbell, who played the game much better and far more cynically – adhered to this hapless dynasty long after the connection had become a liability.

The MacKenzies did at least maintain a stable order on Lewis, free of the feuding and bloodshed that had characterised the last decades of MacLeod rule. But it was not a settlement; it was an occupation. Assorted friends and kin of Seaforth were rewarded for fealty with tracts of Lewis land, at nominal rents and, of course, the obligation to rise in arms for their chief as he demanded. These tacksmen conscripted their subtenants besides – whether they wanted to fight for the distant satrap in Brahan or not – and thought nothing of firing the roofs over their heads should the helots resist.

Accounts of the Seaforth order vary. By the time of the Napier Commission in 1883, it had become fashionable on Lewis to view it nostalgically as a golden age. The first generation of MacKenzie hangers-on were not, for the most part, a bad bunch: they brought (and taught) better agricultural techniques and seem to have been decent to their subtenants, the latest martial adventure on behalf of a Stuart fool permitting. Colin, the first Earl of Seaforth, also made a signal contribution to island religion: he imported from Kintail the Reverend Farquhar MacRae, a bustling man and an earnest, sensible Christian, who found what was to all intents and purposes a heathen community and, in the early months, conducted marriages and baptisms on a near-industrial scale, the crowd on one occasion being so great that 'being unable to take them individually, Mr MacRae was obliged to sprinkle water at random over the crowd with a heather besom'. The calibre of ministers subsequently appointed to the island was – considering the woeful state of Highland Presbyterianism till late in the eighteenth century, and the general disinterest down south in its spiritual welfare – remarkably high, but the impact of even the best churchmen was inevitably limited: all Lewis, till 1722, was just two parishes (Stornoway and Barvas) and thereafter, and until the reign of George IV, just four. One alone – Lochs – was geographically bigger than several Scottish counties.

The fact remains that ordinary Lewis folk had absolutely no security of tenure and the tacksmen had all but the power of pit and gallows over them; there is hard evidence of abuse in later decades. 'The people disliked this new system of land tenure intensely,' writes Donald MacDonald of Tolsta, 'for they were now at the complete mercy of these tacksmen who looked on them as an inferior race and treated them accordingly. Unfortunately, they had no means of redress, since the MacKenzies left the management of their Lewis estate in the hands of their factors or chamberlains who, ably assisted by the tacksmen and the four ground officers (one for each parish) ensured that their subtenants' lives were far from pleasant . . . during the whole of the Seaforth regime, proprietor and tacksmen alike exploited the people with little or no consideration for their welfare.' The island, from the remote chief's perspective, counted for nothing more than a sporting-estate, a pool of reluctant soldiers for his own vainglory and a convenient source of revenue – squeezed out of the Lewis people by rapacious middle-management, who besides creamed off a good deal to enrich themselves.

It is worth stressing the inequities of this time as it goes a long way to explain why the Matheson regime is, to this day, remembered in higher regard and affection than it objectively deserves. In just one detail of MacKenzie oppression, the Earl of Seaforth and his underlings laid claim to everything washed ashore, citing his status as 'Admiral-Depute of the Western Isles'. But driftwood was a vital resource in an almost wholly treeless island, desperately sought for roof timber, and this caused great misery and tension. A plank or beam would scarcely be cast up by the tide before some servant of the estate had painted a bold red 'S' on it – for Seaforth – and recorded its presence.

Nevertheless, it was apt to disappear, and then Seaforth's comptroller would launch a search of houses in the vicinity; on at least one occasion, he ordered pitiless raids and scrutiny of every single home on the island, and any rafters or purlins with the fateful mark were implacably confiscated. In such an environment, it is no wonder that even in the last years of the nineteenth century men frequently drowned by the shore as they fought to catch some big bobbing log; in 1795, as is well documented, a ship from Mealista in Uig – on its way back from Skye laden with timber – had the misfortune to go aground at the hamlet Bagh Ciarach on the Park coast, where the denizens not only seized the cargo but murdered the crew. (The crime was uncovered, by one version, only when a grieving Uig widow recognised her husband's gansey among clothing for sale in Stornoway.)

The town itself was the main beneficiary of the Seaforth era, and its expansion – and its distinct and self-consciously superior development from the rest of Lewis – is also a factor in subsequent events; as it grew to a minor metropolis of merchants, sea-captains, professionals and shopkeepers and coastal traders, it became more autonomous, immune to the whims of lairds and factors, and indifferent to their activities, however oppressive, elsewhere on the island.

Colin, first Earl of Seaforth, soon grasped the potential of the local fishery – the fat ling in deep Lewis sea-lochs, the fine cod and haddock of Broad Bay, the herring in their season – and did his best to build Stornoway in this regard. Seaforth besides, with an eye to the next world, set up a church in every barony of his realm (including St Lennan's in Stornoway, the town's first parish church, which stood on the site of what is now the Royal Bank) and, at his passing, bequeathed a goodly sum to Chanonry for the foundation of a grammar school. (Fortrose Academy – now a comprehensive school in modern premises on a commanding seaward site – remains, to this day, one of the most respected in the Highlands.)

He also won the royal assent – from that thrawn if high-minded incompetent, Charles I – to making Stornoway a 'royal burgh', which meant a good deal more than just a fancy coat of arms. James VI, his father, had already made it a 'burgh of barony' as part of a deal with the Fife venture capitalists. The word 'burgh' means only 'a fortified place' – a town with walls – but a royal burgh was notionally owned by the king himself, to whom rent was paid, and had the right not just to trade with the wider nation but with ports and capitals overseas. Winning the approval of King Charles, though, was one thing; winning any meaningful commitment was quite another. Stornoway had fierce commercial rivals – especially on the East Highland seaboard, those already royal burghs, such as Tain and Inverness. They lobbied ferociously against any such promotion for the Lewis capital, and prevailed. The town remained but a 'burgh of barony', with all its constraints. To add insult to injury, Parliament (no doubt at the behest of these self-interested campaigners) in 1629 censured the earl for encouraging foreign (Dutch) fishermen.

That Dutch connection proved useful to his brother George, the second Earl of Seaforth, for Colin had outlived his only son and George himself was not nearly so good a politician – no light matter in the excessively interesting times that were mid-seventeenth-century Scotland, rapidly reduced to popular and ecclesiastical uproar over the fatuous endeavours of Charles I to impose both episcopacy and a read, Anglican-style liturgy on the Kirk, and then the pact between the Covenanters and the forces of Cromwell in the English Civil War; and finally, after the 1649 execution of Charles I, the endeavours of an earnest but distinctly silly Scottish theocracy on behalf of the very young Charles II. It all ended in tears, with defeat at Worcester and the young king's flight to France in 1651, and the subjugation of Scotland to Cromwell's occupying forces.

George, second Earl of Seaforth, was but a tepid supporter of the Loyalist cause, though that was sufficient to cost much Long Island life: 300 Lewismen were drafted to the king's standard at the battle of Auldearn in 1645 (under the command of James Graham, Marquis of Montrose) and, according to tradition, only three survived.

When George died suddenly – in the Netherlands, in 1651, shortly after the rout at Worcester – his son, Kenneth, was a boy of 16, just launched on study at the University of Aberdeen. The new, third earl hastened at once to Kintail to raise new armies for the king's service, where the sensible Highlanders took one look and told him bluntly he was far too young. Before poor Kenneth knew where he was, there was a price on his head and his estates were bankrupt and in the hands of trustees; in 1653 the forces of the Commonwealth seized Stornoway and soon erected and garrisoned a substantial fort on what is now Point Street. In 1654, an audacious bid to storm this base – the last significant battle ever fought on Lewis – ended in bloody failure despite the best efforts of assorted MacKenzies, and MacLeods of Raasay; they had no artillery, and could not breach its walls. There were afterwards vicious government reprisals on the local people.

In 1655, the impetuous young Seaforth was finally captured by General Monk and held in Cromwell's Inverness garrison. This was really a rather comfortable open prison. Kenneth was allowed out on bail and even to go a-hunting in Kintail, with 'the flower of all the youth in our country, with a hundred pretty fellows or more', and in 1658 married a cousin, Isabella, daughter of Lord Tarbat and a granddaughter of Ruairidh Mor.

Isabella was a force of the first order, popularly charged with one atrocity at Chanonry Point – a myth we shall shortly demolish – and whose surviving portrait shows a woman of more presence than beauty. 'After all men's hopes of him,' mewed one Highland clergyman – Rev. James Fraser – in his *Wardlaw Manuscript*, Seaforth had debased 'himselfe mean spirited to marry below himself, getting neither beauty, parts, portion, relation'. Certainly Isabella brought little of a dowry and, evidently sharp-tongued and imperious, she was perhaps easier to admire than to like: something of her reputation can be sensed in a delicious 1676 diary entry by Brodie of Brodie:

> July 31: my Ladi Seaforth cald; and we being from home, she went to Darnaway.
> Aug 1: my Ladi Seaforth went by and cald not. I reveranc the Lord's providence.

Isabella bore eight infants, lived to a great age (dying only in 1715), took avid and bossy interest in the ambitions and careers of her children and grand-children, and gives every impression of being both an intelligent and distinctly imperious old battleaxe. It is little wonder that Kenneth drank heavily – it was after a protracted boozing party at Stornoway, heading recklessly home in his birlinn amidst a northerly gale, that Iain Garbh MacLeod, Chief of Raasay, was drowned with 16 of his high kindred, a local disaster that begot no fewer than five overwrought Gaelic laments. The earl besides enjoyed occasional dalliance – there was at least one misbegotten son – and he was away from home a great deal. Delighted to be summoned to court in London by the restored, grateful Charles II in 1662, he hoped eagerly for rich recompense after 'ruining his father's interest in the civil wars, though all he had was bad success . . . Yet all Seaforth,' sighed James Fraser, 'gained at Court was the King's countenance and the compliment of carrying the Sword of Honour before the King upon some solemn holy day from the presence to the Chapell Royall and, after service, back again. A farthing of the King's money he never saw, not so much as to repair his castle of Brahan, which the rebels spoiled.'

Kenneth nevertheless travelled to France on a court mission, and otherwise sought distraction and anaesthesia at Brahan, Chanonry or Stornoway. 'I heard of great drinking betwixt the Earl of Seaforth and Aboin,' wrote Brodie of Brodie in his journal on 6 July 1673. 'Alac! God dishonoured and not in al ther thoughts.' The third earl, still only 44, was gathered to his Maker in 1679: the fourth Seaforth, another Kenneth, was 18 and, we are assured, 'adored' by his mother, who no doubt did her best to run his life. It was defined, though, by two things: his subsequent conversion to Roman Catholicism (on the occasion of his marriage to the daughter of the Earl of Powis) and his loyalty to James VII when he was overthrown after the Revolution of 1688, and spurned in turn by the Scots the following year. The fourth earl followed his king to Paris, was rewarded with the paper, Jacobite, titles of Lord Fortrose and Marquis of Seaforth and died – contented in exile, priestcraft and martyrdom – in 1701. 'He was the great joy of my lyf and the support of my age,' lamented his mother, who then tried to decree the education of her grandson, William, the fifth earl.

Isabella had the sense to realise the future was Protestant; her daughter-in-law did not, and William was 'carried out of the kingdom to be popishly bred' against the wishes of both government and Granny. Inevitably, he proved as witless a Jacobite as his fathers; inevitably, he took prominent part in the Rising of 1715 and the latest Caberfeidh ended up – as always – on the losing side. In 1716, the earldom was 'attaindered' and the Seaforth estates forfeit, and William spent the rest of his life skulking on Lewis. William had been dead only six years when Charles Edward toiled through the bogs of the Long Island in confident hope of help and cheer; in all, though, it can be imagined these fatuous romantic endeavours for a dynasty hounded once and twice off the throne for its entire political incompetence did little for the welfare of the Seaforth tenantry.

No trace can now be seen of that first MacKenzie base on Lewis, though Peter Cunningham has established that the 'traditional site of the fort is at the shoreward end of croft number 6 at Seaforth Head. The ruins of early buildings and of a black-house, vacated within living memory, occupy this promontory and were built presumably from the stones of MacKenzie's settlement. Certainly, it is impossible now to identify the original building but, sitting amongst these ruins and looking down the winding Loch Seaforth around which little has changed in three and a half centuries, it is easy to imagine Seaforth's galleys pulling up the calm waters to the beach below. Doubtless there were, as now, seals hauled out on the reefs, a golden eagle soaring over Feiriosbhal and the wake of an otter in the mountain's shadow . . . In 2007, a handsome little monument was erected by the roadside above what is judged to be the locus.

In due time, their authority established, the Seaforths might well have renovated Stornoway Castle to their own comfort, but, after George's witless antics for the doomed head of Charles I, it was pounded to rubble by the guns of Cromwell's navy; and Colonel Lilburne wrote the tough old Roundhead from Dalkeith on 13 September 1653 to advise

May it please Your Excellency – Since my last to your Lordshippe, I have
had a more particular account of the proceedings of Col Cobbett in reducing
the Lewis.

The Lord Seaford had left his bastard brother Governor there. Upon the
approach of our forces he and the inhabitants quitt the fort, where there
were 2 greate guns and 4 sling peeces, and towne of Loughsternay, and fled
to the Hills, but upon Proclamation from Col. Cobbett they came to their
houses, and divers of them brought in their arms. Major Crispe is left there
with 4 companies, and is fortifying Loughsternay, and a little fort in an
Island, which is almost inviron'd by the sea. The Harbore is very
commodious for shipping to ride in with security under the fort. The
27th August Col. Cobbett sayl'd thence and by intelligence sent by the
Marq of Argyll the 3rd instant, he entred Mula Islande, and took in the
strong Castle of Dovert; the 3 shippes sent from Aire, with Captain
Hargreave's Company, mett him before his going into Mull.

Uppon the appearance of these forces they had a generall alarm throughout the Highlands, and pretended to march to the releife of M'cloud, who
they heard was a prisoner.

Stornoway was then little more than the promontory now run by Point
Street, with North Beach and South Beach to either shore, and it was in this
area Cromwell's fort was built: its well survived just into living memory
(behind where the town's cinema was erected in the 1930s, now the British
Legion), and Cromwell Street and James Street probably mark two protective
trenches; the tower was between Amity House and Custom House, glowering
over the narrows into the inner harbour. The one evidence of its existence still
visible today is the curious alignment of the Town House – now the Golden
Ocean Chinese restaurant – by the corner of Cromwell Street and North Beach;
its front elevation was laid along the past barrier of the defensive Cromwellian
trench.

Without a castle – which, cramped and exposed, would have been of limited
appeal to well-connected gentry in what, slowly, grew to be more peaceful times
– the Seaforths needed a rather more central Lewis summer-house, and by the
1719 Rising (we know this, because there are references to William, fifth earl,
and some choice friends laying their schemes in it) Seaforth Lodge had been
built on the fine stance now occupied by Matheson's Lews Castle. We have a
good idea of its rugged but (by the standards of the time) spacious appearance
from a 1798 painting of the town by James Barret, and a later 1819 print –
looking east and south, from behind the Lodge – by William Daniel. In 1798,
too, there was a tantalising description in the Statistical Account that on

'an elevated situation on the other side of the bay, near and opposite the town, is built Seaforth Lodge, a neat, modern house, for the reception and accommodation of Seaforth when he chose to come and visit this part of his estate . . .'. This was no light undertaking: the journey from Brahan Castle on the east coast to Poolewe on the west (the historic port of embarkation for Lewis) could be accomplished only by foot or pack horse, unless one braved a single, meandering and dreadful military road. In 1799, the latest Lady Seaforth nevertheless insisted on taking her carriage: by 15 miles beyond Contin, at Achanalt, the vehicle was not only so damaged she could not continue, but so wrecked it was not worth hauling back home.

The dynasty was already in torrid times. There was an inevitable hiatus under William, disgraced and alienated, and when his son Kenneth at last in 1740 inherited what was left of the Seaforth fortunes, it was merely as Earl of Fortrose. He had, however, been brought up a Protestant and worked hard for respectability, sitting in the House of Commons (first for Inverness, then for Ross) and steadily regaining this and that chunk of the old MacKenzie lands. He refused to have anything to do with the Jacobite cause in 1745, spent his latter years in London and is buried in Westminster Abbey. His son, still another Kenneth, is best remembered for forming the 72nd Highland Regiment (which endured to 1961 as the Seaforth Highlanders) and even regained the 'Earl of Seaforth' title, though only in the Irish peerage and with no seat in the Lords. Kenneth Street, in Stornoway, seems to have been named for him. He died while on passage to India with the troops in which he took such pride, and without leaving a son, the last in direct male descent from the fourth, fifth and sixth earls. All devolved on a second cousin, Thomas Frederick MacKenzie, who gloried in his new estate for just two years before he was killed in a naval action in 1783. His brother, Francis Humberston MacKenzie – born in London in 1755, schooled at Eton and as deaf as a post after a boyhood dose of scarlet fever – was the next in line. (It is for him that Stornoway's Francis Street is named.)

We might say that the last decades of Seaforth hegemony on Lewis were stalked by two monsters and book-ended by a third. Thanks to the excited writing of an amateur folklorist, Alexander MacKenzie, in 1877, it is widely known that the hapless life of Francis MacKenzie saw the awful outworkings of an ancient prophecy – or curse. In local tradition, and as outlined (and indeed embroidered) by that Victorian hack, the 'fall of the House of Seaforth' was foretold by one Kenneth MacKenzie, *Coinneach Odhar an Fhiosaiche*, the 'Brahan Seer'. Born and brought up at Balnacille, Uig, on Lewis, early in the seventeenth century, he had powers of augury and the second sight, using a wee 'divination stone'; he had found favour with Kenneth, the third earl, and been granted convenient employment near his Brahan base. During the earl's absence in France, the widely retailed story goes, the ferocious Isabella summoned *Coinneach Odhar* to give her news of her suspiciously long-gone husband. When at length he told her – humiliatingly, in front of feasting friends and servants, and in a mocking tone – that the earl was not only in Paris having a ball but enjoying thoroughly the company of obliging ladies, Isabella's revenge was swift and horrible. The Seer was condemned to death at Chanonry Point in a blazing barrel of tar, thick with iron spikes and into which he was chucked head-first. (In one version, the earl arrived on the scene seconds too late to save him.)

Once his own doom was certain, *Coinneach Odhar* is said dramatically to have cursed the whole Seaforth line:

I see into the far future. I read the doom of my oppressor. The long descended line of Seaforth will, ere many generations have passed, end in extinction and sorrow. I see a chief, last of his house, both deaf and dumb. He will be father to four fair sons, all of whom will go before him to the tomb. He will live careworn and die mourning, knowing that the honours of his line are to be distinguished forever and that no future chief of MacKenzies will rule at Brahan or Kintail. After lamenting the last and most promising of his sons, he shall sink into the grave, and the remnant of his possessions shall be inherited by a white-hooded widow from the East, and she is to kill her sister.

As a sign by which it may be known that the things are coming to pass, there will be four great lairds in the days of the last, deaf and dumb Seaforth – Gairloch, Chisholm, Grant and Raasay – one of whom will be buck-toothed, another hare-lipped, another half witted and the fourth a stammerer. Chiefs thus distinguished will be allies and neighbours of the last Seaforth; and when he looks around him and sees them, he may know that his sons are doomed, that his broad lands shall pass to strangers and that his race shall come to an end. And of the great house of Brahan not a stone shall remain.

Francis MacKenzie was deaf from his sixteenth year, with some sort of speech impediment – and, in the very last years of his life, mute besides, more by emotional trauma than infirmity. His intelligence, charm and common sense nevertheless saw him prosper in public life: a patron of the arts (he did much to advance the career of Thomas Lawrence); a governor of Barbados; and elevation in 1797 to the British peerage as Baron Seaforth and Lord MacKenzie of Kintail. He did have four sons, three of whom attained manhood – and he did outlive them all. His estates finally fell to his daughter, Mary, who came home from India to take possession as the white-capped widow of Admiral Samuel Hood. She had, as a young woman, been at the reins of a pony-carriage when the steed took fright and bolted; there had been a smash, and her sister – the passenger – did subsequently die of her injuries.

Yet there was not a single publication of the 'Fall of the House of Seaforth' prediction until years after its fulfilment. Yes, there is reference to it in Elizabeth Grant's *Memoirs of a Highland Lady* for the year 1815, when Baron Seafoth was still living and months after the deaths of two of his sons. But her book was only published, posthumously, in 1898; and it would be 90 years before her entire, unabridged text appeared, in 1988. And yes – Walter Scott banged on extravagantly about the Curse of the Seaforths, and even wrote a gooey poem, but nothing was printed before its substantial fulfilment, and, as a man with novels to sell, he had a keen commercial interest talking up spooky stuff.

Indeed, in certain details – long after Alexander MacKenzie's book – the doom of Seaforth as related would not be complete until the mid twentieth century. His great-grandson, James Stewart-MacKenzie, would be created Baron Seaforth of Brahan – but die childless in 1923. A grand-nephew adopted the name Stewart-MacKenzie of Seaforth – and was killed, with his brother besides and within 24 hours, at Salerno during the Second World War. Brahan, rife with woodworm and rot, was inherited by a cousin, Madeline Tyler, who also adopted the Stewart-MacKenzie surname; she could not afford to renovate the old pile, and no one wanted to buy it, so it was levelled to the ground, and – indeed – not a stone remains. The present-day Brahan is the old Georgian stable-block. Where the ancient seat stood is but one great green lawn.

But there is nothing at all to link this with a Kenneth MacKenzie from Balnacille, or any hard evidence that a single 'Brahan Seer' ever existed. The relevant church records show no trial or burning of a clairvoyant at Chanonry Point around 1662 – or at any time. We know that there was someone called Coinneach Odhar – 'Sallow Kenneth' – because the Bannatyne Manuscript, a history of the MacLeods written around 1832, refers to a native of Lewis of that name prophesying doom for . . . the MacLeods. Much more striking is a Commission of Holyroodhouse, issued on 25 October 1577 to Walter Urquhart, Sheriff of Cromarty, and Robert Munro of Foulis among others – and, inter alia, charging them to seek out and arrest six men and twenty-six women charged with 'the diabolical practices of magic, enchantment, murder, homicide and other offences' within the bounds of the Earldom of Ross, the Lordship of Ardmannach (the modern Black Isle) and other parts of the Sherrifdom of Inverness. The last name on the list – almost a century before, as Alexander MacKenzie assured us, an enraged Countess Isabella gave him a new career as barbecue – is one 'Keanoch Ower . . . the leading or principal enchantress'.

The clerk would not have been familiar with Gaelic, nor been readily able to judge gender from such a name, but it attests that some sinister chap called *Coinneach Odhar* was notorious in the Highlands almost half a century before an Earl of Seaforth had even been created. This evidence is reinforced besides by an earlier Commission, dated '1577 January 23', and which also talks darkly of a 'Kennoth, alias Kennoch Owir, principal leader in the art of magic . . . using and exercising the diabolical, iniquitous and odious crimes of the art of magic, sorcery and incantation . . .' And it is worth remembering besides that *fiosaiche*, in Gaelic, is never used for a seer or possessor of the second sight: the term then is usually *taibhsear*. *Coinneach Odhar an Fhiosaiche* means but one thing: Sallow Kenneth the Warlock – or witch.

The occultist's fate is unknown, though others on these writs (centred on an involved, very dark domestic drama in the Munro of Foulis household) were certainly tried, convicted and burned at Chanonry in November 1577. And there was a MacKenzie tacksman – George MacKenzie – at Balnacille, early in the seventeenth century; his mother was a Munro of Kaitwell, closely related to Munro of Foulis, and she would doubtless have known in great detail of recent scandalous events. It is probable she spoke of them much in the new, colonial, MacKenzie culture of the time, and that is how a mangled version took root on Lewis. But the Brahan Seer is not a historical figure: he is a meme. To this day – be it for the 1982 opening of the Kessock Bridge or the commissioning of a new Stornoway ferry in 1995 – journalists still eagerly try to unearth some suitable imprecation from the Seer and, when one is not found, have not the least difficulty inventing one.

There are charming, pastoral *et in arcadia ego* Lewis notes of this Francis Humberston MacKenzie, last in the direct male line of the House of Seaforth – thoroughly anglicised, a pillar of the London establishment, sometime Governor of Barbados (and who of his benevolence tightened up the law on killing slaves, though drew the line at abolishing slavery itself). In 1786 one John Knox, agent of the British Society for Extending the Fisheries, visited the island; unlike Charles Edward, he prudently sailed – rather than walked – from Tarbert to Stornoway, accompanied by Captain Alexander MacLeod of Rodel, who was executing great schemes for that little port. Knox and MacLeod were tired and scruffy, and had not the energy that night to parade in society, so they slummed it in a local inn and sent word to the factor for an audience. Instead, within the hour their landlady rushed into their chamber, shouting 'Seaforth! Seaforth!' and there indeed was the man himself, glowing and implacable; his honoured guests 'were carried irresistibly to the Lodge'.

Knox, like many gentleman of his generation, could not look at a view without thinking of a canvas in frame and was quite charmed, on the morrow, by the prospect from Seaforth Lodge: once the new parish kirk was finished, he declared, 'with a small spire also upon the town-house, and other ornaments which Seaforth's fertile imagination may easily conceive, this place will merit the pencil of the first landscape painter in the kingdom'. And he did not find it too hard to persuade Seaforth and the captain to join him on an expedition to Loch Roag, on the west coast – though, as organised and catered for by Seaforth, it sounds less like a business fact-finding mission than a rather jolly picnic.

A boat was manned and stored with provisions, wine spirits and malt liquor. The weather still continuing fine, we set out in high spirits from the harbour of Stornoway for the Barkin Islands (at the mouth of Loch Erisort). Our design was to go as far as we could by water, and to walk from thence to the head of Loch Roag . . . Here all hands were employed in landing the cargo, and carrying it to the place of encampment. Some brought up firearms, others carried the provisions and liquors; and the rear followed with kitchen utensils. The island was covered with heath, and a fire was instantly kindled under a little rock, where the fish was to be cooked. Every man now took up his station. Seaforth cut up one of the lythe (caught on the passage), which he gutted, washed and put into the kettle. The department chosen by Captain MacLeod was to attend the kettle and supply the fire with heath, which being dry made a fine blaze and facilitated the business on hand . . . When dinner was nearly ready to be served up, Seaforth spread a large tablecloth upon the ground; opened his hampers and kantin [*canteen, containing cutlery*], laid the knives, forks and plates; took out his stores of cold tongue, tame and wild fowl, roast beef, bread, cheese, butter, pepper, salt, vinegar, pickles etc., also wine, spirits, ale and porter . . .'

One can only echo Peter Cunningham's wondering as to what else might have been included in that 'etc.'. But, by the time all this had been leisurely enjoyed, the weather had taken a turn for the worse. The expedition to Loch Roag was abandoned and, though they could make the immediate shore, a sail back to town was impossible. The gentry found lodgings in a local township – perhaps Ranish – and walked back overland 'through mosses and moors now rendered almost impassable. We encountered the storm with a bold face and arrived safely at the lodge.'

Knox was sharp enough to detect, behind the charm of this holiday-idyll mentality, a faltering grip on the affairs of Lewis or any real knowledge of its commerce and conditions. The Seaforths were souring on island taste, and no wonder, when 'the fishery of the island has so long been monopolised by the factor, who pays the fishermen £13 per ton for the ling, and gets, when sold upon the spot, £18. When, to these advantages, are added the various emoluments arising from his office, and his traffic in grain, meal, cattle, etc., his place is better than the rent of many considerable estates in the Highlands. The father of the present factor procured a lease of that office, with all its appendages, for a number of years, six or seven are still unexpired; and it is said that he retired with a pension of £20,000 a part of which he has laid out upon an estate where he now resides.' The 'Chamberlain of the Lews' held an office ripe for untold possibilities in corruption, and successive holders largely fatted themselves on them. The one mercy was that Seaforth himself had no interest at all in commercially motivated evictions, the laird assuring Knox 'that he neither would let his lands for sheep pasture, nor turn out his people, upon any consideration, or for any rent that could be offered'.

Lord Teignmouth thought well of this Francis, last Earl of Seaforth, writing that he 'was one of the most accomplished and princely characters of whom Scotland could boast. His acquirements, classical taste, urbanity and liberality, rendered him the delight of every society in which he appeared, the pride of his clansmen and the ornament of his country.' Sir Walter Scott paid him a still more striking compliment: 'a nobleman of extraordinary talents, who must have made for himself a lasting reputation, had not his political exertions been checked by painful natural infirmity.'

But he is also remembered, with rather more ambiguity, on Lewis for his fevered recruitment of soldiers, especially in Uig, where the 'soldiers of the deaf MacKenzie' were raised in very large numbers, were away for a very long time, served with heroism and distinction and very many of whom came back blind and dependent from Egyptian service against Napoleon. Many, of course, never returned. And there was, besides, the grossly exploitative kelp industry, which by 1793, as Donald MacDonald writes, had 'taken precedence over cattle and horses as the most important trade on the island'. Seaweed, gathered in vast quantities, heaped, dried and burned to a slag, produced chemical necessaries for the manufacture of glass, soap and explosives. From 1776 till the 1820s – its value much inflated by a helpful tariff (under the Salt Act) on imported alternatives, and later the Napoleonic Wars – West Highland kelp was big business: on Lewis alone, some £37,000 was made by the Estate from kelp between 1812 and 1835.

The kelp industry had, in fact, less impact on Lewis than elsewhere because only its southern districts, rent by narrow arms of the sea and full of tidal creeks – Carloway, Uig and Lochs – lent themselves to regular harvest of wrack and weed. Yet kelp was exacted in full measure from tenants by more exposed coasts, even if it were largely the tangle blown ashore by storm and precious as such seaware was for the enriching of tenants' soil and the nurture of tenants' crops. It was grim work, with all involved – young and old – chill and soaking, especially as the usual season was in the early summer, when food-stocks were low and people were hungriest. It took 40 creels of seaweed to make a mere single hundredweight of kelp, and for every pound the laird was finally paid for it, those who had actually gathered and produced the stuff earned, on average, one shilling. 'The people of Lewis,' as MacDonald writes, 'did not take kindly to this new industry, so a certain amount of pressure had to be applied to make them undertake this arduous, unhealthy and far from congenial work.'

Seaforth's high-minded refusal ever to clear his tenantry for sheep should be read in this cynical light; as we shall see, kelp was of especial profit to the greedy lairds the old clan chiefs were fast becoming, because the labour was free – and the people hounded, harried and sometimes literally whipped to the wretched gathering whether they wanted to work at kelp or not. 'The parish of Uig was the first important kelp-making industry,' writes Donald MacDonald, 'and before long the inhabitants developed such expertise that they also kelped in Lochs, Harris, and even in Uist. They were probably forced to do this, as it is recorded that they went to Lochs in 1794, "but not until they were absolutely beat and forced by Mr Gillanders, the factor, who happened to be on his recruiting jaunt at the time." Evidently, they had to choose between kelping and the army. . . . The introduction of kelping into Barvas met with much resistance, as the people detested the work. The factor, however, was determined that their antipathy should be overcome, as to bring in kelpers from outside would dent his profits.'

The unthinking contempt in which many overseers of the exaction held the workforce is evident in this 1821 report from a Mr MacGregor, ground officer at Barvas, who bemoaned still another obstacle to his quota, the

want of boats. As the poor people get no fish they cannot keep boats. There is not a merchant in Stornoway that would give them credit for a pint of tar since they got poor, and if I had not given them a piece of shore timber to repair their boats, I could never get the kelp shipped . . . I was two days and two nights at Shawbost waiting for shipment of the kelp, and the people along with me, without going to a house, and as I didn't allow the people to go to the ebb as usual, for some shellfish or seaweeds, which is their daily subsistence, the last day they were not able to row their boats or stand; only for some meal and bread the master of the vessel was giving them, I could not get anything done. What could be expected of people in such a state?

One is not, after this, greatly moved to note that the last years of Francis MacKenzie, Earl of Seaforth, were clouded by sustained family unhappiness, costly mismanagement of his West Indies estates – forcing stringent economies and the sale of the original lands in Kintail – and stubborn personal extravagance. When Francis died, in Edinburgh, in 1815 – only two months after his last surviving son, a Member of Parliament and by all accounts a very fine fellow – Seaforth affairs were in a perilous state as Mary, so recently the widow of Vice-Admiral Sir Samuel Hood, sailed home from India in mourning at once for her husband and her father.

'Our friend, Lady Hood, will now be "Caberfeidh" herself,' Sir Walter wrote a friend, adding presciently, 'She has the spirit of a chieftainess in every drop of her blood, but there are few situations in which the cleverest women are so apt to be imposed upon as in the management of landed property, more especially of a Highland estate. I do fear the accomplishment of the prophecy that, when there should be a deaf "Caberfeidh", the house was to fall.'

There is ample evidence of the new chief's high character, keen piety, sharp intelligence and warmth of heart. In David Octavius Hill's magnificent painting of the first General Assembly of the Free Church of Scotland – an event she lived to attend, and bless – she looks on amidst a bevy of high ladies from the upper corner, and Mary Stewart-MacKenzie (as she had long been) has a kind, engaging face. But she had none of the ferocity or steely self-possession of the politely lamented Isabella, far less Rory Mor. Incurably domestic and, it would seem, rather timid, she had not long observed the obsequies for her naval husband before wilting into the arms of a new one, the Right Honourable James Alexander Stewart, nephew of the 7th Earl of Galloway. They compromised on the Stewart-MacKenzie surname; and, though the consort's vast self-belief proved distinctly in excess of his abilities, he nevertheless held this and that public position, amassed this and that honour, and quite eclipsed his retiring wife, who to a degree that seems almost incredible in modern eyes submitted herself in all things to his interests and will.

Once and indeed twice offered her father's peerage – in her own right – by successive Tory prime ministers, she refused – her husband was a Whig, with important Whig friends, and she would not risk embarrassing him, especially after 1825, when the wider Lewis estate went bankrupt and it was only by £160,000 of his hard cash that the couple managed to outbid the sinister 'Joint Stock Property Company of Edinburgh' and buy the island from creditors. (They had hitherto owned personally little more than the Seaforth Lodge policies, the mass of the island being hitherto in the hands of a faltering Trust.)

Mrs Stewart-MacKenzie is still remembered for her good works and, especially, for her historic importance as godmother to a new Evangelical religion. (In this, alone, she seems to have had some independence from her husband, who was an ardent Episcopalian; in 1839, as if to assert his own spirit, he helped set up the St Peter's Episcopal congregation in Stornoway, notably the first ecclesiastical division in post-Reformation Lewis: not by 'Calvinist schism' either, but the pomposity of a posh incomer who felt, as is the wont of the species, that the local religion was not good enough for him.)

His lady, though, set up no fewer than five Sabbath schools in Stornoway, which also gave weekday lessons in English, Gaelic, handwriting and needle-work. She tried to foster similar schools in other parishes (though in this her endeavours were largely redundant, as the assorted Gaelic Schools Societies in the cities were already toiling to that end). It was under her patronage – in the bad ecclesiastical order of the day, when the 'heritor' or laird appointed parish ministers and not the people, an order she privately deplored – that the first Evangelical ministers came to Lewis; after the Disruption, she gladly granted fine sites throughout her estates – already fast shrinking – for Free Church manses and churches, and on the most generous terms. But her goodness was practical as well as holy: on several occasions she personally underwrote government famine relief when summers were grim and harvests were bad. Mary 'was possibly the most able of the MacKenzies', writes Cunningham. 'Her talents and influence were devoted to works of Christian benevolence. She had the personal dignity of chief of a clan and moved in the highest circles of society, admired by such luminaries as Sir Walter Scott, who extolled her virtues in verse.'

Concerned at the widespread practice of illicit distillation – with good reason, for the hooch produced was ferocious and on occasion toxic – she sensibly chose not to wage war on home-brew, but instead built a new and lawful distillery, below Seaforth Lodge, by the site now enjoyed by the modern Woodlands Centre. It included besides a saw-mill, a corn-kiln and a carding-mill, all powered by running water. By 1834, others were in operation – at Ness, Shawbost and Carloway – and, by the energies of Captain Benjamin Oliver and his customs cutter, the *Prince of Wales* (it is for this official Oliver's Brae is named), smuggling and illicit stills were in due time suppressed. It was also by Stewart-MacKenzie endeavours that Stornoway required its first town hall, a jail (a disagreeable necessity in any seaport) and its first bank: a branch of the National Bank of Scotland opened in 1830. By 1835 the Lewis Estate was even issuing its own paper currency, in what proved an unsuccessful bid to raise hard capital; a few of those huge, neatly engraved £1 'Stornaway' notes still exist.

It may seem strange this remarkable woman is not more vividly remembered on Lewis. She was, of course, seldom resident on the island and she had not the later flair for publicity of her Matheson successor. But these were bad times. The French Revolution begot a succession of Continental wars – notably the long, Napoleonic campaign – in which very many Highlanders served, including many of those Lewis troops raised by the last Earl of Seaforth. (The dozens of blinded veterans were in time at least granted a special pension, with a further allowance to pay a lad to lead each man around.) Evangelicalism took roaring root from 1822, bringing dignity and literacy and a new community in its train but – in the short term – a force, especially the gentry or those aspiring to join it, thought a divisive and dangerous form of 'enthusiasm', something not too far from the sedition that terrified everyone of property and standing after events in France.

There was predation besides: though it is not now widely recalled, these were years when the Royal Navy was desperate for men, and thought nothing of sending the press-gang into provincial ports and pubs, or even putting cutters ashore simply to seize and bundle aboard anyone who looked remotely fit. A kinsman of my own in Shawbost, Calum MacPhail – who, by the way, was also renowned for the very good dram he distilled unlawfully in a Fivig cave – spent a whole spring and much of the summer hiding in a remote *cleit* (a small, plain dry-stone hut) of A' Bheinn Mhor from a press-gang, practically camped in Loch Shawbost and daily searching for him: it is retailed that he snuck back to his holding at dusk to get on with the croft-work, using the *cas chrom* or 'foot plough' to turn in the manure his wife and children had earlier spread. (He was besides the owner of a gorgeous red silk shirt, secured in Spain during service with the Seaforth Highlanders, which became great currency in itself, such were the favours he could earn by lending it out.) And the kelp industry reached its exploitative peak around 1820 – when 627 tons were gathered, along with a profit of £3,356 – Mrs Stewart-MacKenzie fussed over her Sabbath schools.

At this time, too, in the 1820s and 1830s, there was our second monster, still vivid in local horror-stories as *mac an t-Sronaich*, a vague and almost demonic figure who was supposedly on the run in the moors of Lewis after some ghastly mainland crime; he killed repeatedly, without evident motive, and for fun; he lurked variously in the mountains of Uig and in a bare, troll-like cave by the mouth of the River Creed; and he was finally caught and hanged on Gallow's Hill, high above Stornoway and with appropriate regrets and maledictions.

There was some sort of outlaw; he seems to have been a Robert Stronach, son of the innkeeper at Garve and of his Lewis-born wife, a MacAulay from Uig. And Stronach was probably caught and hanged – though at Dingwall or Inverness, not Stornoway. There are no hard records. But this was an age when a man could still be executed for picking a pocket or stealing a sheep, and some who were known to make discreet provision for *mac an t-Sronaich* (a shakedown in the byre; some bread and cheese and cold meat wrapped in a hand-kerchief) were eminently respectable people: it is even said that they included a cousin married to a venerated local minister. It is unlikely in the extreme she would have succoured a murderer, her kin or no. *Mac an t-Sronaich* – a name all our grandmothers could, even in the 1970s, roll out with the-bogeyman-will-get-you relish – is, really, as much a phantom as the Brahan Seer: a convenient scapegoat for murders in fact committed by the forebear of an inconveniently near neighbour, or for squalid, drunken – and natural – deaths by silly young men wandering home through lonely winter hills.

In 1841, though – at almost the end of the Seaforth reign – a new procurator fiscal was appointed to Stornoway. Donald Munro could not be kept out of town by an alarmed mob, nor is he remembered for his bounty to good causes or the extravagance of his boating trips. Alas, he was no phantasm, but fact. To understand him best, and the battered social structure he came to dominate, we must now closely examine Lewis in the last years of faltering Seaforth power.

3
Lairds: The last of the Seaforths; and how they ran Lewis

There is a darker aspect to the last decades of Seaforth dominion on Lewis, beyond the pieties of Mary MacKenzie-Stuart. And it should be considered against a wider background of considerable change in Scotland, coupled with substantial movement of population to the cities, a new lack of scruple in the management of landed estates and – if anything – a still further imbalance of power between haves and have-nots. It was in this context, even under the self-conscious and sunny paternalism of a socially climbing laird like James Matheson, that so wicked a man like Donald Munro could for so long prosper, and by extraordinary conglomeration of power. But he did not actually introduce an unchecked, despotic style of administration to the Isle of Lewis. He arrived in a community where, thanks to extraordinary maladministration by the distant government (to say nothing of the legal establishment in Edinburgh), and in combination with mounting Stewart-MacKenzie detachment, it was in large part the accepted order. To understand this we must, a little tediously, consider Lewis law and Lewis lawyers.

Scots law is very different from that of England. It has evolved quite separately; the system was never imposed on Scots by an external or occupying power, and it is expressly protected by the Articles of Union of 1707. It has, of course, a distinct vocabulary – sheriffs, not magistrates; advocates, not barristers; culpable homicide, not manslaughter; house-breaking, not burglary. Witnesses in a Scottish court do not swear on the Bible; 15 sit in a Scots jury, not 12; and, in criminal proceedings, there are – like the ancient Romans – two verdicts of acquittal: Not Guilty, and the far more ambivalent Not Proven. 'It is our own peculiar amalgam of Roman law,' writes James Shaw Grant, 'feudal law, borrowings from England, both voluntary and inadvertent, and a faint trace of old Celtic law, which can be sensed now rather than identified.'

There are three chief differences from south of the Border. Scots law is substantially based on statute, not precedent and (setting aside, for the moment, the 'District Courts' for venal offences, where a Justice of the Peace presides) there are two tiers of criminal trial. There is 'solemn procedure', with a High Court judge and an empanelled jury (typical 'solemn procedure' matters would be rape and murder), and the usual 'summary procedure' of the Sheriff Court, the main court of first instance which is convened in even quite small Scottish towns, and where one learned man is both jury and judge over a great range of offences, and assorted civil actions besides.

There are two Sheriff Courts in the modern Western Isles – at Stornoway and Lochmaddy – and the system generally reflects the old and healthy Scots instinct for power devolved and decentralised. And at its core, in every district, is the locally based prosecutor, the procurator fiscal, each appointed by the Lord Advocate (in Edinburgh, the immemorial capital of our Scottish legal system) in the name of the Crown. Procurators fiscal are by training solicitors, and the position, these days, is salaried and full-time. In most rural areas, there is just one fiscal. In a city like Glasgow, there may be over forty. There are besides regional, supervising procurators fiscal to keep a quiet eye on the Crown's work in their province.

The office embodies much greater and more wide-ranging power than is often appreciated. At its heart, of course, the role is of a prosecutor. In allegations of less serious criminal offences, the fiscal decides whether or not to prosecute; prepares the prosecution case; and arranges its presentation and conduct in court, working closely with the police. In a more serious matter, the fiscal decides provisionally whether trial by solemn procedure (with a jury) should be heard in the Sheriff Court or the High Court of Justiciary, which, in the Highlands and Islands context, is convened in Inverness. But he refers the matter then to the Crown Office in Edinburgh, over which the Lord Advocate presides, and, should a High Court case proceed, the fiscal will assist the 'Advocate Depute' in the conduct of the case.

A procurator fiscal's role does not stop there. He can – and often does – direct police inquiries into a given crime. He investigates any complaints against the police (referred to him, perhaps problematically, by the police themselves) that involve allegations of criminal conduct. He must investigate all suspicious, unexpected or sudden deaths, from ordering collection of the remains to arranging a post-mortem and pondering the findings; likewise, unexplained fires or explosions call for his attention (again, with appropriate expert examination) for these, too, may lead to criminal proceedings. In fact, though the fiscal normally operates passively and from police or medical intimation, he may pursue any matter brought to his attention by a member of the public who suggests the law may have been broken.

The fiscal is on hand to give advice to other, locally active government departments on matters of criminal law: again, he may have to pursue cases arising from their work. While Scotland – unlike England – has no mandatory inquest after a sudden death, it is largely by the fiscal's discretion whether or not a Fatal Accident Inquiry is held, and he must marshal and present the evidence. The procurator fiscal makes the initial inquiries, too, when someone dies intestate – without leaving a will – and reports to the Crown Office; he is besides responsible for any 'Treasure Trove' found within his bounds, for he represents locally both the Lord Treasurer's Remembrancer and the Queen herself. (In England, only silver or gold – precious metal – are legally treasure trove; in Scotland, any articles of value can be declared Crown property, as long as they can be held as abandoned and not – like a modern engagement ring – merely lost.)

The system works well and avoids some of the vulnerabilities of the English system, where the police not only arrest offenders but have a substantial role in the conduct of the prosecution, a great strain on community relations in, for instance, a troubled urban ghetto. But on the Isle of Lewis, 200 years ago, local legal arrangements were ill-supervised, clumsy and grossly inadequate, with the result – exploited so ruthlessly by Donald Munro – that the islands were denied in any equitable sense the rule of law. As a consequence – and not least by the good offices of a new laird who might most kindly be described as naive and doting – the Tain adventurer, within a few years, had attained absolute power. 'Agus tha breitheanas air pilleadh air ais; agus tha ceartas a' seasamh fad as; oir thuislich an fhirinn air an t-sraid, agus cha b'urrain ionracas teachd a steachd,' the fearful murmured darkly, from the prophecy of Isaiah: 'And judgment is turned away backward, and justice standeth afar off: for truth is fallen in the street, and equity cannot enter.'

The problem was historic. Late in the fifteenth century, the Stewart monarchy had outmanoeuvred, outflanked and finally destroyed the Lordship of the Isles and the general West Highland suzerainty of Clan Donald without raising any effective polity in its place, save to favour cynical loyalists – notably the Campbells and the MacKenzies – to guard its own flank against the 'wickit Hielanmen'. Whatever the rapacities and ruthlessness of Clan Donald, there had at least been someone on each major island to dispense laws, rule in disputes and administer some sort of broadly respected justice. In northern Lewis, as we have noted, this had been the hereditary office of the Brieves – the chiefs of Clan Morrison. In more recent times (and often, no doubt, less than partially) it had to a degree fallen to local tacksmen. The Established Church had some judicial functions, notably at the level of sexual morality and 'affiliation' disputes – when the paternity of a child conceived out of wedlock had to be established; such cases could still absorb sessions on Lewis as recently as the 1980s. And – until the 1745 Rising – resident clan chiefs exercised 'heritable jurisdiction' in their districts, though this can have had little meaning on Lewis after the death of the skulking William, Earl of Seaforth, in 1740.

After Culloden, a distinctly rattled government for years kept most of the region under nervous military occupation. London abolished the heritable jurisdictions, passed the silly Disarming Acts – which, for some decades and beyond the Crown's own forces, outlawed bagpipes ('an engine of war') and even tartan – and built elaborate new camps and fortifications, such as the spectacular white elephant that is Fort George. But this was only to weaken still further the limited legal structure serving the Highlands and Hebrides since the fall of the Lordship, despite warnings from the Church and others. As early as 1725, as James Shaw Grant notes, and at its very first diet, the new Synod of Glenelg (covering the Outer Hebrides, Skye and Wester Ross) had petitioned Whitehall 'asking that "fit persons" should be commissioned to reside "in some of those places at greatest distance to see the laws duly executed".'

The Kirk's chief fear, no doubt, was Jacobite revolution, the return of Episcopal religion and the general murder of Presbyterians in their beds. Like most entreaties from Scottish churchmen to the post-Union government, it was ignored. Until the late eighteenth century, sheriffs in Scotland – some of whom presided over huge tracts of the country – were responsible not only for appointing 'substitutes' to administer justice in distant corners, but had themselves to salary them from their estates and resources – with the predictable result that as few sheriff substitutes were appointed as possible. In 1788 the government took on this responsibility – relieving sheriffs of this obligation was deemed cheaper than giving them the pay rise they demanded – but the consequences bore little regard for the realities of geography and attracted little government attention.

The plight of Lewis was especially difficult, for she lay within Ross and Cromarty and the county (and judicial) seat was at Dingwall, not just on the mainland but on the other side of Scotland. And communications, of course, even in the reign of George III, were risible. The journey from Lewis to Easter Ross – typically by sailing ship to Poolewe, a rowing boat down Loch Maree and by pony and primitive gig over the spine of the Highlands and by atrocious road to Easter Ross – was fraught enough, as we have seen, even for the Seaforths. A summons to court in Dingwall, as a consequence of what were often malicious actions by the mighty against the weak, caused much 'unnecessary trouble, hardship and expense . . . without serving any good purpose', the Sheriff of Ross and Cromarty, Donald MacLeod of Geanies, himself admitted in 1788. (MacLeod's own suitability for the office – which he would hold for nearly half a century – is dubious; when he was finally edged from office in 1833, someone remarked of this amiable country gentleman that he was respected for almost everything 'except his knowledge of the law'.)

But the Sheriff of Ross and Cromarty was in any event helpless when the first sheriff substitute appointed by the Crown – aloof and largely indifferent in Edinburgh – for Stornoway was a Dingwall solicitor, George Munro, who stayed in Dingwall and kept practising law in Dingwall. Flapping uncomfortably to Stornoway, he then inveigled the court there convened into choosing his own apprentice as sheriff clerk depute 'within the island of Lewis': but that young man, too, remained in Dingwall. And Sheriff Substitute Munro recommended a new procurator fiscal for Stornoway, John MacAllan – also a lawyer or 'writer' in Dingwall. As if these arrangements made not enough mockery of due process, Munro ruled that in civil actions there would be only a day's notice of court action for 'defenders' – those being pursued, for instance, for allegedly unpaid debt – within a given distance of Stornoway, and two days' granted defenders in other, farther parts of Lewis.

This, of course, was for Sheriff Substitute Munro's own convenience – to keep as brief as possible the time he was forced to spend on this westerly and, by his lights, bleak and uncomfortable island; for a tenant in a distant corner of Uig or Park, though, it meant an immediate and anxious tramp to town as soon as a summons came, without time to check records, consult friends and acquaintances or arrange the care of livestock and so on in his absence.

But there was a still bigger problem: the dearth of solicitors. It is self-evident that only a qualified solicitor can be appointed a fiscal, and that, besides, a lawyer can only act for one party in a dispute. And – whatever good intent may have lain behind the one-size-fits-all reforms of 1788 – it is evident that no one in authority cared about Hebridean realities. There were simply not enough qualified men on the Long Island. 'For the best part of a century after Lewis, belatedly, got a Sheriff Court,' writes Grant, 'there was never a period of ten consecutive years, I believe not even five, in which there were two independent legal agents in the town of Stornoway, so that one litigant in every civil case, and the accused in every criminal case, was unrepresented, except on the rare occasions when relatively wealthy people, faced with major litigation, were able to buy in legal advice from across the Minch.'

The consequences of this were somewhat mitigated for the accused in criminal proceedings, because of the Crown's struggle to provide a fiscal. For a while, they tried to serve the whole county with the procurator fiscal at Dingwall. But Munro soon realised that, for Stornoway purposes, he needed a man on the Long Island itself. With entire disregard for ability or equipment, he appointed Donald Ross, who was tacksman of Mid Borve, on the Atlantic coast between Barvas and Ness; the surname, as Grant highlights, suggests he was not a native of Lewis. Worse, Ross had no legal qualifications or even a university degree. In any event, he only lasted a year, being too far from Stornoway even to attempt the job to Munro's satisfaction. He was followed by an Alexander Anderson, who did live in town and seems to have had no attainments or aptitude either, and was not long in post. Thereafter, *ex officio* and by tacit agreement, the solicitor retained in Stornoway by the Seaforths served the authorities besides as procurator fiscal.

One need scarcely enlarge on the folly of this. For one – with the Estate already wielding massive economic and civil power – it was a gross conflict of interest. For another, it tilted the scales of law decisively in favour of the rich. The Seaforths, the forces of law and anyone raising an action had a solicitor on the spot: those they or other wealthy notables sought to arraign, or indict, or summons, had no hope of legal representation.

The horror stories are legion. By the early 1820s, even as his good Seaforth lady floated around funding Sabbath schools, writing cheques to charity and thinking of suitably godly ministers for the next parish vacancy – James Stewart-Mackenzie, her ponderous husband, was organising clearances, especially as the repeal of the Salt Act in 1822 began rapidly to reduce, and by decade's end quite demolish, the profits from kelp and any commercial value in tenantry.

There was no forced emigration overseas, of course, but Stewart-MacKenzie was anxious to increase Estate revenue and wanted to try large-scale sheep-farming on the model demonstrated so notoriously, at the turn of the nine-teenth century, in Sutherland. As Uig had been most pressed for troops by the late father-in-law, it was on Uig too – 200 years ago, a wealthy and even bustling part of Lewis, with fat harvests and fine cattle and a range of skilled tradesmen – that Stewart-MacKenzie focused this experiment. The best chunks were to be rented to Lowland graziers; and their 'redundant' inhabi-tants removed to one exposed chunk of Lewis where, Stewart-MacKenzie thought vaguely, they could develop a fishing industry.

So Mealista was cleared, as were Haclete and Kirkibost on Bernera, and the southern peninsulae of Park were also emptied of their villages. (It should not be forgotten, either, that not a few families in Ardroil were robbed of land so that the greedy new minister of Uig, the Reverend Alexander MacLeod, could enlarge his glebe.) Everyone was offered relocation – Tong, in some instances, but mostly parts of Point like Swordale and Shulishader; and new villages were created at the northern end of that peninsula, like Portvoller and Portnaguran. But many of the families so rudely uprooted preferred (and took) passage to Cape Breton. And we know that as late as 1840, Stewart-MacKenzie did not hesitate – when crofters dared to demur – to raise proceedings for eviction in court.

That year, Sheriff Robert Sutherland Taylor presided for some months at Stornoway, and the record reflects the dour laissez-faire spirit of the mighty in Scotland in those days. He left on record his annoyance at the problems inevitable from 'the circumstances of this Court, where the Respondents have not access to professional legal assistance except at a great distance'. Yet, in the various cases before him on Lewis in 1840, he refused to grant any delay, there being 'no remedy consistent with the expeditious discussion' of the matters.

'Two of the cases were actions for removal at the behest of the Seaforths,' writes Grant, 'and it seems reasonable to assume that, whatever the urgency with which the estate wished to get vacant possession of its property, the tenants being evicted would suffer more from undue haste than the estate from undue delay.' For Sheriff Taylor – no doubt itching to return to his mainland ease – 'expeditious discussion' counted for much more than natural justice, and he was but the child of an age when, badly rattled by the French Revolution, gentry and professional men and those aspiring all over Scotland to join their ranks shuddered openly at anything remotely suggesting 'sedition' – with even the local press of the day only too eager to share in the propaganda.

In July 1839, for instance, the *Highland News* was happy to paint the latest sad little scene in Harris evictions as if cut-throats had been on the brink of bloody revolution. The rapacious sheep-farming tenant of Luskentyre (cleared of its helpless people years earlier for his enrichment) had refused now to renew his lease unless the village of Borve (not to be confused with the Lewis township of that name) was likewise emptied of its folk and added to his fat machair holding. But the people of Borve dug their heels in and refused to shift, and the factor panicked. He sent, incredibly, for troops:

> On Saturday, Lieutenant M'Neill with his party of soldiers returned to Glasgow from the Island of Harris, after an absence of nine days. He has been successful in the object of his mission and, we are glad to learn, without violence. They reached Harris at 7 o'clock on the morning of Tuesday last, the 23rd, and were enabled to leave it at 6 the same evening. All the cottars or small farmers implicated in the deforcement were requested to assemble in the village, and from the body five men, who had been most active in the illegal proceedings, were selected and carried prisoners to Portree. The visit of the military excited the deepest alarm among the poor islanders, who were heard to express in Gaelic their terror that the scene of Glencoe was about to be acted all over again.

'Thus,' burbled the factor, 'terminated an outbreak which, but for the prompt measures of the government in sending in the military, would have thrown the whole of the West Highlands into confusion for many years.' As Bill Lawson dryly observes, this was 'so severe an outbreak that it could be dealt with by calling the people to a meeting and selecting five of them to take to jail'; but, in this climate of public life, the rise of such a creature as Donald Munro can readily be grasped.

As Lawson has elsewhere observed, the fumbling efforts of Stewart-MacKenzie to 'improve' his Lewis estates were, for the most part, as futile as they were witless. 'Most of these schemes were unsuccessful, and their end result was to cause upheaval and misery throughout the island, without in any way improving the financial position of the Stewart-MacKenzies . . . Stewart-MacKenzie had made the same mistake as was made all over the north-west. You cannot merely transport a crofter to the shores and expect him to make a success of fishing. Quite apart from the questions of skill and experience, the fisherman requires a boat and gear, and the new settlers in Point had little chance to gather the capital to acquire either . . .'

It had been difficult enough for ordinary island people before the new legal order subjected them to one or another form of judicial terrorism. About 1831, the farmer of Upper Coll – Roderick Nicolson, one of the local big-shots, who combined the status of tacksman with some prosperity as a shipowner – sought an interdict against the tenants in Nether or Lower Coll, to prevent them setting their cattle to graze among the seaware on the beach. There were some 300 beasts; cattle have a taste for seaweed, with all its minerals and flavours, and they were led down daily by some herd boy or other as the tide ebbed to take their fill, before the waters of Broad Bay flooded back in. The people of Lower Coll (and their stock) had enjoyed this access since time immemorial and not even a laird – as would later be attested in Kilmallie after the Disruption, when Cameron of Lochiel did all he could to deny or hinder Free Church worship – could claim jurisdiction below the high-water mark (though Matheson, in his day, would make a determined try).

But Nicolson had engaged the only lawyer on the island. The poor people of Lower Coll not only lost the case, by default, but were found liable for all legal expenses. And there it might have ended had the Seaforths not, in 1832, sacked their factor, Alexander Stewart – who briefly set up shop himself as a local solicitor. Though lately an agent for Estate oppression, he was now hired to act for the Lower Coll crofters and could personally attest in court both to their rights to graze the shore under their current lease and the costly, labour-intensive improvements they had been forced to promise before they were granted it.

But the skew-whiff order of law in Lewis was perilous even for little men in little cases, far less beleaguered communities fighting to stay on their ancient ground. And Nicolson seems to have been an exceptionally nasty piece of work. One incident around 1834, detailed by James Shaw Grant, shows the capacity of some of the island's luckiest and most well-off men to resort to litigation in the furtherance of what was little more than robbery.

In the village of Tong there lived a Murdo Matheson, who scissored a scant living for himself as a tailor and further reinforced his budget by carrying loads about with his cart and grey horse. One spring he set his cuddy, as usual, to grazing on the Tong moor. The horse enjoyed himself and wandered, then wandered some more. Matheson was not greatly anxious, for he knew word of him would come eventually, and, sure enough, he heard after some weeks that he was trotting around by the dykes of the farm at Arnish. He sent his wife and servant to collect the animal; not only did they recognise the horse at once, but he recognised them, being such a pet – according to Grant – that he would even step into their house in hope of food.

But word of this reached Roderick Nicolson, who scented the chance of winning a free horse. He now claimed the beast as his own, and raised an action against him in the Sheriff Court – and, to further it, retained the services of the only solicitor in town.

As had happened to other hapless Lewis people in recent years, Matheson might well have lost the horse by default. But he was lucky. He had a brave and literate friend, Hugh Brown, who had his own legal ambitions though not, as far as we can now ascertain, any qualifications. His ability is evident. Brown wrote a deft, even passionate plea to the court, pointing out – for instance – that Nicolson's own mount had been sighted on the Lochs moor after the reporting of the Matheson beast at the Arnish Farm boundary and 'unless he were a Pegasus he could not be one and the same animal'. And Hugh Brown set gleefully to giving the greedy Roderick Nicolson his character, in contrast to the honest and saintly industry of Murdo Matheson, who

is a poor, illiterate man without legal advice or assistance, depending for his own and his family's subsistence upon the services of the animal of which the Petitioner so unjustly seeks to deprive him. On the other hand the Petitioner, with whom he has to contend in defending his lawful property, is a rich man and has employed the only procurator in the place to conduct his case. He had the greatest difficulty in getting a person to undertake the writing of these answers and, were it not that he has the greatest confidence in the goodness of his cause and your Lordship's impartial judgement, he would, in all probability, sit down in despair and suffer the Petitioner to carry away his property without opposition.

Brown took care to conclude his entire, elegant argument with the note, 'drawn without fee or reward by H Brown'; and that Matheson himself put his cross to it – and Brown did himself, between 1815 and 1833, serve as fiscal, until there was yet further (and broadly sensible) reform of the creaking Scots legal system and the office thereafter could only be held by a qualified solicitor. The people lost a friend in Hugh Brown; and as the Industrial Revolution devoured the Lowlands of Scotland, the tenets of Adam Smith were applied with all the more rigour to Highland affairs – and that in a free market rigged consistently in the interests of land and capital.

So much of the popular history of this period – and the assorted monuments and memorials to James Matheson himself – paints a picture of a backward, benighted, illiterate island that it is important to stand back and take a long look at the Lewis of 200 years ago.

Certainly it was an island still largely roadless, though rough, unmetalled highways – by the direction of the last Earl of Seaforth, Francis Humberston MacKenzie – now ran to Point and across the island to Barvas. Certainly it was a place where most of the housing (even in Stornoway) was still thatched – though the Hebridean black-house, made with good materials and with reasonable security of tenure, should not be despised: it was warm, well insulated, well drained and sustainably built. And certainly it was 'remote' – all the more so as power, wealth and people generally drained from the countryside into the rapidly industrialising Lowlands; and as local authority was cemented in the burghs of the East Highland seaboard. And certainly, by the mid 1840s – owing to circumstances unwonted, unusual and, as events would prove, short-term – it was an island with real social problems.

But this was not some Third World demesne in need of some lordly paternalist of a laird to 'ameliorate' the lot of its shiftless, whingeing natives. Even by 1800 this was a thriving, outward-looking place, exporting some remarkable and highly educated people, with strong commercial links to the Continent and beyond and – long before the Gaelic Schools Societies or the endeavours of either Mrs Stewart-MacKenzie or Lady Matheson – one of the best educational establishments in Scotland.

The Stornoway Grammar School, founded and endowed by the Seaforths themselves, was in operation by 1680 and was still going as late as 1819, by which time there was a fee-paying establishment in ferocious competition – the Stornoway Academy. Nor were the rural districts forgotten; the Scottish Society for Propagating Christian Knowledge had, by the 1745 Rising, set up establishments at Keose in Lochs and Swainbost in Ness, and by century's end there was at least a third in rural Lewis, at Shawbost on the West Side, by which time the Keose and Swainbost seats of learning seem to have folded, as well as one in Stornoway itself. In 1828, another SSPCK school would open at Loch Shell, and in 1832 two more, at Valtos and Callanish. The SSPCK schools naturally taught Scripture and the Shorter Catechism, and Psalm-singing, but they taught besides handwriting and arithmetic and geometry, and English as effectively a foreign language.

The 'Ladies' Schools', founded early in the nineteenth century by the benefactions of urban Evangelicals, reached Lewis in 1811, when the first opened at Bayble; by 1815 there were eight of them on the island. The ambition of this new generation of Gaelic schools was most modest: they would only teach people how to read the Bible in their native language and, to defuse any opposition from island ministers, it was made a strict rule that their teachers were never to preach or 'exhort', though they were suffered to read the Scriptures aloud on the Sabbath and to conduct prayer meetings. (The complete translation of the Bible in Scottish Gaelic was as we have noted belatedly done; it would be 1828 before a popular edition was available at a genuinely affordable price.) Nor was there any plan for long-term operation. The Edinburgh Society for the Support of Gaelic Schools – the first and most influential – only intended to fund a teacher in a given locality for a year or two; he would then be moved on to a new work of outreach elsewhere. These schools besides attracted much comment because they taught a very high proportion of girls, who had hitherto, save for the governess-reared daughters of gentry, been denied any formal education in the West Highlands.

The success of these new schools, with minimal materials and usually got up in some small thatched cott, was immediate. The first teacher at Bayble, an Angus MacLeod from Skye, opened with just three pupils. Soon he had 60. Three hundred people started gathering each Sabbath to hear him read the Bible. He was moved to Gress after two years, and had soon mustered 150 pupils. Nor was the thirst for learning confined to children – grandparents wanted to join these classes (and did) and at least one perky great-grandmother sought a place in one Society school on Lewis, was happily admitted and duly learnt to read. And several of those schools were sustained by villages, at their own expense, when Society funding ceased – as was the establishment at Galsion and its teacher, John MacLeod, another Skyeman, when he was sacked by the ESSGS at the behest of the jealous parish minister: MacLeod had started to hold full-blown services.

The contribution of these schools to the extraordinary Evangelical trans-formation of Lewis – accomplished with remarkable speed from the early 1820s and sealed by the Disruption of 1843, when practically everyone repudiated the Established Church – owed much to these little seats of learning. For decades thereafter, island churches made a special collection for the ESSGS at the end of each Communion season. 'Cho fad 'sa bhitheas m uir a'; bualadh ri lic,' asserted one great island minister, the Reverend John MacRae, 'agus bainne geal aig bo dhubh, cha bu choir do mhuinntir Leodhas na sgoiltean Gaidhlig a dhi-cuimhneachadh.' 'For as long as the sea beats against a rock, and white milk comes from a black cow, the people of Lewis should not forget the Gaelic schools.'

That illiteracy had hitherto been widespread was undoubted, and little wonder in an agrarian, subsistence economy. In communication with the ESSGS in May 1811, the minister of Stornoway, the Reverend Colin MacKenzie, calculated that, out of the 2,000 people in the town itself and its adjacent townships, 1,333 could neither read nor write, in either Gaelic or English. Of the 800 folk in Point, only 20 could read English, and 6 Gaelic; in Back – about 700 people – only 6 were literate in English, and 2 in Gaelic. It may have been even worse in other island districts. Earlier, in his chapter for the Statistical Account in 1796, Mr MacKenzie had advised there were 40 scholars in Stornoway town's parochial school (the Seaforth Foundation) and 129 at the one maintained by the SSPCK, as well as a separate spinning school, founded as early as 1763, which, within two years, had trained over 400 girls. It was in this establishment Mrs Stewart-MacKenzie took such interest, and by the height of her endeavours there were two spinning schools in each of the island's four parishes. They would survive until the wholesale import of cotton from the Americas hit hard the market for linen, and much value in its skills; the last Lewis spinning school had closed by 1845.

The Stornoway Grammar School, though, was a remarkable establishment: small, yes, and filled largely by aspiring families and pushy parents, and perhaps with more than a hint of the hothouse, but supervised closely by the local Presbytery and drawing scholars from all over rural Lewis. By 1761, it was preparing pupils for admission to university – which, in those days, was usually Aberdeen, and to which apt boys would generally be sent around the age of 14. By 1781, the Grammar School was teaching – and to a high standard – English, arithmetic, religion, Latin and even Greek – this at the time when Greek was not even taught in Edinburgh's Royal High School and the very idea was angrily opposed by university professors. In 1810, the Presbytery would rigorously interview three candidates, all highly qualified, for the position of headmaster, after grilling each on a range of subjects including both ancient languages.

None of this sits readily alongside our cosy imaginings of a distant, straw-sucking Teuchterville. The Academy of Stornoway, which opened in 1817, was still more ambitious. It was private – got up by a pool of 'subscribers' among self-conscious Stornoway gentry; fees were levied for scholars, and there was a board of directors. Subscribers could nominate their own offspring for admission, and others they felt worthy of it. A fee was charged for each subject taken, and the range was impressive – the basics, of course, like English and arithmetic, but the Academy also taught Latin, Greek, French and even Italian, as well as mathematics, astronomy, navigation, natural philosophy (physics) and chemistry; for some reason, the highest charges were for the classes in drawing and stenography. The rector was a Dr Alexander Pollok, and the chairmen were successively Captain John MacKenzie and Lewis MacIver.

MacIver was early in the succession of 'big men' the Long Island has produced in recent centuries – natural leaders, usually blessed with some evident commercial acumen and invariably with a keen brain, common sense and high emotional intelligence or 'people skills', who tend to tread a fine line between popular standing and serious clout in high places and often have a deliciously subversive streak, usually evident in a keen sense of fun – a throwback, to that capacity for riotous gaiety widely recorded in old Norse saga of the best Norse princes. The type endures to this day – in far more decent men, like Sandy Matheson of Stornoway or John Murdo Morrison of Tarbert – and, equipped of necessity with a very thick skin, they go about doing good, mitigating evil and humouring or outmanoeuvring, as need arises, this and that officious blockhead.

One of the earliest on Lewis was John Morrison, tacksman of Bragar and a grandson of John, the last Brieve, slain so unfortunately at Inverkirkaig and gralloched as tempest deferred his burial. John himself was a highly gifted man, the author – around 1660 – of an important, early account of Lewis life and mores, under the pseudonym 'Indweller', and who won a striking compliment from an admiring MacKenzie: that this Morrison had a 'lady's modesty, a bishop's gravity, a lawyer's eloquence and a captain's conduct'.

John Morrison seems to have been among the first pupils of the Stornoway Grammar School, and is said to have won his Bragar tack after giving Seaforth himself a lift ashore on his back at Stornoway. He was a knacky engineer, constructing a sluice and valve that allowed him as he saw fit to drain the brackish waters of Loch Ordais while keeping the Atlantic out, and he managed (characteristic of his island breed) to build and maintain the most cordial relations with the officers of Cromwell's Stornoway garrison while quietly amassing intelligence for passing to Seaforth's men. 'Indweller' begot besides a remarkably talented family, including three ministers, a highly regarded island blacksmith and one of the greatest bards Gaeldom has ever produced, Roderick Morrison, *An Clarsar Dall* ('The Blind Harpist') of Dunvegan.

This Louis or Lewis MacIver was very much in the tradition, another Broad Bay farmer and Stornoway shipowner whom James Shaw Grant describes as the 'uncrowned king of Lewis in his day', and who seems to have exemplified that natural Gaelic ease even with Hanoverian royalty. For the eighteenth century did not pass without another prince setting foot on Lewis, and to rather more relaxed and happy a reception than his Stuart cousin.

On 19 July 1785, HMS *Hebe*, a 40-gun frigate, wallowed importantly into Stornoway harbour – under the command of Commodore John Leveson-Gower – after sailing from Kirkwall; and evidently tarried for some days, for she did not make her next port, Belfast, until 3 August. In fact, the *Hebe* was making a complete tour round the British coast, according to Roger Fulford, which may have been partly for the benefit of a young officer of 20, whose curious appearance – he had a very red face and a pointed head that put many in mind of a pineapple – belied his importance. He had been sent to sea by his formidable parents in June 1779, not yet 14, but by all accounts he exulted in this independence and was eager to put fellow sailor-lads at ease, for it is recorded that shipmates – knowing full well the boy's rank – surrounded him at once with mingled curiosity and ill-ease, until one was brave enough to ask the little chap how he ought to be addressed.

'I am entered as Prince William Henry,' piped the new recruit, 'but my father's name is Guelph and therefore, if you please, you may call me William Guelph, for I am nothing more than a sailor like yourselves.' Later, in 1789 – though only after, chafing at the unusual delay, he threatened to stand for the House of Commons – King George III finally raised his third son to be Duke of Clarence; in 1830 he would assume the throne as King William IV. He was the first – and last – prince of the realm to see New York while it still owed allegiance to the British Crown; he was the last to rule both Great Britain and Hanover, which has the 'Salic law' of succession and, on his death, passed to his brother Ernest Augustus, Duke of Cumberland, fifth son of George III, while the thrones of Britain and Ireland were assumed by their niece, the 18-year-old Victoria and only child of the late Edward, Duke of Kent.

The *Gentleman's Magazine* in 1789 records that the prince had a very pleasant if strait-laced time in Stornoway. Naturally the last Lord Seaforth hastened to meet him. Prince William Henry had a tour of the town and was even taken for a spot of fishing. (No one seems to have suggested he visit Arnish; Charles Edward, actually, had only died the year before.) Local tradition, beyond the pages of respectable journals, relates that the prince – at least when the sun went down – also enjoyed the diversions, in abundance, for which Stornoway still has a reputation and which are rather more to the unregenerate taste of the young British male. Lewis MacIver was soon in

William Henry's little Stornoway set, and Grant records that the future monarch 'got into some sailorly scrapes ashore, with considerable assistance from the locals'.

But this was not the only Hanoverian connection with Stornoway. In 1801, Alexander MacKenzie – the celebrated explorer of Canada – was knighted, just two months after publication of his *Voyages from Montreal on the River St Lawrence, through the Continent of North America to the Frozen and Pacific Oceans, In the Years 1789 and 1793*. Concision was not a virtue of eighteenth-century titles but – though only 750 copies of the book were printed, in beautiful leather binding and with elegant maps (still boasting great blank voids, as if to emphasise MacKenzie's original achievement) – it made the explorer's name.

Though not schooled on Lewis, MacKenzie was born in Stornoway, in 1764 at Luskentyre House on Francis Street – on the site now occupied by Martin's Memorial Church, where a tablet records his nativity. His mother was a locally born MacIver; his father, tenant of Melbost Farm, had been an ensign in the Stornoway Company at Culloden, on the government side. Alexander had a basic grounding at the Stornoway school, but was only ten when his mother died and his father removed the family to New York, where there were relatives. (It was a period when tacksmen by the hundred were quitting the Hebrides and West Highlands for the New World.) The boy seems to have had little formal education thereafter, but he had made his voyages and won his fame before he was 30.

For this Alexander MacKenzie, native of the Isle of Lewis, was the very first man to cross the North American continent – at least, the very first white man – an achievement all the more remarkable as he had little training in navigation, inadequate and obsolete instruments and only a quarter of the men who, in 1803, and at the behest of President Thomas Jefferson, would accompany Lewis and Clark on their much more trumped (and far less impressive) trek across the continental United States. These Americans are still vaunted – as James Shaw Grant acidly points out – as 'the men who opened up the Continent' and did so 'almost without bloodshed'. MacKenzie had done it a decade before, much further north, by foot and canoe, in a more severe climate, at far greater risk – and with no bloodshed at all. MacKenzie planned and accomplished this daunting journey without (as Charles Lamb admiringly remarked) 'the authority, the flags or the medals of his Government'. And, had MacKenzie not done so, the geopolitical consequences could have been epochal: had he not demonstrated this reasonable overland route, the west coast of North America might well have been colonised from the sea – by tsarist Russia.

MacKenzie's first, 1789, attempt was amateurish: he set out to reach the Pacific, and ended up in the Arctic. The one consolation was the great rolling waterway he discovered, which he darkly named Disappointment River. His men bore this embarrassment with kindly good humour, and Alexander MacKenzie then spent a year in London, furiously brushing up his skills in navigation. For the second bid, he took remarkably few instruments, and of curious quality: a compass, which was not graduated; a sextant, of an old-fashioned and antiquated design; a chronometer which ran down relentlessly during the expedition and grew less and less reliable. As far as he could tell, joked Grant in the 1980s, 'the telescope functioned adequately'. But MacKenzie made it and duly published his book, of such impact that several years later Napoleon himself, directing his network of spies and with thoughts of an invasion of Canada by Marshall Bernadotte from the French colonies in Louisiana, managed with signal difficulty to have a copy smuggled out from London.

MacKenzie's knighthood, so soon after his *Voyages* appeared, seems to have been secured on his behalf by Prince Edward Augustus, Duke of Kent and fourth son of George III: but for his death in 1820 – a chill he would certainly have survived but for the crazed, blood-letting endeavours of his doctors – he, and not his daughter Victoria, would have inherited the Crown in 1837. A soldier by profession and a martinet by temperament, Edward was otherwise in his vices of extravagance and meddling typical of all the hapless sons of George III – 'the damndest millstones ever hung about the neck of any Government,' the Duke of Wellington in his hoary old age would grimly recall – but Kent spent much of the 1790s in Canada, brutalising troops, cosseting his mistress and racking up prodigious debt, and he knew Alexander MacKenzie well, taking him on at least one occasion as a travelling companion. One of his very last letters, in 1820, was to the sturdy old Highland wanderer.

That epistle has long lain in the Royal Archives, but the very map of Canada itself celebrates this Stornoway boy – MacKenzie Bay and MacKenzie Point, the Mackenzie Valley and the MacKenzie District and the MacKenzie Pass, and MacKenzie's Rock in what has long been the Sir Alexander MacKenzie Provincial Park, where the triumphant explorer at last scrawled – in melted bear-grease and vermilion – 'Alexander MacKenzie/ from Canada/ by land/ 22d July 1793.' Most famous of all his memorials, though, is his first: that wild torrent of 1789 mortification, now long the celebrated MacKenzie River. The explorer, still only 56, died of kidney disease at Dunkeld in March 1820, on his way home to Avoch in the Black Isle, where he is buried.

But the Canadian adventurer was not the only bold, adventuring MacKenzie from Stornoway. Colin MacKenzie, a grandson of the MacKenzies at Kildun, was born in the town a decade earlier – son of the local postmaster – in 1754 and educated at the Stornoway Grammar School, before beginning a career as a local customs officer. He must have had a remarkable teacher in mathematics – perhaps a Benjamin Mercer, apparently removed in 1774 under pressure from the Lewis Presbytery for, it is hinted, undue worldliness – for he had exceptional mathematical acumen and was still employed at the Customs House when engaged by John Napier of Merchiston to study Hindu logarithms; the Edinburgh nobleman was writing a book about his distinguished sixteenth-century forebear. The commission soon begot a fascination with all things Indian in Colin MacKenzie, and in any event the lot of a customs officer in the West Highlands was both ill-paid and socially fraught. At the age of 28, MacKenzie demitted his position and joined the British East India Company as an officer in the engineers.

At the Battle of Seringapatam, where British forces took on and (despite inferior numbers) defeated the Maharajah of Mysore, Colin MacKenzie earned the undying friendship of Colonel Arthur Wellesley: they shared a dangerous side-action after another officer failed properly to study the ground before attack, and it was MacKenzie's testimony that cleared the future Duke of Wellington from allegations of what would have been career-ending incompetence. (Years later, in a tight spot at the siege of Badajos, the tough old fellow would sigh, 'Oh, that old MacKenzie were here . . .')

After the Seringapatam triumph, Colin MacKenzie was put in charge of the 'Mysore Survey' – an exhaustively illustrated study of the natural history, lore, traditions and customs of the region – and ended up as Surveyor-General of India, mapping the whole subcontinent to the highest standard. It was, of course, to the bidding of a ruthless commercial and imperial adventure, but his research and vast collections are of abiding importance to India's cultural heritage. He funded much of this work from his own resources and hired learned Brahmins to assist him in survey and translation. As James Shaw Grant relates, the Lewis scholar 'collected, and so probably saved from destruction, 1,568 manuscripts in different Indian languages, 8,076 inscriptions, 2,630 drawings, 78 plans, 6,218 coins and 106 images, to say nothing of 3,000 tenures inscribed on stone or copper, and all relevant to Indian history. He also contributed valuable articles on Indian religion to learned reviews and collected, often from wayside fakirs, oral lore which would otherwise have been lost. Despite the fact that the British Raj is now only a memory, and not a happy one for India, the name MacKenzie is still respected, and his collections regarded as of considerable importance.' Unfortunately Colin MacKenzie's original maps, and what must have been a fascinating memoir – seven folio volumes of it – are still missing, perhaps casualties of the Indian Mutiny.

Colin MacKenzie later spent two years in Java, under British occupation at the height of the Napoleonic Wars. He seems never to have returned to Scotland – and was buried in India at his death in Calcutta in May 1821 – but he kept in close touch through his successor as Comptroller of Customs, James Robertson, and funded the building of a fine house for his sister, Mary Carn MacKenzie, which stood by the modern Town Hall and survived till its witless demolition in the 1950s. It was Robertson who, after MacKenzie's death, travelled to London to resolve a dispute over the estate – the late surveyor-general's widow, a woman of Dutch parentage, quickly remarried – and returned in triumph with £30,000 in hard cash for Mary, a vast fortune at the time: 'a very considerable sum,' says Grant, 'and enabled Mary Carn to play the Lady Bountiful in Stornoway for the remainder of her life. And to leave more than a hundred legacies locally when she died.' MacKenzie himself left generous bequests for good Stornoway causes, and the elaborate family tomb at Aignish gives his name pride of place, though thousands of miles from his dust.

The third Lewis explorer is much less known, partly because of his early death overseas, partly because the book that would have won him a global reputation was not published until very many years after his death, and partly because history has persisted in putting him down as a Londoner. But James Morrison, who was sentenced to death (and subsequently reprieved) for his part in the mutiny of the *Bounty*, was a Lewisman, and in fact one of the leading and most sensible figures in the angry overthrow of the notorious Captain Bligh. Morrison had landed in Australia the year that modern Australian history began, spent time as virtual 'king' of Tahiti and wrote the first extensive, warm and detailed English account of life in Polynesia, with rich description of local life and custom: when Christian missionaries first made for Tahiti, it was with a 100-page lexicon of the local vocabulary, alphabetically arranged and accented, Morrison had compiled while lying aboard a Royal Navy prison-ship. He was pardoned, and lost at sea in 1807, as gunner on HMS *Blenheim*. The pages in Morrison's *Journal* about the mutiny on the *Bounty* have been joyously pillaged for years by writers and film-makers; his study of life in Polynesia has only once been published, in 1937, in a very limited edition, and with minimal impact.

The community that Matheson would so patronise and Munro hold in such contempt had, in the last decade of the eighteenth century, produced three pioneers of world-class importance – as in truth befitted an island then with its own extensive shipping and rich in the humane, good-humoured and wandering blood of the Norsemen.

The final years of Seaforth rule on Lewis have a shifting, *fin de siècle* air: a spectacular marine drama (culminating in a notable public hanging); a

disconcertingly convivial funeral, the last of its kind in Highland clan exuber-
ance; yet another officious, vain procurator fiscal; and the last duels fought
anywhere in Scotland.

Meanwhile, a new, sensible and Gaelic-speaking sheriff substitute, John
MacKenzie – a son of MacKenzie of Letterewe in Wester Ross and whose
wife was a daughter of the ageing minister at Uig, the Reverend Hugh Munro
– was appointed in 1813. He would serve the Long Island for almost 30 years.
He remains the only Stornoway sheriff yet appointed to have had any real,
prior knowledge of Lewis – Mackenzie had been a solicitor in the town in his
youth, and served besides as sheriff clerk – but his mainland estate called him
away for what were often long, distracted spells. Besides an undoubted hazard
of deep ties in the local culture, Sheriff MacKenzie was open to pressures an
entire outsider would have quite evaded. Nevertheless he incurred the wrath
of Mrs Stewart-MacKenzie, who seems to have felt the Sheriff Court
insufficiently biddable under his presiding to the whims of her Estate, and
did her best to secure his dismissal; a reminder that at times she was not quite
as nice as she looked (or was at least capable of firing the bullets her husband
made).

The shortage of court time and the lack of decent local facilities – such as a
jail fit for human habitation – led to bizarre court outcomes, especially when
Sheriff MacKenzie and Hugh Brown (the unqualified procurator fiscal) cooked
up expediences that would have done credit to the Brieves. In 1818, one
prisoner left to rot in Stornoway until the courts could get around to trying him
– Alexander MacDonald, a subtenant at Begnigary, had confessed to stealing
seed from a neighbour's barn – wearied of his conditions. He was besides scared
of the probable sentence – a good public flogging, and then banishment. He
finally petitioned Sheriff MacKenzie in these extraordinary terms, pleading

> that your Lordship will consider that he has already been sufficiently
> punished for his crime by being confined so long in this jail, and that as he is
> given to understand that there is no Common Executioner at present in the
> Town of Stornoway, he is willing to accept this office for his liberation, and
> on condition that a reasonable provision will be made to maintain himself
> and his family.

Still more remarkably, Sheriff MacKenzie granted this crave, solemnly
finding the prisoner entitled to the 'fees, perquisites, and emoluments' of
the office, as long as MacLeod did indeed 'consider himself bound to perform
. . . whenever he is called on to do so'. In fact, there were never again to be
executions in Stornoway, but the post of Common Executioner – who, in every

European community, was a general pariah – was notoriously difficult to fill, and MacLeod's nerve had probably tickled the sheriff's sense of humour.

In the winter of 1821–22, a Donald MacLeod – a Bayhead stonemason – lay in Stornoway's squalid Tollbooth, having been incarcerated since August after allegedly setting a boat adrift and stealing some bedding. His trial, he was told, could not be held until April. Using a friend – perhaps Hugh Brown – he wrote to Sheriff MacKenzie, begging simply to be banished from the county, rather than languish in these conditions. His Lordship obliged; MacLeod was exiled for seven years.

On a Sabbath evening in July 1821, tenants of the tacksman at Tolsta Farm saw a wreck some distance from the shore. Regard for the Lord's Day was not then what it would fast become, and a boat was promptly launched by locals eager for the fruits of salvage. The abandoned vessel was a copper-bottomed schooner, lying on her beam ends. Attempts to tow her to shelter failed when a gale blew; in the morning the broken ship lay in a cove by Tolsta Head, and her cargo – bales of paper, barrels of beeswax, jars of olives, bags of aniseed and pipes of sweet oil – washed up everywhere. The tacksman himself waited till Monday evening before sending a messenger on his leisurely way to town to report the incident to the Receiver of Wreck; on Tuesday morning, that official was readying for the march to Tolsta when customs officials sent him scurrying instead to Swordale. They had heard suspicious reports of a boat off the coast there during the weekend.

On the shore at Swordale Roderick MacIver, Surveyor of Customs, found a fishing boat drawn up on the shore and six men – none of them islanders or Gaels – sheltering in an improvised tent on the beach. They claimed to be of the brig *Betsy*, from New York, lost several days earlier off Barra head, and their leader – George Sadwell – said he had been her mate; that the captain and he had quarrelled as she had foundered, and the master had then made off in one boat with five men for Liverpool. He himself, asserted Sadwell, had rallied the rest and made for the Scottish mainland. Unkind winds had forced them ashore on Lewis.

At this point MacIver knew nothing of the wreck on Tolsta. But he insisted on searching their belongings and, though he found no contraband, he found some Spanish cash – silver dollars – in the assorted sea-chests they had brought ashore. And, as he padded away to report, a young lad broke away from the survivors and dashed after him, to Sadwell's evident consternation; and all was soon exposed.

This 18-year-old cabin boy, Andrew Camelier, was from Malta, and he told a very different story. They had in fact been the crew of a schooner from Gibraltar, not New York, and she was not the *Betsy* but some other ship; and her master had been a Scot, Thomas Johnston. He had talked too much one night, in his cups, and let slip the vessel bore not just oil and olives and beeswax and so on, but eight barrels of Spanish dollars – $38,180, in fact. The mate (whose real name was Peter Heaman) and the cook, François Gautier, had plotted, and one night attacked and murdered Captain Johnston and another Scottish sailor, one Paterson – the ship's helmsman – dumping the weighted bodies overboard. Paterson had certainly been dead, said Camelier miserably, but he had thought the captain still alive.

Two other protesting Scottish sailors had been imprisoned in their berth under a nailed-down hatch, according to the cabin-boy, and after a determined attempt to smother them with smoke, had – 'alive but dejected' – been prevailed on to co-operate, swearing secrecy on a kissed Bible. To cut an involved tale short, they had made for Barra, bought a small open fishing boat, and planned to scuttle their ship – which was actually called the *Jane* – in the Minch, before slipping covertly to the mainland with all their cash. But the *Jane* – unbeknownst to them – had disobligingly refused to sink and contrary winds had prevented passage east over the Minch. So they had taken refuge on the shore at Swordale, and buried most of the Spanish silver on the beach. Andrew Camelier the cabin boy (who, as was later implied desperately by Heaman in court, had probably been forced to service as a catamite of the captain and perhaps others, a notorious hazard of onboard life at the time) may well have had resentments of his own, but everything he asserted tallied with what the officials had found out or could quickly check, from the wreck at Tolsta to the huge quantity of dollars soon unearthed from the Swordale sands.

The entire conspiracy collapsed and, in November 1821, Heaman and Gautier went on trial in the High Court of Admiralty at Edinburgh – in a case of some legal importance as it established that, even for a crime committed thousands of miles away and in international waters, men could be held accountable under the jurisdiction of a Scottish court. Both men were duly convicted of murder and piracy, as James Shaw Grant details, partly on Camelier's evidence and not least on their inability to explain how they had both been caught with clothes and belongings of the late Captain Johnston. The jury did not take long to find them guilty. (The dispatch and efficiency of the case is in noted contrast to Donald MacLeod's treatment in Stornoway that same winter.)

'To the misguided and penitent offender the door of mercy is sometimes opened,' pronounced the judge sententiously, 'but against the pirate and murderer it will be for ever shut.' And Heaman and Gautier were condemned to be taken to 'the Tolbooth of Edinburgh therein to be detained, and to be fed on bread and water only, until the second Wednesday of January, when they were to be "taken forth of the said Tolbooth to the sands of Leith, within floodmark, and then and there hanged by the neck, upon a gibbet, by the hands of the common executioner, until they be dead, and their bodies thereafter to be delivered to Dr Alexander Munro, Professor of Anatomy in the University of Edinburgh, to be by him publicly dissected and anatomised".'

The *Glasgow Herald* reported that, in the face of the savagery of this sentence, both men 'received the announcement of their melancholy fate with the greatest composure, and bowed respectfully to the Court'. They were duly hanged – publicly – two months later, on a scaffold at the bottom of Constitution Street in Leith, 'immediately in the centre of the road,' declared the newspaper, 'so that the whole proceedings could be seen a great way up the street. Everything passed off quietly.' Indeed, it was a mannered business, with Heaman bowing gravely to city crowds as a cart drew him through packed streets to the rendezvous with the rope. Both men publicly endorsed the justice of their fate before the traps fell. Peter Heaman and François Gautier would be the last men executed in Scotland for piracy. It would be long before the sight of customs carts – several of them – piled high with silver dollars, trundling through the streets of Stornoway, passed from living memory; it is said that for many years afterwards wifies still went from door to door selling mysteriously acquired beeswax, and that you could not break a large banknote in town without finding Spanish silver in your change.

Mary Carn MacKenzie enjoyed six years of good works and high local honour, and her funeral was attended by John Shore, Lord Teignmouth, orientalist and politician, who had served for four years as Governor General of India and known her brother well. He was besides the first president of the British and Foreign Bible Society, and his delicious account of the obsequies for the old dear in 1827 captures the tension between the panache of one of the last true chiefly occasions in Highland history and his Evangelical disdain for its excesses – practically the last hurrah for a tired, dead religion even as a new Gospel order took fast grip of the Long Island.

During my stay in Stornoway, I received an invitation to attend the funeral of a wealthy old lady, who had made numerous and liberal bequests . . . Immediately after the decease of this lady, a cask of Madeira was opened in her house, a wake had been kept up, and the house nightly illuminated according to the custom of the country. The chief mourner, who arrived in an open boat from the mainland, was a minister, and the funeral was attended by all the principal inhabitants of Stornoway. Our party from the Lodge arrived too late at the house of the deceased to partake of the preliminary refreshments, but we overtook the procession on the road to the ancient cemetery of Stornoway, which is situated on the beach of Broad Bay, about four miles from the town. Another burial place used by the people of Stornoway, near the town, has been so encroached upon by the ravages of the sea, that the bodies will probably soon be consigned to a watery grave . . .

The graves of the principal families are enclosed by four walls forming a sort of mausoleum. That of the lady, whose obsequies we were celebrating, contains a marble monument to the memory of Colonel Colin MacKenzie, bearing a highly panegyrical inscription . . .

In Scotland, the funeral ceremony is celebrated without any religious rite. The minister of the parish attends only when invited, and not officially. He sometimes embraces the solemn opportunity of offering up a prayer among the assembled mourners at the house of the deceased, previous to the departure of the procession, though he may not accompany it. On the present occasion, as soon as we reached the cemetery, the coffin was deposited in the grave with all possible decency, and the whole body of mourners instantly adjourned to a tent pitched in the cemetery, within a few yards of the mausoleum, where we found the tables groaning beneath a plentiful repast. As soon as we were all arranged, a hundred and twenty in number, the minister, who presided as chief mourner, delivered a grace in the form of a prayer; and the minister of the parish offered up another, accompanied by thanksgiving after dinner. The bottle was then circulated and many loyal, patriotic, and complimentary toasts followed; nor was the memory of the deceased forgotten, while the toasts were as usual accompanied with appropriate speeches. The presence of several ministers, and one acting as chairman, no doubt tended to preserve a certain degree of sobriety in the midst of revelry and merriment, inseparable from such a meeting, as the occasion would be necessarily speedily forgotten by the greater part present. But at length the chord was touched, to which the bosoms of the islanders responded, amidst the flow of wine and whisky, with resistless accordance. 'The Chief of the MacIvers' was proposed amid loud applause. The guests now became quite tumultuous, and the Revd Chairman immediately rose up and left the tent, accompanied by nearly all the party.

The expectations of the gleanings of so plenteous a repast had attracted to the spot a multitude of people of all ages, who thronged around and closed in upon the tent, eager for the signal for rushing in upon the remains of the feast. A man was constantly employed in walking round the tent, armed with a long whip, with which he inflicted perpetual, but almost fruitless, chastisement on intruders.

A few of the guests, who had not heeded the example of the chairman, continued long carousing, and one of them was brought to Stornoway on the bier which conveyed the body to the grave.

Lord Teignmouth was an able statesman, of dry humour and profound humanity, but failed perhaps to realise the irony behind the toast to the 'Chief of the MacIvers': a wry tribute-cum-dig to Lewis MacIver, whose relations with the pompous Moderate clergy of the island were evidently fraught.

Yet another procurator fiscal for Stornoway, Thomas Buchanan Drummond – appointed in Hugh Brown's stead in 1834 – was, at least, neither a retainer of the Seaforths nor connected with the Lewis Estate; and a qualified and experienced solicitor. He had occasional good ideas but, as Grant points out, they were for the most part 'lonely swimmers in an ocean of nonsense'. For one, Drummond's occasional sparks of wild genius – he anticipated the formation of Comhairle nan Eilean Siar by a century and a half, suggesting all the Western Isles be made one new county and called 'Lewis-shire'; and, less brightly, called for wholesale and indeed kaleidoscopic redrawing of crofting boundaries, regardless of landscape realities or human consequence – suggest a man of little practicality. For another, not least for his entire contempt for island culture, as one ridiculous letter to James Stewart-MacKenzie on 3 June 1834 affirms, Mr Drummond was both highly ambitious and a pompous ass:

Respected Sir,
      . . . In the first place I would suggest the propriety of changing the name of Stornoway, which has no meaning whatever as far as I can learn, and which to the ear of all Lowlanders sounds harsh, and indeed is often pronounced 'Stormoway' and gives strangers a wild idea of this country which it is undeserving thereof and in lieu thereof I would propose to substitute the name 'Port Royal' in memory of His present Majesty who I observed visited this town in 1793 [*sic*] . . . This can at once be done on your application, and I am sure with His Majesty's approbation, and I know from my having hinted to some of the most respected Merchants here that I meant to apply to get this done that the change would meet with the approbation of the inhabitants – but I court your approbation not theirs, and it is you as the proprietor that has best right to claim the change from His Majesty though I hope you will do me the justice in intimating to His Majesty your wish that it was I, humble individual, that suggested it as a mark of my respect to his Majesty so far, and should His Majesty and you approve of my doing so, I shall so soon as the change of name takes place

commence a small work giving a description of this place and an account of
His Majesty's visit here . . .
    Your most humble servant
    (signed) Thos. Drummond
    Proc. Fiscal
    Stornoway.

Peter Cunningham properly remarks, 'No doubt we have to thank the good
sense of the recipient of this self-seeking and sycophantic letter (with echoes of
Uriah Heep) that the egregious Mr Drummond did not get his way with the
ancient name of our only town, however ungratefully it may fall upon Lowland
lugs.' Drummond, too, betrayed his own ignorance; following the Hebridean
jaunt of James V in 1540, the fine natural harbour on Skye where he spent a
night (and added MacLeod of Dunvegan himself to a pile of chiefly hostages
in his galleon's hold) has since been known as Port-Righ, Portree – the 'King's
Port' – in his honour.

    It was not the end of Drummond's grandiloquence. He continued to threaten
a new book about Lewis – being, he declared, 'already the author of several
works', the project calculated to ensure that 'strangers from all corners of the
country will pour into the place and be induced to reside here . . . the seas and
rivers here, as well as the lands, abound with everything necessary for man's
existence yet all these mercies are, as it were, neglected by the inactivity of the
natives.' Nevertheless – if only men had the sense to take Drummond's advice –
'bareness and misery' would soon yield to 'beauty and fruitfulness'.

    The profitable notions Drummond did have – proper investment in the
fishing industry; the building of a decent harbour with some elected supervising body, the provision of a proper courthouse and so on – were vitiated by
such vainglorious burble. In 1835, Seaforth in any event appointed him both
his 'baron baillie' – whose functions had some similarity to those of the modern
Land Court, settling minor crofting quarrels and levying minor fines – and
political agent. Drummond gained all the more local clout when Stewart-
MacKenzie was shortly appointed Governor of Ceylon and (with his lady)
removed still further from regular contact with island realities. Drummond
died early in 1838, and as another briefly competing lawyer, Roderick MacK-
enzie, seems to have been removed from Stornoway (or perhaps had not the
recognised competence in the first place) Lewis had, for a spell, no solicitors at
all. On 25 April 1838, the latest Lewis Estate factor, Thomas Knox, was
appointed procurator fiscal, 'there being at present no legal practitioner in said
island'; and the Stewart-MacKenzies soon petitioned the sheriff to allow him to
act in civil cases besides, regardless of his lack of qualifications. The tenants lay

more defenceless than ever before Seaforth whims and, well before the sceptre of the Long Island passed to James Matheson, such imprudent concentration of powers was the Lewis norm.

Sheriff MacKenzie had a bad social scrape on Lewis around 1831, partly thanks to the sleekit Lewis MacIver. The magistrate had accepted the Gress tacksman's invitation to come and visit its notable Seal Cave, a sea-fronted grotto whose entrance was (and remains) so narrow that only a tight-beamed craft can enter it. The skiff that day was evidently unstable, for she promptly capsized and both men were flung into Broad Bay. They were soon rescued, relates Grant, 'but MacKenzie, who was a frail old man, was badly shaken.' He was put to bed at MacIver's house and was, no doubt, still a-tremble when the factor of that day, the crafty Alexander Stewart – who would be sacked by the Stewart-MacKenzies some months later – called to gain his signature on a summons for debt.

This was against a notorious local physician, Dr Donald MacAulay of Linshader, who was much more of a merchant, tacksman and grabber than a cooing practitioner with a pleasant bedside manner. He was a brother-in-law of the Reverend Robert Finlayson, the new and very Evangelical minister of Lochs and – like Mrs Finlayson – a first cousin of the skulking *mac an t-Sronaich*. Local tradition recalls him as *an dotair Ruadh*, the red-haired doctor, and that he hated consultations, preferring instead to be advised of a case third-hand and then dispatching his rude manservant to the bed of sickness with some pills or potion (for a handsome fee). One Stornoway lawyer is said to have described him as an 'exceedingly illiterate and ill-tempered man' and Dr MacAulay was certainly what we would now call a 'vexatious litigant', constantly suing someone or other and, not infrequently, the Lewis Estate. In less than ten years, from 1819 to 1828, he laid some 70 legal actions at Stornoway Sheriff Court. The red-haired doctor was besides an industrious lecher, though less than gallant when accused of paternity; he fathered at least two misbegotten weans, and one mother successfully fought him in court (with Donald Munro as her solicitor, in a rare outing for common decency). The monstrous old man finally died in, of all places, West Derby, Liverpool, in May 1852 and at a 'small private insane asylum', which suggests the strong possibility of 'general paralysis of the insane' – tertiary syphilis.

MacAulay was a man any sensible public figure took care not remotely to annoy but, grateful to be alive, and forgetting the rather vicious factor he was dealing with, Sheriff MacKenzie was careless. He seized the summons gladly, dashed his name thereon and declared how delighted he was to be able to sign it. Alexander Stewart spotted a useful bit of ammunition and made sure to repeat the comment to Dr MacAulay, without of course explaining the context. Besides, he had an old score with Lewis MacIver, and feared too convenient an alliance between the Mr Big of the community and the tough old sheriff.

Around 1820, after all, on the sands of Tong, Stewart had been forced to fight a duel with the enraged MacIver. It was the factor's own fault: not only had he started to unload a cargo of coal at a jetty he knew perfectly well was the private property of the Gress tacksman, but when MacIver turned up to remonstrate Stewart had let things develop fast into an outright brawl: he was a much taller man, and as the fat little fellow started to rant he whacked his hand impudently on the MacIver head with such force that the brim of his top hat ended up around his chin. Louis MacIver, now beside himself with rage, flew at the factor, belaboured him with his Malacca cane, and had already drawn blood when bystanders managed to overpower him.

Even today, the most mild-mannered of Highlanders would have found it hard to take such contumely unruffled. Two centuries ago, it was all but unthinkable. As recently as about 1870, the wise old minister of Carloway, Revd John MacRae – *MacRath Mor* or 'Big MacRae', one of the great churchmen of Victorian Scotland – rose to a man's defence when the elders tried to refuse him baptism for his child. Had he not been seen brawling? 'Well, a number of us fishermen were standing at a dyke and a tramp came along and began to spit on us. So I gave him one and knocked him down.' MacRae smiled broadly. 'Give the man baptism,' he decreed. ''*S e as fhiach 'nuair laigheadh e fo na smugaidean*': 'he deserves it when he would not lie under the spits'. Lewis MacIver was as unsanctified as MacRae was holy; that same night, no doubt nursing his mauled hat, he challenged Alexander Stewart to a duel, and next day they met on the tidal flats of the great Cockle Ebb. The tacksman of Gress fired first – and missed. Stewart, who had no mean reputation as a shot, took aim next – and, according to Grant, 'blew away MacIver's whiskers from the left side of his face'. Honour, in the ridiculous code of this sort of thing – which the authorities had been fighting practically since the Reformation to put down – was thereby satisfied on both sides.

Early in 1844, Lewis MacIver ('addicted to quarrelling', says Grant) would apparently fight another duel, but by then he had already made a vindictive enemy out of a new procurator fiscal. Appointed in November 1841, Donald Munro now seized on an opportunity to destroy him.

4

Law: Donald Munro sets up shop on Lewis

We have but two portraits of Donald Munro. He can be seen near the back of a highly stylised and, frankly, indifferent 1847 painting by Robert Grant Masson of the great and good of Stornoway. It purported to show the assembly for the foundation-stone-laying ceremony when work began on Matheson's new Lews Castle: the daub was commissioned by the town's Freemasons – Lodge Fortrose had been established in 1767 – and, naturally, the Masons, in their silly aprons and sashes, are most prominent in the crowd of 84. James Matheson himself, and his lady, are curiously relegated to the back corner. The canvas was at the time described as a 'perfect gallery of old Stornoway portraits, a separate sitting having been taken for nearly every head by the artist who although accounted no great colourist was an adept at catching a likeness'.

Donald Munro – perhaps by his own design – stands very near the new Lewis laird, and is a slim, dark, balding man with carefully tended side-whiskers and a bland, official sort of air. His background remains mysterious and it is hard, at so late a remove now and probing back to a time when records were limited (civil registration of births, marriages and deaths, for instance, did not begin in Scotland until 1855), to find out very much about his upbringing or kin. There was probably, if we could dig back far enough, some link to the Munros of Foulis; and he may even have been related to Finlay Munro, an itinerant Highland evangelist from Tain who preached widely on the Long Island in the early 1820s, with enormous impact, and whose name is still revered on Lewis.

The latest procurator fiscal was of very different stamp. Born in Tain, about 1811, we know from Donald Munro's death certificate that he was the son of William Munro – a general merchant – and his wife, Janet Ross. He seems innocuous enough. The solitary, surviving photograph of the 'Chamberlain of the Lews', taken some 20 years later – in what was still a day of slow shutter-speeds and slower plates and when the subject had to pose stock-still for many moments – shows someone much more sinister.

This Munro, grim and unsmiling, is of stouter build; the sideburns have expanded and now meet in a heavy moustache. He is behatted – in an early form of the 'derby', or bowler hat, the titfer into my own lifetime of the bureaucrat, the foreman, the middle-manager, the Guards officer in mufti – and be-frock-coated, and with more than a hint of the sort of cackling villain who, in early silent cinema, ties a vacuous blonde heroine to cold steel railway tracks. But what locks your attention at once is the stick. It is no cane, but a heavy, menacing thing, and the chamberlain has it raised in both hands, like a sceptre, or, more ominously, like a weapon, as if he were about to batter down some tenant's door.

The Freudian analyst would no doubt have still more colourful takes on this, such as phallic narcissism; certainly, there is no warmth in this image, no intimacy, no vulnerability. This is the Chamberlain of the Lews, in full pomp, precisely as he wished to be seen. It is a portrait – as it was no doubt intended to be – of absolute power; not merely of a man entrusted with authority, but who self-consciously embodies it. The photograph does not announce that Munro upholds the law. It screams, 'I *am* the law.'

He was a dreadful man, embodying not that evil that is at least dashing, or bold, or defiant, but which is mean and malignant, slimy and low. Munro seems, rather, to have been the sort of base individual who made every woman's flesh creep and every man's fists tingle and who, as he grew in power and authority and confidence, grew the more emboldened, seldom missing an opportunity to humiliate.

There was no reason, in November 1841, for anyone to expect this new fiscal to last any longer than his rapid succession of predecessors, or that Lewis would have to put up with him for more than a few years, before ambition took him elsewhere. But hitherto, as James Shaw Grant points out, 'the deficiencies in the legal system in Lewis had been largely negative, arising from the shortage of qualified solicitors, which left accused people, and respondents in civil cases, without representation, and had sometimes led, for short periods, to the amalgamation of the incompatible offices of fiscal and factor. Now a key position in the legal system, and in the life of the island, was occupied by an ambitious and arrogant man who systematically set about accumulating power and flaunting it in the faces of the people whose lives he dominated.'

Munro soon had a talon, too, in the favours of the Estate, which, since the Stewart-MacKenzie retreat to Ceylon in 1833 (perhaps reflecting some financial embarrassment, though it is hard to be certain) was under the executive control of 'trustees' in Edinburgh. The stately couple would later voyage to represent the Crown in the Ionian Islands. As the only lawyer on Lewis, Munro was quickly appointed the Estate solicitor. He was besides the only notary public – the Scottish equivalent of a commissioner for oaths – which gave him useful, privy information of all sorts of deals and bargains. And he had two considerable strokes of luck. Months before his arrival, in July 1841, Sheriff MacKenzie finally retired, on account of great old age – though descendants would remain, to this day, prominent and powerful on Lewis (and still treasure his gorgeous, embroidered waistcoat, a poignant reminder this venerable jurist was once quite the young man about town in an elegant Georgian age). MacKenzie's successors were not of his calibre or local knowledge, and the more likely to co-operate with Munro's legal manoeuvres towards empire-building. And, within a few years, he would have a new laird, a poor judge of situations and a still worse one of character, and in the end all but the last man in Scotland to see through Donald Munro.

This, for now, on 5 November 1841, was but the minor lawyer 'sometime writer in Tain, but later residing in Edinburgh' admitted to practise in the Stornoway Court and 'having taken the oaths to government and *de fideli administratione officio*' became procurator fiscal for the district of Lewis in the county of Ross and Cromarty.

The first on Lewis to feel the clout of Munro's instinct for despotism were the hapless crofters of Park, in various communities around Loch Shell – at whose mouth, on Eilean Iubhard, Charles Edward Stewart had taken brief refuge as he scurried from Stornoway almost a century before. So used is the modern islander to the sadly reduced villages of Park (a district also known locally as South Lochs) in the twenty-first century – homes ruined and abandoned, or reduced to holiday cottages, and townships of thin or even derisory population – that one naturally thinks of the three villages in question (Eishken, Orinsay and Lemreway) as tiny hamlets. And we assume that, around 1842 and however frightful this exercise in landlordism, only a couple of dozen people were affected.

It comes as a shock to find the first great enterprise of Donald Munro was against the homes (and land, and livelihoods) of some 400 people. And Park, indeed, as Roger Hutchinson has emphasised, suffered more than any quarter of Lewis from irresponsible landlordism. Crofting is essentially a pastoral economy and the quality of Lewis moor such that crofters need not just common grazing, but vast tracts of it. However mucked about the Lewis tenantry elsewhere were, they had always the great heart of the island for their beasts. By 1850, the people of the surviving Park townships were quite blocked from it – the district is all but an island, pincered by two great sea-lochs – and at their back lay only the Minch. As late as 1888, obdurately refusing to recognise their plight – or even the good of the untilled land itself – Matheson's silly, preening widow would tell a delegation of crofters that 'the land under sheep and deer is my property and I can do with it what I like.'

A generation earlier, it is unlikely Mary Stewart-MacKenzie, last of the Seaforths, and her career-minded husband knew anything about these Park evictions – though it is certain neither ever deplored them. The decision to clear those townships – and turn their painfully tended land, drained and enriched from bleak bog by centuries of arduous work, into a 'Loch Shell Farm' for one Walter Scott, an incoming entrepreneur – was probably initiated by the Seaforth trustees in Edinburgh, rather than by Munro himself. There was already a tacksman nearby, a Patrick Stewart. He may well have been related to those Stewarts of Bute who were now, as factors and tenant-farmers, causing mayhem and misery south of the Clisham, and later, in 1877, described by Alexander Carmichael as 'the greatest curse that ever came upon Harris': not content with wholesale clearance, they even ploughed the ancient burial ground at Seilebost for crops, so that skulls and bones rolled in desecration amidst its rigs for decades to come. Kin or no to these robbers, the name of Patrick Stewart, tacksman of Park – vindictive and violent – is still execrated in the district; and those of his brothers, partners in wider South Lochs enterprise, are recalled with little more affection.

Meanwhile, the fate now meted out to the people of Eishken and Steimreway, Orinsay and Lemreway, was orchestrated with signal relish by Donald Munro himself. As solicitor for the Estate, he sought in the spring of 1842 to the Sheriff Court at Stornoway – and duly obtained – detailed, summary orders of eviction for 36 named heads of households in the townships along the shores of Loch Shell. Munro besides gave as grounds for this action – and he probably knew the accusation was wholly false – that the crofters had been stealing sheep from the Loch Shell farm. He then, as procurator fiscal, took entire charge of the expedition that would enforce these decrees. And, in early June and with Munro at their head, the goons of the Seaforth Estate marched on Park.

'As the solicitor concerned,' writes James Shaw Grant, 'he was well aware that the decrees he [*had*] obtained became effective only "at the separation of the crop from the ground" which, in Lewis, would have been October; yet, as procurator fiscal, he gave the protection of the Crown to the attempted destruction of the crofters' houses on the 2nd of June, more than four months before the Court orders became effective.' The assault on those townships – practically a punitive expedition – was not just oppressive, it was illegal. Munro had taken cynical advantage of the assorted voids in island justice. The newly appointed Lordship on the local bench, Sheriff Substitute Robert Sutherland Taylor, had only just taken up his post and – as Grant suggests – seems simply to have taken the fiscal at his word and signed what he was asked to sign for the ordained evictions without actually checking back through court records to see what the decree actually granted. It was all the more incredible – and indeed derelict – an omission by Taylor as he not only sanctioned Munro's descent on the townships (which was not just, after all, to serve papers, but to throw the people from their homes and demolish or fire the roofs over their heads) but chose to accompany him.

Of course, had there been another lawyer on Lewis – and had the crofters concerned secured his services – the sheriff would then have heard their case. But there was not. And, had Munro not been solicitor for the Estate as well as procurator fiscal – or had he been the Estate's agent, but not fiscal – then that, too, would have been a hurdle of defence. But he was. The *Inverness Courier* of 15 June 1842 – seldom critical of general goings-on in Gaeldom – reports a gratifying turn of events:

> Another of the painful scenes, which lately have been too prevalent, connected with the removal of Highland cottars, took place at the farm of Loch Shell, parish of Lochs in the county of Ross.
>
> The farm has been taken by an extensive sheep farmer from the south and, with the view of carrying out rural improvements, the occupiers of the soil were summoned to remove.
>
> The Sheriff, Procurator Fiscal and Factor with a part of ground officers, constables and others proceeded to the spot and commenced throwing down the huts.
>
> A number of women then rushed upon the party and drove them off the field without committing any bodily injury except a little rough handling to one of the officers.

It is typical of the Highland press at this period to describe wholesale evictions and then the predatory mass-grazing of long-tilled, long-manured ground by a stranger's sheep – without the least toil or fertilisation at any time afterwards by his own efforts – as 'rural improvements'; it is also a useful reminder to the historians of the Scottish Left that woman's part in the struggle of the people was not invented at the Glasgow Rent Strike of 1915.

Taylor was either chivalrous by temperament or – more probably – shaken by the fury of the South Lochs women. Once they held the field, he quietened his humiliated force and went to talk to these wives and mothers, no doubt with an interpreter. In fact, he ascertained, they were enraged not so much by the evictions – for all the distress and upheaval – but by the reasons given in law for it. Their men had never stolen any sheep and no such robbery had ever been proved, nor anyone ever convicted. They would be forced from their villages if they must, they would not be driven from them as thieves.

Sheriff Taylor was evidently shaken by the anger of these Lewis ladies and, probably, for the first time, began to doubt his own legal ground. He called off his dogs, returned to Stornoway, and passed the problem to Edinburgh. The new Sheriff Principal of Ross – John Jardine – was ordered by the Lord Advocate to go to Lewis and investigate.

Jardine himself was well on in years and had found it inordinately difficult finally to secure his new job in 1833; MacLeod of Geanies had refused to go quietly (unless he were granted a pension no less generous than his retiring salary) and there had been much lobbying against Jardine in Highland legal circles, not least the unkind charge that he was too old and portly to stump about his realms on horseback. The journey from Dingwall to Lewis was still not one lightly enterprised and it is unlikely Jardine was in the best of humours by the time he alighted, perhaps a little green at the gills, on a Stornoway jetty. In the general conduct of Highland governance at this time, he might well have thrown the book at the tenants of South Lochs and the harridans who had so outrageously resisted (the Scots term is 'deforced') the strong arm of the law.

But Jardine's decision, having made due inquiry, was remarkably delicate. No one was prosecuted. The folk of Eishken, Orinsay and so on were instead given time, space and dignity to negotiate their departure. A mutually convenient date was fixed: 28 May (Whitsun) 1843. The determined reasonableness of these terms was not the fruit of judicial loving kindness. It was Sheriff Jardine's tacit acknowledgement that Donald Munro had managed to rope the due process of law in his Ross-shire domains into an enterprise utterly illegal. And it was the worse for Lewis – though, no doubt, the inertia reflected Jardine's awareness that, once you are in a hole, it is often best to stop digging – that he had not the courage to remove Stornoway's procurator fiscal *apud acta* from office. It is unlikely a humiliated solicitor would have long lingered on Lewis, and unthinkable that even Matheson would have put a disgraced one in charge of the entire Estate.

At this juncture, the tenants of the Loch Shell townships had won sympathy throughout a generally restive island – where certain problems were now causing real social pressure, from the growing crisis in the Church to a remorselessly expanding population and acute shortage of land. And the folk of these Park villages, casting about – in the absence of any available law agent – now secured the services of a highly improbable ally, Lewis MacIver.

Capital is not generally found acting from the goodness of its heart on behalf of disenfranchised labour, and MacIver's dealings with his own tenants at Gress was far from blameless. For one, as Donald MacDonald of Tolsta confirms – and like many local big-shots of the time – he profited greatly from 'thirlage', a positively feudal arrangement which oppressed ordinary people: the tenants of Gress were compelled to grind their corn at his mill (the building still substantially survives) and grant him 'multure', or a proportion of the meal so produced – at a proportion which, depending on local custom and the greed of the given superior, ranged from a thirtieth to a twelfth of the precious commodity. And, even if the poor people ground it elsewhere (such as by quern at their own hearth) they were obliged to pay the tacksman a 'dry' multure, in cash or kind. As if that were not bad enough, it was not in the least at MacIver's cost or by his labour that the mill itself was kept in good order – the chores of maintaining every last bit of it, down to keeping the lade clear and the dam intact, and the horrendous and highly skilled, time-consuming job of carving respectable millstones from robust Lewisian gneiss, were entirely the responsibility of his tenants.

There are even stories – and, for all we know, MacIver also went to such lengths – of factors and tacksmen searching tenants' houses to find and destroy querns: according to Duncan MacDonald of Ballalan, the tacksman of Laxay once seized and dumped so many of these handmills off a certain point on Loch Erisort that the locality is still known as *Poll nam Bra*, 'Pool of the Querns'. Incredibly, even one or two ministers – like the Reverend William MacRae of Barvas, father of Dr Charles and a figure still remembered with extraordinary ambivalence on Lewis, both as an allegedly graceless Moderate and as a civic leader who was unusually sympathetic, for the times, on behalf of ordinary island people – enjoyed this cash-crop levy of a hard-won food; in 1833, MacRae actually complained, because despite a huge parish he only enjoyed thirlage over the townships of Upper and Lower Barvas.

And, to cap everything, as Donald MacDonald points out, thirlage 'caused the people much suffering and hardship, for many of the villages were miles, and roadless miles in most cases, from the prescribed mill. The Tolsta tenants were thirled to the Gress mill, five miles over a roadless moor, and even longer if they went by sea. They had to pay the rapacious Lewis MacIver £6 10s a year in dry multures as they preferred to grind their grain at their own mills. The townships of Coll, Back and Vatisker were also thirled to Gress, and their inhabitants were charged every twelfth peck, besides mill services such as thatching the mill and repairing the dam and the lade. The Stornoway mill only claimed every sixteenth peck. The Uig people suffered badly, having to take their grain to the Callanish Mill. Some had to travel twenty miles, or face the dangerous crossing of Loch Roag. This long and difficult journey entailed many days away from home, as well as much unnecessary discomfort. It was not surprising that many tenants preferred to pay the dry multures.'

In a curious why-can't-they-eat-cake? moment, Mrs Stewart-MacKenzie –

who had invested heavily in building that most modern mill at Stornoway, and made sure Lewis MacIver was suitably menaced against interfering with her own levies of multure and thirlage – deplored the old mills of rural Lewis: presumably the egalitarian, community-built Norse mill type, of which a fine example has been restored at Shawbost. She described them as 'wretched hovels, hardly above ground, and only capable of being worked when the burns were full in autumn and winter'. She does not seem to have grasped that that was the only season when crofters needed to use them, or that her complacent disapproval owed more than she cared to admit to thoughts of lost revenue. It is all, again, a grim reminder that oppression in Lewis centuries ago (and generally in wider Scotland) was not about a 'free market', but a thoroughly rigged one or, at least, a curious form of socialism – to the exclusive benefit of the rich.

And it is besides a reminder of the extraordinary complexity of Lewis MacIver, who on a wider stage was grudgingly admired: in 1820, for instance, at the first formal Cattle Show ever held in the Outer Hebrides – all the more impressive as they managed to find a reasonably flat piece of ground for the occasion in Tarbert – he was even one of the judges appointed by the Highland Society of Scotland. Nor was he averse to showing a little affected piety, if a nod to religion seemed politic. Around 1833, a Sir Thomas Johnstone enjoyed a sporting let from the Seaforths, evidently near Gress, for Lewis MacIver cordially called to inquire if he could 'administer to his comforts'. The knighted gentleman evidently assumed MacIver just another local peasant, for Sir Thomas told him rudely to return on Sunday 'to make arrangements about the house'. In some spirit, MacIver advised that 'we are not in the habit of making any bargains on Sunday in this country'. Sir Thomas snorted, and called him a humbug. MacIver later declared the contretemps had 'raised my Highland blood', but seems on this occasion not to have demanded satisfaction at dawn; and when he was later called to account for the row by 'Seaforth', according to Grant – he presumably means Mr Stewart-MacKenzie – the tacksman of Gress was still seething about Sir Thomas Johnstone's 'vanity', 'folly' and 'absurd aristocratic notions'. Many a Lewisman today would sympathise.

Yet MacIver's own exploitation of the vulnerable, and on many fronts, is undoubted. Drawing heavily – as a Tolsta man, born in 1904 and for many years a Lowland schoolmaster – on his own village tradition, Donald MacDonald grimly related in 1978 that evictions and local clearance were by no means the monopoly of a heartless laird or a wicked factor, casting a little light on Munro's allegations of sheep-rustlin' in them thar hills:

Although every tacksman could evict a subtenant, some were more likely to do so than others. The most notorious of these men were Lewis MacIver of Gress, Dr MacAulay of Linshader and Crossbost, and Archibald Stewart of Park. Stewart's favourite excuse for getting rid of his subtenants was for sheep-stealing. He was a most aggressive man, who had no hesitation in manhandling his tenants or anybody else for that matter who happened to cross him. On one particular occasion, he ill-treated some fishermen he found ashore on the Shiants, then part of his tack, as he thought they were there to steal sheep. It was also said that he, and some others, severely manhandled the *Breabadair Mor*, the Big Weaver, a native of Seaforth Head, who had gone to Valamos after some poinded horses [*seized by sheriff officers in lieu of unpaid debt*].

Stewart, with his brother Alexander, a much more respectable man, is believed to have arrived in Park with only sixty sheep, fifty of which were ewes.

The arrogant and insatiable Dr MacAulay, 'a landgrabber and oppressor with an insatiable appetite', made life extremely difficult for his tenants, exacting his 'pound of flesh' whenever possible.

Lewis MacIver, of Gress, seldom needed an excuse for removing his tenants. A shrewd business man, he showed little consideration for anyone who interfered with his plans. His subtenants, in Back and Gress, led an unenviable, uncertain existence. In 1822, his tenants in Gress complained to Seaforth [*i.e. the Stewart-MacKenzies, or at least their factor of the day*] of having been dispossessed of their lands twice in as many years and sent to the 'edge of the town' for no known reason, especially as they had paid their rents on 'the day'.

Sheriff Court papers unearthed by James Shaw Grant even showed that, shortly before he became the unlikely advocate of Loch Shell crofters, Lewis MacIver was joyously pursuing a man from Brenish, Uig, by all process of law. The poor fellow, Malcolm MacLeod, was taking passage to Canada, and the sum involved was but £1 4s 7d – yet the tacksman of Gress demanded that officers of the court be sent to search the very ship for the voyage. The *Lady Hood* was lying off Stornoway awaiting sailing orders for Quebec; her name suggests Mrs Stewart-MacKenzie may herself have organised the transport. They were to seize this MacLeod, cart him off in irons to the doubtful comforts 'within the Tolbooth of Dingwall'. Even allowing for inflation – that would now be a moderate three-figure total in pounds decimal – Grant rightly observes that this 'seems a trivial sum for which to prevent a fellow islander from making a new start in life'.

Later, when the Seaforth Estate pondered a bid from village crofters for direct tenancy of their holdings, MacIver would beg renewed lease of the village of Back – for at least seven years 'as I possess it . . . I pay as much rent as the tenants offered for it and not a shilling in arrears,' he further asserted. He declared he was going to import 'shelly sand' from Bernera to improve the soil – unlikely, as beaches almost the length of Broad Bay are thick with the stuff – and assured the trustees he would soon have 'Back as well improved as any tenant's holding in the land'. So why, a few years later, would this jolly home-grown robber baron be so eager to defend the interests of the benighted folk by the shores of Loch Shell? It boiled down to economic advantage – his own.

Grant has a wry take on this:

> Clearly he was an energetic improver who was adding to the wealth of the island but, equally clearly, he was not prepared to let anyone stand in his way. He made no claim, it should be noted, that he could improve the land above the level ordinary tenants achieved. He merely said that he could equal them. However primitive their methods, the island crofters were land improvers *par excellence*, converting virgin moorland into arable from which the landlord could profit.
>
> The difference between MacIver's attitude to the crofters in Back and Gress and to the evicted crofters of Loch Shell reflects a difference in his relationship with them. On his own doorstep in Gress, he was in competition with his crofter neighbours for the very limited arable land on which their economy depended in a way his did not. In Loch Shell, he was in a commercial partnership with the crofters as fishermen, relying on them to meet his requirements as a curer. At that time the fishermen contracted with a curer season by season: it was nearly half a century before the practice of selling the catch by auction was introduced.
>
> In a small community, anyone yielding as much power as Lewis MacIver did – subject though he was to the even greater power of the proprietor – must have been seen in an ambiguous light by his poorer neighbours. When he was leaning on the crofters, he was an intolerable bully, but, when they were leaning on him, he was a tower of strength. His closest neighbours had the most unfavourable view, but even they must have seen him in a different light at different times, according to the relationship in which they stood to him at any particular moment.
>
> The crofting and the business communities were not opposed to each other: certainly not at all times and in all circumstances. Their interests were interlocked, and both were bound within the conditions and conventions of their day. There was a reciprocity, as well as antagonism, which is

sometimes overlooked when we apply the yardstick of our own experience to a very different situation. Relationships are always more complex than oral tradition remembers or class theories postulate. However oppressive he might have been in another context, in the affair of Loch Shell Lewis MacIver was a white knight, defending the crofters against the worst excesses of the Estate Solicitor.

Grant, scion of Stornoway privilege and monoglot English upbringing and a Moderate, politely mannered United Free religion, neglects other factors. Lewis MacIver wanted to take on Donald Munro because it was fun; because it bolstered his own self-image as a moral, fearless tribune of the people; and for the sheer *élan* of such an enterprise, which had certainly – in his own words in an earlier context – 'raised my Highland blood'. But, as Grant reminds us, 'Donald Munro did not forget the fact and, when the opportunity appeared to offer for revenge, he tried to take it.'

For now, Munro coldly negotiated. As Estate solicitor – and well aware of MacIver's greed for land – he was in a strong position, and a show of solidarity with the people evidently meant more to the tacksman of Gress than the hard nuts and bolts of a good deal, for he did not get one. The terms finally reached on behalf of the Loch Shell crofters, and signed by Lewis MacIver and Donald Munro on 28 June, committed the tenants of the assorted townships to removing on or by 1 May 1843. They would pay all rent due up to that very day; though both men were fully aware the crofters would have to sell their livestock the previous autumn – the thin, tottery beasts had little value after scant winter fodder. And they were not allowed to sublet the grazings to anyone else as grass began to green the slopes in the spring of that year. Stewart would not in the least be disadvantaged by the Estate's show of leniency. Munro – perhaps aware how narrowly he escaped – did not apply for fresh orders of eviction from the Sheriff Court; that hardly mattered as MacIver foolishly signed some paper the procurator fiscal dashed up, attesting that for all legal purposes the warrants of ejection already served remained in force. He besides made himself guarantor for the rent of the townships (£70) and an additional clause levied a penalty of £50 should the tenants default.

This was silly: though MacIver (and the families he represented) had made huge concessions, Munro had committed himself to nothing in return. There was no agreement binding the Estate until the Seaforth trustees and Walter Scott – the incoming sheep-farmer – had solemnly signed one; and MacIver had struck such an imprudent bargain he was already committed to it, whatever terms they might now impose. Scott did sign terms two days later, and Munro at some point (and perhaps long after the fact) craftily added a minute – in his

own hand – recording the approval of the Seaforth trustees, but he signed
nothing committing the Lewis Estate to anything.

There were twists and turns to come. Somehow – this must have been a
desperate plea from the Loch Shell crofters – MacIver won permission for
them both to sow crops on the land in the spring of 1843, and for the men
subsequently to harvest them, though they still pitilessly had to abandon their
homesteads from 1 June. They had won but an extra month's time before
departure with their families, stocks and chattels; only one man from each
household would be allowed to stay in the locale till the point of harvest to tend
the oats, barley and potatoes and – still more officiously – each would be
nominated by the factor himself. 'The watchmen, however,' Grant related
darkly in 1992, 'were not permitted to live in the abandoned family houses: the
agreement makes it clear they were obliged to live in the barns. The houses,
presumably, were to be destroyed as soon as they were vacated. The rest of the
family were permitted to return to cut the corn and lift the potatoes, but only
"as fixed by the Chamberlain".'

At this stricture, Lewis MacIver exploded. It was not merely the pomposity
of such micromanagement. It was an early instance of the spite with which
Donald Munro would operate for the next 30 years. He was himself an earthy
Highlander, well aware of rural realities. He knew perfectly well that a factor in
a town-centre office was in no position to judge the readiness of crops for lifting
in hamlets a long distance away, past high hills and a succession of sea-lochs.
Nor was he any better placed to assess (far less predict) the weather conditions
necessary for a clean, easy gathering of harvest; far less – the point MacIver
seized on – conveying the precious winter provision safely by sea to wherever
the tenants were, at the Estate's pleasure, to be domiciled. He demanded
flexibility: crops could only be conveyed 'when the weather will permit them
going, with their small boats, for loads of top weight' – aware of realities which,
as James Shaw Grant vividly assails Munro's nonsense:

> What a picture that conjures up! Thirty-six families trying to secure the
> harvest, within strict time limits, in the uncertain Hebridean weather, and
> moving large quantities of barley and oats, in the sheaf, in open boats, at the
> time of the equinoctial gales, on a date arbitrarily agreed by the factor,
> without regard to wind or weather.

And Loch Shell is notoriously dangerous. As recently as 1945, over a century
later, six men – all heads of households (and there were only 14 of them) in the
painfully resettled new community of Orinsay – would be drowned on its
waters, in two separate incidents, in a single month. One orphan of that

calamitous summer was the young Calum Kennedy, future Gaelic singer, TV star and accident-prone impresario. These were highly experienced island fishermen, who knew the waters, were free (as Grant points out) to assess the conditions 'and still got it wrong'. But there was no logic at all, of course, to Munro's stipulation. He imposed it because he could, because it was a demonstration of his power and authority, precisely because it would cause strain, trouble and anxiety – and because knowledge of all this gave him the greatest pleasure. It is this conscious enjoyment in evil – not just the execution of evil things – that makes him, even at this remove, so disturbing.

And worse was to come.

Donald Munro had been so eager to clear the wretched folk of Eishken, Orinsay and Lemreway from hearth and home that he had recklessly directed the expulsion months before he had proper legal authority to do so. But there was no such alacrity in finding them new homes. Upset and miserable, acutely conscious of Lewis MacIver's frailty as an ally (and, still more, in dubiety of his motives) the tenants and their families waited for word. And waited. And waited. Finally, in agonies of apprehension – and in, no doubt, an anger they dared not display – they sailed practically as a body to Stornoway, on 29 May 1843 – just three days before they were ordered to quit – to find out whatever was to happen to them.

But there was no answer. Munro himself was in Edinburgh, seeing the trustees; even at this early stage of his career, one wonders who took instructions from whom. In any event, he was still sufficiently short of confidence – and had sufficient sense of self-preservation – not to initiate resettlement without express instructions from the factor. The people of the Loch Shell townships, then, hung wretchedly about Stornoway for three days, until he deigned to return and make hasty, scornful arrangements. The families were arbitrarily assigned to crofts elsewhere in the parish of Lochs – or, one suspects, to existing crofts blithely carved up for them, with no consultation with folk already there. And two of the evicted Loch Shell tenants – a Donald MacLennan and a Malcolm MacLeod – were not granted new holdings at all.

There is no evidence that either man had caused particular offence. Estate papers unearthed by James Shaw Grant do suggest that their families were 'weak and numerous' but – as always, when finding practically anything penned by Munro – we do not know when that annotation was added and to what purpose. Grant may well be correct in suggesting that Munro and the Estate officials feared men lumbered with such a brood could, in future, struggle to pay rent – though they were certainly up to date with their rent by Loch Shell; had there been any arrears, Donald Munro would certainly have flaunted that fact in court. Again, one has to suspect he picked out one or two men, quite at random, for his amusement and because he could.

And one can scarcely blame MacLennan and MacLeod for what they did next: they calmly packed their families and chattels back aboard their boats and, with no credible alternative, sailed back to their homesteads by Loch Shell and occupied them once more.

Donald Munro had an action lodged against them both, in Stornoway Sheriff Court, within the week. And he sent imperious demand to Lewis MacIver for that agreed indemnity of £50.

The tacksman of Gress, as it happened, was not at home. He was far away, in England, on business – another useful reminder that, even in the early 1840s, Lewis was not nearly so parochial a place as we like to think. (He would in fact contract a chill on the trip, and die not long after return.) And when the summons came, his son James – evidently a retiring chap and not generally thought as bright or formidable as his father – went to court in Stornoway in his stead.

One can imagine Donald Munro, solicitor for the Seaforth Estate, procurator fiscal, turning up that day in happy expectation of an overwhelmed young man, stumbling through a case he barely understood in a setting that quite overawed him. And one can imagine, as things proceeded, the smile rapidly vanishing from those thin lips. Young MacIver, according to Grant, 'represented his father as effectively as if he had been a trained lawyer. His answers to Munro's petition read like the work of a professional . . .'

In fact, they almost certainly were: the tacksman of Gress might well have almost drowned him but, as Grant argues, the aged Sheriff MacKenzie and Lewis MacIver had become (and remained) fast friends. Citing the later memoirs of Evander MacIver – another son, and with much of the acumen if rather less of the ruthlessness of his old boy – as hard evidence, Grant reveals that the sheriff himself drew up Lewis MacIver's will (and was, of course, grand-uncle to his boys). It is highly probable, faced with an unexpected courtroom drama in his father's absence, that James sent word at once to the old beak, with a copy of the papers in the case, and received reams of wisdom and argument in reply.

So, with mounting confidence, James MacIver argued robustly that Mac-Lennan and MacLeod had in all fairness kept their end of the deal 'as far as it was possible for any human being in their distressed circumstances' and, in any event, they had no less fair and just a claim to new crofts in Lochs than the other tenants dispossessed from the slopes by Loch Shell. Besides – and he made much of this – his father had not even been on the island, far less consulted, when the new crofts were allotted to the evictees, so he was certainly now released from any contract. Had not MacIver *père*, argued MacIver *fils* – who, by this point, was no doubt thoroughly enjoying himself – not done the Seaforth trustees and all involved, including Munro himself, a great favour by persuading these Park crofters to a voluntary departure, and in good order? Surely better, asserted James MacIver, 'than forcing them out by a party of soldiers at the point of the bayonet'.

In any event, having had quite enough of Donald Munro's little games, MacLennan and MacLeod did not resist the new summons of eviction against them individually. They had quit their old homes without demur and, Grant reports, 'sought shelter with friends': we know nothing of what suffering and humiliation this involved for their families. Donald Munro had already won on his main front even before the case had come to open court; but he was yet determined to wrest that £50 from Lewis MacIver – and, of course, all the legal expenses for an unnecessary and vindictive action, arising wholly from his own capricious refusal of new homes for two Loch Shell families.

The Seaforth solicitor did secure his expenses, but not the £50. Sheriff Taylor had dimly started to draw Munro's measure, and was swayed besides by the arguments in court and the wider reality: that both the crofters of these Park villages and Lewis MacIver himself had faced extraordinary difficulties with 'no ready access to professional legal assistance except at a great distance'.

James Shaw Grant is damning.

The MacIvers, father and son, were in fact acting as amateur lawyers on behalf of a group of people who had no access to a solicitor; who could not have paid a solicitor even if one had been available; and most of whom could not read, write or speak English, and could no more understand the legal documents which determined their fate than if they had been written in Hindustani.

Rev. Robert Finlayson [*inducted as minister of Lochs in 1831, and who would 'come out' with the entire community for the Free Church in 1843*] estimated in 1833 that there were only twelve people in the parish . . . who could write, and only a few males who could speak broken English. It is not that they were averse to education: 50 per cent of those between twelve and twenty-four could read Gaelic, thanks to the activities of the Gaelic Schools Society. This, to the discredit of the Scottish educational system, was a higher percentage than could read Gaelic a hundred years later, after seventy years of compulsory state education.

The destruction of three villages, with four hundred inhabitants, was represented, according to the *Inverness Courier*, 'as rural improvement.' There was, however, no element of improvement involved, even on the

narrowest commercial criterion of profit. The crofters were not in arrears
with their rent. The incoming sheep farmer was not offering more than they
were already paying. The new use of the land was purely extractive,
leaching away, in the form of wool and mutton, the fertility the crofters
had built up through generations of diligent cultivation. The tenants being
removed were not incompetent agriculturists who had been misusing the
soil. Their agricultural activities, in fact, were subordinate to their main
source of income as fishermen, and, occasionally, pilots, guiding stricken
vessels into the shelter of Loch Shell or the even safer anchorage of
Stornoway.

And Grant adds another note, lest we persist in thinking of these South
Lochs people as losers from Hicksville. Finlayson's entry in the 1833 *New
Statistical Account* mentions the gifted boat-builders of his parish, on top of the
usual tailors and weavers and general tradesmen; and one ship built in the Park
end of the parish – 'Malcolm McNeill's brig' – is even mentioned in a letter
about a party of emigrants now lodged, across the Atlantic, in the Library of
Congress. McNeill's brother, Donald McNeill of Ardmeanish, at one time held
as his tack all of the parish south of Loch Erisort – no doubt owing to the offices
of his father-in-law, Colin MacKenzie, who was then factor of Lewis. This
sturdy ship, built just north of Loch Shell – on the shores of Loch Odhairn –
once, according to reliable island tradition, held the world record for crossing
the Atlantic from Quebec. And this, indeed, was an era when locally owned
vessels routinely sailed overseas from parts of the Hebrides we, today, would
dismiss as 'remote': from Scadabay in the Bays of Harris, for instance, a family
of Campbells (of the same resourceful blood as Donald Campbell of Scalpay)
not only cured herring in great quantities, but – far into the nineteenth
century – sailed their own ships, laden with it, to ports on the Baltic and
to Russia itself.

Lewis MacIver had lost neither his spirit nor his dangerous, most Highland
hauteur and, early in 1844, by one account, he again insisted on settling a
difference by pistols.
    This time the fuse had been lit by a Mr MacLeay, a much younger man and a
new Collector of Customs, who took understandable and close interest in the
movement and freight of locally owned vessels, some of which of course were
operated by the tacksman of Gress and which routinely voyaged to and fro
foreign parts. One suspects the Exciseman had good grounds for suspicion –
MacIver would have been scarcely human, by the mores of the time, if he had
not imported quantities of tobacco and liquor on which no duty had been paid,

if only for his own use; and in any event assorted illicit imports remained rife along most of the West Highland coast. There was, besides, widespread resentment in the country at how the expenses of the British state were funded not by general taxation of banked or earned wealth, but almost exclusively from a bewildering range of taxes and duties on things consumed by the mass of ordinary people. Now, in Stornoway, there was a ferocious quarrel and in some context – no doubt voices were raised, as ears twitched eagerly nearby – the Customs official publicly accused Lewis MacIver of smuggling.

The 'King of Lewis' was so enraged he demanded an immediate duel; and MacLeay was so angry himself he was daft enough to accept. They did not even wait to secure a referee or organise 'seconds', but instead stumped off forthwith to a field near the Cockle Ebb, about three hundred yards west of the house of Goathill Farm, which is still there. The field at that time was worked by a tailor called MacKenzie, and when the furious pair happened on the tenant – probably already brandishing their guns – he was pressed into immediate service to hold their coats.

So, in full and wrathful solemnity, MacLeay and MacIver took their stances, glowered darkly, awaited their turn, took aim – and both, mercifully, missed.

In very Lewis fashion, MacIver seems almost immediately to have been chastened by the sound of shot and the acrid reek of gunpowder; MacLeay, too, grasped the silliness (and the danger) of the situation. He graciously now apologised and off they went, practically arm in arm, to the tacksman's pleasant town-house, which stood at the junction of Church Street and Kenneth Street where the town's police station stands today, and duly drank – at length and, it is probable, repeatedly – to one another's health, and no doubt with draughts of something potent and either home-distilled or imported, and on which not a penny of duty had been rendered the Revenue.

There was much quiet enjoyment in town over this strutting cock-sparrow affair. Donald Munro, though, could not believe his luck: duelling had long been outlawed, and here was his chief local bugbear engaged in scandalous criminality. He dashed out forthwith to garner statements: the tailor (still rather affronted) sang like a canary, and Munro besides wrung testimony from a passer-by or two who at least owned to hearing gunshots. Then, joyously, the procurator fiscal transcribed the lot and, with a righteous covering letter, sent word of the case to the Crown Office in Edinburgh. In his excitement, he quite forgot that, while high authorities might well have sanctioned prosecution in a general case of duelling, they were scarcely likely to welcome such proceedings when one of the accused was a senior customs official.

Much as an island policeman who has behaved foolishly is dealt with to this day, MacLeay was in short order transferred quietly to the customs round in another, distant port. Munro's instructions came back swiftly, and they were emphatic: there was to be no prosecution. His rage and chagrin might readily be imagined.

One must, though, point out, that this is but Grant's version of the dramatic gunfight; he offers no documentation, save for a newspaper article written many years later by John N. Anderson, a remarkably gifted Stornoway citizen and a formidable post-Great War Provost. Certainly, as Grant avers, he had as a young man worked with Donald Munro in the chamberlain's office. But Grant has also written elsewhere of Anderson's fateful weakness for drink, which finally destroyed his abilities, his career and his reputation, and reduced him to near-dereliction in Edinburgh, writing brilliant but disordered epistles, on any old scrap paper, to Stornoway friends from squalid city lodgings.

Peter Cunningham has another account of what might, conceivably, be an earlier MacIver and MacLeay collusion; but he has contemporary documentation of it, it is much more likely to be the only occasion they ever exchanged shots and Donald Munro cannot conceivably have been involved. On 5 September 1835, Thomas Knox – then but a minor Seaforth retainer – anxiously wrote his distant master, James Stewart-MacKenzie, in a letter surviving in the Seaforth Papers:

> On Wednesday last, the 29th current, about 4 pm, a hostile mutiny took place at the north east end of the Goathill Grounds near Seaforth's well, between Collector MacLeay and Lewis MacIver, the former supported by the Controller, the latter by Mr William Fairbairn, and after exchanging shots once, the parties separated.
>
> The Collector rents MacIver's house in Kenneth Street and being somewhat troublesome as to repairs and alterations, workmen were employed in taking a floor out of one of the rooms and putting in a new one.
>
> On Monday afternoon MacIver called about the expense, words were exchanged of an unfriendly nature, and the Collector attempted to strike MacIver with his stick.
>
> The consequence was a message by Mr Fairbairn to the Collector and the meeting just mentioned. Nobody hurt – fortunately, for there was no surgeon present.

Whenever it happened – and one must regard the Knox account as the more authoritative – this was, as far as can be ascertained, the very last duel fought in Scotland, if of no benefit in any way to the schemes of Donald Munro, half-bested in court in the summer of 1843 by the amoral little tacksman of Gress. But events were suddenly moving elsewhere to his very great advantage.

On 24 September, quite quickly and with not much fuss, James Stewart-MacKenzie died. Fatuous as he seems to us in many respects, and ill-judged and cruel as had been some of his 'improvements' on Lewis, his disconsolate widow – her old MacKenzie estates already much contracted – felt unable to manage her island without him.

It is impossible to view this good-hearted if naive woman without ambivalence and her ponderous husband with serious respect. Of her own carriage in wider society – and in some exotic, uncomfortable parts around the globe – there is no doubt. 'Circumstances afforded full play to her peculiar talents and graces of manner and deportment,' cooed Lord Teignmouth, 'whether accompanying her father during his government of Barbados, or as wife of Admiral Sir Samuel Hood, when commanding on the Indian Station, or enjoying the personal dignity of chief of a clan, or moving in the higher circles of society . . . Her talents and influence were devoted, like those of her sisters, to works of Christian benevolence.'

Yet, beyond that due exercise of feminine gifts in one of the very few realms of life at the time, beyond children and kitchen, where they were permitted, her undoubted abilities were never devoted to the intelligent management of her estates or the real, material betterment of her tenants. The Stewart-MacKenzies deserve commendation, certainly, for implacably dismantling the middle-management, tacksman layer of oppression over ordinary Lewismen. But it also served – as Lewis MacIver's late career attests – to remove men who could, on occasion, serve as tribunes instead of petty tyrants, and who ended up in quasi-Darwinian struggle with crofters for the same scanty patches of worthwhile ground. Donald MacDonald of Tolsta is too glib when he asserts that, in buying all Lewis from the claws of Seaforth Estate creditors in 1824, it was for James Stewart-MacKenzie 'a gross mistake on his part, as it led him further into debt'. The competing bidder, as Cunningham relates, was a ghastly Lowland outfit, the Joint Stock Property Company of Edinburgh – comparable to the private-equity vultures of our own day, who would simply have asset-stripped the island as one wretched cash-cow and, in all probability, reduced it to the depopulated desolation that is most of modern Mull; and MacKenzie-Stewart's friends in high places did, as MacDonald concedes, materialise in the nick of time with honoured overseas offices to grant the pair some latter dignity.

He is on surer ground in asserting the self-evident truth that the Lewis dominion of the last of the House of Seaforth 'was marred by a lack of money, recurring famines, the failure of the kelp industry, unemployment, an ever-increasing population, and a husband whose imaginative ideas for increasing his rapidly diminishing income were not matched by his power of accomplishment . . . after the failure of the kelp industry, he tried to recoup his losses by concentrating on fishing and sheep-farming, unfortunately without much success.'

But MacDonald goes too far in declaring that the 'many deserted townships in Lochs and Uig are reminders of his sheep farming policy that caused untold misery to many defenceless people,' comparable to Joni Buchanan's likewise sweeping claim that the 'interiors of the hilly parishes of Uig in the south-west and Park in the east were put under sheep farming during the first three decades of the 19th century and the people, for the most part, cleared to Canada.' By comparison with many other parts of the West Highland in an unscrupulous age, very few villages on Lewis were forcibly cleared of their inhabitants, still fewer were abandoned permanently of tenantry, no one was forced into emigrant ships for Canada – virtually all were offered alternative holdings on Lewis – and it is naive to think the likes of Kinlochresort or Steimreway would, unmolested, still support communities today, when so many localities in Gaeldom never served with eviction orders do not.

'For many years the Highland Clearances were a taboo subject,' said Bill Lawson, launching his Angus MacLeod Memorial Lecture at Garyvard, Park, in 2006, 'rarely mentioned, certainly not in the teaching of schools in the Highlands – in fact I probably heard more about the Highland Clearances in my schooldays in Ayrshire than my wife ever did in Point. Now the pendulum has swung the other way, and everyone whoever moved house was driven out by a bad landlord, with the house roof in flames over their heads . . .'

And, concluding a brave, but rigorously argued and well-documented, case that night, and in no way trivialising the real evictions and the undoubted degree of distress and suffering inflicted, Lawson marvelled:

that Lewis seems to hark back to the bad days of the Clearances more than any of the other islands do, and yet, as we have seen, it was the island least affected by them. I think that this may, paradoxically be in part because the Lewis clearances resulted in so little emigration . . . most cleared families remained on the island, and the land which had once been their family's home was readily visible, perhaps even on a daily basis. It is perhaps only to be expected that the memory of so personal a loss would remain as an open sore, but what is less justifiable is the way in which many people seem to have lost sight of the reality of what happened in Lewis, and have begun to invent a fake history in which everything which ever happened in a clearance anywhere in the Highlands must have happened in Lewis also. Does this matter? I think that it does, if only because propagating a fake history hides the reality of what actually happened, and blinds us to the true causes of problems which still remain in the community and in the economy of the islands . . . If a township such as Lemreway is losing its population, it is easy to blame it on the clearances of 1842, and ignore the fact that it was resettled in 1858 – and most of the problems have arisen since the latter date. Angus MacLeod's own township of Calbost is now virtually empty, but it was never cleared, and none of its numerous cottar families had come from any of the clearance townships. If Baremsavay had not been cleared, would there still be families living there today? I very much doubt it.

The last of the Seaforths did not long hang about her western realms to ponder her own personal loss. Mrs Stewart-MacKenzie had already sold off the last of her estates in Kintail, Alexander MacKenzie recalled in 1877, with a sort of horrified relish, 'the sunny braes of Ross, the church lands of Chanonry, the barony of Pluscarden . . .' Now she rid herself of the Isle of Lewis; and spent the rest of a final, surprisingly long and – one suspects – contented widowhood at Brahan, where in 1867 she died. And there Mary MacKenzie, widow of Sir Admiral Hood, relict besides of Sir James Stewart-MacKenzie, was, on 28 November, afforded a great funeral, 'the grandest in the Highlands since her father's,' says Cunningham, 'and as much for an age now gone as for herself'.

On Whitsunday 1844, and for the sum of £190,000, James Matheson had taken possession of the Isle of Lewis. He refused – as, too, did his Matheson successors – ever to take the oaths of the Craft and join Lodge Fortrose; but on 28 June that same year, exactly a month after he had become laird, the records of Stornoway Freemasons add the name of a new initiate: Donald Munro.

5

Matheson: How a drug baron won Lewis; and how he ran it . . .

A middle-class, highly ambitious boy, eager to make a great deal of money and with no scruples as to how he does it, pairs up with a like-minded youth and, after dabbling in this and that, hits on the considerable profit to be made by selling drugs in a given, vulnerable community. When the feeble authorities protest, and try and stamp out their trade, our ruthless pair pull strings in high places and, besides, orchestrate vicious gang-wars. Finally, years on, our man has a vast fortune. He wins a trophy wife, buys a rural estate, builds a vast and luxurious home and turns himself into quite the country gentleman, living the sweet life and wielding enormous local power as a result of his loot, amassed on the back of untold human misery, degradation and bloodshed.

Would not the newspapers have a righteous fit? Would not politicians trip over one another to condemn? Would not royalty be sure to shun, and clergymen no less to deplore? There are still such people in Britain, some with a veneer of respectability, and others whose close links to gangsterism and evil – while not quite demonstrable enough to land them in prison – frequently attract the righteous ire of middle-class tabloids. But when, early in the nineteenth century, James Matheson did exactly this, it was to near-universal admiration and applause. By the time he bought the Isle of Lewis, he was a Member of Parliament. In 1851 – and on entirely false pretences, taking credit for a vast charitable endeavour that was no such thing – he was even made a baronet. In his own lifetime, he enjoyed near-uncritical regard in wider society and, to this day, his effective (and absolute) monarchy of the Isle of Lewis has won little criticism.

'On the whole,' Joni Buchanan has rightly observed, 'history has treated him with remarkable generosity.' It has, by contrast, been singularly unkind to the last laird of Lewis, Lord Leverhulme, who – though scarcely less the paternalist, and all the more stubborn – had far more commercial and humanitarian sense and was never remotely tainted by criminality. Only one of his contemporaries – the father of the modern Conservative Party, Benjamin Disraeli – seems truly to have seen Sir James for what he was – 'a dreadful man, richer than Croesus, one

McDrug, fresh from Canton with a million of opium in each pocket', – and that was an indirect, *roman-à-clef* shot in the politician and adventurer's novel, *Sybil*; Peter Cunningham suggests besides (though it seems improbable) it was actually a dig at Matheson's old partner-in-crime, William Jardine. In any event, as Whigs, they were Disraeli's detested political opponents.

To this day, with Sir James himself now far beyond living memory and almost a century after his Matheson heirs finally sold Lewis, he and his lady cast a very long shadow. Walking in the grounds of Lews Castle, there is still the sense of exploration, and indeed intrusion, into someone's private garden, as you pass splendid specimen trees or amble up some artfully curved walk or study a carefully framed 'prospect'. On the castellated promontory of Cuddy Point, there is an adoring tribute to Sir James by – improbably – his mother-in-law; near the River Creed, on another elegant walk, a sort of Italianate grotto is some hundred yards along from an 'Iron Well' – with a drinking-fountain bubbling, day and night, its sulphurous refreshment – dedicated to a toff in the Matheson circle who used to drop by in his yacht each year. By every access into the castle policies, there is some watchtower, from the baleful Porter's Lodge at the main entrance to the Boatman's Lodge overlooking the Inner Harbour, and from the low bunker at the Marybank entrance to the alert fortress by the Creed.

From Porter's Lodge, the stately pair could sweep behind what was then the built-up town by a specially built drive – called, then, Mary Road – to their Sunday rites at St Peter's Episcopal Church, there being no other church on Lewis good enough for them. (It would be late in the laird's era before it was renamed Matheson Road, and plots feued off for villas by the new Stornoway gentry; it was a condition of sale that they planted trees by the roadside, to make the Matheson trot to Holy Communion all the more grand an avenue.) At this run's very end there was no escape from the pair, for the highway to matins debouched at last onto James Street, named this time in the husband's honour. Another new highway, rolling west of town to Sandwick and Point, was Perceval Road, also named after the lady of the manor; and Perceval Square is still at the heart of Stornoway, snug by the inner harbour.

Not far from the mock-Tudor hulk of the castle Matheson built is the vainglorious Matheson Monument, a great marbled thing with a cupola over a sort of battered, faintly butch Venus de Milo. After many years of neglect, vandalism, encroachment by trees and ensuing popularity as a trysting place for casual liaisons, it was restored in 2005 and unveiled anew to curious pomp. The extravaganza overlooks Stornoway Harbour like a battery of aristocratic cannon, and is faced on all sides with adoring inscriptions in which words like 'opium', 'factors' and 'evictions' do not appear – all, save perhaps for the one finally commemorating herself, worded by the Matheson widow.

The encomium to Sir James is far too long (and embellished with capitals, italics and other forms of Victorian emphases) to inflict here; but it highlights the late landlord's many averred virtues and a long prosperous career, climaxing, 'In 1844 he added to his Highland possessions the Island of Lewis which henceforth became his chief place of residence, devoting the remainder of a long and useful life to ameliorating the condition of the inhabitants of that Island. H.M. Queen Victoria in 1850 testified to her sense of his noble benevolence during the Famine of 1845–46 by creating him a Baronet of the United Kingdom. . . .' On another face of the costly stone, 'Well done, thou good and faithful servant. Enter thou into the joy of the Lord. Matthew XXV 21.' And on still another – after the relict, in turn, had gone to the house appointed for all living, 'On this Monument is added the name of Dame Mary Jane Matheson who, during her husband's life, aided him in the benevolent and philanthropic works carried out for the benefit of the Island of the Lews and its inhabitants and who during eighteen years of lonely widowhood endeavoured to fulfil the trust he had imposed in her . . . "She hath done what she could." Mark XIX, 8.'

Finally, relentlessly, on the fourth blank of marble, 'In life a consistent Christian, possessed of those special virtues conducive to the happiness of others and truly has it been said of him "That he was a child of God, living evidently under the influence of His Holy Spirit." In person he was a tall, handsome noble-looking man with a beautiful placid expression of benevolence and a winning kindness and dignity of manner.'

Sir James certainly took a fine photograph; all surviving images show a visage serene, saintly and faintly smiling. Certainly he was an earnest churchman – if a convert to Episcopacy from his native Presbyterianism; certainly he bequeathed a splendid woodland in the great arboretum of the Lews Castle policies; certainly he built a vast and largely surviving infrastructure of roads, piers and bridges; and there are yet those who insist he outlaid far more money on Lewis than he ever recouped. (But the records do not support this; much as he did spend, in essence Matheson regarded Lewis as a personal playground, a Shangri-La: much of his expenditure, even on roads, was for his own amenity. He and his agents undoubtedly tried to wrest as much money back from the tenantry and townsfolk as possible; and, especially in the early and famine-fraught years, people were readily squeezed as cheap or even free labour.)

Sir James Matheson was, at best, a well-meaning paternalist; he was far from a competent one; he was an appalling judge of human capacity and middle-management character; and the record of his island dominion is as thick with mud as marble. The truth is that his actions as landlord (and still more the actions of those, like Donald Munro, who ministered to him) were oddly divorced from his self-image: the noble, upright benefactor, oozing good works and moral probity. In reality – conditioned by many years of business in the Indies and Canton – he operated as an Eastern potentate – a 'Chinese mandarin,' James Shaw Grant concluded in 1992, 'absolute in attitude, but benevolent in intention; doing everything with, as he saw it, a high moral purpose, but strictly in his own terms and in his own way.'

Matheson might well have won a gong – indeed, a hereditary knighthood – for his 'untiring benevolence in relieving the inhabitants of Lewis during the famine'; it was, as we shall see, wholly undeserved. And, as Iain Fraser Grigor notes, Sir James,

> part of whose fortune was requisitioned to prevent widespread starvation, disapproved strongly of what he called the lavish waste of money in the government's famine-relief programme. He thought it better for the poor people to labour for their means of sustenance – 'that they ought rather to earn their food by toil, than eat the bread of idleness and pauperism' – and so set his own tenants to work on his estate for just enough food to keep them alive and working. Perhaps his eastern experiences helped him to balance this delicate equation: for the greatest portion of his truly huge fortune had been made in the China opium addiction trade, which he had once recommended to a friend as 'the safest and most gentlemanlike speculation I am aware of.'

The remarkably enduring legend, on Lewis and abroad, of Matheson as the best of Highland landlords sits curiously alongside the seldom-studied Conditions of Let for his Lewis Estate, run up by his Edinburgh lawyers in 1849; the fact that they were largely standard for the period renders them no less disturbing to an age far less feudal.

Crofters caught poaching were to be charged double rent on their holdings for a year – in addition to any fines and penalties levied in the Sheriff Court. All tenants, 'in going to kirk and market, or to ferry, or other place of resort' – like church, or school – were at all times to use, and only use, the footpaths and roads designated by the Estate. All tenants were in thirlage to the mills of the Estate, whether they had mills of their own or not and even if the appointed premises (with its detested cut of their labour) were a very long and gruelling distance away. Married couples were absolutely forbidden to live in the home of either set of parents. Every crofter, Grant additionally highlights, had to make 'three tons of kelp per annum, at a price dictated by the factor, under the threat that, if the kelp was not to the factor's liking, or anything

happened to it before it was safe on board ship, the full value would be added
to the rent. And the

> tone of the Matheson administration is best reflected in the final condition:
> 'The proprietor, being very desirous of promoting education . . . and
> having provided . . . various schoolhouses and schoolmasters at his own
> expense . . . the parents or guardians . . . of any child who may be absent
> from school for fourteen days continuously, without being able to assign a
> reason for such absence . . . shall be held to have incurred the proprietor's
> grave displeasure, which shall be considered as excluding [*them*] from those
> marks of grace and favour which he is always desirous of dispensing to his
> well-conducted tenantry.'
>
> Sir James's interest in education was real enough. But so, too, was his
> appetite for lavish praise and obsequious crofters . . .

James Nicholas Sutherland Matheson was of the middling tacksman class in
Highland society and was born, in October 1796, in the parish of Lairg,
Sutherland, the second son of Captain Donald Matheson and his wife,
Catherine MacKay. By local standards, the family were comfortable; Captain
Matheson – who died in 1810 – held the lands of Shiness, and did business in
India. Young James was not just Highland, but post-Highland – he spoke no
more than a few words of Gaelic, if any – and, by late life, post-Scottish, of
Anglican religion and, one suspects, the studiously acquired accent of English
gentry. But he came of moderate money and was well educated, being sent
successively to Inverness Royal Academy, Edinburgh's Royal High School and
the city's university. (Classmates – as Lady Matheson laboriously reminds us
on that memorial, lest we think her husband learned his letters alongside the
brood of crofters – included 'The Right Honourable David Dundas; David,
Lord Marjory-Banks; Sir Robert Christison, Bart.; the second Lord Brougham
and Anthony Adrian, Earl of Kintore.')

Matheson began working life as a 17-year-old in a London 'counting-
house'; at 19, he sailed for India, to like employment for Messrs Macintosh
and Company in Calcutta, a firm owned by his uncle. He does not seem to
have got on very well and they 'let him go'; it seems the last straw was when
the young man forgot to send an important document, provoking his uncle to
dismiss him around 1820. No doubt mortified, struggling to find his niche,
young Matheson made for Canton in China. Valuable things came out of that
great, though, by the early nineteenth century, very tired, land – silks, tea –
and Matheson dabbled in assorted little ventures in both, by himself, or in
partnership with others, to no great success. Then he fell in tow with another

Scot, William Jardine: this proved the making of them (like in ambition, energy, focus and amorality) and the great house of business they founded in 1832, Jardine Matheson and Company, was of such roaring and unprincipled success it thrives to this day. The vast, fabulously rich Jardine Matheson empire is still renowed for its internal and Byzantine intrigue and the notorious games (immortalised in a thinly veiled James Clavell airport novel) to be 'Tai-Pan' – head of its empire or, in rough equivalence to the Mandarin, the 'Big Shot'.

There was nothing in the least wrong with buying silk and tea and ginger and porcelain and all the other dainties of the mystic Orient and shipping them home to a grateful Europe. The evil lay in how Matheson and Jardine decided to pay for them. It was no light matter to raise hard cash to buy such goods from the Chinese, who expressly insisted on payment in silver; British merchants, their currency long founded on the gold standard, could only source silver from Europe, at additional trouble and charges. Besides, neither man – the archetypal 'Scotchmen on the make' who so typify this period, to the point of being satirised in its fiction – was the type who cared to part with precious metal. Yet the Chinese – who have always cared still more passionately for money, and are extraordinarily fascinated by it – had no appetite for British goods in kind. At first, no doubt, too high-minded to follow their predecessor's trading custom, the young men reasoned themselves back into it. There was a great and insatiable popular appetite in China for opium. In Britain, it was freely available – then, and for many more years to come – as a mental and emotional crutch, usually steeped in alcohol for the popular over-the-counter medicine (and woozy trip to La-La Land) of laudanum. The Chinese, though, had discovered its still more extraordinary properties when smoked, and with such dire consequences for the life and culture of what had once been perhaps the world's most sophisticated civilisation that her government now did its best – with little conviction and less avail – to ban its import.

The stumbling Chinese Empire was no match for such as Jardine and Matheson. Soon they were buying enormous quantities of opium in India, selling it by auction in Calcutta – in full knowledge it was being snapped up by the middlemen who smuggled it, more or less brazenly, into China – and then vested that fortune not just in sought-after consumables from the great country, but besides 'developed enormous interests in banking, insurance and shipping', writes Joni Buchanan. 'They traded in tea, silk and cotton but cash from the sale and transportation of the opium underpinned all of the company's trade. James Matheson wrote in 1833, "The command of money which we derive from our large opium dealings and which can hardly be derived from any other source gives us an important advantage."'

To make matters worse, the self-righteous Scot debased even the Christian faith, as James Shaw Grant related in 1985, finding

> time to take a very active interest in social and educational enterprises in Canton. He established the first English language newspaper in China, *The Canton Register*, and was the principal supporter of a missionary school. He was undoubtedly a philanthropist, but there was another side to his activities. One of his first associates in China was an eccentric Pomeranian missionary named Gutzlaff, who claimed to have converted more Chinese than any other man in history, and almost certainly dosed more Chinamen with pills. His missionary activities were sufficiently important to gain him an entry in the *Encyclopaedia Britannica*, but the association earned Matheson the reputation of going round China with the Bible in one hand and opium in the other. There is more than an element of truth in the charge.

The Chinese grew the more desperate to beat the dreadful physical and social cost of opium addiction, and to stem the remorseless outflow of silver, relates Buchanan, but to Matheson all their laws and decrees were 'so much waste paper'. Even when his own nephew, Donald Matheson, quit the business in quiet disgust, his uncle was still insisting that he had 'never seen a native in the least bestialised by opium smoking'. One suspects he had never made much effort to find one. Matheson, as his future tenants in Lewis would learn, had a gift for overlooking things he did not want to see. In 1839, the frantic Chinese finally abandoned attempts in law for the exercise of full military force – blockading their ports, stopping and searching ships, arresting Chinese opium-dealers and (for the first time) sentencing them to death, and even going so far (under a new commissioner of Canton) to blockade British merchants in their own factories and deny supplies until they finally stopped shipping drugs into the Empire.

So the British, not least at the urging of Jardine Matheson and Company Ltd, went to war. The government in London had earlier yielded to pressure and agreed to take possession of all the available opium in British hands and yield it to Chinese authorities for confiscation. Ministers now cynically decided some short, brutal bloodshed was preferable to actually paying the promised compensation to British traders.

With huge military and technological advantage, the outcome of the conflict was never in doubt and, in 1842, the Qing Empire was forced to sign humiliating terms of peace in the 'Unequal Treaty' of Nanjing. In the House of Commons, a newly elected Member, William Ewart Gladstone (then a High Tory) declared that if there had ever been 'a war more unjust in its origin, a war more calculated to cover this country with permanent disgrace, I do not know'.

Though he never set foot in the town – and only once, with mild interest and from the deck of a passing yacht, ever beheld it – Gladstone's mother, Anne MacKenzie Robertson, had been born in Stornoway.

A second Opium War would follow, after still more ruthless demands and provocations by the European merchants and their tame governments, from 1856 to 1860, and be settled in an agreement just as one-sided at Tianjin, to British advantage and with still heavier Chinese indemnities in silver; it would be 1870 before the disgusting trade was finally put down. By then, of course, Matheson had long retired to Scotland, with all his loot, to play the Highland laird. On quitting the East, as a fawning 1878 obituary reminded his country, he 'on that occasion received an address from the native merchants of Bombay expressing their high sense of the judgement and fairness he had displayed during the crisis which arose in Eastern mercantile and political circles owing to the war with China . . . through their having seized some opium, against the importation of which into their country they had protested. For this service Mr Matheson was presented with a piece of plate valued at £1,500.'

In 1843, back in Britain, the blithe drug baron succeeded his old henchman Jardine as MP for the rotten-burgh division of Ashburton; from 1847, Matheson (with no greater difficulty, on a minimal electorate) would sit for Ross and Cromarty, and in 1868 pass that representation to his nephew as if it were a set of golf clubs. He also bought a chunk of Sutherland – the Achany estate – but evidently remained on the look-out for territory still grander.

And on 9 November 1843 – surprisingly late in life – Matheson married Mary Jane Perceval, who came of English gentry and with a colonial twist. Born in Comberflory, Somerset, Henry Perceval had established himself prosperously in Spencerwood, Quebec, though Mary Jane herself seems to have been born, in 1820, in Edinburgh. For a time Mr Perceval served on the Canadian province's Legislative Council. There seems to have been some kinship with Spencer Perceval – Britain's only assassinated prime minister, shot by a furious bankrupt in the House of Commons lobby in May 1812 – though, as he was a son of the Earl of Egmont, the link was tenuous and perhaps optimistic. Nevertheless, the martyred premier's portrait would hang for many years in Lews Castle, all the better to promote thoughts of the connection. Matheson no doubt hoped for children, but – and this did little for the moral development of either – the union proved barren. There is evidence besides that Lady Matheson grew shrewish and domineering, convinced just a little and to the last she had married beneath her.

Matheson came into his Lewis estate at a time of turmoil and trouble, the advent of his new regime – and the departure of the Seaforths – being just one dislocation. In May 1843, a year previously, the Kirk had been rent by the Disruption. There had historically been far more probationers – those trained for the ministry, but never settled to a charge or ordained to its functions – than she needed; and the sudden advent of the Free Church (with scores of new congregations begging for pastors) and the no less sudden creation of many Established Church vacancies, opened up vast new employment prospects, not just for all those 'stickit ministers' but for men who had been forced to make do with demanding, far-flung charges in the Hebrides and West Highlands. All of a sudden, delightful alternatives were available. Of the six ministers in Lewis, four had 'come out' for the Free Church; by the end of 1844, three had speedily accepted calls to pastures new, as did the adhering Established Church minister of Stornoway. This flight of their natural leaders – at a critical moment in island fortunes – has never been forgotten on Lewis, and begot a sour streak of island anticlericalism that endures even in the twenty-first century – for, as Donald MacDonald of Tolsta observes, it 'caused much confusion and bitterness throughout the Island'.

But there had besides been almost a decade of sustained economic crisis; and not the sort of austerity of which we complain now – a general climate of belt-tightening, foregoing luxuries and putting off expensive purchases – but of true hardship, hunger and starvation. From 1835 there was a run of indifferent summers, bad weather and poor to calamitous harvests, combined with a crash in the value of cattle; the winter of 1836–37 had been particularly dreadful as, confident of an upturn in stock prices, islanders fed much of their seed-corn and potatoes to feed up the beasts that summer.

The people of Lewis, as in the West Highlands generally – and, still more notoriously, in rural Ireland – had grown too reliant on the potato. It had been introduced to the Outer Hebrides only in 1743, by MacDonald of Clanranald – though some lines in Martin Martin's memoir of island travel suggest it was known, at least in the Inner Hebrides, in 1695 – and at first there was great popular resistance. It is said that the tenantry of South Uist did mulishly plant potatoes at the chief's behest, and tend them, and rig them, and in time unearth them; but finally they came and flung the tubers at his feet, announcing that while the great Clanranald might indeed command them to grow these strange things, he could by no means compel them to eat them.

The advantages of this new staple, though, were quickly grasped. Potatoes were far less vulnerable than standing corn to rain, wind and tempest; they were much easier to store (usually buried in straw-lined pits); the calorific yield, per square yard planted, was much greater; their easy use greatly reduced dependence on mills and the hated thirlage; and, supplemented by milk, butter and cheese, potatoes were practically a complete food. By 1780, this American native was the mainstay of all the Hebrides and its inhabitants were wholly dependent on it for half the year, as attested by striking figures retailed by W.H. Murray from just one parish in Skye. In the 40 years between 1801 and 1841, the grain product did not vary (some 1,600 bolls of oats and barley in a year), but the population burgeoned from 2,555 to 3,625 – and the potato crop from 5,000 barrels to 32,000.

The general population explosion in the West Highlands in these decades of the early nineteenth century – peaking around 1841 – put enormous strain on land and resources. In Lewis, for instance, it climbed from a mere 6,386 (fewer people on the whole island than now live in Stornoway) in 1755 to 8,371 by 1791, 10,092 by 1811, 14,541 by 1831 and 17,037 a decade later. In fact – and in stark contrast to practically everywhere else in the region – it would continue steadily to rise until the Great War, more evidence of the Lawson analysis that the Lewis clearances were largely a movement of people about the island than expulsions from it.

The causes for this extraordinary expansion are complex. The potato was undoubtedly a big factor, and the advent of smallpox vaccination – it is mentioned by visitors to Stornoway before the close of the eighteenth century – another. As the superstitious practice of applying filthy poultices to the umbilici of newborn infants was firmly educated out of the community, the ravages of infantile tetanus (the 'fifth-day sickness') disappeared; however it would be late in the nineteenth century, and only thanks to a strong-minded Free Church minister, before the strange folk of St Kilda abandoned such folly. The booming business in (largely illicit) whisky and the jerky development of the fishery were others, as indeed was the kelp boom. But, as we noticed in passing earlier, the landlords themselves (including the House of Seaforth) had manoeuvred to restrict their tenants' choices and economic independence for their own ends, especially when unusual (and short-term) factors granted rich profits from kelp. While to much less an extreme on Lewis than was general, the best agricultural land was taken from the people for incoming sheep-farmers; and the people themselves were forced into the new crofting order, on plots of individually rented land (and shares in indifferent common grazing) incapable of entirely sustaining them, as James Hunter observes:

No man could support himself, his wife and his children on the produce of such a holding. And that, in fact, was the intention. To feed their families and pay their generally exorbitant rents, as landowners knew very well, crofters would require employment outside the comparatively limited range of agricultural activities which had been sufficient for their non-crofting predecessors. And the only such employment available, of course, was the kelp industry . . . the crofting system was a beautifully efficient form of exploitation. By limiting the amount of land at the family's disposal, by charging a high rent for that land and by paying extremely low prices for kelp, island lairds provided themselves with a workforce which was as much at their mercy, and as firmly under their control, as any set of slaves on a colonial plantation.

As we have noted, there was an aversion among Hebrideans generally to the wet, unpleasant work of cutting, floating, bringing ashore and processing kelp, especially in the knowledge that, per ton, they earned only a tenth of what the landlord was paid for it. The instinctive reaction in many quarters was to emigrate. By early 1803 on Skye, for instance, fully two-thirds of all Lord MacDonald's tenants in Sleat were planning passage to North America. He – and other lairds, like Lord Seaforth – played for time, said soothing things, and contacted friends in high places. By that autumn, and by legislation in Westminster, the cost of transatlantic passage was set at a minimum deliberately beyond the reach of the poor. 'The emigration is entirely stopped now,' Lord MacDonald's factor wrote smugly, 'from the Act of Parliament which puts it out of the poor people's power to pay the increase of freight.' Adam Smith's free-market doctrines had, again, a decided limit.

On Lewis, throughout this period, the Seaforths and their men on the ground had actively encouraged large families. By the turn of the century, it had become the norm to marry very young; indeed, men tended to be younger than their wives. A new crofting economy made it a positive advantage – in the short term – to have large families: the more hands the better for a myriad of tasks. Within a generation, though, as should have been foreseen, it created pressures that led to the widespread, unofficial division of holdings between family members and – but for the dramatic measures finally adopted by Matheson and his henchman – Lewis today might yet abound, like Skye or Barra, with such addresses as 'Third of 8 Leurbost . . .' or 'quarter of Croft No. 12, North Tolsta . . .'

Certainly, as Cunningham relates, Matheson took over an island 'in a parlous state. Many of the population of 17,000 were in a wretched condition. A contemporary newspaper described them as the worst fed, the worst clothed and worst housed peasantry in Britain.' And Joni Buchanan does not greatly exaggerate in her assertion that 'by the time the island was sold in 1844, the legacy of the Seaforths' centuries-old proprietorship of Lewis was an impoverished people and a pitifully underdeveloped land'. Then – catastrophically – in 1845, the potato crop failed, as the blight already afflicting much of the West

Highlands (and Ireland) hit the Isle of Lewis. It failed again in 1846, and the blight lingered until 1850; on top of poor grain harvests, indifferent fishing (for which there were inadequate boats, tackle and facilities) and atrocious prices for cattle, the island gently starved. There were no longer enough seed-potatoes even for planting, as W.H. Murray notes of the general Hebridean context, and destitution

> changed to famine on a vast scale, beyond all local control or remedy – a situation that would nowadays be declared a national emergency. The Westminster Government refused funds, but set up a Colonial Land and Emigration Department to compile statistics. The granaries of the southern shipping ports were full, yet the government gave no direction for the distribution of grain. The people affected had neither voting rights nor representation in Parliament. As late as 1850, at the worst of the famines, the Free Church was still appealing to the Secretary of State for aid. Apart from starvation, the people were suffering cold from lack of clothing. They had no change of clothes day or night, were using meal bags for under and over-garments, and all went barefoot in winter. . . . Emigration was the only solution to gross over-population and its consequent evils of abused land and famine . . . A solution to the Highland problem was thus presented to the lairds. A few were themselves in desperate straits: most were absentees, and Lowlanders; yet the haste in which they acted was despicable. One Robert Chalmers had spoken their mind: 'Of late years the landlords have very properly done all they could to substitute a population of sheep for the innumerable hordes of useless human beings who formerly vegetated upon a soil that seemed barren of everything else.' The substitution was called improvement. The idea that a landowner had the right to do with his property and tenants as he saw fit had supplanted the clan ideal of trusteeship, and bore the most poisonous fruit ever grown on the Atlantic seaboard . . .

Thousands of Highlanders would certainly have died but for the efforts of appalled leaders in the new Free Church, struggling throughout the 1840s against widespread landlord hostility. A large yacht, the *Breadalbane*, had been gifted to the new denomination by Lowland subscribers; she was a 30-ton rigged schooner, described as 'large, fast and excellent', and had been designed to convey peripatetic Gaelic ministers and much Christian literature up and down the western seaboard. She was quickly adapted, now, for a Free Church famine-relief programme, and delivered great quantities of meal throughout the region. It is largely on account of the *Breadalbane* and this endeavour that, in contrast to Ireland, fatalities from the crisis were so limited in the West Highlands.

But she could not do quite enough and her movements, inevitably (and no doubt by oversight) were dictated by the prevalence of Free Church people. Where there were very few – like South Uist, the community that suffered most between clearances, famine and despotic landlordism – the eyewitness testimony is appalling. The Reverend Norman MacLeod, one of the outstanding men of the post-Disruption Established Church, was shaken by what he saw on a visit to that island at the height of the crisis. 'Deplorable, nay, heart-rending . . . on the beach the whole population of the country seemed to be met, gathering the precious cockles . . . I never witnessed such countenances – starvation on many faces – the children with their melancholy looks, big-looking knees, shrivelled legs, hollow eyes, swollen-like bellies. God help them, I never did witness such wretchedness . . .' It was the sort of scene our own generation would associate with Ethiopia.

The plight of Lewis was complicated by the Disruption and by the ensuing turmoil in Poor Relief, still the notional responsibility of the Established Church and administered by local kirk sessions. Care for 'paupers' would soon, as a consequence, be the direct responsibility of landlords – a burden Matheson had not, in 1844, envisaged. Tenants were no longer a source of soldiery, to the bloody grass of Auldearn or the greater glory of a deaf Seaforth; they were no longer useful, kelp-reaping worker ants. All of a sudden, ordinary Highlanders were a liability.

Until 1849, Matheson would refuse to seek any help or support from the belatedly erected Highland Relief Board. Instead he bought and imported great quantities of meal; and it was in the genuine belief that he, from the goodness of his heart and for free, had given food to the starving that, in 1850, the queen conferred a baronetcy.

The truth was much darker. Matheson had not enriched himself by habits of unconditional philanthropy. His abiding reputation is because he resisted, in these years of hunger, the stratagem of practically every other Highland landlord: wholesale evictions and forced emigration overseas. In South Uist, for instance, the vile Colonel John Gordon, who had acquired the estate from a bankrupt Clanranald, hunted down his 'redundant' tenantry with policemen, guns and dogs. Even the parish minister enthusiastically joined in, a shocked observer wrote, directing operations like a slave-hunt on the African coast. Men were bound hand and foot and tossed into boats like cattle, as carts conveyed helpless women and howling children to island quays: Gordon besides simply confiscated – stole – all their belongings, from livestock to implements to mean sticks of furniture.

But Matheson had great schemes; work that needed to be done. No food was bestowed gratis on desperate Lewis people. Meal was only offered in exchange for labour – hard labour – on this and that lairdly project: the building of new roads and the repair of existing ones, the construction of quays, the erection of dykes and the digging of drains and the planting of marram to secure the sandy dunes on western shores. And – amidst all this island anguish – work proceeded serenely on his new stately home.

Most of Seaforth Lodge was pulled down and a new, grandiloquent Lews Castle began from November 1847 to arise, built to the cod-baronial design of Charles Wilson (whose other erections include Glasgow's Park Circus, General Post Office and the Gartnavel Asylum) and from Dalbeg granite, hewed out on the West Side by thin and gaunt-eyed men, and drawn the breadth of the island by weary carters. The building – 'a handsome evidence,' writes Peter Cunningham, 'in the extravagant style, with crenellated turrets and parapets, that was so popular with the newly rich at the time' – was completed in 1850. The Matheson arms still smile pompously from above the *porte cochère*, or covered carriage entrance, at the head of a stately drive winding up from the Toad Hall silliness of the Porter's Lodge. Internal apartments abounded in 'attractive pilasters, ceilings and mouldings', and all looked out over a ha-ha (a hidden parapet in the ground, in the stead of an unsightly fence, so that sheep and so on might prettily graze in the distance without imperilling the gardens) to the harbour and town below. The 'private gardens' and great conservatories were in time stocked with gorgeous flowers, tree-ferns and other exotics readily imported through Matheson's many contacts in the East a hothouse furnished grapes and peaches, and extensive kitchen-gardens and orchards were besides laid out to the west.

Most famously – though the papers detailing so extensive a project have not survived – the boggy land of moor and summer shieling about what had been Seaforth Lodge (bits of which can still be seen embodied in the back of the new château) was planted out as a great woodland. It is thought Lady Matheson herself largely designed the planting of these 300 acres, established at first by shelter-belts of conifer, rhododendron and sycamore, and over the years filled with copses, shrubs, a remarkable range of specimen trees from every continent, with pleasant walks and carriage drives that seem, to this day, to echo to the tap of hooves and the faint rustle of crinoline. It is also believed, locally, that the Mathesons imported a lot of soil. Many plants still here survive at their north-westerly extreme in Europe and, in the intervening century and a half, birds and beasts – from rooks to tits to finches to the pipistrelle bat – have since established themselves gratefully on Lewis.

A Manor Farm was also established and a large 'Dormitory' – which

survives, though all but derelict – was erected at 'Marybank' – lands by the
Bayhead River and also named in honour of his lady, which (with Maryhill)
would be laid out as a crofting community only after the Great War. This stark
building, at a good and discreet distance from the castle and behind what is now
a contractor's depot, housed in scant comfort most of those engaged in the
construction of the castle and the reinvention of its policies.

The fatuous Reverend George Hely-Hutcheson, an early priest of St Peter's,
and who enjoyed 20 years' run (from his chosen base at Soval Lodge) of island
fishing and shooting for his studious Matheson pains, enthused of those early
days of their state '. . . when the castle was lighted up, the rooms and corridors,
and staircases decked out – above all, that beautiful ball and music-room
thrown open, which used to remind me so of Almack's in its palmy days when I
was a boy, and the Redouten-Saal at Vienna – it was a pretty sight to see . . .'
But other comments, rather less flattering, Peter Cunningham deliciously
attributes to an 'unidentified snob':

> Opposite Stornoway, on the other side of the bay, is the castle of Sir James
> Matheson, which ranks among the very first in the Highlands after
> Dunrobin. Its close proximity to the town, however, we should fancy
> must be a very grievous drawback. Its frontage is exposed to the public gaze
> of every profane tourist or Stornowegian and while commanding a very fine
> and extensive view of Stornoway Bay and the blue hills of the mainland, it
> has little of that retired privacy which the occupiers of such castles generally
> contrive to find . . . Sir James and his lady kindly grant the use of the
> grounds for recreation to the Stornoway people, a benefit which the citizens
> of close-laned towns would highly value . . .

In fact, such access was restricted and episodic; in all, Lews Castle cost
£60,000 to build – and the sprawling parkland, between draining and planting
and roads and bridges and gatehouses and so on, a full £49,000.

And it is generally forgotten that two entire villages were obliterated to make
room for Matheson's general *et in arcadia ego*. The people of Ranol were
completely removed, partly because their township ran up to the summit of this
parkland and because their children and livestock were too near the castle by
half. Their long-tended *feannagan* – rigs – can still be discerned in the slopes of
the modern golf course, laid out in the western reach of the castle policies after
the Second World War. And the original village of Bayhead – not to be
confused with the street of that name by the inmost reach of Stornoway harbour
– was dissolved, so that its hard-won fertile ground could become the Manor
Farm. (In turn, from the late 1960s, this – some of the very best farmland on

Lewis – has vanished under hideous council housing and street upon street of modern bungaloid character; the site of the farmhouse itself is now dominated by a derelict dairy and the ennui of the Caberfeidh Hotel.) The townsfolk of Stornoway itself – many of whom, even well into the twentieth century, would keep a house-cow – were besides deprived of their winter grazing. And, as we shall see, the regal Matheson pair would go to still more ruthless lengths to protect their amenity.

James Matheson had been grandly entertained to a Stornoway public dinner in the early autumn of 1845 and – according to the *Inverness Courier* on 10 September – prettily promised that he planned 'to draw forth the energies of the islanders, to employ a Highland factor and to employ islanders wherever possible'. The building social crisis gave him abundant scope for the hard use of his tenantry and it was only exacerbated by his new chamberlain, a ruthless fellow from Sutherland, John Scobie, who served his laird from 1845 till 1850. Donald MacDonald of Tolsta, in a rare lapse, asserts that this man 'was just and generous' in all his dealings. That is scarcely borne out by the record, though it may reflect general Tolsta relief after the demise of Lewis MacIver. Scobie was an austere man; he exercised (on behalf of his master) a grasping covetousness. He had been hired not least for his knowledge of 'improvements' in his own native county, where the ducal house had its own curious ways of managing 'aborigines', as the infamous Patrick Sellar described the Sutherland people.

For all the talk of Matheson's untold generosity in a time of want, in cold fact he won that baronetcy on false pretences and on the back of three outrages. First, as Joni Buchanan angrily details, 'Matheson instigated "work-schemes" as an alternative to emigration. It was a response that singled him out and staved off emigration for about four years. However the schemes were as exploitative as they were compassionate; instead of helping the people on the edge of starvation the schemes served the estate's purpose well by using a substantial pool of labour to effect estate improvements at minimal cost.'

Secondly, as James Shaw Grant has demonstrated, the 'relief' was not free in any form. John Scobie, with or without Sir James's authority, charged every last pound of meal issued to the crofting recipient's rent. 'The vast arrears which the years of failed harvests had inevitably created were thus swollen quite unmanageably and the whole economy of the island was threatening to break down.' Expanding this further, in 1992, Grant explains that the 'meal distributed to the Lewis crofters in the Hungry Forties was not a gift from Sir James, as many people, both then and now, have assumed. The meal was sold to the crofters. At cost price, admittedly, and on credit, because they could not pay, but it was added to their already enormous arrears of rent.'

Third – and it is astonishing how few have touched on this infamy –
Matheson and his lackeys even charged the helpless population for food they
themselves had imported for free. From 1849 Matheson availed himself, like
other lairds, of the Highland Relief Board. What cost him nothing was then
turned to profit. 'During the potato famine,' reports Buchanan, 'large quantities of meal were supplied to Highland estates at government expense. But

> in Lewis, the Estate distributed the relief meal only in exchange for labour
> on Matheson's work-schemes. Similarly, seed-potatoes supplied by south-
> ern charities were sold at 25% of the market value – and if the tenant could
> not meet the cost of the potatoes or the relief meal it was added on as
> another item of rent under the heading 'balance of destitution meal'. Where
> crofting land was drained the rents were raised. Road tax was added to the
> crofter's rent where township roads were constructed. And, invariably, the
> meagre wages paid by the estate had conditions attached – one-third was to
> go on payment of rent, and if the labourer was in arrears of rent a portion of
> the wage was kept in lieu of payment. In an impoverished community,
> where rent arrears and other debts were endemic, the schemes were seen as
> yet another instrument of repression, and offered no possibility of improv-
> ing the crofters' lot.

The mandarin of the East had turned human suffering, on a considerable
scale, to his own advantage, and even Donald MacDonald concedes that the
activities of the Highland Relief Board were largely 'for the benefit of the
proprietors who thus had their properties improved at no expense to themselves. At no time was the land improved without the crofters having to pay for
it.' By 1850, the Lewis community – families and entire townships – were
effectively bankrupt, many facing great backlogs of obligation and rent, which,
in the present land-based economy, they could not hope to repay.

Even so, the wholesale social engineering about to break could have been
averted had Sir James, as he now was, possessed informed judgement or heeded
sensible advice. The central difficulty was that Lewis was not his business, but
his hobby. He had heaped his gold, he had more riches salted away than he
could possibly spend and he had no real interest in commercial development.
While 'Sir James was determined to collect all the rents that were due to him,'
Grant quite properly asserts, 'he was a wealthy man and felt no urge to invest
speculatively in the hope of increasing the rent roll still further.'

Closely examined, most of the much-vaunted Matheson schemes for industry and improvement are marked by inane lack of study or expertise; or a
view of commercial realities already obsolete; or a lack of elementary business

sense – and, through all, a want of common sense and an extraordinary capacity for appointing managers who were incompetent, or corrupt, or both.

To be sure, Sir James – and quickly – did important things for Stornoway itself. He built a jail and a 'ragged school'. He constructed the first waterworks on the island – utilising Loch Airigh na Lic, west of Marybank; the reservoir was only superseded in the 1930s by Loch Mor an Stairr, north of Newmarket on the Barvas Moor. As well as this Stornoway Water Company, he founded the Stornoway Gas Company; well into living memory – it would be 1931 before electricity reached the town – this lit homes and businesses, and it was long a Stornoway boast that 'we got gas before Greenock'. He besides took to do with the harbour – we shall study later drama there – and built two big new quays and an esplanade. Yet his much-vaunted 'Patent Slip' – which was really one great, winched shipyard sort of thing, its timber ruins still visible in James Shaw Grant's boyhood and running across Shell Street – was a white elephant even at its beginning, suited only for the fabrication of timber-hulled craft even as shipbuilding was shifting wholesale to vessels of iron and, later, steel.

It had cost £6,000 of more opium loot. Yet even by the late 1860s the Patent Slip's heyday was gone. 'The place will sadden them,' wrote R.M. Stephen around 1910, with Stornoway children in mind: he was a Free Church 'stickit minister' – a probationer who was never called or ordained to a charge, and whose posthumous and melancholy *Glimpses of Portrona* has much local colour of the Victorian town. (We shall understand all the more that melancholy when we meet his parents, George and Catherine, who were all but beggared by Munro and Ross.) Born in Stornoway in 1861, Stephen himself could but dimly remember much activity. 'The bones of the Slip are still there; there is even some flesh left on them; but the soul is fled.' No longer could one see 'the great engine working and the great wheels go round, or joining the carpenters as they drew the cradle up by hand to the accompanying shanty: "Rio! Rio! Rio! Rio!, I'm off to the Rio Grand . . ."' When Matheson had bought Lewis in 1844, Stornoway had boasted 11 shipbuilders; by 1885 this had peaked at 13. By 1898, there was but one; none would survive by the early 1930s. Had he invested in modern facilities for the boats people actually wanted – as opposed to timber skiffs, smacks, wherries and schooners – things might have fared very differently.

The oversight is even odder as in 1846 Matheson himself had ordered and laid on his own fat little iron paddle-steamer (named the *Mary Jane*, naturally) to give Stornoway its very first modern, timetabled, steam-driven mails and 'packet' service. She voyaged weekly from Stornoway to Glasgow and back, with calls at Oban, Tobermory and Portree, to say nothing of pausing for 'flit-boat' stops and this and that locality en route; on alternate Mondays she sailed straight to Lochinver and back, and on the other Mondays to Portree. From 1849, Sir James also used another ship: the tactlessly named *Marquis of Stafford* (he was heir to the Duke of Sutherland) chugged between Stornoway and Poolewe; much later, the paddle-steamer *Ondine* carried the Stornoway mails directly to Ullapool.

He disposed of the *Mary Jane* in 1851 – probably because David Hutcheson & Company (which concern would later pass to the young partner David MacBrayne) launched their extensive West Highland shipping enterprise that year. But she survived, old and stately as she was, for very many years, most of them in Hutcheson/MacBrayne hands, as the *Glencoe*, still remembered for her ancient steeple-engine and for the chilly sign in her steerage accommodation, 'This cabin has accommodation for 90 third-class passengers, when not occupied by sheep, cattle, cargo or other encumbrances.' The *Glencoe* – latterly the Skye mail-boat – would be withdrawn only in May 1931, in her 86th year and to widespread regret, and shortly before demolition at Ardrossan was photographed incongruously (but on purpose) alongside MacBrayne's new *Lochfyne* – a gleaming diesel-electric screwship.

And, of course, the baronet built roads; there were but 40 miles of rough highway when he bought the island. His men also raised new stone bridges to such a standard that, narrow as they were, one (at Laxdale, and now a notorious bottleneck at peak periods) bears to this day the heaviest modern vehicles; another, right on the Harris border, was part of the Western Isles 'spinal route', uncomplainingly coping with the largest articulated lorries, until its redundancy in 2005.

But Sir James for nine years doggedly defended a dispute over that same Harris boundary in the Scottish courts – an earlier round of hostilities had been waged by Alexander Hume MacLeod against Seaforth from 1804; and was resumed in 1847 by the 'Tutors of the Earl of Dunmore' – from seeming bottomless pockets, until lawyers grew rich and judges grew famous, and to little purpose, and finally to the very House of Lords. There is still, near the long-abandoned hamlet of Crola in deepest Uig, a stone memorial raised by Matheson's orders to the high jurist finally summoned to see the border for himself. It reads only: 'Lord Kemble, Lord Chief Justice of England, sat here, 3rd September, 1853.' We might rather remember the man from Morsgail, *Calum Mor an t-Sruth*, according to Grant, who agreed to bear the monument all the way to this lonely spot, were he given twice the usual rate. So he 'carried the huge stone five miles across the moor on his back, and then walked five miles home to collect his double pay – four shillings. In modern money – 20p.'

The lairds ended up, by the final 'interlocutor' of 1856, taking a chunk each of what were in any event the scant and worthless acres in debate, and neither

Dunmore nor Matheson gaining quite what each insisted were their rightful marches.

Sir James besides, as early as 1845, hired two of the land-reclamation experts of his day – a Mr James Smith and a Mr Dean – to survey Lewis and see what usable land could be won from the general central bog for more agricultural tenancies. They settled on various localities for the wheeze, most on the West Side and including Galson, Barvas, Shawbost and Carloway; but the main works were inland at the deep peat of Lochganvich – '890 acres of moorland on a gentle slope,' as Cunningham outlines. 'These were wedge-shaped and laid out in ten-acre fields, enclosed by ditches and turf walls. Clay marl, shell sand from Bernera, guano and dissolved bones were applied, all at a cost of £2,202. One of the present tenants remembers his father finding in a peat-bank one of the leather over-shoes worn by the horses in these operations.' The new Arcadia, as fondly envisaged, was even named 'Deanston' after one of the great men. But – as any crofter could have explained to Sir James – such an endeavour was quite pointless so far from the coast, where rack and seaware could not readily be brought to the rigs and where there was no hope of ancillary fishing.

Lewis could well have supported a whisky industry. The skill was available and there were plenty of crofters to grow grain and good peaty water to lend the product atmosphere. But, in one of those howling, almost hilarious twists of history, Matheson, who had made so much out of Oriental addiction, was a righteous teetotaller, who would all but have gone to the stake rather than sully his name at such a trade. So still another island enterprise went by the board. Matheson instead enthused over deposits of clay at Garrabost in Point, and by 1860 had brickworks bustling away at what is now Claypark; roof-tiles were moulded and baked there too. But such tiles were ill-suited to the extreme windiness of the Lewis climate (in any event, even after the Second World War most households still lived under thatched roofs) and, with the incessant wet and driving rain besides, only the toughest glazed brick, unless the walls were rendered, was a credible building material. Nor, being heavy, of relatively low value and far from suitable markets, could either product be profitably shipped across the Minch. The Claypark enterprise is another instance of boyish Matheson enthusiasm eclipsing any commercial logic.

But the farce was only compounded by its incorporation with still another ill-conceived enterprise, the 'Lewis Chemical Works' beyond Marybank and by the River Creed, all geared for turning peat into profit.

Peat is but a mass of hydrocarbons and, in the mid nineteenth century and before great reserves of oil had been found underground, far less tapped, it made perfect sense to process it for this and that. And, once they were up and running, after construction in 1859 and near-cataclysmic explosion in 1860, the

Lewis Chemical Works were briefly the most advanced in the world, widely publicised and attracting many expert visitors – all anxious to see, in a rapidly industrialising world, any source of oils that involved neither plants nor animals.

All that the works by the Creed did yield was what could have been a lucrative anti-fouling paint for boats and a still more valuable lubricating oil for engines – had its three wise men, Dr Benjamin H. Paul (incapable of suffering fools gladly, a fatal weakness under a laird who hired dozens of them), Henry Caunter and Donald Morrison (who built it all in the first place) not constantly bickered; had it been thought through with any practical grasp of principles these days assumed among most 16-year-olds now embarking on their Higher Chemistry; had a range of valuable tars and gases not been allowed to belch filthily into the atmosphere, instead of being tapped in a fractional-distillation tower or at least burned off as a source of cheap heat; had not badly supervised managers started watering down this or that product to meet a bulk order; and had not three separate works on three distant sites (including the end-product refinery by Garrabost, some 6 miles from the Creed) mocked all business sense.

It cost as much, as Fred Silver details in his excellent essay on the whole forlorn business, to manhandle – by an uphill rail-track – wagons of Garrabost distillate up a short one-in-thirty incline as to bring the raw tar from Marybank to Garrabost in the first place. In all, an idea with real commercial potential was ruined by ignorance, mismanagement and Matheson's own failure either to choose the right men or impose proper supervision from the start. By the time he grasped what had to be done, he was a tired old man and the first oil wells were already being tapped in America. The works finally closed in 1874.

In 1850, John Scobie left the Matheson service, and a new chamberlain took up what was now a highly fraught Lewis position: John Munro MacKenzie. By this point no one could deny the woes of rural Lewis. Households by the hundred groaned under the burden of debt. Most people were hungry and all were anxious. Holdings everywhere had been divided between adult offspring; in some distances, they were divided again. Meanwhile, James Matheson, who disliked columns of red in his books – they offended his sense of rural idyll, his self-conceit as a well-beloved patriarch and especially his tidy mind – was now determined to regularise the situation. Grant puts it bleakly: Sir James 'wanted to get rid of those who were irretrievably in arrears with their rent, and re-let the land to those who could pay.' The bad payers would be blown away like the chaff – to the Americas, anyway; those who did render unto Caesar what was Caesar's (presumably, in Matheson's curious cosmology, because of greater character and capacity) could then inherit the earth.

The problem was all the more pressing because, despite everything, the rate of increase in the population showed no sign of slowing: indeed, it would increase between 16 per cent and 21 per cent through every decade of the century. Besides, as so many had not paid rent in some years, those who did actually meet their dues now restively felt they were subsidising others. They wondered aloud why they should bear the exactions of the Lewis Estate when others – as it seemed – were getting away without rendering a penny.

Sir James was not inclined to forced, even violent emigrations on the Sutherland or North Uist model. Apart from anything else, it was bad for his image, and this was a salient point after the events of 1849 in North Uist, which commentators on the Lewis situation tend to overlook. There was determined effort that year to clear 600 people from crowded townships in the parish of Kilmuir – communities like Dunskellor, Middlequarter and Malaclete. The people had simply refused to go. At length, in high over-reaction, 33 constables were shipped from Oban to remove them from their homes by uniformed might. (The abuse of the police in this fashion, here and through many other outrages of Highland landlordism through decades to come, has bequeathed to this day a lingering distrust of the constabulary in the culture; though one officer of quite another stamp would play signal part in Donald Munro's downfall.) There were dreadful scenes – and no wonder, for no alternative accommodation was available and no ships of emigration were even imminent, far less in sight.

As houses were roughly de-roofed, physical struggle ensued and four men were arrested. The Free Church minister – himself the victim of dreadful treatment by the laird – had to be begged to come and calm the situation. The police scuttled back to the mainland with their captives, who were duly tried and convicted at Inverness – but, to widespread surprise, the jury nevertheless begged for clemency and the presiding judge, Lord Cockburn (one of the most interesting men of his age) added some acrid comments of his own. 'They had nothing but the bare ground, or rather, the hard, wet beach, to lie down upon,' he grated. It had been said – or, really, insinuated – that 'arrangements' had been made for these tenants and their families, from babes in arms to gnarled great-grandparents. It had besides been claimed in court that a ship 'was to have been soon' on the coast. But, for the time being – nevertheless – the people's hereditary roofs were to be pulled down, and all exposed to the cold, wet Atlantic elements, 'and the mother and her children had only the shore to sleep on, fireless, foodless, hopeless.' Lord Cockburn sentenced the men minimally – four months – and, with ample time in prior custody to take off that, they were out shortly, in time to join their families on weary passage to the New World.

Cockburn's remarks had been widely reported and widely read, and for the first time what was going on in the Highlands and Islands (including widespread, vindictive measures against Free Church congregations) began to win Lowland attention and Lowland anger.

Sir James Matheson had, then, to be careful. He would send for no constables; there would be no unpleasant incidents to embarrass him in the papers. Those who could pay rent would be encouraged – with delicate menaces – to clear their obligations; the rest would be given opportunity to emigrate to Canada. He would arrange their relocation there; he would pay their passage; he would organise the shipping and he would even (this with a deft eye on public relations) send with them a Free Church minister, whom he would personally recruit, for the good of their souls. John Munro MacKenzie, the new chamberlain, 'would have the unenviable task,' records Grant, 'of selecting those who were to emigrate, re-letting the land to those who remained, organising the ships on which the emigrants were to sail, and recovering in the process as much of the rent arrears as he could.' With wholesale redrawing of croft boundaries – generally in smaller holdings in what were already pretty crowded villages – it was not only a dramatic reorganisation of all Lewis but a thankless task for the new factor.

John Munro MacKenzie was an able man, a fine man and one of the very few high officials anywhere in Lewis through this century who should command respect. His name is still blackened because it has suited some, then and since, to hold him culpable for all the details in execution of a plan he had not conceived and which, deep down, he probably deplored. He also – unusually, for he had not done it before and would not do it again – began a daily diary on 1 January 1851, made his last entry on 31 December, and at once let off the exercise. It was not a journal of anguished reflections, or some diabolical master plan, but a cool curt record of dates and doings, meetings and facts – 'more of a time sheet,' as James Shaw Grant has noted, 'than a personal diary,' though there is enough colour and occasional acidity to make it absorbing. Unfortunately, since its recovery among family papers some two decades ago, some have quoted it selectively and out of context to the blackening of his reputation.

We do not know, as Grant observes, why MacKenzie started keeping a diary then; and why, having begun one, he abandoned it after one precise, entire calendar year. But it was a year of gruelling responsibility, and it was a business, we may fairly suspect, he viewed with profound unease.

For one, MacKenzie was no outsider: he was a son of the late, old but goodhearted Sheriff MacKenzie. Family tradition holds that the new factor was born in Stornoway, he spent most of his youth on Lewis, he was of course a fluent Gaelic speaker, and his descendants have remained both prominent and extremely useful on Lewis to this day. His grandfather, the Reverend Hugh Munro, had been minister of Uig; two of his uncles had served in the 78th Regiment – Seaforth's – and, with hundreds of other Lewismen, helped deliver Wellington's famous victory at Assaye. Decades afterwards – a thoughtful gesture that says much for John Munro MacKenzie – he obtained campaign medals for the few surviving veterans, largely in Uig, though by then few were fit to come to the ceremony at Glen Valtos where these honours were belatedly presented. He could also be extraordinarily fair, able even – under one official hat – to reverse, on hearing appeal, decisions he himself had made under another official hat. Yet MacKenzie could, when he was convinced people were, as we would say, trying it on, be both wily and tough.

When he had left Stornoway for the first time, in 1837, the parish minister – the Reverend John Cameron – had supplied a warm testimonial: that this John MacKenzie was 'a young gentleman of amiable disposition, genteel in his manners, affable in his conversation and mild in his deportment – that he is a young man of promising talents, respectable acquirements and moral abilities – though tall he is but young and used to make a respectful appearance in his classes'. Down south, John Munro MacKenzie – we know this from the application letter he wrote for the post of chamberlain, which survives – apprenticed in civil engineering, became a highly regarded 'resident engineer' on various new railways in the Glasgow area, and had already an excellent 'situation' when he sought to succeed Scobie, earning 'nearly £500 per annum . . . However, I would prefer to assist you,' he told Matheson sagely, 'in the improvement of my native land, which I know you have so much at heart, but of course would not think of giving up my connections in this part of the Country without expecting a liberal remuneration. My knowledge of Engineering would I consider be of great use in carrying on improvements in a new country . . .'

That last holds a big clue to MacKenzie's profound unhappiness as, uncharacteristically, he took up a bound blank volume that New Year of 1851 and started to record his daily deeds.

He was smart enough, no doubt, to grasp that the programme of emigration Sir James had insisted upon (and which could, with some elision of mind, be regarded as 'voluntary') would make little or no demographic difference. In the event – as MacKenzie in all probability foresaw – 'the natural increase in the population, in little more than four years, replaced the eight hundred who left in 1851,' notes James Shaw Grant. 'At the end of the decade, in spite of the exodus of 1851 and subsequent years, the island's population had increased from 19,711 to 21,056.'

But – worse still than being pointless – this orchestrated emigration was largely unnecessary. There was a simple solution to the population crisis of

1851, though it required a little Matheson patience, some deftly focused civil-engineering expenditure and a few more years of providing relief for the destitute: to retreat from a land-based, agrarian economy and invest massively in the harvest of the sea.

As lairds elsewhere had done on still bleaker a coast – that of the north-east Lowlands of Scotland – Sir James Matheson should have built harbours and piers all round the coast of Lewis, furnished boats and tackle (on easy terms of credit), sat back and waited for the profits to roll in. The richness of the seas about Lewis – especially in the mid nineteenth century – is beyond dispute. The great sea-lochs were already famous for their ling; in their season, twice a year, herring boiled off its crags and beaches by the million. The game fishing needs no introduction: Lewis boasts untold trout fishing and some of the best salmon waters in Scotland. On John Knox's visit in 1786, on three days that August he oversaw exploratory netting of the Tong Pools on the tidal sands of the Cockle Ebb. On 17 August, just one little stretch – drawn once – yielded 29 salmon, 128 trout and 1,468 flounders. The next day, two pools were tried: 139 salmon, 5,128 trout and a few flounders. On 23 August, they were broached again, and this time gave up 143 salmon, 143 trout, 'and the flounders I did not count, but they were a great heap, about 7 or 800. Everyday an immense number of herrings, sprats and cuddies were caught.'

The simple, patient fix for the whole Lewis difficulty was the determined development of the fishing industry. It was obvious to John Munro Mac-Kenzie. It is obvious to us. It seems incredible it was not obvious to Matheson. But he refused stubbornly to admit its potential, to grasp that even local curers and merchants (far less the island fishermen) had not the capital to build harbours and sea-walls themselves – and in any event could not, in the face of a laird who owned every square inch of Lewis land. Save for Stornoway, and a few sheltered sea-lochs in the south and west, there were no safe natural harbours and nowhere at all beyond Stornoway where catches could be landed, processed and sold, save for the later badly designed and constantly silting works at Port of Ness. Worse still – especially on the bare West Side and the coast of Broad Bay – there was no secure, easily reached shelter for boats in trouble. It was not merely that, as a result of Matheson obtuseness, the rich fisheries of Lewis were eventually plundered by mainland fleets. As a direct consequence, dozens and dozens of Lewis fishermen were drowned.

John Munro MacKenzie, this grey New Year's Day, robbed of the chance to see what he could accomplish in stone and concrete and new vibrant industry, could but settle down and placate his employer's obsession with emigration. Within a week – in a rare miscalculation – he decided to consult Donald Munro.

6

Clearance: A crisis, a factor and an emigrant ship . . .

Donald Munro had not, in 1851, yet attained the supremacy he would for so long exercise and still more relish; and, as John Munro MacKenzie toiled to 'regularise' the tenantry of rural Lewis – growing with each passing month much less nice and pleasant – the procurator fiscal's role was largely limited.

But he was still throwing his weight around and, the colourful Lewis MacIver aside, had only met one serious defeat. Within months of his arrival on Lewis, in 1842, the adventurer from Tain – in his capacity as solicitor for the Seaforth estate – had not only immersed himself gleefully in the rout of Loch Shell, but foolishly taken on the Established Church – or, more accurately, the kirk session of the parish church in Stornoway which, that side of the Disruption in 1843, remained a formidable force in affairs and had control of the Poor Fund.

The provision of this relief in Scotland at the time, such as it was, bore little relation to our modern ideals of a welfare state. It was a mean aid grudgingly given, and for which only the most desperate applied, such were the humiliations through which one was dragged. Its parochial administration saw untold, cynical games as a given kirk session tried to wriggle out of obligation to this or that desperate case and, hopefully, pass it on to another kirk session. The fear that human tragedy might become a 'burden on the parish' features again and again in contemporary records, and determination to minimise the strain on limited funds is a large reason why so much Presbyterial procedure seems almost clinically obsessed with cases of 'ante-nuptial fornication', babies conceived before or outwith wedlock, and especially sustained determination to establish a child's paternity. But, as Drummond and Bulloch explain, it was a creaking, vaguely inhuman system based on barnacled old law. The Kirk's

ancient responsibility for the poor had gradually been slipping from her hands and its end roughly coincided with the Disruption. In 1843 the care of the poor in Scotland was still based on an Act passed as long ago as 1579. It drew a distinction between the ordinary poor, those so disabled that they could not work, and the occasional poor, who were sick for the time being but otherwise able-bodied; and for this second group no help was available. This had been the law of a poor country where every man had to work hard but where the family ties were strong and local communities intimate, and behind it was the assumption that people would normally have kindly relatives and neighbours at hand who would not see them perish because of some temporary need. For the others, children under fourteen, old persons over seventy, and those permanently handicapped, there remained the small charities of the local kirk session paid out of collections, charges for mort cloths, occasional mortifications for the poor and – not least – the fines imposed on those guilty of the sins of the flesh. This system has been described as 'a regulated and legalised scheme of begging, supplemented by voluntary assessments and the charities of the Church', and the last great attempt to make it work – by Chalmers at St John's in Glasgow – served only to emphasise the fact that, whatever it may have done in small communities, it could not cope with the ills of industrial society. . . . Poverty was no longer confined to a few families among comfortable neighbours but existed on a massive scale, concentrated and isolated in areas of its own. In any case, the temper of the age was changing and the inclination to solve the problem of poverty by neighbourliness and generosity was fast fading. Country ministers who wrote the Statistical Accounts in the seventeen eighties had seen it in personal and Christian terms, but their successors who wrote the Second Account half a century later saw it through the eyes of economists . . .

Donald Munro was not a man who would ever be noted for seeing anything in 'personal and Christian terms', but when, in May 1842, he grandly wrote Colin Leitch – session clerk of Stornoway – it was on behalf of the Seaforth Estate and almost certainly at the instigation of the factor, then the hard-nosed Thomas Knox. The solicitor from Tain demanded that he himself (in the name of the Estate) be put in charge of the administration of the Poor Fund, that he be granted the right to attend all meetings of the kirk session that dealt with Poor Fund affairs, and that he be given sight of all relevant documents.

The sheer effrontery of this decree will immediately strike most island believers today. A kirk session (which deals, for the most part, with highly personal matters: admission to baptism or the Lord's Supper and the occasional correction of erring church members) is not open even to communicant members, far less the general public. It meets invariably in private, its minutes are private, and any elder who divulged business from it or broadcast details of its discussion – in all Presbyterian denominations, to this day – is open to serious sanctions.

In terms of the Poor Fund, the Munro insistence was no less outrageous. The monies were gathered by the kirk session. The Seaforth Estate contributed nothing and had, in law, in 1842, no responsibility whatever for the care of 'paupers'. It is difficult to see this decree of Knox and Munro as anything other than officious vainglory, and a greed for highly sensitive information. Leith, the session clerk, wrote back quite properly in flat refusal; and Munro then imperiously wrote the parish minister.

The Reverend John Fraser replied in silky firmness. 'I have seen your correspondence with Mr Leitch and I have heard of you tendering your services to Mr Knox, at two guineas per day, to force the Session Records. Trade must be slack with you when you have no other butt than the Poor Funds and the members of Session.' He nevertheless undertook solemnly to place Munro's epistle before the next meeting of the session – held, he explained, on the first Wednesday of each month; the subtext here being to make sure Munro grasped no special diet would be called on his account – and would advise of the outcome.

Munro kept on pressing, evidently with insinuation and threats, for Cameron had to write him again in July. The records, he said, would be shown to him in good time, and the Estate would then be assured there was 'neither fraud, deceit or extravagance found in the distribution to 200 paupers in a population of more than 5,000 . . .' But there was more from an angry minister. 'Should you press the case, I shall sooner go to gaol than submit to Mr Knox till I have his special mandate from Seaforth for making such a demand.' This was a shrewd shot. The Stewart-MacKenzies, as Mr Fraser knew, were far away and all but inaccessible in the Ionian Islands; and it was most unlikely they had authorised this initiative by their lackeys.

But there is a terrible indefatigability to Donald Munro. He could not readily win word from Mr Stewart-MacKenzie but he could certainly contact the Seaforth trustees in Edinburgh. In short order, he had persuaded these distant Edinburgh lawyers to issue a 'mandate', ordaining Thomas Knox to inspect kirk session records and sit in as a veritable monarch at their meetings. Knox, in turn, gladly signed still another mandate – vesting this Seaforth pomp in Donald Munro, solicitor and procurator fiscal.

The Stornoway kirk session, though, were not readily intimidated, and dealt coolly with the latest assault when they met on 1 August. They were happy, they intimated, to accept a mandate from trustees that gave such authority to Thomas Knox. The laird – the superiors or 'heritors', who maintained the local kirk in the Established order – had some right of access, or to confer that access on their named agent. But they could not accept Knox had any authority to transfer it to Munro, or that the trustees would have sanctioned it. The steadfastness of the Stornoway session on this matter is striking, as Grant points out, not just because the three members were all men of the highest economic and professional standing – Rev. John Fraser himself, the Comptroller of Customs and the Sheriff Clerk Depute – and could scarcely be painted as raving Jacobins, but because, in the church crisis about to come, Mr Fraser would not even join the Disruption. 'The resistance to Munro came from the very heart of the Establishment.'

Now he sued, raising a Sheriff Court action – in the name of Knox – against the Stornoway kirk session, demanding all the access they sought and, besides, an award of expenses against the session (which would, of course, fall into Munro's own grateful pockets). The case was fraught and at first messy – the 'answers' first furnished by the session showed 'so wide a deviation from the accustomed and prescribed form of pleading' that the sheriff ordered their withdrawal, and an amended version had to be lodged instead. Though many papers in the case are missing, the wrath of these sturdy men is evident against 'those who contribute nothing to the funds' and who had so pressed 'a most ungracious and invidious request'. It does not sound as if either Knox or Munro ever went to sermon. Whatever their piety, or lack of it, they lost, especially once Sheriff Substitute R.S. Taylor discovered that Munro had lodged the action before he had even approached the kirk session with his mandate (which, as Taylor ruled firmly, Knox had no authority to transfer to him in the first place). 'The significant point, however,' Grant muses bleakly, 'is that an organisation like the kirk session was able to stand up to him: the crofters and private individuals could not.'

Certainly, nothing seemed to dent the Munro rapacity, the Munro arrogance or the Munro confidence, which waxed year upon year and through three decades until, fatefully, it became delusional. There was besides the bewildering array of Munro hats – if nothing to the galaxy that would adorn him once he won the entire confidence of Sir James Matheson. In 1849, for instance – and the papers survive – Donald Munro issued seven summonses for removal, against sixteen Stornoway tenants, and in four different capacities: as, in his own right, a 'heritable proprietor', righteously throwing out folk from buildings he owned; as a solicitor for the Seaforth Estate (concerning those renting their property); as a solicitor for this and that private individual; and even as procurator fiscal, on behalf of the Crown and taking ruthless possession of a house or 'immovable estate' in a case of intestacy, where someone had foolishly died without making a will and the Crown was final beneficiary. He was besides moving to build what James Shaw Grant would later describe (anachronistically, but without undue hyperbole, for his own Stornoway forebears endured much at its hands) as a 'legal mafia'.

On 21 February 1851, Munro was joined in practice by his own cousin, William Ross; and it was as 'Munro and Ross' they would subsequently conduct private legal business. And more besides, for Ross was appointed deputy fiscal to his cousin soon after his arrival and, in due course, to the still higher pomp of joint fiscal. Such exaltation is all the more curious as there was evident unease at his admission to practise in Stornoway Sheriff Court. Sheriff George Deas, who presided, added a curious note to the 'interlocutor', that as 'the applicant has only been examined by the single Procurator practising before the Court at Stornoway' – which was Donald Munro, of course, his own first cousin – 'the Sheriff thinks it the safer and better course to admit the applicant in the meantime as a practitioner in that district only, leaving him to apply of new if he shall afterwards desire to practise elsewhere in the Sheriffdom.' Deas had evident doubts about William Ross's entire suitability – though, in common with his peers, he deemed him quite good enough for the Outer Hebrides.

As Grant very properly points out, the fact that Munro needed a partner at all suggests there was ample work in Stornoway – and on Lewis – for two solicitors; but it would have been far better for the community had another, competing lawyer hung up his shingle. Instead, the two men – in strangling alliance – had a general monopoly of legal business, a situation ripe for cruelty and corruption. They were determined, as we shall see, to stamp on any potential rival at law, and were greatly reinforced not just by Munro's later and near-supreme power as chamberlain but by their own determined nepotism. When the Harbour Trust was founded – and there lies a tale in itself – Donald Munro would serve as de facto chairman, with William Ross as secretary and treasurer. Munro would chair the four parish school boards on Lewis – Ross was clerk and treasurer to each. Ross would besides, for some time, be the Inspector of Poor in Stornoway and his son, John, would serve his apprenticeship in law with the pair. Meanwhile, Munro's nephew – John Rose – would be conveniently appointed both ground officer for Stornoway Parish and clerk in the great chamberlain's office. Still another chamberlain's office employee would collect the Poor Rates; in his last years on high, yet one more would be agent for Matheson's mail-steamer, the *Ondine*. And, to cap everything, they even had a man in Edinburgh: William Ross Skinner was a qualified 'SSC' – a Solicitor before the Supreme Courts of Scotland, lest any Munro and Ross scheme reach the Court of Session and threaten to become mucky.

'In a small community,' sighs James Shaw Grant, 'some degree of pluralism is bound to occur in the filling of public offices which are necessarily part-time, but the concentration of power within the chamberlain's office in Lewis was unique in Scotland, as was the control exercised by the chamberlain and his relatives over the judicial process, both civil and criminal.'

There were besides extraordinary strokes of good luck. First, and most disastrously, Sir James would make Munro chamberlain – coupling at a stroke the administration of every foot of Lewis to both an avaricious solicitor and the prosecuting might of the Crown. Second, Munro and Ross were able to block or scare off almost every lawyer who thought of opening up shop in Stornoway: the one they did fail to outmanoeuvre was an accident-prone incompetent. Finally – and for much of the critical period between 1851 and 1874 – Andrew Lothian MacDonald, appointed in 1843, was Sheriff Substitute for Lewis. MacDonald, personally, was a decent man. In the practice of law for 17 years at Tobermory, Mull, he won just praise as the 'Poor Man's Lawyer' for all the legal work he carried out, free or for a nominal charge, on behalf of ordinary islanders.

And he was of good Highland blood, of family from Keppoch, Morar; besides, MacDonald was a Roman Catholic, which for the time made his appointment to such high public office most unusual. 'His appointment to Lewis was greeted with much suspicion when his religious adherence became known,' writes Frank Thompson, but 'that attitude soon changed and he became highly regarded in the Lewis community. Although at first he was greeted as "An Dubh-phapanach" ['*the Dark Papist*'] on account of his religion, this soon changed to "An Siorra a chur Dia oirnn," ['*the Sheriff granted us from God*'] as the community realised that his religious background did not affect his fair and unbiased judgements. For that he was justly respected.' But Thompson documents none of this supposed Stornoway bigotry – he even concedes that Protestant ministers were among the signatories to a testimonial presented to the sheriff on his 1871 retirement – and there has never been any tradition of sectarian tension, on the bigoted Lowland model, in Lewis or anywhere else in the West Highlands. And, however MacDonald comported himself on the bench, his conduct of Sheriff Court administration was infamously weak. Instance upon instance suggests a man easily intimidated by Munro and Ross and who too frequently abetted their agenda.

Surrounded by relatives and dependent hirelings, and operating a legal monopoly under a complacent laird, a timid sheriff, a remote and indifferent Crown and with a host of public offices and positions of commercial power in their hands, Munro and Ross would rampage through a quarter century of Lewis history like a cartoon witch and her familiar.

The distress of 1851–52 is still remembered on Lewis – if, in the context of wider and still more terrible goings-on in the West Highlands, perhaps more sorely than it deserves – and confused in some degree, through the generations, with the earlier and much more serious disruption (especially in Uig and Park) under the Stewart-MacKenzies. The removals of 1851 had an especially bitter sting because so many left their homes (and, in some instances, the island) under the cloud of unpaid debt, a reproach almost as shameful, by the values of the time, as the smear of thievery so resented by the wives and mothers of the Loch Shell townships. And, as we have already noted from Bill Lawson, the fact that most turfed from their abodes in 1851 were merely relocated elsewhere on Lewis only reinforced the whole upheaval in local folk-memory – to say nothing of the resentment caused in the villages that had to make room for them. My own MacAulay great-great-grandparents, from Kneep, were among many decanted from assorted Uig villages into Shawbost; and there are still those in that village who talk of themselves, darkly, as 'old Shawbost', distinct and superior to the riff-raff dumped among them in the year of the Great Exhibition.

It is frankly impossible, besides, to believe that every family, without exception, forced to remove elsewhere in Lewis was behind with their rent. One suspects households whose affairs (by Providence) were in good order, or could be quickly rectified, were nevertheless ensnared in a programme delivering much to Matheson's immediate interests under the cover of saintly humanitarianism. Certainly, many of the townships now cleared were rented out afterwards, no doubt at profit, to tenant-farmers.

For some, the disruption was repeated; many children faced several read-justments in a lifetime. 'A four-year-old Tolsta boy, John MacDonald, carried the tongs when his parents had to leave their home in 1852,' Donald MacDonald relates. 'The family had to flit once again the following year to the Moine, unreclaimed peatland on the outskirts of South Tolsta. The factor was extremely generous, for he did not charge rent for this bog-land for the first two years. In 1922, seventy years later, the boy returned to the village from which he had been evicted as a child.' The confusion in local place names exemplifies the bewilderment of the time: old John MacDonald finally came back to what been North Tolsta, but was now New Tolsta – and the part of the lively community laid out today as North Tolsta is actually the old South Tolsta.

What strikes us still more, as Grant points out, is how such huge social engineering was accomplished in such good order. 'The most remarkable fact, having regard to what was happening elsewhere in the Highlands at the same time, is that the mass exodus from Lewis was carried through without the intervention of a single soldier or policeman, and with no civil disobedience of any sort. The explanation lies largely in the terms that were offered. However they appear to us today, they provided the emigrants of 1851 with an escape from an intolerable situation.' He adds elsewhere, less convincingly and citing no source, 'Many of the emigrants afterwards expressed gratitude for their release from an intractable poverty.' That is now hard to ascertain, for little or no tradition survives among their Canadian descendants. Certainly, no one pushed away to some other quarter of Lewis (and often to a cool reception) felt the least obligation to the noble baronet; and – for Lewis as a whole – the 1851 recasting was, as Grant puts it, 'only one incident in a process of oppression which lasted, and indeed intensified, for another thirty years.' Besides – as is widely overlooked – Matheson only funded the Canadian emigration costs when forced to it; he tried to the last to pass the cost to the government and there are frequent references in MacKenzie's diary to a petition about the 'State of the Country' to this end.

The island's travail has also to be considered within a wider shift in Scottish (and Christian) attitudes generally to poverty and misfortune. It may not have been the necessary and logical outcome of the Industrial Revolution, which emptied rural communities into wretched urban masses and reduced people to so much labour (and expendable at that), but it was certainly the fruit of general acceptance of Adam Smith's and quasi-scientific analysis of an untrammelled, free-market economy – and the failure of the Kirk, to say nothing of dissenting Presbyterian groups like the Secession Church, to subject this to anything like intelligent Christian critique. For some years after the Disruption, it seemed the new Free Church might well take a fresh and radical approach. But her leadership was largely rooted in the Lowland middle class (whose natural pleasure lay in disapproval of supposed working-class vices). Besides, the new denomination was wholly dependent on the givings of her people and rapidly became an outfit where money talked. Ministers grew loath to say anything to disturb the prosperous men who were their best contributors. (An odd consequence of this was that, shaken by the Disruption as she was, the Established Church never quite lost widespread grip, at least in sentiment, of Scotland's Lowland poorest, and by 1900 had quite eclipsed her Presbyterian rivals in their adherence.)

Men like Sir James Matheson, in a new era of enterprise, slept at night because this had become a land which, for long given to a providential view of history – the Most High, as was earnestly believed by most eighteenth-century Scots, had certainly willed the destruction of Roman Catholicism and the Stuart dynasty, for had not great storms once and again frustrated their endeavours at invasion and reconquest? – now took, likewise, a providential view of money. To be rich and successful attested the Lord's smile of favour. By contrast, to be poor, wretched and unfortunate – and this became wide-spread Scots opinion – was surely born of some degree of moral failure; at least a want of thrift and industry. Even men like Thomas Chalmers – whose goodness and spirituality are undoubted, but had, like most gentlemen of his age, a mild horror of the rabble and a great horror of sedition – toiled not to fight poverty, but to reduce 'pauperism': the burden of that misery on the resources of others.

The Disruption, the universally low standard of poor relief and the serious fear of bourgeois Scots that the slums might yet breed terrible epidemics (spreading without regard for class or residence) all contributed to the new Scottish Poor Law of 1845. Like virtually all Scottish legislation of the period it was no more than the very recent, precedent-setting English Bill in a minimal kilt.

The Scottish Act finally removed such as remained of her responsibility for pauper-relief from the Kirk and, while retaining a parochial administration in which churchmen had some part, establishing an order funded largely by urban ratepayers and, in the countryside, 'heritors' – the lairds – all now under a statutory obligation to care in Scotland 'for the problems caused by the rapidity and inhumanity of its economic development', as Drummond and Bulloch rightly put it. One can now grasp Sir James's sudden alacrity to do something about the plight of his tenantry.

Dramatic schemes for New World emigration apart, the most visible (and notorious) fruit of this was the erection of 'poorhouses', for there was now a near-total prohibition on 'outdoor relief', or benefits in cash or kind to people in their own homes. (Stornoway's 'Combination Poorhouse' would not, however, open till 1897, and only the truly desperate – many, if not most, with severe learning difficulties or mentally ill – ever lodged in this bleak *Tigh nam Bochd*, 'home of the poor.')

There was besides now an obligation in law to care for the 'sick poor'. All parish boards were made accountable to a Board of General Supervision, sitting – like most agencies of the Crown – in Edinburgh. Most, though not at all, of the traditional fines levied to support a parish Poor Fund were abolished – though offences under the 1832 Day Poaching Act still won amused ministers a little money for parochial purposes far into the twentieth century. Yet many well-off Scots, as Drummond and Bulloch point out, were irate, and

there was much criticism, but not from the standpoint of Christian charity. The industrious, it was said, were now to work to support the lazy; there was to be no distinction between the poverty caused by misfortune and the poverty caused by vice; none between the deserving poor and the undeserving; industry and frugality were being discouraged, charity stopped and movement to the towns increased. But this was unjust, for the Commissioners themselves fully shared the harsh outlook of their critics. Hunger, they considered, was the best incentive to work, and hard work and thrift paved the road to prosperity . . .

It was in this Spartan spirit that the new Poor Law operated from the start. The poor dreaded its inspectors, were deeply humiliated at having to accept its dole, and regarded the poorhouse as the final degradation. Probably they starved a little less than under the old system, but otherwise there was little gain. No written record fully conveys the deep bitterness and resentment created. What lay at the root of the trouble was not the Victorian legislation but the spirit in which it was drafted and operated, the conviction that poverty was the fruit of idleness and vice, that an empty belly was the best urge to make a man an industrious citizen, and that the community owed the debris of society no more than would keep them from dying on the streets. Though this has been dignified with the name of the 'Protestant Ethic', it was a repudiation of the social outlook of the Scottish Church from the time of *The First Book of Discipline* [*John Knox's manifesto for a new Scottish order in 1560, with radical proposals for education and welfare*]. As apartheid has been justified in South Africa on the strength of some scriptural texts, so there were Victorians who found texts to justify this outlook, but its true origins lay in the teachings of the economists and the hard society they had created. Poverty in Scotland was never effectively dealt with until the legislation at the close of the Second World War.

It is no coincidence that as Scottish Presbyterians in the early Victorian era so rapidly threw off the old social conscience of their faith, by its last decade they were busy repudiating its core theology – a movement far more vigorously resisted in the Highlands and Islands, where the two had never been divorced in the first place. The Mathesons, at least, had some sort of self-conscious *noblesse oblige* and in their personal lives – in local charities, with their servants and employees and so on – are remembered for many dainty acts of individual generosity and kindliness. It was exercised, though, by some faculty quite divorced from Estate policy and general overlordship – and that enforced by the likes of Donald Munro, a gleeful social Darwinist to whom people were but cattle.

It was Munro who now complicated John Munro MacKenzie's plan for recovering rent arrears and, if necessary, the subsequent re-lotting, removal and emigration ships: Munro, critically, who ended what had been the factor's genuine intent to go about Lewis in a bid to exhort, encourage and persuade, rather than pound on crofters' doors with a big stick. Nothing in MacKenzie's journal suggests any heartfelt enthusiasm for emigration, and little enough that he ever reconciled himself to it as anything beyond a desperate expedient for desperate people.

What is evident even in the opening pages is his own prodigious workload, marked in this eventide record by some mild disregard for punctuation and grammar and routine reference to the welfare-for-work projects under way. One soon has a picture of John Munro MacKenzie, a conscientious man, already tired, trying less than successfully to justify his master's schemes to himself but determined to deliver them to the best of his ability. And one is oddly reminded of Henry Mollinson's Mr Farquharson character in Alexander Mackendrick's 1949 Ealing film, *Whisky Galore!* – that world-weary Highlander and customs officer who knows just how a game against the forces of an alien order is played, and cannot but admire the way his own people play it, even as he cynically trims his nails.

Friday 3 Jany 1851

Went to the office, and was engaged writing letters – and giving tickets to members of Fishermens Society – Went over Plans and Specification of Terrace wall, & advertised same for contractors – Went to Melbost to see work doing in repairing Roads by Statute labour. Proceeded to Aignes to arrange with Mr Alexander about repairs required at his Steading, spent a considerable time with him in endeavouring to arrange matters, but Alexr being rather drunk we separated without coming to any conclusion, he said he would leave at next term rather than stand to the bargain made at our former meeting – The Steading cannot be put into any state of proper repair under £300 – I do not think it would be any great loss should Alexander leave, he is such an untidy farmer & never in his sober senses – Went to Garrabost & inspected the Tile Work which seems to be doing well at present – Proceeded to Bayble to see work doing on crofts, the people are more anxious than ever to work now, as we are wishing to Stop them –

Thursday 9 Jany

At office going over Dft Memorial regarding State of the Country with Mr Munro – was called upon by the Banker & Mr J McLeod regarding arrangements for a general illumination this evening & a public meeting in the Mason Hall in honour of Mr Matheson being created a Baronet – Wrote Revd Mr McRae with Dft of Memorial & Mr Mathesons letter on the subject – Went to Castle & arranged with Mrs Watson to have the building illuminated – Arranged various matters with Mr Howitt, gave books & maps to teachers. Went to Square and examined feet of ponies, was glad to see that they were much better & on a fair way to recovery William having given them more exercise of late outside – Returned to office and had meeting with McNab regarding his a/c for the Castle Works, wrote Mr D Mackenzie Holm for an account of all cash materials etc given to McNab by

Mr Scobie – also to Mr Gair for a/c of Steamer freights – Mr McNabs a/c
for the Castle building amounts to £20,368.3/2 which with materials
furnished such as Stone, Iron beams, Hardware etc, will amount to at
least £30,000 – Attended meeting in the Mason Hall which was most
respectable, and all seemed to rejoice in the honour paid to the Proprietor,
this appeared even more evidently in the manner in which the illumination
was conducted, every house was lighted even the most humble in Bayhead
& Inaclete – There was not a window dark in Stornoway except Mr John
Reid McKenzie's who is always an exception of every general rule however
proper it may be –

Friday 17 Jany
    Went to office and wrote several letters for the Packet to Sir James
Matheson, Mr Wilson Glasgow etc Had meetings with various parties about
settlement of a/cs etc – Went to Soval to attend Poor Law Meeting – Mr Allan
Ross was appointed Inspector, the Revd Mr Reid & I voted for Mr Wm Ross
the Stornoway Inspector, but were outvoted by the other members who held
that the Inspector should reside in the parish – Mr A Ross is in the mean time
appointed Interim Inspector, the state of the votes being referred to the Board
of Supervision to confirm Mr A Ross's appointment – Mr Ross is the Free
Church Teacher of Lochs, which I stated as an objection to his holding the
office of Inspector, as he could not faithfully perform both duties, to which he
answered that he intended giving up his school – Mr Ross is a very respectable
person & I have no doubt will perform his duty of inspector faithfully
& regularly. The Memorial to Govt on the State of the Country was read &
approved of by the Meeting – Went over the former Inspectors a/cs & find
him to be due £19 to the Board, but which will be reduced to a few pounds if
he produces vouchers for several items not allowed in his a/cs – Considered
several applications for relief & admitted a few. The people of this parish
(except the district of Carloway) are on the whole very well off. Having still a
few potatoes and plenty of fish – The people of Carloway are very poor &
much crouded, a number of them should be sent to America – got home
at 11 P.M.

It is evident from this meeting both how almost all of any authority in the
Estate still adhered to the Established Church; the mental tricks MacKenzie
was already forced to play on himself (instinctively voting with the parish
minister of Lochs, who had not two people attending sermon, and for an amoral
Stornoway solicitor against a local candidate for inspector of poor whose
suitability for the post MacKenzie entirely acknowledged) – and his sheer,

murderous workload, with untold responsibilities and incessant travel, on foot or by horse, in all weathers. What is still sobering, and evident in these three extracts alone, is the chamberlain's huge reach in Lewis affairs and his colossal personal power – if, for the moment, in the hands of a decent man.

Yet it is typical of someone like Donald Munro that no one can long draw close to them, or interact with them in any business, without somehow themselves being defiled. John Munro MacKenzie's position was difficult enough, especially as he knew the truth of the Lewis situation and in the bitter light that it was far more (and humanely) retrievable than his employer would ever acknowledge. He could but make the best of his brief.

First, the factor tried to establish some sort of consensus among Lewis residents of influence and standing – or, as some might more cynically put it, at least ensure that as many hands as possible were dipped in the blood. He sounded out ministers, schoolmasters, the members of the parochial boards and so on. He was besides reinforced by Sir John MacNeill, chairman in Edinburgh of that Board of General Supervision: he struggled to the Outer Hebrides, was shown around Lewis, and over a bottle of wine one night by some pleasant fireside in the new Lews Castle was readily brought to the mind (if he did not have one already) by the chamberlain that emigration, and on a substantial scale, was vital. Sir John in fact personifies the worst of ruthless, Manchester-Liberal, laissez-faire High Victorianism – let the market rule all, though the heavens fall – and presided over a new order of 'relief', which, when considered in detail, makes the Matheson administration at this pre-Munro juncture seem scarcely less tender than Oxfam. 'It must give us pause, as we read the *Diary*' as Grant remarks of the MacKenzie jottings, 'to think that the crofters were better off, under the regime the Chamberlain was reporting on, than they would have been under the "care and protection" of the British Government.' With the militia reinforcing naked greed on Harris and policemen stripping roofs on North Uist, it is hard to disagree.

The chamberlain, though, had an undoubted headache in Stornoway shop-keepers and merchants, reflecting the increasing estrangement of town from country and certainly the divergence of interests. They were not, of course, opposed to an emigration scheme – however benevolent in conception or execution – on its merits. But many were owed substantial sums by distressed crofting tenantry. They wanted their dues and convinced themselves it was only a low scheme by Sir James to regularise his own books, while – as James Shaw Grant puts it – 'leaving them to whistle for their money'. MacKenzie was well aware of this immediate self-interest, but had limited sympathy. He was already trying to impose some order on his own immediate problem: how to achieve widespread, voluntary passage overseas, and how it might be encouraged. One rough but simple solution was starting to form. Some townships were wholly dependent on the land for their support and wellbeing; there was scant to nil prospect of any recovery from amassed arrears of rent, and these villages should simply be cleared. In others, already winning some wealth from the sea – or with real prospects of doing so in the near future – there was some hope of recovering Sir James's outlay and there need be no hard-sell of emigration.

It was on that rough basis that Tolsta and the Broad Bay villages of northern Point, like Portnaguran and Portvoller, lost no families to Canada (though both were mightily put out in other respects, with the general redrawing of croft bounds and the dumping of additional families). North Tolsta (the present New Tolsta) was cleared for one cynical reason: to create a lucrative farm, which was spared from crofting till the Great War. Carnish and Reef in Uig, though, were to be cleared; and Dalmore, between Carloway and Shawbost, and Galson, up towards Ness, both, besides, became farms. Reef (which included part of what is now Kneep; we should not forget that most of the villages emptied of tenantry under Matheson were eventually resettled, though in some instances not for many years) was a particular headache for Mac-Kenzie. The people had already been served with eviction notices by his predecessor, John Scobie, between 1848 and 1849, but were most reluctant to quit. In other districts – we have seen his view of Carloway, above – it was not hard to persuade himself of manifest poverty. 'The people of Mid Borve are destitute of all means of support & also much in arrear of rent. The people of Melbost Borve are not quite so ill off, tho' much in arrear.'

It is possible – though unlikely, given an abiding island capacity to nurse a grievance – that John Munro MacKenzie could, merely by patient persuasion, have tempted sufficient islanders to Canadian passage. It would certainly have been much the better for his own reputation. But it would have been far from easy. For one – and few outwith Gaeldom have ever grasped this – there is an extraordinary, emotional attachment to land in the Hebrides. It is not just the love of a given place. Nor is it merely some sort of bottom-line insurance against utter destitution, on the premise that with five acres of marginal arable (the typical Lewis holding) you will at least not starve; though that alone was reason enough, and certainly the obsession of enough Great War veterans, to destroy Leverhulme's ambitions for Lewis even 70 years later. It is a singular passion for land you have personally drained, turned, dug, sown and harvested, and it is all the deeper if you have worked this soil all your life as your fathers before you for generations. And there is a telling story from the aftermath of the Park Deer Raid, in 1887: one young man had promised his grandmother in Calbost to bring back some soil from Steimreway, where she had been born. He forgot and grabbed a handful in Calbost itself, sure she would not know the difference. The old lady grabbed it, sniffed it, even mouthed a little – and then told him coldly it was mere Calbost earth, from a certain patch of ground – she would know it anywhere – and not at all from her lamented, promised land.

Sir John MacNeill, in his city arrogance, would, shortly, made public mock of a Skye crofter who through two decades spent six months of the year labouring on a Lothian farm, in order 'that he might continue to enjoy his croft and comparative idleness for the other half-year in Waternish'. Apart from the obvious question – did Sir John ever wield a spade in his life, even in hobby? – Grant rightly denounces that attitude which regards such 'attachment to land as an eccentricity, almost an absurdity, and a barrier to progress. They have not stopped to enquire whether it is really an attachment to the land, or something much more fundamental: a recognition that human beings are social rather than economic animals, and that the dominant culture in a state is not necessarily the best.' It was (and remains) the general ethos on Lewis. And, deep down, it was the chamberlain's ethos too.

But MacKenzie met with serious, practical difficulties in his show of high-minded and most public fairness. For one, the records of debt to hand were far from reliable. In one village, crofters flatly denied the amount of meal put down had ever been given them. In other villages, folk insisted they had paid for the subsistence on receipt. There were, in that place, local ground officers – two brothers who could neither read nor write and could not conceivably have memorised, over a number of years, details of untold, personal, and by the standards of Matheson riches utterly trivial transactions, on which now the entire future of families could hinge. It is unlikely the arrears so fiercely disputed were cancelled. What is certain is that they were never collected – though doubtless extorted, in time, from the new tenants – and what is still more evident even from the chamberlain's nightly log is that, as he trundled around Lewis, very, very few crofters and their families volunteered to go.

Again, writers in this weepy page of Lewis history have neglected the wider context. It was not merely that island folk beyond their eyebrows in Matheson debt thought emigration a splendid idea, as long as other villagers did it, or that they lacked drive and initiative and the pioneering spirit of Viking forebears. Nothing in general Lewis history gives any credence to that. It was that they knew full well an Atlantic voyage on a typical emigrant vessel was a deadly business and – again – news of those forced from the Uists and elsewhere was circulating widely at the time. Down south, some from the families forced so horribly from South Uist and Barra by Colonel Gordon's thugs and hounds and pet policemen had managed to escape: people in Edinburgh were shocked to see, on their own streets, wretched Barra refugees 'in a state of absolute starvation', most without even a few broken words of English. In Canada, immigration officials – hard men who thought they had seen everything – revolted at the spectacle of broken, bedraggled and near-skeletal arrivals from these Outer Hebrides, their clothes reduced to rags and stained and reeking with their own filth, who owned nothing but these desperate threads and, stooping and humiliated, squatted on Canadian piers and begged at Canadian corners for a crust of old bread.

Crossing the ocean at this time was hazardous even for the confident, as a walk round Stornoway's Old Sandwick Cemetery, or even the quiet old graveyard at Tolsta will attest – drowning of village sons all over the world; lads like William MacKenzie of Cromwell Street, Stornoway, 'who left Greenock in the ship "Ceylon" 1865 and was never heard of'. It had evidently sunk unseen and with all hands. Many other headstones in the old Sandwick ground alone commemorate those drowned in the world's oceans: the memorial raised for John MacGregor, a Stornoway joiner who died in 1877, lists among his offspring two sons lost at sea, and a third who succumbed to fever in Glasgow. Only 65, the father had survived them all.

The best and most seaworthy merchant-vessels, like Sir James's own stately tea-clipper of 1850, grandiloquently named the *Stornoway*, bore expensive goods: fine fabrics, tobacco, spices and tea and coffee. Shabbier ships bore livestock; those still leakier and creaking were relegated to the freight of timber and, when they grew too dubious even for that (decks leaking, masts and timbers half-rotten, ropes cast about the hull and bound to keep the failing structure together), they were then deemed fit only for emigrants: from northern England, from Ireland and from Scotland. Such vessels tended besides to have the worst and most disreputable crews. In just one six-year period – from 1847 to 1853 – at least 49 emigrant ships were sunk or wrecked. Most simply vanished. And all this was known and retailed and reported all over Lewis. A reluctance to commit themselves to the perils of the deep seems, in this light, a perfectly rational decision.

If James Munro MacKenzie had hitherto resisted what Donald Munro kept pressing him to do, he did not – as the scale of popular determination to stay grew evident – hesitate long. He yielded to the procurator fiscal's counsel at last, and Munro duly served notices of removal on every tenant MacKenzie listed. It suited Munro, certainly, as an ambitious solicitor to Sir James Matheson, to expedite the proprietor's plans; but there were besides the fees to be amassed by processing every last eviction through Stornoway Sheriff Court. (For that matter, as fiscal, he still enjoyed no salary, but was paid pro rata for every successful prosecution; it is no great surprise to discover that once he was paid a steady wage by the Crown, the rate of recorded crime on Lewis fell remarkably.) And, as James Shaw Grant chronicles, from that point on

MacKenzie seems to have abandoned the attempt to persuade. He went round the villages, day after day, explaining the terms the landlord offered and putting the finger on those who were to go. Decisions were dictated almost entirely by the state of the rent book. If the head of the house was physically fit, and two years behind with the rent, the whole family was bound for Canada . . . Those who were readiest to emigrate were those who had been moved from their original homes by the Estate on a previous occasion. This suggests that the pull of friends and community was the dominant element in the crofters' reluctance to leave. Where ties had already been loosened it was easier to make the final break. Some also appear to have had second thoughts. A few who at first refused to emigrate later followed the factor to another village to say they were willing to go. Whether willing emigrants or not, in June, when the *Marquis of Stafford* arrived in Loch Roag to take the first party to the Clyde, they were there with their pathetic bundles, ready to go. The factor claims that, on board ship, some of them thanked him for having resolved their difficulties and given them a new chance in life. That may well be true.

They were given biscuits as they clambered aboard (from little boats, ferrying from shore and back); they were sold utilitarian tinware; and they were besides offered new clothes 'at a price', though in the end many were given gratis to the utterly destitute. Before the anchor was lifted, the Free Church minister of Uig – the Reverend John Campbell – preached and prayed; and a Gaelic psalm was 'given out' and sung. The chamberlain himself joined them on board for the last Lewis duties. So did Donald Munro. He, however, alighted at the last moment, content only to show face. John Munro MacKenzie accompanied them for the first, fraught trip round northern Lewis, by Ness and Tolsta, to Stornoway.

Thus 400 people, most from Uig and some from Carloway, began their passage to the New World. Details of that first island leg alone – up to the Butt of Lewis, beam-on to the relentless rollers of the Atlantic, to pick up yet more emigrants at Port of Ness (they arrived at 4 a.m. on that stormy night, and John Munro MacKenzie had to get ashore at once, if only to escape briefly from the stink of vomit), are miserable enough. Local fishermen at first refused to take out any emigrants, until the chamberlain gave peremptory order. Then, in turn, the Uig emigrants refused to admit the Ness passengers. There was, they insisted, smallpox in the district, and in any event the vessel was already crowded – so short of covered accommodation that dozens had to stand in the open. The *Marquis* had already given up, and was well on its way to Tolsta, when MacKenzie finally found the argument to have the ship turned round.

If the large vessel for the Atlantic voyage, already awaiting them at Troon, had not enough passengers, he thundered, it would not sail – and all the Uig people would be stranded there and at their own expense.

So the *Marquis of Stafford* did beat ignominious retreat to Ness (though that spirited Uig stand does suggest this was not the clichéd Clearance of powerless, martyred losers). And there was in turn more trouble at Stornoway. MacKenzie did not want the ship to berth alongside, lest many highly unhappy and seasick travellers now abandon her and vanish into town. But the captain quite defied instruction simply to anchor in Glumaig Bay: he had to collect both his wife and his furniture, he asserted, and, whatever might do for Hebridean crofters and their children and grandparents, she would step aboard at the pier like a princess. Besides, the ship was now so awash with sick it had to be properly cleaned, or he could not possibly sail. In the event, the quays were so jammed with fishing boats the ship could not come alongside, and MacKenzie won this argument.

Perhaps in deliberate spite, the master then vanished for hours, socialising long in Stornoway. No crew made any effort to clean the decks of the *Marquis of Stafford*; though for five long hours rain came down in curtains and rods, drenching a good many of those on board, as the brave captain made all his leisurely 'arrangements'.

Another ship, the *Barlow*, made like passage later from Loch Roag, with a still greater host of Lewis people and with misadventures and delays of her own, not least the officiousness of Customs: her master had forgotten the official, printed, contract tickets for every soul on board, and even the chamberlain could not persuade the jobsworths of the Revenue to accept handwritten slips. She sat for days as a young clerk, Murdo Morrison, travelled to Glasgow and back for the vital proper tickets; and was then delayed for hours more when it emerged she was eight bolls of meal shy of the statutory minimum for her complement of passengers.

Both ships made it to the Clyde; and everyone made it to Canada: a few ended up building new lives on the Saskatchewan prairie, and communities named Barvas and so on can be found there to this day, though even by 1911 there seemed surprisingly little folk-memory of a Hebridean past. There can have been still less after a railhead was opened at what became (by the suggestion of a postmaster, Murdo Mciver) the town of Stornoway, and shortly a heaving metropolis, 'with, *inter alia*,' reports Peter Cunningham, 'five elevators, a school, a bank, a Chinese restaurant, two garages, five general stores, a telephone exchange, three churches, an egg-handling station and butcher's shop . . .' In Quebec, transplanted Lewis communities – like that at Lingwick – held on for decades, with Presbyterian Communion seasons and

Gaelic fellowship meetings and so on; but they have long disappeared under a surrounding and hostile Francophone culture.

John Munro MacKenzie had failed to prevail on Matheson to leave off emigration schemes in the first place; he had compromised with Sir John McNeill; and he had finally all but sold his soul to Donald Munro. Of the remaining years of his stretch as Lewis viceroy, the less said the better. He cleared Reef simply by starving them out: all the men were denied work on Poor Relief schemes. He clawed back rent arrears by every stratagem, most desperate, some low. He directed assorted ground officers to attend cattle sales, spy on crofters and report transactions. MacKenzie and his staff visited townships, remonstrated and threatened, seized livestock in lieu. On one Borve raid, things came close to high comedy. Poinded beasts had just been painfully herded together when the party was ambushed by artful villagers; young and old sprang out yelling from all directions, scattering cattle and horses and sheep in chaotic fright. The chamberlain held his nerve, negotiated coldly, and some men did shamefully cough up rent. His final, favourite and usually effective expedient was to ban the cutting of peats until arrears were settled in cash, or a cow given up in lieu; as peats can only be dried, in an average Lewis summer, through May and June, any delay ensures damp fuel and fitful, sulky winter fires – and this did produce results. Yet, the more MacKenzie resorted to such means, the more inside him died.

In 1854, he quit his position and removed to the mainland, doing business in Cumberland and later the Lowlands. The contents and farm-stock of his island home, Sandwick Cottage, were advertised for auction on 25 May: they included, among much else, a mahogany sideboard, with dining tables and a set of 12 chairs to match; carpets and rugs, fenders and fire-irons, coloured engravings, curtains and 'spoon-boxes'; a French bedstead; two oak children's cribs; a 'Staffordshire China dinner set', tumblers and wine-glasses; eight Britannia metal dish-covers; an eight-day clock; six Ayrshire 'milch cows', a draught mare, two ponies, a plough . . . An entire life and past was sloughed off, as if he could not bear to carry off a single souvenir.

John Munro MacKenzie finally ended up a minor laird himself, proprietor of the Mornish estate on Mull, with a handsome house in a beautiful setting overlooking golden sands. Years later, he was visited by Colonel MacLeod of Drynoch, whose sister was married to the former Lewis chamberlain's brother. Colonel MacLeod, about to sail to Canada, was enchanted by the spot, and in 1883 – deputed to name a new city in Alberta – he remembered that place, and that hospitality; and he called it Calgary.

At Whitsun – 28 May 1854 – Donald Munro, solicitor, procurator fiscal, was appointed Chamberlain of the Lews.

7

Chamberlain: Donald Munro and his reign of terror

Donald Munro, in the fullness of his power and the multiplicity of his offices, would terrorise Lewis for over 20 years, with almost entire impunity and the serene connivance of his proprietor. We shall look at the notable enormities in detail: the deceitful game he and Sir James played over Stornoway harbour; the sustained legal terrorism Munro and Ross waged against one Stornoway family; and, of course, the final, spectacular assault on the people of Bernera, which at last detonated to the chamberlain's ruin. But it is not, really, singular outrages that Munro is still remembered on the Isle of Lewis, nor on their account his name is yet spat with such detest. It is for a thousand little oppressions and incident upon insult – tiny things, humiliating that individual or oppressing that household, in one sustained narrative of malignity, through over two decades.

The varied little spites were bad enough in themselves. What has embedded his reign so deeply in the psyche of a proud and warm-hearted people was the contempt behind them, a contempt made manifest continuously, by a man who believed himself utterly secure and knew he could destroy livelihoods and lives. It was all the worse because he was no Lowlander, but a Gael like themselves; and because there seemed no meaningful motive behind his conduct save a sort of gloating, pointless hate; and his constant taunt – a threat all too often made reality – still echoes in the popular mind, in the alien Gaelic of Easter Ross – 'Cuir mi as an fhearan thu!': 'I'll have the land from you!'

Such was the Chamberlain of the Lews who, as Donald MacDonald records, from 1854 'had absolute sway over the whole Island, holding no fewer than seventeen public offices, naturally the most important ones, while his clerk held the others which were too trivial for his attention.' The real wonder is not that such a frightful human being could have won all this power. Once one has studied the career of Sir James Matheson and taken a long hard look at his character, it is evident that he had absorbed more of the cruel mores of the East than he had ever realised. It made a dangerous cocktail, on top of all the assurance of his age in the entire virtue of untrammelled free-market capitalism and the absolute duty of government to stay clean out of the way of men as they made themselves filthy rich. Besides, looking at Matheson's imbecilic industrial enterprises on Lewis, we have noted he was a rotten judge of men. The real marvel is that the people of Lewis put up with Donald Munro for as long as they did.

To be sure, in the island townships there was no security of tenure: it would be 1886 before Highland crofters won such a basic right, 16 years after the peasantry of rural Ireland and only after massive extension of the franchise elected four Crofters' Party men to the House of Commons.

And it was, too, the case that the only people who could (and did) resist the more despotic endeavours of the Estate were the merchants and professional men of Stornoway. Apart from capital and self-confidence, they were besides 'feuholders', actually owning the land on which their homes stood. This naturally granted substantial security – but the interests of comfortable Stornoway people were not, for the main part, bound up with those of the tenants in 'landward' Lewis. Indeed, it is only since the Second World War – and largely in my own lifetime – that the social gulf between Stornoway and the folk of rural Lewis has largely collapsed, because of the loss of Gaelic, in the main part, as a community language and because the advent of the motor car has effectively suburbanised the island.

Even in the 1950s, very many people in such places as Shawbost, Tolsta, Uig or Ness only came to town once a year – usually on *latha na drobh*: the day of the cattle sales. And the contemptuous Stornowegian terms for the local country bumpkins survive to this day in the colourful local argot: a *lourag* (a girl from the outlying villages), a *Maori* (anyone from out of town); or a *maw* (someone from the real sticks, like Ness or the West Side). Even people from the villages immediately adjoining Stornoway, like Sandwick or Laxdale, are the *susnochs*, just a little below the salt; and the folk of Newton – historically the most blue-collar part of old Stornoway – are the 'crabs'. As recently as 1960, there were still hundreds of very old people in the West Highlands – most, probably, on Lewis – who spoke no English. My MacLeod great-grandmother at Cross in Ness, who died that year at the age of 84, had only once in her life – in the mid Fifties – ever left that district, to be seen by the optician in Stornoway, which was a great adventure for her. And not a sentence in English ever crossed her lips.

The gulf between town and country was still manifest reality in the boyhood of James Shaw Grant, born in Stornoway in 1910. The 'line of demarcation between Gaelic and English was sharper than it is today and, although there was a great deal of Gaelic spoken in Stornoway, the frontier of language and the frontier between town and country were roughly the same . . .

On latha na drobh the country folk came to town, but not as fishermen returning to assume their week's work in the vessels which had lain in the harbour even in their absence. They came as crofters, driving flocks of sheep, or herds of cattle. Or riding in little red and blue carts, or brown varnished pony traps. Or leading shaggy horses to the sale ring.

They came from a world that was quite unlike my own, even although at that time many Stornoway families kept a cow or two, as my grannie did, and cultivated an allotment at the back of the town.

And they came in such numbers that Cromwell Street looked as if it might burst apart with the pressure of slow-moving humanity, in the evening, when the market was over and the day's earnings were being liberally spent in the pubs, and we youngsters were reluctant to go to bed, lingering on the streets late into the night in the hope of seeing a fight, which we very often did.

I suppose the girls from the country districts came to the market too, but if they did I have no recollection of them.

It is the boys who march vividly before me as I write. Tall gangling youths with a lumbering athleticism in their gait. The product not of organised games or work in a gymnasium, but of tramping broken moorland, scrambling on cliffs, and jumping in and out of restless boats launched from rocky geos [*narrow rifts in rocky cliffs*] or open beaches.

All of them wore caps. Huge cloth caps that seemed many times too big for them. Their floppy brims were generally supported by a willow withy frame so that they stood out like sunhats or sombreros without a crown.

And corduroy knickerbockers [*breeches*] unfastened at the knee so that they hung halfway down the leg, looking as inadequate and untidy as the caps were excessive but kempt.

Many of them carried walking sticks or, if they didn't, the purchase of one was the first priority when they got to the fairground, with its stalls and its circus, and its coconut shies . . .

His 1977 reflections – in a book, not a newspaper column – are still more illuminating:

I was not myself a Gaelic speaker, although my mother's folk had been, and the Gaelic-speaking villagers who came into town . . . and who lived in thatched houses and earned their living as crofters and fishermen, seemed to me almost a different species from my neighbours in town.

With true urban arrogance, I rather looked down on the slow-moving country folk from the hundred crofting villages which lie round the rim of

Lewis, all but three of them on the coast (for the sea has always been more important in the Lewis economy than the land), but I changed my opinion when I found myself competing against them in the local [*grammar*] school. They had to sink or swim in English from the day they entered the Infant Room, whether they understood it or not, but, despite the disadvantage they suffered of having been taught to read and write through the medium of a 'foreign' language, I found it hard to keep pace with them when we met in the senior classes . . .

When I visit Doune Carloway . . . I think neither of the mystery of the brochs, nor of the bloodstained history of Lord Macaulay's ancestors, but of a dark-eyed girl who was in school with me half a century ago, and whom I once saw for a fleeting moment when we were proudly driving down the West Side of the island in our first motor car. She had laid aside the modest finery she wore in school for the dark striped skirt, the black blouse and shawl which was the typical wear of country women in those days. Her skirt was protected by an apron made of sacking, and on her back she had a creel of peats supported on a 'dronnag'. She seemed an entirely different person from the girl I knew: temporarily, but completely, re-absorbed into the village environment.

I had never before realised that I, a middle-class product of the town, was more tightly confined within the prejudices, pretensions and aspirations of my class than the crofter's daughter who moved with facility and grace between two different cultures, and two very different styles of life.

It was the very first time Grant – then a sixth-form pupil at school – had ever seen anything of Lewis much beyond Stornoway. His honesty and self-knowledge, even as a mildly swotty teenager, were unusual for his town generation, and they give some idea of the charm between the commercial capital of Lewis and the ancient, agrarian society of the rest of the island. Indeed, its baleful reality had significant consequence till the final advent of a new Western Isles Council – Comhairle nan Eilean – in 1975; for Stornoway Town Council had far more standing, and made much more noise, and had many more friends in high places, than the generally rackety 'Lewis District Council' which actually represented many more people.

And there were strange, dark little anomalies. Almost all the men drowned in the *Iolaire* disaster of 1 January 1919 were from rural Lewis, but the jury at the subsequent Public Inquiry (granted only after great clamour) was empanelled exclusively from Stornoway ratepayers; the Iolaire Disaster Fund, which raised in the end over £25,000 for distraught widows and desolate orphans and frail old parents, was got up and administered exclusively by Stornoway men.

Save for their miscalculations over the harbour, Donald Munro and his master decades earlier were generally careful to stay on the right side of town opinion; relations in fact proved much more fraught under Matheson's widow. Without that clout on their side, and indeed held in general and amused disdain by Stornoway's complacent burghers, the crofting community was largely defenceless – especially as the years succeeding the hardships of the 1840s and their messy resolution in 1851–52 were of noted Stornoway success. Indeed, as early as the year Munro was enthroned, John Munro MacKenzie's hopeless bid to convince Sir James of the potential of fishing was sadly vindicated, as MacDonald records. 'The expansion of the Caithness fisheries brought such prosperity to the Lewismen who went there for six weeks every July that, by 1854, practically all arrears of rent had been repaid and household plenishings were more plentiful than ever before.'

There were other elements in the protracted Munro rule. For one – and this was a perfectly reasonable hope, bearing in mind just how many there had lately been – few, at first, expected him to serve as factor for very long. Everyone else had made off for the mainland (or been sacked) after just a few years. For another, emigration – largely, after 1851, to the mainland and especially to Glasgow – was a safety valve of sorts; relieving to some degree (though not nearly enough) the remorseless demand for land. Nor should we underestimate the new moral and spiritual restraint of the new religion, or the reality that island ministers (and only one or two in all the nineteenth century were actually natives of Lewis) were loath to challenge secular authority. In any event the clergy were largely protected from Munro's little games. Parish ministers (of virtually no popular standing after the Disruption) were inevitably Matheson pets, for he personally as heritor appointed them; and Free Church ministers lived in manses, farmed their glebes and preached in churches on land the new denomination had bought, soon after the Disruption, on very easy terms from the well-disposed Mrs Stewart-MacKenzie. (They nevertheless smouldered in quiet sympathy with the crofters, and in the later struggles of the 'Crofters' War' never threatened any involved with church discipline.) Yet, at last, as Donald MacDonald records, and in large measure by Munro's own reckless follies over a people who 'were law-abiding and docile, the time came when their patience was exhausted'.

From the first, Munro asserted his authority by written law – only the rules of the Lewis Estate, of course, though with all the other offices he held (including, critically, procurator fiscal) it is little wonder most islanders could scarcely tell them from Acts of Parliament. He did not just codify these requirements, prohibitions and general tenets, he grossly expanded them, in the knowledge that the more numerous and detailed regulations become, the harder it grows even to remember them, far less to keep them. The statutes of the Lewis Estate in 1849 were, as Donald MacDonald points out, 'despotic' enough; the micromanaging fullness of those conceived, phrased and finally put down in cold hard print by the chamberlain, in both Gaelic and English and in a fat little pamphlet, were all but intolerable. They were, besides, officious and meddling in the extreme; even today, portions are in some detail all but incomprehensible, as a glance at the 1879 edition of Codex Munrovus (published a few years after his fall, but mostly his composition and almost all in his tenor) attests:

Any tenant who, before the term of Martinmas, 1881, shall execute in whole or in part, improvements upon his lands in terms of Article 1 here-of; and shall also erect a dwelling-house and offices on his lot, or make alterations on his present premises, in accordance with Article 2 here-of; and who shall further observe the Rules and Regulations hereinafter specified, shall, on the completion of such house and offices to the satisfaction of the proprietor or his factor, receive a lease of his present possession to endure until Martinmas, 1893, without any increase of rent.

For wasteland, thoroughly improved by trenching and draining and brought into a proper state of cultivation, and for sufficient stone fences, enclosing a croft or lot, meliorations will be allowed the tenant at the end of the lease as follows:

In order to fix the amount of the meliorations, a certificate will be granted by the factor at the end of each year, in a book to be retained by the tenant, of the nature of the improvements executed by them during the preceding year, shewing the date and the extent of the same, and the estimated value there-of at the time, and at the end of the lease, five per cent will be deducted from the amount for each year the tenant shall have possessed the lands after the dates of the outlays made by him. Should the tenant be removed from his occupancy before the end of the lease, on account of any contravention of these Articles, or from any other cause, he shall be allowed meliorations in the above proportion, at the date of his removal.

The dwelling-houses to be erected by the tenants on their respective possessions, shall be built of stone and lime, or of stone and clay pinned and harled with lime, or with stone on the outside face, and turf or sod on the inside, and roofed with slates, tiles or straw, or heather with divots, which heather and divots the tenants shall have liberty to take for this purpose from such places only as shall be pointed out to them by the ground officer of the district; each house to have at least two apartments, with a glazed window in the wall of each, and a closet or small room, with chimneys in the gables, or other opening for the smoke in the roof; the thatch or covering not to be stripped of or removed for manure; the byre to be built at the end or the back of the dwelling-house, as the site may admit, and to have a separate entrance. In the byre a gutter to be formed for the manure, which shall be regularly removed to a dungheap outside.

Any tenant, whether possessing a lease or not, who shall build such a house to the satisfaction of the proprietor or his factor, shall, in the event of his being removed, or otherwise quitting the croft, be allowed meliorations for the same by the proprietor or incoming tenant, at the value of parties mutually chosen.

It is evident even from these 1879 provisions – one could not bear to read much more of this stuff – that crofters had no meaningful rights; the Estate's power to remove them for 'any other reason', beyond breach of the Untold Commandments, is expressly reserved. And, while a heavily conditional security of tenure is outlined, in practice few could hope, and still fewer ever afford, to attain it by the works prescribed.

There was little or no recompense for improvement to houses and holdings, until expressly granted by the Crofters Act; indeed, it could even jeopardize your tenancy. The contempt for the traditional black-house – and general incomprehension of its features and ecology – is no less evident. (Dung stored outside had lost much of its worth by planting time, as the rains of winter washed nutrients away; the warm bodies of family cattle under the same roof helped to heat the house; only the bottom layer of straw was removed each year by tenants, as it had some manurial value – the previous year's top layer was then put on the turves in its stead – and so on.) As in so much else in this narrative, the assumptions of a self-consciously superior (and certainly far more powerful) culture were laid oppressively on ordinary Highland people.

And there were many more 'Articles'. If you allowed others to squat on your croft, you would be evicted. If you overstocked your land, you could again be evicted – and certainly fined, and perhaps the excess of stock confiscated by the Estate. 'Herds' – boys or girls to prevent animals wandering, in an era before galvanised-wire fencing – had to be appointed by each village annually; sheep had to go to the hill in April, and herds watch them at all times. Pigs could only be kept in sties (in reality, there were scarcely any swine on Lewis, and – at least until the advent of shaggy-jumpered incomers – they have never been kept on Barra).

Lewis crofters were allowed to trap rabbits; on no account, however, could they shoot them. You could only keep a dog with the express permission of the factor – and for a fee. The Estate, too, ordained – precisely – where on the relevant village moor you were allowed to cut peats; to cut them anywhere else was strictly forbidden – and mere Lewis crofters could not possibly be trusted to supervise such a weighty matter by themselves. No green, grassy turf was ever to be cut for any purpose. Muir-burning was allowed – but under strict control. Heather, rushes and 'bents' – marram grass – would not be pulled or cut, save at appointed places, on appointed days. Special permission had to be obtained to cut seaweed. Illicit distilling and 'shebeening' were absolutely forbidden. Only the official roads and paths could be used for going anywhere. Tenants had to contribute to the rates. Every township had to appoint a 'constable' – notionally to oversee all crofting operations, though such men were invariably unpopular, and in any event the real authority lay with Munro's resident goblin of a ground officer. All land disputes were to be referred at once to the great chamberlain; local resolution was not allowed. And, of course, only the laird – Sir James Matheson, until his death in 1878 – could hunt deer, grouse, salmon and sea trout and brown trout, for they were held his exclusive property. The proprietor besides had the right, at his will and pleasure, to 'enclose and plant land, build houses, shut up or alter roads and streams, and straighten marches'.

A sort of common sense underlay many of those requirements. Straying livestock could (and certainly would) devour precious crops. Peat-cutting, and the harvest of other plant-cover or dune-binding materials, has to be regulated – as common grazings committees or the odd environmentalist quango does in our own day – and it was reasonable, after the crisis of the 1840s, to rule firmly against 'squatting' – the proliferation of cottars – and the subdivision of holdings. But all this could have been overseen and enforced perfectly well by villagers themselves – after all, it was in their own self-interest: even in the early twentieth century a Lewis township more than once rose as one to tear down a squatter's home if it had been erected against the wishes of the community. What Munro had deliberately devised was a grossly centralised, tyrannical order with rules so many and so highly detailed they were almost impossible to keep, which fed information and plaints and local difficulties constantly back to his office, and granted him abundant opportunity to meddle all over the island. And he had besides, underpinning all this, the ferocious terms of the original 1849 tenancy agreement – and, beyond any codification anywhere, full freedom to decree whatever came into his head.

'Any tenant who contravened any of the Rules and Regulations (of which only some have been mentioned),' Donald MacDonald relates, 'would have his lease terminated immediately, and on being informed in writing, would have to remove himself or be liable to a summary ejection.' That was a euphemism for Munro's hirelings materialising to pull the roof off over your head. MacDonald adds dryly, 'Apart from these written regulations, and a few unwritten ones, the tenants were free to do whatever they wished.'

Even aside from the way it was operated, such a ridiculous code was guaranteed in itself to infuriate a Lewisman, especially as more and more were drawn into the seasonal fishing, first at Caithness and then, as the century matured, round the perimeter of all Great Britain – for the great shoals of herring circumnavigated the coast, and boats followed by the thousands, from Wick to the Ross-shire coast, and the shores of Moray, and by Fraserburgh and Peterhead, Aberdeen and Stonehaven and Montrose and Arbroath, and by Fife and East Lothian, and so on round by Great Yarmouth, Lowestoft and so on. So, in time – as girls at the gutting – did thousands of young Lewis women. They sent cash home, and came back with cash, and new and lovely things – it was a great occasion in many an island home when your Anna or Mairi or Peigi came back with her kist and flung it triumphantly open. But these young people acquired something else too: the experience, year upon year, 'engendered a new confidence,' MacDonald rightly points out, 'widened their horizons, and developed their ability to deal with strangers.' In time, in Hebridean affairs – and especially among lads who went to fish, in season, on the coast of Ireland – this would be highly significant in the erosion of despotic landlordism.

But, of course, it was not just these arbitrary statutes that oppressed, it was the people who enforced them. Local constables were apt to favour friends and relatives, and certainly themselves. The ground officer's eyes were everywhere, watching, assessing; not just his purported business – boundaries and natural resources – but which households were doing well; who seemed to have new, pleasing possessions; who had adult offspring away and sending money back; who did well at the cattle sales. Hearts sank constantly as, over the boundary bridge or down the school brae, the detested *earraidhean* – the messengers of the Estate – came in sight; they almost never brought good news, it was almost always of more deprivation or another imposition, and it was delivered invariably in tones of smug relish. And, stumping about over all, or plotting from his offices in Carn House – once, well within living memory, such a fountain of Lady Mary's generosity – was Donald Munro, like a squat black spider in a great sticky web; save for the frequent, scary occasions when he went abroad in landward Lewis.

Certain big enterprises blacken the Munro reputation in the pages of island history. But it is the particular hurts – and the monstrous demands of his vanity – that people in island townships today largely remember, and which have done more damage (in Lewis, at least, if not Canton) to the reputation of Sir James Matheson, for all the might Munro so abused was vested in him by His Radiance. 'He had so wormed himself,' Daniel McKinlay would write of contemporary Lewis after Munro's final ruin, 'into the confidence of the proprietor, that he was allowed to manage the people and the estate without any control; and he ruled them with a rod of iron. The crofter-tenants-at-will were quite at his mercy and nothing was done to improve their lot,' – and, even after all the drama of Bernera, and when newspapers the length of Britain feasted on the outrageous management of Lewis, Sir James would still defiantly assert he would stand by Munro 'as long as he lived'.

Beyond the fatuity of Matheson and the evil of Munro was a Highland order wicked in itself and in which there was, really, no meaningful rule of law, so weighted was it in the favour of the landed and powerful and on the premise of their unfailing benevolence – and an order that positively promoted poverty, indolence and hopelessness, and which just happened, as Joni Buchanan explains, to be especially bad on the Isle of Lewis:

> The fact that Lewis crofters remained 'tenants-at-will' throughout the period of recovery and until the passing of the first Crofting Act in 1886 was indicative of poor estate management and a considerable obstacle to improvement. The land was held on a presumed verbal lease, commonly of one year's duration. Their status could command no redress in law and subjected the class to the absolute and arbitrary power of the landlord. Security of tenure for a period of five to six years could only be granted if certain conditions were met. These included the building of a suitable house; the payment of all arrears of rent; and enough capital to stock the land. Munro MacKenzie said in his evidence to the Napier Commission that 'these leases were not much asked for by the tenants . . . as they were too slow in doing their part.' . . . the estate was not slow to capitalise on the crofters' lack of formal rights.
>
> There was no question of compensation for improvements either to the land or to the dwelling. Writing in 1878, MacKinlay condemned the estate's failure to issue long leases and quoted the observations of a Mr Smith who was the tenant of Galson Farm: 'Without a lease the crofter has no incentive to improve or drain his land, as his doing so would only tend to a raise in his rent; and being merely a tenant-at-will he is simply dependent on the factor or the ground-officer for a roof to cover himself and his family.
>
> 'At the present moment you will find families, crowded together, living off the produce of one lot; and but for the sea-fishing at home and the herring fishing on the east coast, combined with the liberality of some of

their neighbours in giving them patches of land, they would certainly starve. On the whole the effect is demoralising, and the poor people seem to have fallen into something like a state of indifference as to what their future may be.'

The tenant-farmers of Galson and elsewhere had done well under the regime and feared that their large holdings might be 'resumed' and turned back to crofts at the decree of the government: Mr Smith had his own motives for implying the folk around him were so many apathetic losers. It is important to hammer home the point that the whole Highland system positively discouraged the betterment of homes, holdings and village facilities, because the myth of Highlanders as lazy, backward and indifferent to their conditions was much vaunted by the Victorian press – especially by complacent, travelling 'gentlemen-writers' – and is aired in the media and in high places even to this day. Even in communities run by factors less depraved than Munro, under lairds less detached and careless than Sir James Matheson, it invited serious trouble to draw attention to yourself by initiative and industry, as James Hunter explains:

> The people who lived in such conditions, of course, did not do so willingly. Their landlords, however, had imposed on them a system which made it inevitable that bad housing would be all but universal. The key to that system was an all-embracing insecurity which ensured that, should a man be tempted to build himself a superior house, his rent would be increased automatically to take account of his holding's enhanced value. Indeed, he might well be evicted if his landlord, his landlord's factor or some other hanger-on happened to be looking for a better than average croft for someone to whom the estate management owed a favour. Such occurrences were common and they acted as a powerful disincentive to improvements of any kind.

Compared to most of the Hebrides, Lewis had – in truth – got off lightly. She has changed hands remarkably few times in her history. Communities were not obliterated wholesale, with thousands forced into emigration ships and thousands more moved about the island, and then moved again, even as others were brought in from other West Highland districts – the sort of protracted upheaval inflicted on Harris in the first half of the century, leaving an abiding sense of dislocation and a very different sort of community and temper.

And, while there were untold injustices, there is not much evidence on Lewis of the sort of demoralisation that so disturbed – from the 1870s – the robust land-reform campaigners like John Murdoch, whose new newspaper – *The Highlander* – was emerging, in Hunter's words, as a 'persistent, unbending and extremely effective critic of Highland landlords'. When he first came to the Uists, Murdoch could not even gather an audience for public meetings, so terrified were local tenants that they might be thrown from their land and homes merely for being seen in his company. Murdoch knew his Highland history; he knew that, almost within living memory, the community of the Uists – and like places all up and down the western seaboard – had been renowned for music and poetry, commerce and industry, fat harvests, hospitality to visitors, succour for the vulnerable and the old glory of Clan Donald. The new atmosphere appalled him:

> We have to record the terrible fact that, from some cause or other, a craven, cowed, snivelling population has taken the place of the men of former days. In Lewis, in the Uists, in Barra, in Skye, in Islay, in Applecross and so forth, the great body of the people seem to be penetrated by fear. There is one great, dark cloud hanging over them in which there seem to be the terrible forms of devouring landlords, tormenting factors and ubiquitous ground-officers. People complain; but it is under their breaths and under such a feeling of depression that the complaint is never meant to reach the ear of landlord or factor. We ask for particulars, we take out a notebook to record the facts; but this strikes a deeper terror. 'For any sake do not mention what I say to you,' says the complainer. 'Why?' we ask. 'Because the factor might blame me for it.'

Even by the standards of his time, Donald Munro's carriage as lord of all he surveyed has still power to shock. As that 1874 pamphlet retailed, he demanded everywhere an obeisance that would have embarrassed Queen Victoria. 'The poor people complain of their thraldom, and the petty tyrannies to which they are subjected. To give examples – though they will appear almost incredible – if a small tenant enters the official room of the chamberlain with his head covered, his hands in his pockets, or with apparently unwashed face, he is by that functionary fined; and if offence is given him – though it would appear to be more frequently taken than intended – or if his behests are not at once obeyed with becoming meekness, the poor crofters are immediately threatened with ejection from their lands. Everyone acquainted with the character of the Highlander and Islander knows the terrifying effect of such a threat . . .'

Munro liked regular, stately, baleful progresses around Lewis; his flunkys in each locality kept him informed of all goings-on, and the proprietor's impressive network of new roads allowed easy jaunts by horse and gig to most corners of his local empire – a signal advantage over all his predecessors. It is also remembered – as Mor MacLeod relates – that he even carried his personal throne wherever he went; a great chair, a 'carver' with arms, to lend the Chamberlain of the Lews special state, as he commandeered this schoolroom or that parlour and deigned to levy the dues of Sir James from a cowed peasantry.

And Donald Munro was especially given to fines. He levied fines at every provocation; and when there was no provocation; and whenever he felt like it. There was a man at 7 Uigen, Mor MacLeod of Brue related in July 2010, a Donald MacLeod, who lived near the Free Church minister, Rev. John Campbell, and used to visit him to hear the latest stories from the newspaper. MacLeod was perhaps a little simple, for he could not read himself and used publicly to marvel how the man of God seemed to know of everything that went on in the world. Rent day fell in the district, and MacLeod – like everyone else – went to wait on the great chamberlain, cap in hand, and duly handed over his precious coin. And as he turned to go (there might have been something of strain or vexation on his face, or there might have been nothing at all save the factor's whim of the moment), Munro snarled at him to come back. ' "Tasdan eile air do dhrein," ' says Mor, 'that's what he said, "Another shilling for your scowl!" And he wasn't a bright man, Donald, and he handed over another shilling without demur . . .'

That was a favourite gambit of Munro; the bark of 'Tasdan air do dhrein!' is still widely associated with him on Lewis. It was not just the venom of the man that so unsettled the people, it was that his antics were so capricious.

James Shaw Grant's own grandmother was fined one day as Donald Munro was strutting by at the head of the Local Volunteer Company, sweaty and resplendent in uniform, the drilled and musket-toting militia tramping in his train. She had a peat stack in front of her house, and so he stopped and levied an immediate penalty, for the peats had affronted the dignity of his office and his parade.

There was a man at Ness, Murdo Smith – *Murchadh Chaluim Tailleir* – and he was away at the fishing, doing fine, and he came back to find Munro's men ripping the thatch from his Skigersta home, with his terrified wife quaking below; she was a Margaret MacKay, and the last child born on North Rona, says James Shaw Grant (for his wife was their descendant). And

> Murdo put his wife and his belongings into a boat and made his way to Tong where he was lucky enough to get a croft, but the malevolence of the factor followed him there. When the rent fell due, he walked to the village of Back, several miles distant, to pay it. Munro refused to take it because he

was a few minutes late. He was ordered to be in time at the next collection, the same day, at Aignish, on the other side of Broad Bay. Munro drove off in his gig for Aignish while Murdo, who had neither horse nor gig, took off his shoes and raced across the sands, against tide and clock, knowing that failure would cost him a fine, or perhaps the loss of a second croft.

In 1880, some years after Donald Munro was finally put out of crofters' misery, a romantic novel was published in London: a 'three-decker Victorian romance,' says James Shaw Grant – *The Love of His Life*, by Cosmo Cumming – though Grant quite properly adds that this hunk of Celtic Twilight kailyard trash (evidently in the wake of William Black's *A Princess of Thule*, a recent and gorgeously junky heedrum-hodrum bestseller) 'failed as a novel. The writing is turgid, the story convoluted and the characters wooden, but there are passages which spring to life.' Grant himself can only bear to include choice extracts after converting the writer's frightful phonetic notion of a Highland accent ('It iss a fwet tay you fwill get for the rents') into sensible Standard English. In any event, 'Cosmo Cumming' did not exist; the author was John MacRae, by birth and background a Harrisman, schooled at Inverness. And, for a while, he had worked as a clerk in Donald Munro's Carn House office and must often have accompanied the Chamberlain of the Lews on his sorties into the townships of the island.

That is significant, for the first third of the tired old tome, entitled 'Israel in Egypt', stars a frightful Hebridean factor in what are really the only pages worth reading in a general waste of perfectly good tree, for they are from genuine MacRae experience and there his involved story flames momentarily into life. And, just in case anyone back home quite failed to grasp the author's inspiration, the villainous overlord is one Donald Black (arch Gaelic mischief on MacRae's part, for *Domhnall Dubh* is a traditional island tag for the Prince of Darkness, Satan himself). And moreover – John MacRae was not a subtle fellow – *The Love of His Life* is 'Dedicated to Donald Munro Esq., Lews, In Grateful Remembrance of His Constant and Valuable Sympathy.' Normally one would deplore this sort of thing – joyously kicking a man when he is down – from a cocky fellow with pretensions to authorship. But MacRae has left us a genuine memoir of just how Munro carried himself amidst the people of Lewis – though with little evidence of talent sufficient to keep Thomas Hardy awake at night.

At this time Mr Donald Black, the Factor, was wont to make a tour round the land over which he was the real king, with the object of collecting rents from those who might not have been able to settle arrears at the more important autumn collection. The past season had been memorably bad. The crops had entirely failed; there had been little or no fishing; and, to crown all, a disease came among the sheep and cattle, which destroyed many of them. But these circumstances had no softening influence upon the native severity of the tyrant factor. A vicious laugh of brutal joy came from him as he stood in his coach-yard, wrapped up in a coat made of several grey seal-skins, and coughing through an enormous comforter that that covered the lower and the redder half of his face.

'Hogh! hogh! It is a furious day to drive on, Tom. But so much the better; the scoundrels will get wet enough. I'll pay them for their confounded impudence. All ready there? Look sharp, confound you . . .'

'All ready, Mr Black; step in, sir, please.'

'Step in, you fool. Where is that idiot Campbell? Ho! There, you lazy idiot; be here at once, or you can walk to Rossy. Look sharp!'

'Yes, Sir,' said the servile Campbell, as he stepped into his accustomed seat behind, after waiting an hour for his majesty's pleasure . . .

The thirty or forty men who had had come up to give their utmost farthing to the inexorable factor had arrived at the time stated in his notice, and had now been more than an hour waiting for him . . .

When he had made himself fairly comfortable, and got seated in his chair of state in the . . . little inn, with his meek scribe before him, Mr Donald Black summoned a few of the dripping cottars to appear.

The first who came to the table, cap in hand, and saluted the factor with becoming respect, was an elder of the church and knew a little English.

'Good morning, Mr Black. It is a wet day you will get for the rents.'

'Hush! What's your name? Where do you come from? Campbell, turn him up. Kenneth Smith, Barney. Number 265. Have you got the rent? Why did you not pay this before? Eh? Look sharp with it and stand back. You were smoking, man. Stand off. Hush! I don't want to hear any nonsense. Next man there . . .

The next man came up like his friend and imitated him in giving respect.

'Good morning? Do you call this a good morning, man? Stupid brutes. Watcher. I saw you before. What's your name again? Number what? Speak out, man. Less noise, there. Any arrears there, Campbell?'

'Yes, Mr Black,' and Campbell read some pencil notes on the margin of the rent sheets. 'Sold a cow to a drover at Christmas; has plenty of money. A rogue and a scoundrel.'

'I thought so. Well what have you to say for yourself, Alexander Thompson? Eh? Sold a cow? Where's the money? Look sharp! Do you think I have nothing to do but wait here all day for you?'

'Well, Mr Black,' the man commenced to explain, 'I had no potatoes; I was unsuccessful in the fishing, and my wife and family were starving; what could I do?'

'Confound your wife and children. That's always the cry. Wife and children! Why do you have a wife and children? I'll manage every one of you. Double his rent, Campbell. I'll see that you have no more children. A fine thing for you to spend his Lordship's money feeding too many children. Deacons and rubbish in a church, too! Fine Pharisees and rogues you make. But I'll sort you. Campbell, mark opposite his name – Summons, sell out, too many children; lazy scoundrel. Next there . . .'

It would be unfair to inflict much more of MacRae's deathless prose on these pages. Yet still more harrowing vignettes follow – a poor, shivering widow ('I'll put you out of your land, and you can go where you like'), an elderly fellow who presumed to turn up with something on his face ('Ah, here is an old divine to be sure; with plenty of snuff about him. What do you mean, sir, by coming into my presence in that state? Go out this minute and wash your face.'). And – this does disturb, because it sounds like something that actually happened and that MacRae witnessed – a still more feeble old fellow hirples in, who in 'his extreme weakness required to rest upon his stick before he could straighten his bent back in order to see and salute his superior. Impatient with this movement, which the wildest savage in mid Africa would have beheld with pity and reverence, the factor sprung at him and, violently pulling his cap off, flung it through the doorway.'

Such was Donald Munro, Chamberlain of the Lews, procurator fiscal, chairman of this, director of that, treasurer, secretary, baron baillie, tax-man, notary public, harbour commissioner, commanding officer of the Local Volunteer Force; and thus he was pleased (it is unlikely MacRae greatly exaggerates, and it is supported by another eyewitness account) to conduct himself. The affected, gentrified, stage-villain English is almost certainly authentic – even by the turn of the nineteenth century, Tain Gaelic was pretty derelict – and the factor's evident contempt for religion (and especially Free Church religion) sounds besides horribly plausible, especially in an age when Highland Presbyterianism was mocked, in the public prints, no less than it is today.

We shall look in detail at grave legal crimes in Stornoway itself, but one dreadful episode is still remembered with anger in the villages by the Butt. On 18 December 1862, 31 Ness fishermen sailed from Port of Ness (the only, though ill-designed, facility then anywhere save at Stornoway and Carloway) to lay their long lines. They were far from shore and the local waters – where there is a menacing swirling confluence of the Atlantic and the Minch – are never to be treated lightly. Perhaps they took chances; perhaps days of bad weather had denied them work and straitened their circumstances. What is certain is that they were caught in a sudden, ferocious storm, and their five open boats all foundered or disintegrated, and every one of them – man and boy – was lost in what is still remembered as *Am Bathadh Mor*, 'The Great Drowning'.

It was more, in the bleak world of Victorian Scotland, than human tragedy: it was social and economic catastrophe for their wives, children, siblings yet ungrown – for families were then apt to be large – and old dependent parents. There were 31 such kindred – to say nothing of the 71 orphaned children and the 24 shattered widows – 7 of them, this December of 1862, with child. One old woman, Grant relates, had lost a husband, a son and a son in law in an earlier fishing calamity (probably the Drowning of 1841, when my own great-great-great-grandmother, Margaret Morrison of Habost, lost her first husband). This appalled woman was now bereft 'of her only surviving son and her only surviving son-in-law, leaving three widows and five orphans in one house, "with scarcely a potato to eat."' The Reverend Donald MacRae, Free Church minister of the parish, nevertheless declared there were other grieving families still worse off. 'The backbone of our fishermen is broken,' he lamented.

This was precisely the sort of situation that did rouse the social conscience of Sir James Matheson. A public meeting was called for 19 January 1863 in Stornoway. Two committees were formed to arrange relief: one in Stornoway, fat with businessmen and gentry, to raise as much money as possible, and a 'Local Committee' in Ness, dominated by the Established and Free ministers, which would 'advise' on the distribution of funds. It is typical of the Matheson era that even ministers in the district itself were not to be trusted in charge of such munificence; and almost inevitable that the convener and treasurer of both bodies was his well-trusted chamberlain, Donald Munro.

There was a very rich gone-away-done-well man from Stornoway in London, William Donald Ryrie, and he set up in the capital a committee of his own. Even in a day when terrible things happened almost routinely to the poor – coal-pit collapses, factory explosions, great blazes in the slums and so on – the Ness disaster was widely publicised and attracted great, genuine sympathy. The Queen herself made a donation. So did the Prince and Princess of Wales, and many of their rich friends. Within weeks – and a full third of it had been raised by Ryrie – the Fund burgeoned with £1488 2s 4d.

There was an initial distribution of cash to the widows and families. And that was the last they saw of it. Soon, many households were straitened. Children began to go hungry; clothes faded to rags. Neighbours could have helped, but had burdens and needs of their own; anyway, had not a great collection been made by the gentlemen of Stornoway? There was never an audit of the Disaster Fund, which somehow ended up – and, even when the scandal was exposed, he never gave any explanation – in a bank account in Donald Munro's name and under his own solitary signature. All the money was at his 'unfettered discretion': meanwhile, the Munro minions kept him up to date with the hatches, matches and dispatches of Ness (indeed, the Local Committee for the Fund was strictly instructed to inform Munro at once of any change in family circumstances) and for over five years the Central Committee was not once called and did not once meet.

Had the chamberlain simply stolen the money, that – vile as it would have been – might at least be comprehensible; but there is something about this man, even 12 decades after his death, still more creepy than a common thief. There were payments from the Disaster Fund – but only on rent day, and only for rent, and only for those (almost all women) who were in their own right tenant of a croft; and not a widow nor bent old mother was allowed to handle a penny. Munro had even a sly little ritual. He sat in his big special chair in his selected Ness lair on rent day, with both big books by him – one recording the local tenancies and their tallies, one for the Disaster Fund. When an afflicted relative was next in the queue, and at last stood in his majestic presence, he balefully counted out her rent (and only her rent) from the Disaster Fund cash. Once it was all tantalisingly on the table, she had timorously to touch his pen on that account book. The money was then swept imperiously off the table into the bag for the rent, and he recorded that payment in his other book. Yet the chamberlain gave no receipt for the rent, and the sum credited to her related only to that rent, and not to her needs, whether she had 'one dependent child or six', as Grant dolefully details. And if she remarried – and some simply had to remarry, if they were lucky enough to attract a kindly husband as they struggled to raise children in a home too often scant of fire and food – she was removed at once from the Disaster Fund list. Her entitlement was over. 'Munro relied on the new husband to pay the rent. He had to, or he would lose the croft . . .'

There would be a sequel to this. For now, in all his offices and in every conceivable tier of local power, Donald Munro reigned as any implacable tsar. And there was still another wicked game. When a family was evicted for arrears of rent on Lewis – between widowhood, misfortune or disabling illness, it happened often enough – the house and tenancy, naturally, were fast bestowed on another. The Estate could not have property lying empty, land untilled and rent unpaid. The new tenant was not just obliged thereafter to pay his own rent;

he was responsible, besides, for clearing every last farthing of outstanding arrears. Again, he had to – or be without a croft. 'The whole community,' states James Shaw Grant, 'lived, from day to day, under the perpetual threat of eviction. They adapted their lives and their attitudes to accommodate that fact, just as they adapted to the wind and the weather. Insecurity was a rule of life: an act of God before which you could only bow your head. The most important duty was to have sufficient money in your hand, on rent day, to meet the demands of the Factor.'

And even that guaranteed nothing, if those empty East Highland eyes turned on you and yours like a cobra.

There was a family at Bosta on Bernera, Mor MacLeod remembers. The mother was widowed, but they worked hard, and hung together, and coped, and the lads went away to the fishing and did well, and sent money back, and they began – just a little – to get on. Word of this reached the Chamberlain of the Lews. One day, without warning, they were evicted – the croft taken off them in an instant, his men sent to throw them out of this house. The old woman ended up in some bleak little Bernera bothy; the two daughters were ordered far away, over to Shawbost, a day's journey by sea and foot. 'And the folk felt so sorry for them there,' remembers Mor, whose grandmother was a Shawbost woman, fostered with her much older and childless married sister at Earshader, and who regularly went back and forth, 'for they would cry all the time, broken-hearted, homesick . . .' You ask, stupidly, why Munro would do such a thing. Mor's eyes lock on yours with incredulity, as if you are dim, as if you do not understand. 'Because they were prospering. They were getting on so well. And he *hated* that. He hated people who "got on". He wanted the people kept down. And Donald Munro threw them out because he *could* . . .'

There is an awkward pause.

Mor closes her eyes, and leans back, and starts reciting, and you recognise the stanzas at once, for they are from the greatest Gaelic poem of the nineteenth century – a period generally noted for the most frightful, hackneyed dross – and you are pulled away in moments to another world, far from the twenty-first century and its kit-houses and clamour and miseries and social-networking websites, far from English, and into a world and a culture all but gone. And you see, as she saw seventy or eighty years ago in other eyes that had in the flesh and in their prime beheld him, that man in black, that fat man, on his gig and with his stick, or pounding the table by his cash box and his big bound book, summoning back that fearful old gentleman to fine him a shilling; and the chamberlain cackled, and he liked it.

And the verses – the final, terrible warning from Mor's long-dead kinsman,

John Smith – *Seonaidh Phadraig* – of Earshader, on the house appointed for all living and even for this Donald Munro – pour forth, in that 95-year-old voice of a great woman of Gaeldom and in matchless, godly solemnity.

O criothnaich measg do shòlasan,
Fhir-fhòirneirt làidir chruaidh!
De 'm bas no' m pian a dhoirteart ort
Airson do leòn air sluagh?
'S e osnaich bhròin nam bantraichean
Tha sèid do shaidhbhreis suas;
Gach cupan fion a dh'òlas tu,
'S e dòir nan ainnis thruagh.

Ged thachradh oighreachd mhor agad,
's ged ghèill na slòigh fod smachd,
Tha 'm bàs is laghan geur aige,
'S gum feum thu gèill da reachd.
Siud uachdaran a dh'òrdaicheas
Co-ionnan còir gach neach,
'S mar oighreachd bheir e leine dhut,
'S dà cheum de thalamh glas.

'S e siud as deireadh suarach dhut,
Thus', fhir an uabhair mhòir,
Led shumanan 's led bhàirlinnean,
A' cumail chàich fo bhròn;
Nuair gheibh thu 'n oighreachd shàmhach ud,
Bidh d'àrdan beag gu leòr;
Cha cluinnear trod a' bhaillidh ann,
'S cha chuir maor grand' air ròig.

'N sin molaidh a'chnuimh shnaigheach thu,
Cho tàirceach 's a bhios d' fheòil,
Nuair gheibh i air do chàradh thu
Gu sàmhach air a bòrd.
Their i, ''S e fear mèath tha 'n seo,
Tha math do bhiast nan còs,
On rinn e caol na ceudan
Gus e fhèin a bhiathadh dhomhs'.'

O tremble in your pleasures,
Oppressor hard and strong!
What death or pains can fairly be
Your wage for folk you've wronged?
The grieving sighs of widows
Are what inflates your wealth;
And every cup of gurgled wine
The tears of paupered wretch.

Though your estates should be so vast,
And armies yield to you,
Death has the strictest law at last
And you must bear its rule;
That's the lord who will ordain
An equal share for all –
He'll grant a shroud as your domain
And two strides of green sod.

That then your squalid border,
You man of swelling pride,
With your summonses and orders
That made the people cry;
And in that quiet inheritance
Your bragging will pipe down;
No factor there in arrogance,
Nor vile official's scowl.

The squirming worm will sing your praise
For your delicious flesh,
When finding you laid out all straight
A spread without a breath;
And chortle, 'Here's a fat one in
Just right for crawly beast,
Since he made many hundreds thin
To make himself my feast.'

Something chills, though the sun yet beams outside, twinkling on the tiny waves of Loch Mor Bharabhais; and it is as if we glimpsed beyond our common end to the pit itself. And all are still.

8

Babies: How Munro and Ross, Solicitors, destroyed a Stornoway family

In July 1857, as families in rural Lewis rationed what remained of the last harvest and looked to the skies as their frail crops slowly, slowly ripened towards that autumn's labour, the Stornoway Horticultural Society held its annual show – and competition.

Most of the best people in town turned up; they had submitted vases of this and baskets of that. From the new Castle, its grounds and its private gardens and its glasshouses now steaming with exotic fruit – plums and cherries and grapes and peaches and nectarines, as Fred Silver describes in his dark little chapter – came a Mr Conlon, who served as head gardener under the Mathesons and was that year's judge for the Horticultural Society's assembly. This, no doubt, explains the outcome in keenly fought categories – and in favour of the Chamberlain of the Lews. For it was indeed 'Munro who took many of the top prizes – including first for the Best Six Cut Roses, first for the Six Best Pansies, first for the Best Three Early Cabbages and First for the Best Early Carrots.' Conlon, as Silver, poker-faced, concludes, 'may well have had personal reasons for feeling that Munro, Factor of the Estate for four years by then, was the appropriate recipient . . .'

Donald Munro, as we noted, had not the life-defining hold over the townsfolk that he enjoyed over families in the crofting, subsistence economy of the wider Isle of Lewis. It is unlikely that his signal success as a gardener – assuming, which is improbable, that he had actually tended those carrots and pansies and so on himself; and that they were indeed the fruits of his own soil rather than insolently commandeered from the hothouse glories of Lews Castle – endeared him in any way to Stornoway society. Nevertheless, as Silver observes, 'one must have the suspicion' that opponents in self-consciously dainty cricket matches found it convenient to lose to the Matheson team, which Munro personally captained; and a certain menace underlay even the chamberlain's conspicuous gifts and gestures. In July 1869, for instance, Donald Munro presented a painting to the local Freemasons, showing 'the capture of whales in Stornoway several years ago': and Silver has a detailed chapter on the herding – on several occasions – of a school of cetaceans into the confines of the port on various occasions between 1820 and 1882, followed by their brutal slaughter, with the crudest weapons seized on to hack and bludgeon the beasts to death: the details are too horrific to repeat here.

In all his hats and through many years, defeats for Donald Munro himself were understandably rare. One of the very few (significantly) fell in January 1851, a few months before he was appointed factor. Among his powers as procurator fiscal was the responsibility to launch legal process for the committal of 'lunatics', though the detail of this as spelled out in law was of little relevance in the Outer Hebrides. The fiscal was, for instance, obliged to announce the case by advertisement in the local press, but the nearest newspaper was published on the other side of Scotland. And, as the island did not boast a mental hospital – and would not, until the charmless doors of the 'Combination Poorhouse' were opened in 1897 – the only place to confine the patient was Stornoway's little prison. 'So far as the patient's family was concerned,' writes James Shaw Grant, 'the stigma of jail was added to the stigma which then attached to mental illness itself. The patient was immediately removed ten, twenty, thirty, perhaps even forty miles from home, with the prospect of being sent, eventually, to a mainland institution, where any link with the family was almost irretrievably broken.' But,

> In January 1851, Donald Munro applied to the court for an order committing a crofter from Garrabost 'to the jail of Stornoway *ad interim*' because he was 'in a state of Lunaticy (sic) Furious or Fatuous and threatening danger to the lieges.' The Sheriff Officer, with two assistants, was sent to Garrabost to seize the patient, but his wife refused to admit them. They went to get 'two farm constables' to help them force their way in, but, by the time they returned to the house, the neighbours had surrounded it and they couldn't get near. That incident appears in the criminal statistics as a serious breach of public order. In the perception of the local community it was a victory – a rare event! – over a remote, alien autocracy personified by Donald Munro.

Such success was rare indeed. In 1861, James Robertson MacIver – son of the ferocious old Lewis MacIver and heir to his father's business and assets – finally went bankrupt. He was universally liked and, as the eminence of a highly respected island family, who had long had a nose for business and a keen sense of the realities of local power, retained high social standing even as misfortune piled upon incompetence. For though he had inherited his father's interests as 'farmer, fishcurer, shipowner, merchant, money-lender, and general public figure,' as

Grant dolefully retails, James Robertson MacIver had little of his force and none of his acumen. His father had not long died – from that unfortunate chill – when the MacIver's ship, the *Peggy*, foundered with a cargo of salt fish: James had not bothered to insure the £1,000 vessel. He continued in this hapless way, even as relatives tried to help or counsel as they could. In his last year as factor, John Munro MacKenzie had taken only two half-days off from his depressing Lewis duties, but one was to take his wife and a little party of friends to see the Callanish Stones, newly exposed in all their glory after Sir James had hired crofters to remove five feet of accumulated peat, and the other was to attend the sale of James Robertson MacIver's furniture as his financial troubles deepened.

There is an unfortunate Stornoway tradition – as the awkward history of the Harris Tweed industry attests – of empires raised by smart men finally run into the ground by inept and foolish heirs. But James Robertson MacIver was still held enough of a gentleman to be invited to the grand dinner flung at Lews Castle for Sir John MacNeil – even after the roup of his classy household effects. And it was a decade later that, pursued by a Glasgow merchant, all he had was finally sequestrated.

It was not just, as Grant points out, a humiliation for him. It was a calamity for the local economy; so entangled were the affairs of James Robertson MacIver with assorted little local businesses and so many were the assorted crofter-fishermen to whom, blundering along in his ill-tended fish-curing business, MacIver had advanced funds for nets and general gear. As factor, Munro's role in the unfolding horror was limited: he had only to evict MacIver from his fine lands at Gress (and Little Bernera, something of a MacIver family seat) and solemnly lodge a claim for outstanding rent, though the odds of recovering any money seemed slim. But, as the only local solicitors, Munro and Ross, Writers At Law, hoped for far fatter pickings. And they were inevitably engaged by the 'trustee' in distant Glasgow, a William Copland – on behalf of Robert Coltart, the avenging creditor – to hunt down anyone on Lewis who had owed James Robertson MacIver money.

Through 1861, and with undoubted relish, Munro and Ross lodged no fewer than 43 civil cases at Stornoway Sheriff Court, and in 42 of them either Donald Munro or William Ross appeared personally for the pursuer. Most of them were for the recovery of debt; at least eight were in direct connection with the MacIver bankruptcy. And the most ruthless and roughly handled fell on a single fishing crew in one Lewis village.

On 17 September 1861, with his assistant in tow, John Henderson – Sheriff Officer at Stornoway – headed out for the township of Back. He had all the necessary papers, and it was his mission to seize the property of the crew of the

Dove, a sturdy open fishing-boat, which (with its tackle) was to be sold at the decree of William Ross. The craft – conveniently beached nearby – was to be auctioned on the spot; the nets and other valuables, however, had to be collected from assorted homes, a signal complication. It is little surprise that when Henderson reached Back, and as he began in all his importance to read aloud the legal warrant, an unhappy and very angry crowd quickly formed. He was – he would claim – threatened with violence, even when he had 'explained the consequences for anyone who obstructed him in the execution of his duty'. But the implacable villagers took a hold of his horse and cart, turned them round and drove them 'a considerable distance' back along the road to Stornoway, and no doubt said many loud and colourful things. We might be a little cynical about Henderson's later claim that he and his henchman were besides assailed 'by threats of the most violent kind, repeatedly threatening to take my life, and throwing turf and stones with which I and my assistant were repeatedly struck'.

But help was at hand, for William Ross now appeared, 'in his capacity as Judge of the Roup,' as Grant sarcastically explains. 'Or was it as a solicitor representing the Trustee in James Robertson MacIver's sequestration? Or was it as Joint Procurator Fiscal concerned with the maintenance of law and order? Or was it as legal agent for the Lewis Estate, which was also a creditor in MacIver's sequestration, and of which all the debtors were tenants-at-will, with no security whatever? The crowd did not wait to enquire which of his many hats the [*Joint*] Procurator Fiscal was wearing. They turned and ran.'

The sheriff officer and his accompanying muscle now deemed it prudent to recover their courage, no doubt bolstered by pointed and appropriate remarks from William Ross. They turned as one and trundled again into Back, where Henderson (evidently not a Gaelic speaker) intoned the warrant once more, and Ross – looking coldly about him – repeated the terms darkly, loudly, in the language of Eden. They then made straight for the sturdy thatched home of George Morrison, skipper of the *Dove*, and (with Roderick Campbell, a Stornoway blacksmith, as witness) John Henderson strode into its dusky interior for a bit of poinding. But, while removing the articles he sought, 'we were jostled and buffeted with turf and manure by men who were concealed in corners . . . and by Morrison's wife throwing water about us until our clothes were entirely covered by filth.'

At the next house, that of a Donald MacIver, no resistance was offered; Henderson got what he wanted. At the home he raided next, though, there was – by the sheriff officer's own account – a very noisy, violent reception, with men 'concealed in all corners' in a cottage whose mean windows had been deliberately blacked out, belabouring him from all sides. Henderson thought better, after emerging from this buffeting, of entering still another black-house, full of men, some of whom had stones or peats in their hands, evidently bent on using violence. I considered it dangerous to proceed further. I ordered the cart to proceed to the place of sale with such effects as had been collected, when some hundreds of the population, chiefly grown men, followed the party, yelling and hooting, and throwing peats and stones. Two or three came over and endeavoured to push me into a pool of water on the roadside, and one of them took off my cap and threw it into the water. About the same time I got a severe hit with a stone on the left wrist, and another on the right shoulder, both of which have caused me a considerable amount of pain. They then followed the cart and, on overtaking it, took out the lynch pin which caused the wheels to come off and upset the contents. I then declared myself deforced and protested that the said Deforcers had incurred the penalties of the law provided and accustomed in such cases.

It is unlikely, had John Henderson come under a shower of missiles as dangerous as he suggests, that he would have expressed himself in terms quite so correct, elegant and Latinate. Certainly he was deforced, though – as Grant points out – had he indeed been subjected to a hail of rock from hundreds of furious Lewismen – he 'would have been martyred, just as surely as St Stephen. Whatever stone-throwing there was must have been sporadic and the work of youngsters.'

It seems that, at this juncture, the assorted officials thought better of the entire enterprise – at least for the afternoon – and skedaddled back to Stornoway, no doubt to the jeering joy of the people of Back. But still the farce was not abandoned. William Ross simply returned to court and obtained authority to appoint another day for the sale. It was solemnly advertised – in strict letter of the law – by posters nailed to the door of the parish church. As this was in Stornoway itself, and as no one in Back attended Established sermon anyway, he had the sense to tack another on the door of the local village school; and poor Henderson the sheriff officer was sent round the township again to deliver direct notice to every last fishermen. This time there was no crowd, no shouting, no violence of any sort. He found only locked doors, and locked they remained despite imperious knocking. All Henderson could do was roll up his missives, and wedge them into such cracks and lockholes as he could find.

The *Dove*, her nets and her gear were duly 'exposed for sale' at the appointed day on the sand and shingle of Back. Ross was there – presumably as judge of the roup, though one could never be quite sure with him – and an auctioneer, and an accountant, and Henderson the sheriff officer. But nobody else turned up. There was not a single customer, and soon everything had painfully to be carted away, at still more trouble and expense for which the distant trustee was no doubt shortly billed by Munro and Ross. 'Even if they did eventually find a buyer,' Grant points out, 'no one would have been a penny the richer, except William Ross and the officials he had employed. The value of the poinded goods was set at £41 15/ . . . Even if they had fetched that sum, there would have been nothing left for the creditors of James Robertson MacIver, once the legal expenses had been met.'

The affair was still more discreditable as – having a sensible grasp of the situation – the fishermen of Back were quite willing to meet the debt, granted time and fair warning. What they would not (and could not) tolerate was a high-handed bid to seize boat and tackle and in an instant halt their trade and prevent them fishing, earning and feeding their families. When William Ross raised a much more straightforward court action against them, they were soon able to pay him £19 in hard cash. The whole melodrama had been engineered not to recover what was due to the hapless, unwitting trustee, but to maximise billable expenses for Ross's own business. Now, though, he could pass all the Back documentation to Donald Munro himself – for the full wrath of the criminal law.

Five men – four barely 20 – at Back were shortly charged with 'resisting, obstructing and deforcing' a sheriff officer in the execution of his duty and, as Grant grimly puts it, 'appeared before a jury in an elaborate show trial for which no fewer than forty witnesses were called.' The fishermen had, of course, no solicitor and, as we must often if tediously notice, for most of this period no other agent was available anyway. They were represented in court by their minister, the Reverend Donald MacMaster of Back Free Church, a tough and able man from Lochaber who did his best. Two of the men were finally acquitted and three others were sentenced to a month in prison – a month, of course, when they could not fish, work or support their households, though as they had already lost their boat and their tackle their vindictive confinement made little difference on that score.

Grant adds much detail of a 'preliminary examination', conducted complacently by Sheriff Andrew Lothian MacDonald – in Gaelic – and observed with relish by Donald Munro, as witness, and a clutch of other officials. Each of the men was interrogated alone, they had no representation of any kind – Mr MacMaster was not allowed to attend – and, even by the standard of the time (far less our own) it was manifestly irregular and unjust. Some of the men were questioned not once, but twice, 'in the presence of a formidable array of officials, including the Factor, who held the fate of all their families in his hands, and who did not scruple at any time to use his power . . .' And, as Grant further points out, the record suggests very close and indeed 'leading' questioning; one of the accused is oddly quoted, 'I did not see him with his hand to his face as if he had been struck.' Such, however, was the rule of law on Lewis for much of the nineteenth century; the preposterous order of things under Matheson apart, the conduct of this episode does indicate how biddable Munro and Ross found Sheriff MacDonald.

Two of the nastiest exploits of Munro and Ross, however – purely as rapacious, billing-by-the-hour solicitors – were against close relatives of James Shaw Grant himself; naturally, he devotes a very large portion of his 1992 book, and in exhausting detail, to how Donald Munro and his other half pursued his Stornoway forebears 'through the Courts for over thirty years in a maze of trumped-up lawsuits which surpass the notorious case of Jarndyce v Jarndyce in Dickens's *Bleak House*. My granduncle, my great grandmother and my grandfather were successively bankrupted in the process. My grandaunt and my granduncle were imprisoned for debts they didn't owe. Their children had to buy back the family home at a public roup in Edinburgh, although it had been taken from their parents quite illegally. The sorest blow of all was the loss of their twin daughters, who perished as infants from neglect and malnutrition, because of the inhuman behaviour of those whose duty it was to protect the innocent and maintain the peace.'

That is perhaps the most horrific detail in a process so protracted, so determined, so avaricious and – ultimately – so pointless as to cast doubt on such a cant phrase as the 'banality of evil', and in which William Ross (who cleverly survived his kinsman and partner's disgrace, and died as a wealthy and powerful man) was no less culpable than the Chamberlain of the Lews.

James Shaw Grant's grandfather was George Stephen, a 'young man from Boddam', an Aberdeenshire village by Peterhead. Like many enterprising seamen, he ended up working with a characterful Stornoway sea-captain, John MacKenzie – as that skipper's mate on a Stornoway-owned brig, the *Freeland*. They survived assorted colourful adventures, from a Masonic ball in Tunis to attack and boarding by Barbary pirates, who only spared their ship, their cargo and their lives when the leader of the cut-throat crew recognised the Stornoway captain from that Freemason's bean-feast – being, it turned out, of the Craft himself. And, like many clever young 'coves from away an no empty' – incomers who are well off – Stephen in 1844 accompanied MacKenzie to Stornoway and fell rapidly in love with a local girl, Catherine Morrison – his captain's niece. In December 1846 they married.

They were a bonnie, popular pair. George Stephen, as a mutual relative described him many years later to Grant, was 'slightly built, exceedingly wiry and full of spirit. His hair and beard were jet black and through two piercing, laughing eyes there looked out at you a shrewd, practical man with a keen sense of humour and a kindly affectionate nature.' As for his wife, Catherine, she was a 'tall, handsome woman, of a quiet and gentle disposition, with a shrewd and intelligent mind, and somewhat reserved manner . . . It felt like a benediction to be in her presence, recognised as a relative and addressed in kind and affectionate words.'

George Stephen, of course, continued his career at sea – in an age when that entailed very long absences and protracted silences, and when a wife not possessed of good sense and keen emotional discipline could reduce herself to a lather of worry over the hazards of the deep. But the new Mrs Stephen was an eminently wise woman. She was also a kind one, loyal to those who were loyal to her and tied by blood or the bond of marriage; in this her husband was like-minded, and it was a small thing – their generosity, from relatively modest means, to Catherine's uncle Colin Morrison – that comprehensively destroyed their lives.

It remains the case on Lewis that enterprising men like to have more than one business going at once; and Colin Morrison was not just a fish-curer but a publican – an awkward combination, for prosecution of the herring trade forced him to tie up capital for long periods, whereas running a local boozer called for a fast turnover. Something upset his cash flow and a wine merchant in Glasgow began to pursue Morrison for payment. Catherine Stephen gave her uncle £11 – no mean sum in the 1850s – to sweeten the amassing creditors; when her husband George came back from sea, he in turn cheerfully lent the additional sum of £30. He had been in Australia – even leaving his ship for a time to join in the gold rush, to no evident fortune – but had come back with £200 handed him in Melbourne by his wife's brother, Angus, in December 1854. It was neither a loan nor a gift, but it was entrusted to George Stephen in warm, confident terms, for him to bank or otherwise use in the interests of the Morrison family.

He chose – as was quite proper – to invest it in a handsome house on the Stornoway seafront, No. 1 Newton, and the property was eventually (though too late) put in the name of his mother-in-law, Annabella. 'It was, in fact, as distinct from legal fiction, the joint home of Annabella Morrison, her daughter and son-in-law [*the Stephens*] and was open to any other member of the family who had need of it,' Grant records. It was, in all, the sort of typical, informal, affectionate arrangement that is still – even today – to a degree island practice; but so obvious an asset was, in times of trouble and vultures, all too ready to catch the eye of greedy solicitors. And the Stephens continued to help Annabella's son and Catherine's uncle, Colin Morrison, as best they could and ultimately to no avail: in October 1855, his many creditors had him declared a bankrupt and proceedings for sequestration began.

But no fees nor juicy profit were in prospect for Munro and Ross, save for a few niggardly sums to be earned on local commission: the liquor merchants William Weir & Company were the main creditor and a Glasgow accountant, David McCubbin, was appointed trustee on behalf of creditors down south. The Stornoway solicitors now plotted. To win serious pickings, they had to round up Colin Morrison's creditors in town and – if they could secure enough – they could outvote those on the mainland and have the distant, city trustee removed in favour of their own creature.

George Stephen – who had lent his wife's uncle that £30 – was foolish enough, for all Grant's plea that he had been 'persuaded, against his natural instincts', to fall in with this proposal. (He would always maintain that William Ross had summoned him to his office and swear an affidavit already prepared, with the assurance that he would incur no cost: Ross and Munro insisted in turn, through the Byzantine twists to come, that Stephen and other creditors had approached them to instruct them as their solicitors.) What is certain is that Stephen did submit a claim and sign a mandate 'authorising Ross to vote on his behalf at any meeting arising out of the bankruptcy', and in March 1856 a meeting of creditors in Glasgow was attended by the gruesome twosome's Edinburgh-based kinsman, William Ross Skinner, who fought to have McCubbin removed as trustee. There was robust discussion. Neither side agreed who had a majority of the signed-up creditors and therefore a majority of the valid votes. The chairman finally decided it was McCubbin. But the chairman (and the creditors down south) did not have a pet sheriff at their disposal.

At Stornoway Sheriff Court, weeks later, in May 1856, Andrew Lothian MacDonald ruled that McCubbin had indeed been removed by a lawful majority. A new trustee was appointed, on the motion of William Ross Skinner: one Donald Fowler. The record, Grant relates, describes him as 'an accountant in Stornoway'. George Stephen would later claim, as mounting woes engulfed him and his family, that Fowler was in fact an employee of William Ross. Ross indignantly (and in strict correctness) denied this: Donald Fowler was actually employed, he declared solemnly, as a 'clerk or accountant to the Chamberlain of the Lews whose counting house is in a separate part of the town from the office of Munro and Ross'. He did not draw to Sheriff MacDonald's attention that the chamberlain was Donald Munro; and that he was not only his first cousin but his partner as senior solicitor in Munro and Ross. MacDonald must himself have known; he did nothing.

McCubbin had not travelled to Stornoway for this hearing and, of course, there was no other local lawyer who could have attended on his behalf. He now appealed to the Court of Session against Sheriff MacDonald's ruling. But his opponents argued that McCubbin had simply lost by default, being absent, and not because MacDonald had made any judgement on the merits of his claim over that of Fowler. The Court of Session decided (by a majority) that McCubbin should indeed have gone to Stornoway, and dismissed all his appeals 'except that defended in the name of George Stephen', whose claim for £34 13s 4d was one of the largest.

It is difficult to relate the rest of the long, long business – unfolded in very great detail by James Shaw Grant – without slowly losing the will to live; but Munro and Ross now fought an ongoing process in the Court of Session for George Stephen, at his expense and without his authority: he was back at sea, sailing to Russia as mate of the *North Briton*. On his return to Stornoway, early in September 1856, Stephen was appalled to find a letter from William Ross not only telling the mariner he had fought a case in the Court of Session he had never heard of, but that he had lost, and that he owed costs of £49 to David McCubbin – and must pay it immediately. When Stephen angrily confronted Ross – reminding him of his assurance that he was not at risk of incurring any expenditure – the solicitor blandly denied such an undertaking had ever been given. (Nor did William Ross at this time break the news that, the sum claimed by McCubbin aside, Munro and Ross had already jotted up on their accounts the sum of £74 2s 10d George Stephen owed them as well, for their expert and unceasing legal endeavours on his behalf.)

For now, George Stephen knew nothing of that detail, and had little time to argue. He quite properly repudiated any claim for £49 against him from Donald McCubbin and, by the end of September he was away again, joining the *Eagle of Liverpool* as first mate on a voyage to China. It would be three years before he returned to Stornoway. Meanwhile, Munro and Ross steadily progressed Colin Morrison's bankruptcy, greatly to their own advantage – their fees finally ate up almost two-thirds of Morrison's available assets – and to the consequent loss of the creditors, who ended up with much poorer recompense in their clammy hands (3s 9d in the pound rather than the 10s in the pound which had first been offered McCubbin and which he had foolishly declined).

Colin Morrison, in January 1858, was at last discharged from bankruptcy and able to resume trading. Now the birds of prey started implacable pursuit of the couple who had tried to help him, which, in George Stephen's absence – his ship finally sailed from Liverpool in early November – could only be waged, for the time being, against his wife. First, McCubbin moved: a 'messenger-at-arms' – in the fantastic medieval attire of the period – assailed No. 1 Newton, announcing himself by arcane decree and conducting a 'most strict, diligent and minute' search of the house in front of the distraught Catherine Stephen and her mother. Whoever this messenger-at-arms was – it was certainly an employee of Munro and Ross – the word sent back to the distant McCubbin (which one or both of these judicial terrorists certainly sanctioned) was a despicable lie, that 'the debtor had absconded for his own personal safety, and his family and servants denied all knowledge of him.'

Then Munro and Ross – instructing their Edinburgh minion, William Ross Skinner – raised an action in the Court of Session against George Stephen, for their own (and quite improper) account, now fattened to £85 3s 11d, and deliberately suggested to the distant law-lords that their prey had 'conveyed away his property, drawn all his funds from the bank, and had left Stornoway "to evade the diligence of his creditors".' Donald Munro and William Ross knew perfectly well that Stephen had simply left in the course of honest duty as a seaman. The Court of Session did not and, in February 1857, granted them decree against Stephen for an only slightly reduced sum. They then mysteriously 'assigned' the claim to William Ross Skinner, to begin his own action for sequestration – probably in a feeble bid to distance themselves personally from Stornoway uproar, and perhaps for some mild financial advantage besides.

In June 1857 (as Stephen still innocently sailed the ocean) the Court of Session granted Skinner's application; in July, the Sheriff Substitute in Stornoway, Andrew Lothian MacDonald, 'confirmed William Ross as Trustee in the sequestration and transferred to him Stephen's whole "estates and effects heritable and moveable and real and personal wherever situated . . . for behoof of the creditors" in terms of the Bankruptcy (Scotland) Act 1856.' And, on 16 December 1858, Mrs Catherine Stephen was 'cited to appear before the Sheriff Substitute at Stornoway to be examined in her husband's sequestration.'

Donald Fowler, who had somehow now escaped Munro's hegemony and was trying to set himself up as a competing solicitor in town, now surfaced to represent Mrs Stephen and had taken care to gain a doctor's 'line' – and not just any doctor, but Dr Charles MacRae himself. Mrs Stephen was pregnant. 'Dear Sir,' wrote the sturdy physician, 'I have at your request visited Mrs Stephen who is obviously *enceinte* and, by her own statement, verging on her *accouchement*. In such a situation I am of opinion that any unusual mental excitement or physical exertion might prove hurtful to her.' Fowler quite reasonably expected that, on such unimpeachable authority, Mrs Stephen's interrogation would be postponed without date. But he had reckoned without either the cold malice of William Ross or the extraordinarily weak character of Andrew Lothian MacDonald – and the filthy minds of both.

For George Stephen had been away from Stornoway for over two years and it seems (though the precise record does not survive, save for a much later note of 'unfounded allegations') that William Ross bluntly asserted he was not the father of the child (in fact, Mrs Stephen was carrying twins) and that she had been guilty of adultery. This was without foundation: nothing we know of her character suggests that, her husband certainly never accused her of it, and the children had in fact been conceived in Liverpool, where the Stephens had been briefly reunited in March 1858, between his two China voyages. (It was then common practice, as Grant relates in understandably anxious detail, for Stornoway wives to travel there for a little time with their men, especially when the gap between voyages was too tight for easy travel, worthwhile respite on Lewis and subsequent return.)

So Sheriff MacDonald blandly rejected Dr MacRae's certificate and, two days later, Catherine Stephen was hauled into court – literally; she was too great with child to walk. A cart bore her from the house to the courtroom, and then her mother and the attending midwife carried her inside. This was a time, as would remain the case for almost a century to come, when women in advanced pregnancy simply did not appear in public; Mrs Stephen, quite apart from Ross's vile insinuations, was hysterical. Sheriff MacDonald, in all his pomposity, nevertheless tried to administer the oath, until the midwife spoke up in robust and pointed terms; the court record notably failed to record them. William Ross then dared to suggest the Court 'grant warrant to commit her to the prison of Stornoway until she is prepared to express her readiness to be examined in terms of the Statute founded on in the petition', but that was too much even for Sheriff MacDonald. At Fowler's request, he belatedly granted an adjournment. Mrs Stephen was borne laboriously home; ten days later, she was safely delivered of twin daughters, though only after a protracted and gruelling labour, the more so perhaps for her ongoing alarm.

There would be little respite for this terrified woman: three months later, at the behest of Munro and Ross, Catherine Stephen was once more inexorably hauled into Stornoway Sheriff Court, chaperoned by her mother, and sworn in. She was then subjected to a barrage of questions about her husband's financial affairs – of which she knew scarcely anything – till she grew incoherent and finally quite uncooperative. Again, Ross ruthlessly demanded imprisonment – this time to loosen her tongue – and this time Sheriff MacDonald granted it.

Catherine Stephen was confined in the cells from noon to eight o'clock in the evening, as her infants wailed unfed at home and her breasts ached; and then hauled back into court once deemed sufficiently composed. She was there interrogated, without respite, until almost eleven at night. She was finally allowed to go home in a state of near-collapse, and for several days afterwards was 'unable to leave her bed or to give suck to her infant children, the milk having left her'.

The babies had been in perfectly good health when their mother was compelled to these vicious proceedings. Five days after Catherine had been hauled to court, tiny Hectorina Mary Stephen succumbed to bronchitis; Grace Stephen, the following day, died in convulsions. Only one male relative – the infants' granduncle, Murdo Morrison – was around to make arrangements and register the deaths; all the younger men were at sea. Anywhere else in the country, the death of these children would – especially amidst general town outcry – have been investigated by the Crown, but in Scotland, it was a matter for the procurator fiscal, and in Stornoway the joint fiscals were, of course, Munro and Ross. But they had scarcely time to think of Catherine Stephen now, far less her dead babies: they had turned their full attentions to her mother.

George Stephen, shortly before leaving for Liverpool, had had the wit briefly to consult a Glasgow solicitor, grasping that the arrangements for the house on Newton Street should be regularised and that the lawyers in Stornoway could on no account be trusted. The law agent in the city would later write Catherine with some counsel on how to deal with another attempt at poinding (she had evidently been in touch with anxious detail of the November 1856 bid) and the Newton Street home was now put in her mother's name. William Ross, from 31 August 1857, had been relentlessly chasing the ageing Mrs Morrison 'for the reduction of her title' to the house, alleging there could be no lawful sale or transfer when George Stephen was already bankrupt and that the 'disposition' in her favour was but 'a gratuitous deed granted for the purpose of defeating the just rights of his lawful creditors'. Mrs Morrison robustly defended the action – asserting, which was no doubt the truth, that she had paid £200 for it – and might well have won, but for the absence of some crucial witness (probably her son Angus, who had first popped up with that £200 in Melbourne) which forced her to press for an adjournment on 28 March 1859, as a jury was about to be empanelled. Without the case even going to proof, huge expenses were awarded against her – £135 5s 10d, by the approval of the same Sheriff MacDonald – and Annabella Morrison, too, was now all but helpless before Munro and Ross, who could now 'gain control of all her assets, including the house, by pursuing her for a contrived debt, just as they were pursuing her son-in-law'.

The case was duly brought, defended hopelessly by Annabella and lost – all on 21 December 1859; and control of No. 1 Newton passed implacably to William Ross. Not content with that, three years later, in October 1862, he brought a second action – for the expenses in the first – and the morass of debt deepened still further as she fought to regain title to her home. Meanwhile, on 1 August 1859 – he had just arrived back in Stornoway after all his eastern sailing – George Stephen was arrested for debt, at the instance of David McCubbin and, as Grant describes, for

> want of a debtors' prison in Stornoway he was incarcerated in an ordinary cell, as a common criminal, and languished there for six months. He was, however, liberated, 'without being called on to pay any portion of the debt,' as soon as McCubbin realised that he had not authorised the litigation in the Court of Session out of which the claim had arisen. Skinner, in later proceedings, accused McCubbin of 'refusing the bankrupt any aliment for his support' while he was in prison. This must be one of the most hypocritical complaints ever penned by a Solicitor to the Supreme Court. There are numerous letters in the Stornoway Sheriff Court records from debtors in other cases, imprisoned at the instance of Munro and Ross, complaining that they were destitute and pleading for help which they did not get. And, as we shall see, Munro and Ross themselves treated Stephen, while he was McCubbin's prisoner, with a degree of malice and contempt which can only be described as evil.

Had it not been for the fury in town about the fate of the little Stephen twins, Munro and Ross would certainly have evicted their mother and grandmother from No. 1 Newton – a stately home, by the standards of the time, with two floors and slated roof and roughcast walls, in sharp contrast to its thatched, modest neighbours. But the lawyers dared not. They let out the front of the house (which had always been rented to others by the family) and the little curing station at the property's rear, and pocketed the proceeds. It would take the Morrisons a quarter of a century to regain No. 1 Newton – and at the last only by buying it back outright.

Meanwhile, the grotesque ordeal continued. Donald Fowler's attempt to build a competing lawyer's business in Stornoway failed; he retreated to Dingwall and went bankrupt in his own stead. The trustee appointed was William Ross Skinner, who was soon chasing Annabella Morrison and her son Colin, the hapless curer and publican, for yet another debt (£40 5s 6d, allegedly owed the state of Donald Fowler for legal services he had rendered them). The list of duties and disbursements on their behalf tallies to more than 75 items, and much of the demand was for travel costs supposedly incurred when Fowler had gone to Glasgow or Edinburgh to defend Annabella Morrison against William Ross's original action for reduction of title.

Both Annabella and Colin denied vehemently they had ever authorised Fowler to do any legal work on their behalf, or ever instructed him to go to the city, or that they had ever been sent an account by him for these phantom

services. In fact, Colin Morrison insisted Fowler actually owed him money –
for liquor run up on a tab at his public house. At most, it seems Annabella –
who could neither read nor write – had sought Donald Fowler's aid in sending
correspondence (at the time of Colin's own ordeal under debt) to his pursuing
wine merchant in Glasgow, Mr Taylor; but why had Fowler not billed her?
Perhaps, as Grant suggests, he had actually been Mr Taylor's hired agent in
Stornoway – and it is notable that Skinner never chased Catherine Stephen
herself for services Fowler had undoubtedly done her as a brief, floundering
Stornoway solicitor, for the simple reason that the Stephens had themselves
settled his bill without any difficulty.

'Whatever the reason,' Grant rightly points out, 'Mrs Morrison was now
being asked to pay her pursuers for the protection she had sought, unavailingly,
from their own harassment.' What is certain is that a decent and hardworking
family, meticulous as to their affairs (save perhaps for the faintly rackety Colin)
had been sucked into an entanglement of lawyers, determined to enrich
themselves by every conceivable stratagem and even if it accomplished the
ruin of innocent people. There is a word for illness occasioned inadvertently by
the endeavours of doctors and medicine, 'iatrogenic'; there should be one for
people whose substance is devoured by grasping solicitors in some parallel –
and unmitigatedly wicked – moral universe. And this affair alone should put to
rest ridiculous, partisan tributes by his enduring co-religionists to Andrew
Lothian MacDonald, Sheriff Substitute for Lewis. He was an 'amiable and
accomplished gentleman', a witness would tell the later Napier Commission,
but who simply could not maintain the 'position and dignity' of his office
against the 'arbitrary power' of Donald Munro and William Ross.

Somehow, even from the misery of his prison cell, George Stephen mustered
the emotional energy to fight back, with the aid of yet another briefly toiling
Stornoway solicitor whose bid to build his own business did not long survive
the determined machinations of Munro and Ross. We do not even know his
first name: only that he was a Morrison. Yet, on George Stephen's behalf, he
mounted a counter-offensive with energy and determination, which drew
embarrassing attention to the multiplicity of legal hats worn by the Scrooge
and Marley of the Outer Hebrides and the doting witlessness of the present
sheriff substitute.

What Morrison wanted was a 'recall' of the sequestration of his client – the
lifting of his bankruptcy. That could only be done by application to the Court
of Session; to prepare it, Morrison needed sight of all the papers in the case,
held in the Sederunt Book of Stornoway Sheriff Court. Munro and Ross flung
up every obstacle they could in the young pup's path. First, Ross declared
he could not see it, as in all probability he would 'have to take criminal

proceedings' against George Stephen. Then, when Morrison craftily asked for copies instead – if access to the original was out of the question – there was but another blank refusal. Morrison then raised an action in the Sheriff Court to gain access to the proceedings in the Sederunt Book. William Ross countered by declaring the action should not even be allowed to proceed until Stephen had lodged a 'bond of caution' – money to cover all legal expenses incurred, should he lose the case and his opponents then find themselves out of pocket. As William Ross had no doubt calculated, to this Sheriff MacDonald lazily assented.

But Morrison promptly appealed, and the sheriff principal overruled Andrew Lothian MacDonald. There was no rule, said Sheriff Cook flatly, requiring a bankrupt to find 'caution' for expenses. So at last the case could proceed, and Morrison rather enjoyed himself in his 'Condescendence', or submission, observing that 'Mr Donald Munro, Chamberlain of the Lews, acted as agent in the Sequestration, his partner, the Respondent (William Ross) as trustee, and James Milwain Wither (an employee of Munro) as "Commissioner", with the only known creditor being William Ross Skinner, "as assignee of Munro and Ross".'

But George Stephen and his solicitor were up against men who had long forgotten how to blush. And, besides, they were at the mercy of Sheriff Substitute MacDonald, who finally ruled on 23 September that they were indeed entitled to copies of the Sederunt Book – but found both sides liable for their respective expenses. So both immediately appealed (again) to the sheriff principal: Munro and Ross, naturally, against the judgement; and Morrison, on behalf of Stephen, against considerable costs. The case presented by this obscure personality is as trenchant as it is right:

> Throughout the whole course of the proceedings it will also become evident to your Lordship that every opposition which an action could admit of, both dilatory and on the merits, was given by the Respondent [*William Ross*] to the claim now properly recognised by his Lordship the Sheriff Substitute . . .
>
> The Petitioner, when he left this country and went abroad, in the exercise of his lawful calling, did so under the conviction that he owed no one a debt of any description. He had all his lifetime earned as much as served, with honesty and independence, to support him and his family, in their own frugal and humble walk in life; and he was due no debt whatever. But, on his return home, this dream of independence and security was to him, but too surely and speedily, dispelled.
>
> He found that in his absence, without his knowledge, most certainly without his consent, and entirely against his desires, he had been involved in

a *mare magnum* of litigation. Large accounts of law expenses had been incurred or fabricated against him; he was rendered a Notour Bankrupt; his estates had been sequestrated; his family and relatives had been oppressed and persecuted, in a manner and by proceedings more akin to those which might be supposed to take place in a Despotic country and at the hands of irresponsible agents than in this free and enlightened Kingdom, and under its just and benign laws, and ultimately he was himself immured within the walls of a criminal cell, though only a civil debtor, where he has since been kept in close confinement, and from the depths of which this *limited demand* to your Lordship was made . . .

William Ross's response runs to 40 immaculately handwritten foolscap pages, launching with black reflections on 'reckless bankrupts with unscrupulous agents' and asserting that the language used by Morrison was a 'libel on the just and benign laws of this free and enlightened Kingdom'. Why should the commissioner in a bankrupt case (the obscure James Milwain Wither, a wage slave of Donald Munro) be put to all the expense of copying out long papers at the behest of a bankrupt who had avowed he had not a penny to his name? And why should he, William Ross, be expected to hang about in the prisoner's cell with the Sederunt Book while copies were being made?

The arrogance – and the sense of entire invulnerability – that would finally destroy Donald Munro and his evil empire are already apparent here in 1859, 15 years earlier. Who were the creditors and agents and commissioners in this case, demanded Morrison? Why, only Ross himself, and his Edinburgh agent, and his clerk. 'The Petitioner has been the Alpha and the Omega of the whole of the proceedings.'

Sheriff Principal Cook, it seems, in large part agreed. On 25 October, while upholding Sheriff MacDonald's belated mind that George Stephen should have access to all documents in his own sequestration, he dismissed that sheriff's inexplicable view on expenses. Were Ross's position to be upheld by the court, Sheriff Cook tartly commented, George Stephen would have been reduced 'to the position of an outlaw'.

Four Court of Session judges finally heard George Stephen's appeal, after considering – and dismissing – almost the final bid of his pursuers to deny him, when William Ross Skinner (on orders from Stornoway, of course) tried to persuade the Court to rule that Stephen was obliged to 'find caution'. For one, as the Lord Ordinary – Lord MacKenzie – properly pointed out, an undischarged bankrupt was in no position to do so; for another, it would be but to grant Skinner a decree by default, winning all the expenses he wanted while escaping any investigation into the merits of the whole claim in the first place;

itself only granted Stephen had been away at sea and unable to respond. Besides, the trustee in the bankruptcy, William Ross, had an obvious personal interest in the outcome, 'adverse' to those of the bankrupt. The four judges at last ruled in December 1863, and unanimously found in George Stephen's favour. Mr Stephen had never owed the legal expenses for which he had been so hounded. But Scots law was, in the High Victorian years, still a bleak thing; and Stornoway was a long way away. George Stephen remained an undischarged bankrupt; and No. 1 Newton was still in the hands of his vindictive enemies.

He and his mother-in-law three years later brought actions of their own in the Court of Session, against Munro, Ross and Skinner, and on the grounds – as the suit laid for George Stephen put it – of their 'unjust, nimious, oppressive, illegal and malicious and unwarrantable acts'. But their forlorn endeavours in law did not get far. There was – as one might have guessed – no messenger-at-arms in Stornoway to serve summons on the principal defenders, and the old and frail Mrs Morrison began an involved process in Edinburgh to gain permission to have the summonses served instead by the local sheriff officer. Her health broke first. She died in 1868, aged 75. George Stephen, who could not long entertain any legal action – he had to return to sea to support his family – died at his business, off Africa's Gold Coast, worn out by repeated bouts of malaria. He was only 49, and his remains were laid to rest with minimal ceremony in the ocean. His wife, Catherine, passed away three years after that, also only 49; it is said that she died of a broken heart, but their lives had been broken irretrievably long before.

No. 1 Newton ended up in the possession of William Ross Skinner, after long, involved and vicious legal games, being finally wrested from what remained of the Morrison family title in 1880 and declared 'irredeemable'.

But there was a curious, rather gratifying providence. On 1 October 1881, Skinner used the property as security for a personal debt of £150, borrowing another £100 against the same asset a month later. In November 1883, Skinner died – leaving both sums unpaid – and in due course his creditors (lawyers, of course, trustees of the estate of the late James Parris) raised an action against both Skinner's heirs and the current, mixed bunch of tenants in the property. The action was not defended and 'decree' was given to these trustees, who promptly put the ill-starred Stornoway house up for sale. After three un-successful attempts, it was finally sold at a public roup in October 1884, for £295, along with the two bonds Skinner had signed when taking on those debts, and which were worthless. The new owner, with some emotion to his eyes, was Roderick Morrison Stephen, younger son of George and Catherine.

9

Port: The plot to steal Stornoway harbour; and how it failed . . .

It was a moist, faintly sticky day in August 1864 and, rather to their surprise, two senior manservants had been summoned by Sir James Matheson: William Edward Martin, his grave and stately butler; and Thomas MacKay, whom the baronet retained grandly as his personal piper.

If they had been alarmed by so unexpected a call to the Presence, it soon emereged that Sir James wished them only to witness his signature to a document. They knew what it was, and what it meant. They also sensed, in his chill if elegant manner, that their 68-year-old employer was in far from a sunny mood.

They stood deferentially behind him, as the clerk from the chamberlain's office – or was it from that of Munro and Ross? – fussed with the papers. And they watched from under suitably downcast brows as Sir James Matheson fumbled with spectacles, dipped a nib, signed this page, and that, and then – as instructed – followed him to the desk, to sign themselves.

The old man straightened; moved to the windows. He looked down over his ha-ha and his elegantly planted 'prospect' to the town of Stornoway over the harbour, with its sand and gravel strands, its minimal quays, the banked brigs and schooners for the most part high and dry on the beaches, their bowsprits jutting across the nearest town streets. There were many men working, here and there; little boats under way by the power of oars. On a mound of rock stood one ruinous 12-foot column – or angle – of old stone, all that now remained of the ancient Stornoway Castle, as built by the Nicolsons, held long and at defiance by the MacLeods, and finally knocked to uselessness by the cannons of Cromwell.

Sir James Matheson had amassed untold fortune, taken on a vast Chinese empire, intrigued and lobbied, engineered war and turned the fate of governments.

He breathed a little heavily.

He had had just been comprehensively bested by a bunch of Highland curers, traders, sailors and shopkeepers.

And he did not like it.

Stornoway, as James Shaw Grant wrote many years ago, is at once the most Gaelic town in the kingdom and the most anglicised town in the Hebrides. But its glory is the magnificent natural harbour from which – dating back at least to the last century of the first millennium – the Vikings bestowed its name. *Stjorna*, in Old Norse, is a steering place or anchorage; *vagr* is a bay. And at the time of wholesale Viking conquest, along the seaboard of north-western Europe and north to the Faeroes and Iceland, throughout Orkney and Shetland, the Hebrides and Highland coasts and down to Ireland and Man and indeed even as far – tentatively, but in determination – as the remote northern capes of the American continent, this *Stjornovagr* was a strategically important base, as Catherine Mackay details:

> The bay at Stornoway provided all the essential elements for land-based winter quarters required by the Viking settlers. Sheltered by the embracing arms of Arnish and Holm, with deep water and accessible at all states of the tide, the bay was like any Norse fjord. A flat sand bar at what is now the Point Street peninsula not only protected an inner harbour but also gave ideal conditions to beach and careen the longships for repair. The water-courses at the Creed and Bayhead gave ample supply of fresh water and flat land at Inaclete and Bayhead provided for cultivation and camp building to provision and shelter colonists and settlers. Thus, more than one thousand years ago, Stornoway evolved as an important base and staging post in the sea-borne Viking empire.

The port was important enough to make a skerry just off the promontory of what is now Point Street the obvious place for some sort of fort or fastness, but there was no thought of developing the harbour itself, or anything that could be dignified as a fishing industry, until that greedy twinkle first lit in the eye of King James VI. That was occasioned less by his instinct for enterprise than reports of Dutch fishermen who, from 1594, started to visit Stornoway, harvested the seas, and happily imparted their secrets and skills. We forget that the people of the Netherlands were then the foremost mariners in Europe, that a surprising number of our nautical terms (yacht, helm, sloop, deck, dock, keel, skipper and so on) are of Dutch origin, and that one early map of the Western Isles – in 1654 – is by a Dutch cartographer, Joannis Blaeu. As Fred Silver explains, these knacky fishers were by mid seventeenth century pretty established:

Dutch herring fishermen with their well-organised herring busses had been working off the islands since 1628 and had made as much as £7,500 in three months selling their catch in Europe. The Dutch were resident in Stornoway with a factor and workforce of six based in the town. They had a storehouse and a 'pretty dwelling house'. The islanders were more accustomed to subsistence or chance harvest from the seas – for instance, around a hundred whales had been captured and killed in the lochs in 1629 and the meat preserved by smoking, as they did not have salt available . . .

Captain Dymes [*officer of the Cromwellian forces*] praises the excellence of Stornoway harbour for shipping in all weathers, and also the way it is easily defended. He points out that Stornoway's open location means that it gets the sun all day; both 'fire and water' are easily available, presumably from the peat cutting which he also describes and from local wells, and he adds it was 'alsoe the place which hath bene always most frequented both of the inhabitants and strangers. . . .

According to John Knox, of the British Fisheries Society, writing in 1786, several Dutch families settled in Stornoway in the previous century 'on account of the fisheries, but they were unfortunately driven away, during the war between England and Holland' which would have left accommodation vacant in the town.

The Dutch quit more than empty apartments; with their flight, improvements to the harbour simply ceased, and – even as Sir James glowered from his drawing room in 1864 – it was over a port which would seem pretty crude to us today, but had altered very little since the late seventeenth century. By 1800 Stornoway was much more important as a trading harbour than as a base for fishing. There were not the boats, the gear or really the skills for proper exploitation of the sea's wealth, especially amidst the Seaforth kelp obsession and the increasingly chaotic affairs of that great family. There were plenty of men in the lively little town with the foresight to see what the harbour could truly be and the vision to execute it. But they could not, from their own resources, raise the necessary capital. And there was besides the issue – as so often in Highland history, and to this day – of land ownership, granting enormous power of interference (or flat obstruction) by the proprietor.

As early as 1816, the businessmen of Stornoway started to raise funds for the building of a proper public pier, essential if goods and fish were properly to be landed, quickly and in great quantity. For the most part, their vessels had to be beached, or taken alongside basic harbour walls only as high water permitted. Quite a few townsfolk had, at their own expense and for their own

enterprises, built little jetties in front of their houses, but nothing on the
scale required. Those who could not, in 1816, spare money for the proposed
quay were glad to offer their labour, gratis, for any project. Mrs Stewart-
MacKenzie took benevolent interest, and personally gave 100 guineas – almost
a quarter of the likely cost. She also agreed to the establishment of a Quay
Committee to run the port and, in 1825, granted Stornoway a charter to allow
the election of a Town Council as a 'burgh of barony'. (There was actually no
need for this condescension; James VI, as had been evidently forgotten, had
made Stornoway a burgh of barony for the dark purposes of the Fife
Adventurers.)

So a basic public quay was built and the new, rather frail, little council took
charge of it. But the legal powers necessary for full promotion (and defence) of
Stornoway harbour interests, and the power to raise substantial loans, required
express legislation in Parliament; in this – despite determined approach from
the town in 1834 – Mrs Stewart-MacKenzie had little influence over her foolish
husband, whose obsession remained the fat profits he was convinced lay in
sheep-farming.

In any event, his subsequent appointment as Governor of Ceylon removed
the pair from the scene and, with deadening effect, meaningful control of Lewis
passed to the Edinburgh lawyers who henceforth managed the estate as
trustees. They glanced coldly at Mrs Stewart-MacKenzie's charter and declared it invalid: she had never the legal power to grant it. Thus the island
'lagged behind the rest of the country,' laments James Shaw Grant, 'not
because the people were lazy or ignorant, but because, in the tightly structured,
over-centralised British system, the inhabitants could do nothing to help
themselves, unless a remote, uncaring, ill-informed and sometimes hostile
Parliament first gave them leave.' The situation was besides compounded, as he
points out, by the self-preserving position of Scots lawyers then and since –
minimising the liability of their clients, distancing them from obligation,
entanglement or trouble.

The nascent Town Council gave up the ghost in 1838, and there remained
but a doughty local Committee – formed from those who had subscribed to the
appeal two decades earlier – which tried to run the port as best as it could,
though it had no authority in law and little meaningful power. Nevertheless the
townsfolk continued to save and to donate, to put money by, and to amass a
fund by which proper works might one day be built.

We have already noted the entire lack of interest by Sir James Matheson in
developing the Lewis fishery. He took the implacable view that any capital for
developing piers and so on should be raised by the industry itself. He did lay on
the first steamer connection to the mainland; he built a few little jetties; and –

on the determined cheap – he had the hulk of an old barque, the *Amity*, wedged by the shore (on what is now King Edward's Wharf) as a larger though most makeshift pier. He built besides, as we have seen, the grand but rapidly obsolete Patent Slip, fit only for the construction and launch of timber hulls in what was now, emphatically, an age of iron. Behind all this lay two principles still more deadly – his determined, authoritarian paternalism (whatever happened, he must control it), and an even more selfish, silly instinct, much bolstered by his languid wife: the desire to protect the immediate amenity of his home, his view, his grounds and his gardens from the clatter and smells of industry and the sight, close at hand, of busy working men.

The men of Stornoway had raised a substantial sum of money, and there was now talk of the realisation of significant harbour powers (perhaps by a private Bill in Parliament) – two things all but irresistible to the Chamberlain of the Lews, Donald Munro. Whatever his rampaging in the countryside, Munro had taken general care (not least for the better prosecution of his lawyers' business) to keep civil, if less than affectionate, relations with the important men of the town. He now approached them with what seemed an eminently sensible proposal. Why not enlist the services of Sir James – both as the local landlord, and their Member of Parliament? He would certainly press for a private Bill. And, as construction would be an expensive business, they might choose besides to make over the funds they had gathered as their own contribution to the cost.

The surviving members of the original Harbour Committee gladly agreed to this, and – as Munro urged – decided humbly to petition the proprietor. So a 'memorial' was drawn up, and signed by all the Committee members, and quite a few other Stornoway eminences – curers, feuars, merchants and shipowners. Townsfolk generally were pressed to sign, but for the most part they hung back – 'whether from apathy, or distrust of Donald Munro, does not appear,' writes Grant, but if 'it was the latter, they were quickly justified'. Neither Munro nor Sir James Matheson had any intention of begetting an autonomous, publicly accountable harbour body over which they had no control. Indeed, Sir James had no interest in seeing the construction of a proper, modern harbour at all: the earnest men of Stornoway, in all good faith, had been gulled into a trap. And, in this instance, Sir James Matheson cannot credibly be exonerated by any suggestion he was unaware of his factor's dealings. The noble baronet knew exactly what he wanted, he knew exactly what had been done and he now ruthlessly pursued his own private interest.

What Sir James really wanted was personal, outright ownership of the 'foreshore' – that part of the land between the marks of high and low tide.

As local laird, he already owned everything above the high-water mark (save for gardens and sites feued off and sold here and there) and the Crown owned all the ground, including the seabed itself, below it. It is unlikely there was more than a trace of greed in this scheme. Sir James was already fabulously rich. But there was certainly a desire to control, for many men – from curers to minor traders in deep waters – plied their business on this and that little pier jutting out onto tidal mud and sand. And, most of all (and one suspects Lady Matheson whined in his ear about it, time and time again) the bustle and infringement and the smells of all this activity impinged often on their Lews Castle idyll.

From time immemorial, for instance, Stornoway fishermen had used the foreshore on the Seaforth Lodge side of the bay to beach and repair or clean their craft, and to 'bark' their nets – a preservative process essential before the advent of man-made fibres. Great vats of hot 'cutch' (a sort of pungent tea brewed from a mix of oak-chips and 'catechu', or extract of acacia wood) were brewed over open fires on the beach, and the precious nets steeped in them, against rot. Those old enough to remember the scent of cutch, like Grant himself, insist that, rather like coal-tar soap or Dettol, it was 'distinctive and pervasive, but not unpleasant'. But it was an unwelcome reminder to the Mathesons that their manicured paradise was cheek-by-jowl with a working harbour. And all those busy fishermen (no doubt roughly and at times scantily dressed, and on occasion not backward either in exercise of ripe seamen's language) at the bottom of their garden undoubtedly gnawed at their pretensions. It was bad enough, besides, that the townsfolk made so much salt herring. What would happen when they thought of kippers?

So, having won the endorsement of Stornoway business by low deceit, and with a promise of all their painfully raised money, Sir James Matheson, MP, did precisely nothing. Sir James Matheson, laird of the Lews, by contrast moved immediately, drawing up a formal request (another 'Memorial') to the Lords Commissioners of the Treasury: could he buy the entire foreshore of Stornoway, to the harbour entrance and beyond even that? After all, the foreshore bounded 'his private pleasure ground and policies'. Yet it was occasionally 'taken possession of', he lamented, by fishermen for purposes 'offensive in themselves and attended, in some instances, with risk of injury' – at least to his prized plantations and shrubberies.

In fact – a point Sir James rather laboured – he was confident he already owned it, under the Royal Charter granted by James VI; he was nevertheless graciously minded to stump up cash and put the matter beyond doubt, lest there be an expensive legal action. Besides, Sir James oozed, the late proprietrix had made a grant of this and that chunk of foreshore to this and that Stornoway gentleman, who had then built piers or quays. He wanted graciously to confirm these bestowals, but how could he when it was not certain whether he owned the tidal ground or not? Nevertheless – between a lush of silky phrases and community-minded murmurs, as Catherine Mackay's account makes plain – Sir James was determined to get it cheap; and his 'petition to the Government . . .' complained that feuars were able

> to occupy or build upon the foreshore, each man according as it suits his fancy or as he may deem it conducive to his own interest, and to convert the foreshore thus unwarrantably occupied, to purposes which seriously inter-fere with the public thoroughfare and convenience.

He had no wish, Sir James said, to secure any personal benefit whatsoever and he felt that, as proprietor of the island and of the burgh, he was

> in a situation which fairly entitles him to expect a grant of the foreshores of the bay of Stornoway, from Arnish lighthouse on the west to Upper Holm on the east.

Sir James further submitted to the Lords Commissioners that, since the foreshores in question were incapable of being turned to any directly profitable or rent-yielding purposes, therefore the price ought to be an extremely moderate one.

Their Lordships handed the matter over to the Commissioners for Woods and Forests (now the Crown Estate) whose legal adviser Mr Horne WS, Edinburgh, asked Sir James to make an offer. Mr Horne felt that there was no need for a special survey and report since there was no pecuniary advantage to Sir James. He only wished to protect the lands against the encroachments of the sea or the acts of individuals. Mr Horne therefore recommended acceptance of his offer of £400.

Thus the foreshores of Stornoway Harbour passed into the complete control of the Matheson Estate. Sir James Matheson now had what he had asked for in his submission – the power to 'grant titles on such conditions as shall tend to the good of the general community and enable him to prevent erections that not only interfere with that but which are turned to uses at once offensive in their own nature and calculated to impair the healthiness of the town.

It was a lie, submitted in the cynical knowledge that this was still – emphatically – an age of deference, especially to the very rich if mildly titled; and that it was most unlikely anyone in the service of the Lords Commissioners would even think of making for Stornoway, in all its here-be-dragons distance from the capital, to ascertain the position for themselves.

Sir James was instead out, as Grant rightly puts it, to win 'absolute personal control over the destiny of the port, the town, and indeed the island'. The Mathesons did not give a hoot for the 'healthiness of the town'. They wanted nothing that would in the least intrude on their expensively crafted Arcadia, or cause any grand visitors to start, sniff or wrinkle a blue-blooded nostril; long after Sir James was dead, Lady Matheson herself would prove wholly obstructive to the continued development of the port, delaying works vital to the local economy for a good many years. They were both children of their age and in the worst, high-handed strain of nouveau-riche arrogance, having few of the instincts of the old (and best) Highland gentry they so pitiably aped.

But Sir James and his lady and their malignant factor had forgotten two realities: as a politician, in the House of Commons, the laird could be readily embarrassed by deftly directed agitation; and they had no immediate, untrammelled and terrifying sanction over most Stornoway people. The bark of 'Cuir mi as an fhearan thu' would be of little avail once the townsfolk tumbled to their game. And Donald Munro, in his baleful excitement, had lost no time in posting his imperious missives, once the formal disposition from the Crown – dated 14 January 1863 and giving Sir James title to all he wanted – was in the proprietor's soft white hands.

On a day later in January 1863 rather many townsfolk – active men of drive, initiative and business; the odd capable woman – were aghast to tear open their post and find triumphant decree from Donald Munro, Chamberlain of the Lews. Most began, 'I think it proper to apprise you that Sir James Matheson cannot in future recognise your right to let your pier for curing or boat-building purposes, or to execute any right or ownership over the same . . .' Mrs MacKenzie of the Lewis Hotel was told, in her own epistle, that 'neither she nor her late husband had a vestige of right' to the jetty on South Beach adjoining their premises, which they had built at their own cost (with the full consent of the Stewart-MacKenzies) and had been accepted without demur by the Mathesons for nearly 20 years. It dawned on everyone that Sir James was now simply requisitioning – seizing – that and every other construction in the harbour, to run as he saw fit, for his own convenience and to his own profit. It dawned on everyone that Sir James now had an entire stranglehold on the fortunes of Stornoway. It dawned on everyone that incomes they had enjoyed for years – and decades, in some cases – had been ruthlessly commandeered to the landlord. It dawned on everyone that they had been conned.

Considering the infamy, the response of the men and women who mattered in the town was one of remarkable restraint. A public meeting was fast agreed on, and duly held at the Masonic Hall – the new building, in use to this day, on Kenneth Street – on 11 February. It was chaired by Kenneth Smith, a prominent businessman whom everyone called 'California', as he had spent some years in America. Though furious, the townsfolk were shrewd and clever. They deliberately took up ground of mildness and sweet reason, determined to leave Sir James as much room as possible to retreat without losing face. First, they elected a Provisional Committee, of eight people – and took care to include Donald Munro – to 'confer with Sir James Matheson, in order to ensure his powerful co-operation in promoting the commercial prosperity' of their burgh and besides regulate the 'sanitary condition of the town'. They would meet Sir James the following day. They also passed a motion welcoming any endeavour to gain additional quayage in the harbour, while insisting any such improvements be executed 'under public management'. And they passed a third, faintly oozing declaration, averring 'the greatest solicitude for meeting the views of Sir James Matheson, in everything that tends to the prosperity of this community'.

Considering the provocation, this was studied civility. Unfortunately, they were dealing with a laird who saw deference as but his most basic due and could be relied on to mistake gentleness for weakness. The meeting at the castle was an entire failure. They found Sir James cold, lofty, uncomprehending, unbudging; not genial, but distinctly grand, cross at such civic impudence. He lectured them, in some pomposity, quoting screeds from the opinion of an Edinburgh advocate he had engaged. And they were then dismissed.

The Committee was promptly convened again, on the 17th, and – darkly noting that Sir James 'did not enter into the spirit of the resolutions' – resolved that another public meeting be held. At this point, a messenger panted in, with a letter from the laird. It was in parts conciliatory, offering to consult with their body – if Captain Donald MacKenzie (whom Sir James evidently thought his reliable servant) were besides added to it, and if it were agreed that any future members all be feuars. Then the Matheson fangs were bared. All the money raised over the years, by the original Quay Committee, must be 'at once transferred to my name, as trustee and superior of the burgh, and, as such, the only legally-constituted authority vested with any right of property in the quay, for the public benefit, as was explained to you by the opinion of eminent counsel read at our meeting'.

He would use the funds, boomed Sir James – and letting slip his true priorities, the beauteous air of his gardens – to fill up a hole near the Lewis Hotel, which was 'notoriously a great nuisance, polluting the atmosphere, during and after the herring season, especially in warm weather'. (He betrayed his own ignorance. There is to this day such little tidal exchange in the Inner

Harbour that the slack water by the juncture of Cromwell Street and North Beach is still known locally as 'Lazy Corner', where scum and flotsam linger.) Of course, he pompously concluded, 'any proceedings adopted by me will be for the public good, in consultation with the Committee'. Whose role, it was evident, would be no more significant than that of a compliant wife. Besides – and here there was a note of martyrdom – it was to be hoped their welcome 'assurance' would follow in 'better results than the plans I propounded as far back as 1846 for the improvement of the town and the comfort of its inhabitants – at my own cost but in which nothing was done owing to their supineness and indifference'.

It was arrogant. It was outrageous. It was candid insult. And it was a huge mistake. As if this grand harangue were not enough, there was another epistle enclosed too – from Donald Munro, who was not present. It graciously authorised the Committee to read Sir James's communication aloud at the proposed public meeting – but any objections they had must first be discussed with him, the chamberlain.

Now the gloves were off.

In markedly chillier language, the Committee replied at once. They had been established, they reminded the proprietor, to co-operate with him. They were not a mere committee of consultation. And they were in no position to foresee what objections might be raised by those who chose to attend the public meeting. That was now arranged for a few days' time – 20 February – while the landlord's rant was made generally known throughout town.

The mind of Stornoway was at once evident when the rally convened. The Committee was unanimously endorsed by those and another 11 men were elected to it. Malcolm MacKenzie, another local entrepreneur, dismissed Sir James's delusions as 'arbitrary and likely to operate against the welfare of the community'. On the morrow, their chairman – Kenneth Smith, 'California' – sent a letter to the castle, making sure the laird grasped the seriousness of the alarm among businessmen of the town at the Matheson position. He had just stripped the long-standing Committee of Management of rights they had exercised, unhindered, for 40 years. Their 1860 offer to transfer garnered funds for wholesale harbour improvements to Sir James had been expressly on the basis that he would work to secure an Act of Parliament, in full liaison with them. Now, said MacKenzie darkly, with the 'peculiar circumstances' forced upon them, 'the Committee cannot consent to have the public money trans-ferred to Sir James's name, nor avail themselves of the pleasure of acting as a Committee of Consultation in giving effect to the claims put forward by Sir James.' If he now helped them – even at this stage – to gain that Act they needed, the town was more than happy to spare him the trouble and expense of all future harbour improvements. At least, warned Smith – with the faintest menace – the proprietor should 'obviate agitation', and not act on the views he had expressed.

The Committee then calmly made their usual, annual arrangements to organise an auction for the subcontracted job – with a cut of the funds – of collecting harbour dues; and thought deliberately (and aloud) about how they might gather 'the written assent of the inhabitants' for their plans to better the port. The message from both moves was plain: we are in charge. Sir James Matheson would have been wise to back off. Instead, he and his factor determined to push their luck.

The roup of the dues was on 23 February, and the winning bid was from a locally based curer, Andrew Gibson. Before night had fallen, a letter from Donald Munro was thrust in his hands. It was blunt, imperious and rude. Sir James quite disowned the 'pretended sale' as 'illegal and incompetent'. If Gibson dared either to let out quays or gather dues, he would sue.

This was a stupid ploy: to prevent Gibson gathering dues was one thing, but to deny facilities for curing herring all but demolished Stornoway's economy at a stroke. It seems, incredibly, Munro had not grasped this; when it dawned on him, the chamberlain tried to make arrangements (in the name of Sir James) for letting the piers and stretches of quayside himself. The Committee wrote at once in firm protest to Sir James. His immediate response was legal action.

Within days (and no doubt Munro, Ross and Skinner were all joyously involved) the laird of the Lews had brought a Court of Session action against 63 separate men of substance in town – all connected with the Committee and most, if not all, hitherto the beneficiaries of assorted waterfront property. By force of law, he would wrest from them all the money raised through several decades – even from years long before he had bought the Isle of Lewis – and besides make them accept that he, Sir James Matheson, had sole rights over the harbour. He alone – and exclusively – had the right to enlarge the quayage, without interference, and to dues so far collected. Even more absurdly, he raised a separate case against all those who had built piers: they had, he asserted, never a right to do so (blithely ignoring the fact that in not a few instances they had been expressly obliged to erect a jetty in the charter of their feu).

A glance at the names affords ample evidence of a proprietor increasingly bereft of common sense or grasp of reality. A truly smart man would have settled on just one test-case – a popular target, ideally the most disliked businessman in town. Sir James instead had summonses served on practically everyone of importance. As Grant delineates, the list not only numbered shipowners and curers, but 'also includes the two local doctors, a bank accountant, a retired naval captain, the Inspector of Poor, the light-house keeper, and Donald Munro's own cousin and partner, William Ross'. That last is interesting: it could have been sly tactics or, more probably, an indication that, while all too happy to set to his master's bidding, in this regard Donald Munro had not that much influence over Matheson desires and determination in the first place. It is difficult, in fact, not to see one overweening force above all on Sir James in this whole ridiculous episode – his insistent, bigoted and socially ambitious wife. And, in the light of this conduct alone, it is extraordinary how kind local history has been to the Mathesons.

The laird was in any event naive to think that, at this late stage, the incensed citizenry of the town would bend the knee. The Committee immediately hired a suitably qualified Edinburgh solicitor – a Writer to the Signet – but, determined as they were (and even before he gave his mind) they knew they faced long odds. By will and temperament and greedy experience, Sir James Matheson and his lady lived as Eastern potentates; the Matheson pockets were all but bottomless; he had a proven zeal for the law – had not the Harris boundary row ground on for years? – and, having bought the foreshore from the Crown, it seemed probable the Court of Session would find in the proprietor's favour. Their own resources were thin and many named as defenders would not, or could not, contribute to the legal costs. (Everyone knew what had happened to George Stephen and his family.)

Lewis people, though – and, perhaps especially, merchants maritime – are both cunning and tough. With no easy way out by the courts, the Committee resorted instead to politics. They were not all – by the involved and unjust property-qualification that then determined it – electors; it would be a lifetime, in fact, before women (and several women were defenders) won the vote. But they were all Sir James's constituents. If they could not beat him, they could acutely embarrass him. It was time to change tactics. They called still another public meeting, expressly seeking the town's mandate to take the whole question to the House of Commons.

It was a packed house and the tone of the Committee was no longer nice and pleasant; as Kenneth Smith's speech from the chair makes plain, a tone of righteous anger now gripped Stornoway. These proceedings of Sir James

> are so much at variance with common justice, and so much opposed to all late legislation upon harbours, the subject demands the attention of Parliament. It is not usual, I believe, to alienate from the Crown the shore of public harbours, in favour of private individuals. The grant does

not in any way meet the requirements of this harbour; it does not provide for any legitimate improvement, and it is proper that we should know the pretext on which the grant was applied for, and the object for which it was given.

For all the proprietor's pained boasting of everything he had done for the community, none of the Matheson promises had been kept. Instead, the trade of the port had been blocked; and the Estate had even tried to shut the fisheries.

He threatens parties here for making use of private piers, built at their own expense, on their own property. He tells them they have no right to use them. That he is to take them for his own private use – for the public benefit. Are we tamely to allow ourselves to be deprived of our public rights? Those who went before us kept their ground nobly. Posterity would brand us with infamy, if we surrendered ours . . .

As if this were not bad enough, the next speech was still more calamitous for the laird – for it came from Matheson's own nominee to the Committee, Captain Donald MacKenzie, and the tone was anything but supportive. Mackenzie was furious. At great trouble and expense, he had built a pier on his own South Beach property, but Sir James had leant on him and wheedled: could MacKenzie not give up the jetty, so that the street be made an elegant public promenade? In all good faith, Captain Donald had complied – and what had Sir James done then but promptly built a pier of his own beside it, and let it out for curing herring and to his own profit? It was, stormed Captain Donald MacKenzie, 'a piece of gross injustice'. Still another Stornoway eminence, Murdo MacKenzie – a leading merchant – savaged this 'hole-in-the-corner job with the Woods and Forests', mocked Sir James Matheson for 'superfine sophistry' and deplored him for 'legal spoliation' – a deft euphemism for stealing. These sentiments – and everything else said that night – were endorsed to a man by the crowded hall.

So a formal Petition to Parliament was drafted, demanding a public inquiry into just how Sir James Matheson had intrigued to buy the Stornoway foreshore from the Crown, and so readily accomplished it. Within a week, it bore 292 signatures – over half the men of Stornoway. 'About fifty,' notes James Shaw Grant, 'described themselves simply as feuars or householders, but sixteen were fishcurers, thirty were shipowners, master mariners or ship-masters, thirty-six were fishermen, thirteen coopers, thirteen ships' carpenters, two sail-makers and three ropemakers. Twenty-three merchants also signed, along with eighteen shop assistants, the banker, the Sheriff Clerk Depute, an architect, a druggist, an accountant, a cabinet-maker, a blacksmith, two porters, a pensioner and a tinsmith. Even Sir James's own gamekeeper signed. The shoe-makers were particularly active. Thirty-three put their names down to the petition. This is not surprising. Down even to my own boyhood, the shoe-makers' shops were the great academies for theological and political debate. In fact the tradition is not yet wholly dead . . .' It would indeed survive until the lamented closure of Smith's Shoe Shop in 2006, a hub to the end for the articulate men of town.

In a matter of weeks Sir James Matheson had united practically everyone of importance in Stornoway against him, and been quite outmanoeuvred by their firm, early show of patience and courtesy. Now, as a deputation travelled to London and secured the services of Sir James Fergusson – Conservative MP for Ayrshire and a rising star under Derby and Disraeli, whose contempt for Matheson was well known – the laird of Lewis was publicly humiliated, and the press beginning to take unnerving interest in his lordly goings-on on Lewis.

Yet, even now, Sir James could not quite face reality. First, beckoning Donald Munro, he resorted to black intimidation. The chamberlain somehow obtained a lithograph – a sort of proto-photocopy – of the petition, and hung it grimly on the wall of his Carn House office. Then, one by one, those who had signed were asked to call by. 'Is that your signature?' he would glower. If it were, they were then confronted with two choices. They could sign – on the spot, right now – a counter-petition Donald Munro just happened to have to hand, withdrawing their names and repudiating the town's cause. Or they could be awkward – in which case, the chamberlain declared, there would be no more jobs for them from the Lewis Estate, no more contracts, no more work. Despite this blatant – and for some all but bankrupting – threat, the signatories largely held firm, buoyed by the growing rumble of concern, support and moral outrage down south and in the newspapers.

Second, Matheson and his Edinburgh lawyers launched a wild, somewhat inept public-relations campaign, issuing a 12-page statement, which – as Grant details – rebutted 'all the charges made at the public meeting, and setting forth once more all his benefactions, including the building of an Industrial Seminary, a ship-building yard, and the only quay, north of Oban, which vessels could approach at all states of the tide'. He had even, they added – in a faint note of bathos – 'given an enclosed Bleaching Green for the use of the town'. And his old ally of the 1851 evictions, Sir John McNeill, was most pained on the Matheson behalf. 'It is remarkable that conduct so liberal should have failed to gain as its reward the gratitude of the population,' he thundered. 'The people of Lewis appear to have no feeling or obligation of thankfulness for the aid that has been extended to them by the proprietor but, on the contrary, regard the exaction of labour for wages as oppression. The best informed persons believed that there were able-bodied men in Lewis who would starve, and allow their families to starve, rather than earn their subsistence by ordinary labour.'

It was a squalid attempt both to bracket – the better to pander to prevailing Lowland prejudice – the commercial men of Stornoway with the 'peasantry' of rural Lewis, and still another hackneyed outing of that enduring smear: the feckless, ungrateful and lazy Highlander.

The same document from these frock-coated Edinburgh agents of the Lewis proprietor also advanced what was little more than a lie – that, during the famine of the 1840s, just after he had acquired the island, Matheson had granted free passage on the paddle-steamer *Mary Jane* to anyone who wanted to make for Glasgow and the south for employment. This may well have been true: what strains credulity is the claim that, in just seven months in 1847, nearly 2,300 Lewis people had availed themselves of it – more than an eighth of the entire Lewis population. And, even allowing for folk hopping aboard the ship from other West Highland ports as she puffed down the coast, 'there must have been a quite remarkable exodus,' James Shaw Grant observes sarcastically, 'in search of jobs, from the island where, according to the government's official adviser, heads of household would rather see their families starve than work for wages.'

Few of the specific claims of Matheson largesse could bear close scrutiny. The 'Female Industrial School' – on the corner of Keith Street and Scotland Street in Stornoway – had indeed been built, and opened by Lady Matheson in January 1848; it was a fine establishment, and over many years produced a succession of strong, clever and skilled Stornoway women: the disgraceful political games surrounding the decaying premises in 2010 discredit our present local authority. But it was not the first such school – Mrs Stewart-MacKenzie had opened similar facilities – and other bodies, not least the new Free Church, built schools on Lewis too. The Patent Slip, dated and unwieldy, was already faltering. As for the supposedly magnificent quay, that was but the rotting shell of the *Amity*, approached by rickety timbers and of such character there was a prominent notice to warn the public it was less than safe and could only be used at their own risk.

The Edinburgh declaration did not delineate, either, just how much of the Matheson bounty had actually been expended for his own pleasures – Lews Castle and the gardens and arboretum; or all the lodges and shooting-boxes for this and that sporting amusement, such as those at Grimersta, and the Italianate extravagance of Uig Lodge – still brooding over the sands of Ardroil

– and the cod-baronial charms of Morsgail Lodge, a favourite bolt-hole of Lady Matheson, completed in 1850 as her husband toiled to have his tenants shipped out to America in their hundreds (ideally at government expense). Indeed, close perusal of this 1863 document – and later information released by Matheson's heirs for the Napier Commission – does not support at all the near-universally accepted myth of a great Matheson cornucopia: a selfless laird who spent far more on Lewis, and for the good of his ungrateful tenantry, than he ever recovered.

He had spent £11,680 on school buildings and teacher's salaries – but £19,289 on just two of the sporting establishments, Morsgail Lodge and Uig Lodge. He had outlaid £33,000 on 'meal and seed for the crofters in the destitution years' – but practically all of that, then and later and even from succeeding crofting tenants, had been clawed back in rent, to say nothing of untold man-hours of unpaid labour in lieu. Six thousand pounds had gone on the Patent Slip – but a cool £33,000 on the inept and unsuccessful Lewis Chemical Works. Roads and bridges (and here Matheson's achievement is undoubted; there had been only 44 miles of road on the whole island at his arrival, and over 200 by his death) had cost the opium baron £254,593 – but he had outlaid £100,495 on the 'Castle building and offices', including all that planting and landscaping. Besides, as we saw, whenever a road was built to or through a crofting township, the rents there were promptly raised. In the raw figures, the £99,720 spent on 'building houses and reclaiming land' looked an impressive charity indeed – but Donald MacDonald is scathing:

This expenditure, however, was not all loss, nor was much of it spent directly for the benefit of crofters. Of the £99,720 spent on the building of houses and land reclamation, nothing was spent on the housing of crofters, as was all too evident, and up to 1853, only £8,471 10/ was spent on their lands with a further £3,000 later on. All of this was eventually repaid. Education certainly benefitted from Sir James's generosity, and the expenditure on roads and bridges benefitted all sections of the community, even if they seemed to lead to manses, farms and shooting-lodges. . . . It was intended to have a road encircling the island, but this was never done. Even today, roadless gaps still exist from Mealista to Aline, Eishken to Lemreway, and from Skigersta to North Tolsta. Until 1923, South Lochs [*Park*] had only township roads and footpaths.

The £30,000 spent on meal and seed for the crofters was not all loss, as the cost was added to their rents and repaid, more or less in full. The Estate therefore had the benefit of their labour in return for the meal which was in fact supplied by the Highland Relief Committee.

The sum of £11,000 spent on emigration was partly offset by the increased rental received from the new farms which replaced the cleared townships of Reef, Carnish, Doune Carloway (later given to the Mangersta tenants), Dalmore, Melbost Borve, North Galson and North Tolsta (now New Tolsta.)

The fish-curing houses proved to be a very profitable investment. The rental for the storehouses in 1883 was £38, and that of the fish-curing stations £145. [*That was just the revenue for one year; they had cost Sir James only £1,000 to build.*] The Patent Slip more than paid for itself, but the experiment to extract paraffin from peat, and the Garrabost brickworks, were failures. In any case, the crofters' houses were built of stone and turf and not of brick, and at the time of the paraffin experiment fish-oil was used for lighting, so this loss should not be debited to the crofters . . .

Despite continued, indefatigable belief in the entire benevolence of Sir James Matheson, his Lewis purchase had proved a nice little earner, as James Shaw Grant argued convincingly in a *Stornoway Gazette* column around 1983 (and included in his fourth, 1985, anthology of these thoughtful pieces). It had been estimated

that Sir James Matheson spent over half a million pounds on his Lewis Estate, including the purchase price, a vast sum of money at that time, and all the product of his Chinese trade.

But it was not a gift to the people of Lewis. Not by any means. A writer in the *Celtic Magazine* of 1882, while praising Sir James Matheson's liberality, calculated that if one excludes the Castle and the Grounds, which were in his personal occupation, the Lewis rents gave him a return of around 3¼ per cent on his capital outlay. Which, with the interest-rates prevailing at the time, was a pretty good return on an investment in the peat-bogs of Lewis.

About £12,000 of the total was spent on assisting 2,231 Lewismen and women to emigrate. The emigration was 'voluntary' in that it was not induced by a physical clearance, but by economic pressures, which were producing the same movement of population, at the same time, all over Europe.

Sir James, of course, could not be exclusively blamed for the emptying of much of Lewis – notably South Lochs, the quarter that suffered most from many decades of irresponsible landlordism, and suffers still. (The lack of that road from Eishken to Orinsay, and the failure ever to resettle Steimreway, despite a faltering attempt in the twentieth century, has been largely in the interests of a local proprietor, who continues to play dark games with the Park community.) But Roger Hutchinson's acrid summary of Lewis management generally should lay firmly to rest the Matheson legend:

> Traditional Gaelic attachment to the land meant that any form of private charter which removed it from the communal, clannish township and placed it into the assets column of an individual's accounts was regarded as being as illegitimate as common theft. Throughout the nineteenth century this simmering grievance was exacerbated by a good deal of actual common theft.
>
> Estate sheep farms were built and expanded upon what had previously been common grazing or arable land. Whole vast areas of moor and heath were enclosed and turned into game parks: playgrounds for the shooting of grouse and deer, where a common native of Lewis dared to set foot only in the very real danger of being captured or arraigned as a poacher of 'private' wildlife. Between 1818 and 1886 almost 50,000 acres of the peninsula of Park in south-eastern Lewis had been methodically fenced off, firstly for sheep-farming and latterly as a deer-run. Age-old villages were emptied; their names – Valamos, Ceann Chrionaig, Ceannmore – would henceforth be heard only in legend or in song, and their ruined walls would turn to ridges in the bracken. Many of the dispossessed emigrated to Canada or to Scotland. Those that stayed huddled together on tiny plots of land in the vestigial coastal communities: by 1881 an estimated 1,700 people were crowded into nine villages in Park. Those nine villages had between them just 181 crofts. The Matheson Estate itself would admit grudgingly in 1883 that it had spent £100,000 [*sic*] on 'improving' its land – of which huge sum only the pitiful fraction of 1.5% had been newly invested in crofting townships.

Concluding, this 1863 Lewis-baiting, Stornoway-bashing rant from a remote Edinburgh law office 'denied that Sir James had agreed to apply for an Act of Parliament to regulate the harbour. It denied that he had acquired any new rights when he purchased the foreshore. It asserted that he alone had the power to levy dues, and that he had taken over the piers (which other people had built) merely to prevent the appropriation by private individuals, for their own exclusive benefit, of what should be left common or public. In other words' – Grant concludes with a flourish – 'Sir James was the public. Louis XIV could not have put it better.'

But the Sun King of Lews Castle was already buckling before the heat, the opprobrium and widespread newspaper scorn (and the chortling of political opponents) over what was now a national scandal, the 'Foreshore Question' of Stornoway. It dawned at last on Sir James Matheson that, in the court of public opinion, he was beaten. The only way out was to compromise, and on terms that would preserve at least the appearance of some Matheson control and the stateliness of his reputation.

He quietly instructed talks.

On 4 February 1864, his lawyers wrote another missive – this time to the Commissioners for Woods and Forests, who had sold Sir James all that weed and mud, sand and shingle in the first place – to announce curtly that 'the big Quay case, as they call it in Stornoway' had been amicably settled. That same day, the Committee in Stornoway themselves sent word (in some satisfaction) to Sir James Fergusson, telling him to step down from battle-stations.

Sir James Matheson, months later and on this August day, glowered down his gracious lawns to the boats afloat in the bay, the activity of the quays and the wherries and dinghies, schooners and brigs and the odd wee steamer tied up alongside. Guts, smoke and a whiff of 'cutch' faintly troubled his nostrils. Behind him, he could feel the gaze – inscrutable, impassive – of the man-servants and the lawyers who had just watched him sign away all the power he had sought – and was it not his right? – to a properly elected Harbour Commission, with seven members and full power in law to regulate the port, levy dues, borrow great sums for great constructions. He, at least, had kept the power to appoint three of these commissioners, and the sheriff could choose a fourth. But three would be elected by the people of Stornoway. It was change – democracy – and a troubling hint of a new sort of country, a very different future.

And he had herself to face, all over again, when they dined tonight.

10

Bernera: How the Beast took on a
people – and lost

By 1874, Donald Munro – Chamberlain of the Lews, chairman besides of this
and clerk of that, to say nothing of vice-chairman of the new Stornoway
Harbour Commission (he usually presided at its diets, as Sir James – who held
the top role – seldom bothered to turn up) was at the height of his pomp and
power.

Munro and Ross, Solicitors, besides sat at the centre of the local rule of law,
quashing most attempts to overturn their monopoly. In December 1862, for
instance, a lawyer from Lochbay in Skye – Gordon MacLeod – sought
permission to practise at Stornoway Sheriff Court. In yet another example
of his unfitness for the bench, Sheriff Substitute Andrew Lothian MacDonald
put scrutiny of his application immediately in the hands of William Ross and
Donald Munro – the two men with a self-evident, commercial interest in
keeping MacLeod out. They pronounced him unqualified and unfit, and
maintained their objection (even when MacLeod produced abundant evidence
of his competence) – and their stance was upheld by Sheriff MacDonald.
MacLeod's bid to practise in Stornoway was denied.

As the harbour row gathered pace in the months following, leading men of
town grew anxious. Six months later, in May 1863, they quietly approached an
Edinburgh solicitor, Napier Campbell, whom we have already met in the
Stephen case. They urged him to set up a Stornoway practice and no doubt
briefed him besides about the fate of Gordon MacLeod and the weak nature
of the sheriff substitute. Campbell was attracted at once to the opportunity,
and simply bypassed MacDonald altogether, going over his head to Sheriff
Principal Cook for permission to 'practice in all the courts in Ross and
Cromarty'. It was readily granted, and Campbell quickly established himself
in Stornoway. The rage of its legal establishment can be imagined.

Campbell was bright and determined, though his judgement was unequal to
his intelligence. He made his name immediately by launching a bid for more
accountable local democracy, campaigning for the recognition of Stornoway as
a 'police burgh, so as to give the people a status to defend their public rights'.

The Estate – and Sir James Matheson – were aghast to imagine any sort of elected town council. But there was no way of blocking the aspiration: the necessary law (which could be easily invoked on application) was already on the statute book. Unable to thwart the bid, Donald Munro joined it – putting his own name atop the signatories of the application, and as James Shaw Grant wryly continues, 'the Town Council was not long in existence before he was Chief Magistrate, presiding over its affairs. He was unable to stop the runaway horse, so he got on its back.'

For a time it looked as if Napier Campbell would pose an abiding threat to the sustained abuses of Lewis order, despite the ill-veiled chagrin of Andrew Lothian MacDonald. In August 1863, Campbell appeared before him to defend a crofter on the edge of town, John Beaton: three of his cows had strayed onto Goathill Farm and been greedily impounded by the tenant, Alexander Gerrie. The farmer insisted on 7s 6d before he would release the beasts – money Beaton did not have. On a friend's counsel, the crofter offered instead 3s 3d, which was still twice the amount stipulated in the venerable law (the Winter Herding Act of 1686) that applied in this case. Gerrie promptly upped his ransom to a full 15 shillings and when – unsurprisingly – John Beaton could not produce this, the farmer instructed William Ross. The solicitor glowed at the prospect of billable expenses. He told Alexander Gerrie to hand back two of the cattle, lock up the third and bring an action against the poor crofter seeking authority to sell this hapless cow – thus covering both the damages to his grazing and the regrettable cost of these legal proceedings.

But Napier Campbell was waiting for them on their day in court and, while he made frivolous objections besides – Campbell had a tendency to grandstand – he presented a robust case, as Grant outlines; pointing out, for instance, that the 'poindfold' in which the prosperous farmer had confined the cow

did not conform with the law, because not enough fodder and drinking water was provided. That an offer of compensation, in excess of what the law demanded, had already been made in front of witnesses. That the damage the cattle were alleged to have done had not been independently assessed. And that the sum claimed was so small the action should have been raised in the Small Debt Court, where the legal expenses would have been very much less, even if the crofter lost the case.

Yet Sheriff MacDonald could not veil his spite against the new upstart of a solicitor, dismissing every single line of defence in blistering language – 'utterly valueless', 'pure nonsense', a 'wretched quibble' and 'the height of absurdity' – and found for the Goathill farmer, Alexander Gerrie. Angry letters were exchanged between Campbell and Ross, and it might have gone badly for the hapless crofter had not William Ross been now under mounting scrutiny from the Court of Session, where poor George Stephen had begun his case against bankruptcy. The established Stornoway lawyers decided they could not risk still another imbroglio that might attract attention from Edinburgh. The bewildered Gerrie was told firmly to settle for 13s 3d in damages, and to abandon any claim for legal expenses.

But Campbell would be neutralised in 1870 by his own folly, when he recklessly conducted the defence of the retiring Aignish farmer, James Alexander, whose usual, sozzled condition had so annoyed John Munro MacKenzie in 1850. Alexander had still won 19 years of renewed lease; but by its final months was over 80, losing his memory, and probably wrecked by alcoholism. The Estate wanted him out and, in the last year of his tenancy (without remitting any rent or offering any compensation) ordered him to leave the two best fields on Aignish Farm uncultivated, so that the new farmer would have full profit from them. Alexander – who boozily forgot – cropped them anyway; and, in the name of Sir James, Donald Munro applied vindictively for an interdict. Napier Campbell was engaged for Alexander's defence and there followed a blizzard of bills, demands and litigation far too involved to detail here, as well as foolish letters from Campbell straight to William Ross. One, in that lawyer's absence from the office, was opened by his clerk, the young John Norrie Anderson – and, unfortunately for Campbell, its wild contents were defamatory.

Munro and Ross saw their chance: an action was promptly lodged in the Court of Session, for £1,000, by their Edinburgh stooge and kinsman William Ross Skinner. Napier Campbell dared not defend the case, and had no choice but to retract his allegations; decree was duly given in favour of William Ross. With cool cunning, though, Ross let it lie. He made no effort to press the advantage home, move for his loot and bankrupt his competitor. The decree sat there, like a bomb waiting to go off, against the day Napier Campbell again dared become difficult. His threat to the Lewis regime was over.

Though James Shaw Grant understandably devotes page upon page to the saga of the *Arrow* – another Sargasso Sea of litigation and billing that all but ruined his grandfather, Roderick Morrison – it is too involved and depressing to go into here at great length. The *Arrow* was a handsome schooner effectively gifted the Stornoway mariner, in May 1873, by his brother-in-law, Roderick MacKenzie – handed over to him, by local custom, in a Stornoway pub (the Crown Inn, which is still there) merely with a shake of hands and before witnesses. The present brought Morrison nothing but misery. He fitted it out handsomely at his own expense, hired a skipper – he had not himself a master's ticket – and embarked proudly on his first voyage, to Stettin on the Baltic with a cargo of cured herring. He was glad to be a shipowner at last and to be spared long voyages, away from his family, in the service of others and all over the world's oceans.

Disaster struck on the way back. As she made for Sunderland with a cargo of timber, the *Arrow* was battered by equinoctial gales and, running for the safe haven of Elsinore in Denmark, was beached by the storm and badly damaged. The bill for salvage, refitting and repair charged by the Danes was substantial, and her hapless owner had to borrow the money locally to raise the bills. Morrison returned to Stornoway shaken, in heavy debt and much burdened of mind, but – granted time – would have cleared all his obligations.

Time was denied him. Within months, the Danish commission-agent had assigned the debt to a Lossiemouth shipowner, William Anderson, who promptly instructed Munro and Ross. The *Arrow* was promptly 'arrested' – with a legal notice nailed grandly to her mast in Stornoway harbour – and could not leave, could not sail, could not trade. Even so, her sale would at least have freed Roderick Morrison from his entanglements; but Munro and Ross had now got wind of her unorthodox transfer to his name and lodged besides joyous actions against her original owners, scenting rich pickings in both damages and legal expenses.

'It was a juicy morsel,' writes Grant grimly, a 'case which would inevitably be contested in the Sheriff Court, creating work and fees for the local partners and might, with luck, spill over into the Court of Session, where William Ross Skinner could join the gravy-train.' Meanwhile, the vessel lay defenceless, unwatched, uncared for, at North Beach as the lawyers haggled and 'the boys made a playground of the *Arrow*, the vandals and the thieves moved in, while my grandfather was stranded ashore, unable to earn a penny for the maintenance of his family, or the payment of his debts. Eventually he took the only course open to him: he abandoned the *Arrow* and signed on as mate, on a long foreign voyage.'

The ship never sailed again and unguarded, unmaintained, she deteriorated so rapidly and became such an obstruction the Harbour Commissioners finally had her towed to Goat Island and beached. (The necessary order was signed, with no evident embarrassment, by the Commission's clerk – William Ross.) The case was delayed continually, of necessity, by Morrison's long absences at sea as he tried desperately to provide for his family. By March 1875, when her sale was finally agreed by both sides, the best offer made for the hulk was £45.

Ross still had not the sense to give up. He sued everyone in sight; he lodged this writ and that action; and once and twice was beaten in court: there was a new man on the bench now, Sheriff Substitute Charles Grey Spittal, of more character and discernment than MacDonald, who not only found twice in favour of the assorted defenders but awarded expenses against Munro and Ross's clients. They ended up being billed for thousands of pounds, on top of their own legal expenses. Roderick Morrison himself, nevertheless, was ruined by their frenzied endeavours, and reduced to the humiliation of *cessio bonorum* – a sort of controlled bankruptcy (roughly equivalent to the modern English arrangement of an Individual Voluntary Agreement) which allowed dignified and honourable closure in this sort of nightmare. Even this was fought to the last by Munro and Ross. They lost, in the end, and they lost expensively; the rotting timbers of the *Arrow* would lie for decades near the Newton foreshore, taunting the Morrison family; her ribs were still to be seen when Grant himself was a little boy, during the Great War. Long before the final conclusion of the saga, however, Donald Munro's tyranny was over.

Fred Silver, in an important little essay on the Chamberlain of the Lews and with deft research into long-neglected sources, in 2009 unearthed two new glimpses of Munro at work – and the instinctive hunger, widely found among island people, for knowledge and learning and personal growth.

One young man, Robertson MacAulay – the son of a Lewis-born skipper, born himself in Fraserburgh in 1833 – came to Stornoway as a child of 10, lodging with his aunt. Still only 12, he secured a labouring job. Yet the lad, as David Boucher retails in the *Canadian Dictionary of National Biography*, possessing 'only the rudiments of education but imbued with the Scottish penchant for self-improvement . . . devoted his evenings to unremitting study, concentrating on mathematics. He promptly secured an apprenticeship with the local solicitor and procurator fiscal. MacAulay's foray into law awakened his social conscience. As an officer of the court he was obliged to evict crofters. The experience convinced him that economic security was the bedrock on which the wellbeing of families depended. The death of his father in 1847, when he was fourteen, cruelly reinforced this view.'

For Robertson MacAulay grew increasingly disgusted with his job and – even before his boss had attained the giddying heights of Chamberlain of the Lews – grew more and more repelled by the loud, ugly, vindictive ways of Donald Munro himself. MacAulay gave up his situation, found others in Stornoway and then in Aberdeen, and – in 1854 – he emigrated to Quebec, brooding still on the question of providing for one's family against the hardest, unforeseen turns of providence. Robertson MacAulay took a novel new view into a notoriously cynical trade – that life insurance is an absolute moral trust – and, by absolute honesty and faithful adherence to its words, Sun Life, under his leadership, became one of the greatest concerns in the world, with abiding impact on the insurance industry. The integrity of your own policies today, and the putative wellbeing of your loved ones amidst possible tragedy, owes, perversely, much to the character of Donald Munro. Thomas Basset MacAulay, heir to his father's empire, was a noted Lewis benefactor after the Great War, and besides a noted breeder of cattle: most of the world's Holsteins, the pre-eminent dairy cow, are descended from his personal herd.

And a 14-year-old boy from Ness, Roderick Campbell, would many years later – in 1901, in thoughtful autobiography – remember his own encounter with the ghastly chamberlain, in the late 1850s.

Campbell was then at the lowest rung imaginable in the economic ladder of Lewis – an unskilled cattleherd in the employ of the Estate, who had spent hardly any time in school and fretted as he watched other, more fortunate boys pad by the Manor Farm into town for their lessons. Campbell's account is especially important as it reinforces John MacRae's account in the 'Cosmo Cumming' novel. And the courage of this lowly child before Donald Munro cannot fail to move us. As Campbell recalled his early servitude, decades on:

I spent my days alone in a large walled park of about forty acres, having as sole companions a dozen or more Irish cows. I had plenty of time to spare for deep meditations, the first and foremost subject being my future prospects. At last out of my daily meditations grew the audacious resolution to ask the bailiff to allow me to go to school two hours in the forenoon and two hours in the afternoon. In return I was willing to sacrifice all my wages. I was prepared to point out to the bailiff that, as the park was walled, my being there made no difference whatsoever to the cows; they would eat and digest just as much grass in my absence as in my presence.

I went to Sandy Buey, the bailiff. He received my plea with a smile, which showed me that my proposition was to be left indefinitely considered. A higher authority, however, was the understeward, the inexorable Estate Factor himself. And with bated breath and beating heart, and limbs quivering like an aspen leaf, to him I went. A perilous business I felt it to be to face a man so powerful and in religious matters, as I had been taught, so 'unsound'. On being ushered into the august presence of the titular governor of the Long Island, I felt as if seized by a sudden attack of lockjaw. . . . Munro sharply asked my business. Drawing my slender frame up to its full height, I boldly repeated the logical proposition concerning the cows and the grass which the bailiff had treated with such scant respect. His face, anything but amiable in his better moods, gathered itself into a grimness altogether terrifying.

'You impudent fellow, your audacity surpasses anything in my experience. Do you think I am going to feed and pay you to go to school? You
could learn nothing if you did go to school. Fishing and planting a few
potatoes need no schooling. Nonsense! Impudence! Away with you instantly!'. . . . I pled long and earnestly, asking at last but one hour daily. But
my remonstrances might as well have been addressed to the stones of the
street for all the impression they made upon him. Finally he got so angry
that he told me he would send me to prison instead of to school if I did not
leave his office sharp, for he didn't want an idiot in his service. The threat of
prison was more alarming to me than even the monotonous prospect of
watching the cows eat grass, so, choosing the least of two evils, I then and
there threw down the seals of office with the titles and emoluments of 'herd
loon' upon the floor and speedily found myself in the street.

Munro is here credibly described – storming, malicious and irrational, even
capable (and he was, after all, procurator fiscal) of threatening a trembling child
with jail. Roderick Campbell went to school. In time, he too sailed for Canada,
where he built a distinguished career with the Hudson's Bay Company.

The incident he so vividly describes confirms abiding folk-memory on Lewis
– not least from Mor MacLeod – that Munro actively opposed the betterment
of ordinary island people and detested the spectacle of those he tried to keep
in serfdom 'getting on'. Fred Silver observes that 'in a fierce exchange of views
in *The Scotsman* newspaper after Munro lost his job as factor almost twenty
years later, a Stornoway man was quoted as saying, "Mr Munro took no interest
whatever in the education of the people – his great aim was to keep them in
thorough ignorance. It was very different with his predecessor – for Mr Munro
MacKenzie, during his reign, took the greatest possible interest in all our
schools, and had them regularly examined in his own presence . . ."'

Yet Munro's many hats included the chairmanship of all four parish school
boards on Lewis – and, from 1872, with the advent of compulsory education
and the absorption of most Free Church schools into the public system, his
power seemed set to be still further extended. The 1872 Act did, in fact, very
little for Lewis: no single event, in the long term, proved more catastrophic for
the Gaelic language than the advent of enforced education in the medium of
English.

Nor were the new buildings now demanded in terms of the regulations –
conceived, of course, for Lowland conditions – really suited in design or
materials to island realities, far less the scant funds locally available. All that
slate and glass, for instance, had to be imported at great expense, as did most of
the timber. And many of the new schools developed in the last decades of the

nineteenth century were – to save expense – erected in the middle of nowhere, between two villages and to serve both of them. That at Knockandhu, for instance – at a junction, on a most exposed site – served the children of Keose and Laxay into the present century. The calibre of staff, too, at many of the new schools was highly variable: knowledge of Gaelic was no longer a requirement, the dregs of the teaching profession (alcoholics, incompetents, psychopaths) unemployable anywhere else seemed easily to gain charge of Long Island schools, and, even in my own lifetime, in certain island districts, dreadful teachers were still able to taunt, beat and terrorise children.

Meanwhile hundreds of scholars, in all weathers, had to trudge across open moor to reach such establishments, each dutifully toting a peat for the fitful schoolroom fire, often sitting for the entire day in soaking clothes and with no solid food between morning and night. This may well have been a factor in the 'consumption' already creeping into the island through the migrant labour of fishermen and herring-girls, and – it had hitherto been unheard of on the island – there was no 'herd immunity'. By the twentieth century, tuberculosis was the curse of Lewis, bearing away dozens of young lives every year, and would remain a serious problem until after the Second World War. The new premises had other dangers besides. At the end of the Great War, for instance, the source of a serious diphtheria outbreak in North Tolsta – which killed children and even parents – was finally traced to the filthy school latrines.

For years, truancy dogged island schools; inevitable when families were expected to pay new 'school rates' (however modest the dues might seem to us now) and in a subsistence economy where the labour of even young children, in planting crops or tending cattle, was held important. Few families in rural Lewis saw any need for the new, highly disruptive order in the stead of the simpler, much more humane schools it had overthrown – especially when the boards that ran them were dominated by the factor's creatures, mostly English monoglots who squabbled incessantly. Besides, as Donald MacDonald points out, to island parents the whole thrust of education 'encouraged their children to leave them, a matter which had the full support of the Estate officials. Parents had not forgotten that, a few years before, the first prize in a competition for all the island schools was a single ticket to Australia. There were no competitors.'

In the wake of the 1872 Act, and with control of every school on the island tumbling into his hands, it is easy to see how Donald Munro, by 1874, had begun to behave as if he were invulnerable. And, not least as a consequence of an accident in China, he had just gained power over a new and subsequently famous grove of academe.

Alexander Morrison Nicolson was one of the very first men from Lewis to qualify as a marine engineer. Born in 1832, he was the son of that unpleasant Stornoway fish-curer, Roderick Nicolson, who had so dishonestly fought for a poor man's horse. All his boys proved enterprising and, by contrast, decent. Alexander did well at school, served an apprenticeship with J. & G. Thomson Ltd of Govan – the family shipbuilding firm which later moved down to, and indeed established, the new town of Clydebank – and then made for the Far East to explore business opportunities there. By 1865, he was joint partner of a large shipbuilding and iron-foundry concern in Shanghai, China; and he was still only 33 when he died horribly – killed by an exploding boiler on one of his own ships.

But, young as he was, Nicolson had taken care to draw up a detailed will; he had left what by the standards of the day was a good estate – £6,672 – and expressly stipulated that a third of this was to be donated 'to the most approved charitable institution in my native town for the education and rearing of destitute children in the hope that I may be the indirect means of rendering some assistance to the children of some of my oldest acquaintances'. Though among the named executors, his father had just pre-deceased him; how best to accomplish the late Alexander Nicolson's wishes fell to his no less resourceful brothers. Stornoway then boasted four schools and (no doubt with an eye to Alexander's own achievements) they soon decided MacKay's School the most suitable. This was an informal but most effective set-up, founded by the eponymous John MacKay of Newton, which not only taught navigation and skills in mathematics, seamanship and other technical subjects to island lads, but coached experienced mariners to attaining master's tickets and so on.

But the building was inadequate and the site confined. It was decided to erect new, larger premises on a better spot, and Sir James Matheson granted ground on Sandwick Road. Much of the money went on building what became known as the 'Clock School' – though the tower would not be added until 1902, nor the clock for three years after that – and a house for the headmaster. What was left was endowed to his salary and augmented by Sir James. Alexander's brothers, too, dug deep to augment his bequest – and continued to make donations for years thereafter – and it speaks volumes for the Lewis enterprise of their generation that, as James Shaw Grant would retail in his 1987 guidebook, *Discovering Lewis and Harris*, that one

was a cotton-planter in Mississippi. Another was a woollen manufacturer in Yorkshire. The third was a farmer in Australia and the fourth a chaplain in the Brigade of Guards. Not one was resident in Lewis, although they belonged to the clan which had been established in the island for at least seven hundred years and had been dominant until the MacLeods took over.

The 'Nicolson Institution', which for 20 years taught only primary pupils, opened in 1873; from 1888 it was the 'Nicolson Public School' and it was further strengthened by the 1896 closure – and transfer of pupils – from the Free Church School on Francis Street. (That building was added to the Nicolson campus and serves, these days, as the local museum.) Since 1901, it has been the renowned Nicolson Institute – a school which has, over the decades, fed Britain and the Commonwealth with hundreds and hundreds of bright, gifted and resourceful young people, and which caused delicious shock in 1956 when a team of Nicolson boys beat scholars from all over the United Kingdom in the BBC's *Top of the Form* programme. The Nicolson was then a grammar school but, in the 1970s and with little difficulty, became a comprehensive; and, since the regrettable closure of Lews Castle School in 1998 (a faintly blue-collar but much loved technical secondary) has been the only six-year secondary school on Lewis. There is still abiding Stornoway anger at the wanton demolition in 1972 of the original Clock School premises to erect a hideous sports centre – itself now obliterated; the 1902 tower alone survives.

For now, from early inception of the new academy, trustees were appointed to manage the new establishment; and the new sheriff substitute, Charles Gray Spittal, was appointed chairman. Donald Munro took office as clerk, as if he had not enough powers elsewhere, and all seemed serene until – and to his evident chagrin – the trustees decided that post should be held *ex officio* by the newly appointed headmaster, John Sutherland, who had hitherto run the town's General Assembly School. Apart from anything else, the records indicate it would 'save expense' – which suggests that some sort of salary, or at least honorarium, went with this clerkship, and no doubt with many of the other posts Munro had clawed to himself over the years. But he proved most loath to relinquish this one, and, when he was removed from it, he flatly refused to hand over the records – even at the express command of Sheriff Spittal himself.

The jurist had no choice but directly to approach Sir James Matheson, the one man the chamberlain, the procurator fiscal and the this-that-and-the-other of Lewis dared not defy. So Munro had at last to surrender the books. When Spittal took a look, he could scarcely believe his eyes; Munro had repeatedly tampered with the minutes, quite distorting the record with adjustments and marginal notes and so on, blithely altering decisions the trustees had made by entirely proper process at meetings he himself had attended. Sheriff Spittal was so enraged, he ripped out all the defiled pages and rewrote the entire record himself, with meticulous accuracy and in his own hand. Somehow, years or months later – perhaps even after his fall – Munro again got his hands on the

Nicolson minute book and added a self-serving nine-page account, from his black perspective, of events.

It is a telling tale. The Chamberlain of the Lews was, by 1874, slowly losing touch with reality; if it were forced upon him in forms and shape he did not like, he rewrote it to his own satisfaction. *I am the law . . .*

The Law, as personified in Donald Munro and to his entire satisfaction, now turned a malignant eye on the people of Great Bernera.

It was the mistake of his life.

The 1860s and 1870s – as Iain MacPhail, a highly respected Dumbarton resident and of first-generation Lewis descent still best known for his taut 1974 account of the Clydebank Blitz detailed in his last book, *The Crofters' War* – were a period of notable Highland change. These years

> have been described as the 'heyday of British capitalism'. Britain was then the leading world power, indeed the only real world power: its textile, iron and steel, engineering and shipbuilding industries were all booming and its overseas trade expanding each year. It was also the 'Golden Age' of British farming, just before competition from the United States, Canada, Australia and New Zealand brought ruin to the farmers. Both in industry and farming the burden of taxation was slight, and successive Chancellors of the Exchequer sought to abolish income tax. The Highlands and Islands, although remote from industry and the area of intensive farming, benefitted to a certain extent by the 'spin-off' from the buoyant economy of the Victorian heyday. This was the period of 'Balmoralism', when wealthy English and Scottish magnates vied with one another in acquiring sporting estates and erecting neo-Scottish-baronial dwellings in which to spend a few months each year. Deer-stalking, grouse-shooting, salmon-fishing provided employment for only a few and almost inevitably clashed with the interests of the indigenous inhabitants . . . The 1870s, as it can be argued, were years of a rising standard of living among the crofter-fishermen of the north and west, and a number of impartial observers bear testimony to this. Indeed, it was partly because standards began to decline in the 1880s that the Crofters' War developed. But the same impartial observers were not blind to the numerous grievances of the crofters . . .
>
> Relations between crofters and tacksmen or farmers were seldom good: complaints were made of the loss of the best grazings to neighbouring farmers without a corresponding reduction in rent and of the encroachment by farmers on the common grazing, which, when there was no adequate dyke or fence, was thus reduced. Complaints also arose out of the

impounding of crofters' stock which strayed. Tenants with shooting rights could be more troublesome than farmers. Deer were sometimes pursued by sportsmen into the cornfields at the Braes in Skye. According to John Nicolson of Sconser, 'It would give the apostle Paul himself enough to tell of it. The women would be quietly herding and would have to fly home because of the bullets.' Where deer fences had been erected, as at Sconser near Sligachan in Skye, they were inadequate as protections for the crops. In the interests of shooting tenants, dogs were forbidden at Sconser, Glendale and Raasay . . .

They were also years, as Iain MacPhail details, of renewed Evangelical fervour: the Revival of 1859 remains Scotland's last great spiritual movement, and saw remarkable scenes in the Highlands, not least on Lewis. There were, besides, steadily improving communications: the railways reached Inverness, then Oban and then, in 1870, Strome Ferry. The Hutcheson/MacBrayne empire of sturdy steamers continued to expand. The telegraph finally reached Lewis in 1872. The Caithness and east coast fishery remained generally a lucrative source of income for Lewismen who did not mind long periods away from home, though some seasons were poor. (The local fishery, thanks to Matheson's obduracy, remained fraught and very dangerous; nearly 300 Lewis fishermen were lost between 1848 and 1883, most of them from want of decent local harbours.)

But there were further cultural developments. We have already touched on one: the imposition of a new, unpopular and anglicising education system on the people of the Hebrides and to their additional, immediate expense. And we have touched on another: the rapid shift in economic exploitation from tenant sheep-farming (for which thousands had been wantonly removed from their ancestral land) to the development of sporting estates, which saw an end to the Clearances but brought new harassment to crofters.

There was besides through the 1870s what MacPhail describes as 'a tremendous upsurge of Gaelic sentiment and a growing awareness of their Gaelic heritage among the exiled Highlanders and Islesmen in the large cities – Glasgow, Edinburgh, Greenock, Aberdeen, Dundee, Inverness. This Gaelic movement manifested itself in various forms – in Gaelic poetry, in Highland societies, in Highland newspapers and journals, in the campaigns for a Gaelic Chair in Edinburgh University and for Gaelic in the state schools. Although primarily orientated towards preserving Gaelic tradition and culture, almost all of these manifestations contributed indirectly towards bringing the condition of the crofter before a wider public and eventually towards the rectification of their grievances . . .'

It would be the 1880s before there was significant and organised agitation for crofters' rights and land reform in the Highlands and Islands. Yet, long before that, it was a heartfelt and articulate cause among Highland émigrés in Scotland's cities, where the laird could no longer intimidate, the factor no longer evict. And it was coloured too by events in Ireland, where – fuelled by a new political nationalism in a land run for centuries by its English conquerors and with signal incompetence – keen campaigns and brave, talented leaders demonstrated what could be accomplished.

And thus it was that the people of Bernera were first provoked beyond endurance by Donald Munro, and then humiliated him in Stornoway itself, and further devoured his dignity in a distant courtroom; but it was the furious, pamphleteering opinion in the south which finally brought him down.

Bernera is a sizeable island on the west coast of Lewis, dominating Loch Roag and separated from Earshader (on the mainland of the parish of Uig) only by the narrowest of sea-straits; in 1953, a single-track but handsome road-bridge, still in use today, was completed over this channel. As Mor MacLeod, born in Earshader in 1914, can recall, even in the 1920s there was no road to Earshader itself and the district was still most readily accessed by sea. Mails were delivered by motorboat and those who had business in town generally walked through the ancient tracks and paths of the wider parish to the 'Uig ferry', then crossing by boat to Callanish or Breasclete. Her own grandmother – a sister of my great-grandfather in Shawbost – once, in the early 1870s and around the time of this drama, made her excited way by foot and boat from Earshader to Shawbost. A long trek; but word had reached the lass, still in her teens, that the village's Psalmody class were to learn a new tune, and she wanted to be there.

This splendid old lady – who bequeathed much of her vast storehouse of lore and knowledge to her surviving granddaughter – died in 1936; she was the very last person to be buried on Little Bernera, the ancient graveyard not just of its much larger neighbour but the people of Carloway. The advent of the motor car has completely altered perceptions of Lewis; even for Mor's generation, it is still a landscape – a coastline – instinctively travelled by boat and envisaged from the sea. It was not the Atlantic that held terrors for our forebears, but the vast tracts of uninhabited and eerie Lewis moorland, which people were loath ever to cross on their own. 'In the road', in the argot of an island township, is down to the safe and familiar shore; 'out the road' is to the emptiness of bog beyond.

Bernera is essentially a fishing community and her people are resourceful sailors; she is besides today distinguished as, really, the least religious part of rural Lewis, where Sabbath observance has largely gone by the board and the Free Church forced to shut up shop. But she is acutely short of good land. Only in the north, around Bosta, is there some verdant machair and, while her coast abounds in good little coves for boats, croftwork in Bernera townships (Bosta in the north; Tobson, Valasay and Haclete — it was then a rented and indifferent farm — in the west; Breaclete and Barraglom in the middle; and Kirkibost, with a decent little harbour in the east) was of the arduous order generally associated with the Bays of Harris. Potatoes and corn had largely to be grown in *feannagan* or 'lazy-beds', the most unjust term in Scots agriculture. Such rigs — many little bigger than a dining table — involved backbreaking work, carved out painfully with a spade amidst ribs of rock and fed with creel upon creel of dung and wrack; but there was no alternative on land not readily ploughed.

As the island boasts besides a great deal of fresh surface water — Bernera is so shredded with lochs and lochans that she looks, from the air, as if she has been blasted with a shotgun — grazing is at a premium. From time immemorial, the people of Bernera have taken their cattle across the straits of a summer to munch the moors of mainland Uig, and their historic land was a great tract of territory between Loch Langavat and Loch Resort. Donald MacDonald suggests that when the cows were removed in the late autumn they were put on the various little islands at Loch Roag.

From 1850, when Matheson formed the Uig Deer Forest, the Bernera people were a little more confined, to 'the moor of Beinn a' Chualein', writes Iain MacPhail, 'stretching from the Uig road as far as Loch Langavat, and abutted by two Atlantic inlets at either side: Little Loch Roag, to the west, and Loch Ceann Hulavig, to the east.' They had been commanded besides to build a wall to separate this common pasture from the playground of their laird, and to maintain this dyke for 20 years at their own expense. But still the people of Bernera could swim their cows across those narrows to Earshader — and, in due season, swim them back again — and it is said the women were always borne over first, so that they could stand on the shore and call to the family cow, the more to encourage her unwonted swim.

And, unfortunately for the people of Great Bernera in the early 1870s, each of these sea-lochs thrusts into prized hunting grounds — Scaliscro Lodge and its deerpark and salmon to one side, and the still more sensational salmon-fishing of Grimersta on the other. In 1871, the Lewis Estate decided to organise these as lucrative sporting estates, not just for Matheson diversion but in lease to visiting gentry.

It was this, as the economic focus of the Mathesons rapidly shifted from sheep and chemicals to the rod and the gun, that brought the Bernera folk into rude collision with Donald Munro — and especially Grimersta, which still holds the record (set some years later, in 1888, when a delirious Mr Naylor landed 54 fish) for the most Atlantic salmon taken on one rod in one day. The river itself is brief and foaming, fed from a maze of lochs and ultimately from Loch Langavat, the largest and most majestic on Lewis and Harris, gouging deep into both and adjoining no public road.

Indeed, so boiling with salmon from a host of island rivers is Loch Langavat that its riches are probably the main reason Sir James Matheson, for all his new roads, never laid one between Scaliscro and Aline. By the same logic, if by the aegis of a different estate, the highway to Tarbert, to this day, takes the awkward route down to Ardhasaig rather than by the obvious line east by Maraig and down to Urgha – where it would pass a stretch of fine fishing lochs in grand, lonely country of Gleann Lacasdal, the 'vale of salmon'. And, as recently as 1973, a later Harris laird tried to have the public road to Husinish diverted, entirely at public expense and by the intrigue of a powerful member of Inverness County Council who had been his Eton contemporary, away from his Amhuinnsuidhe Castle lair and the mouth of another notable salmon river. (Sir Hereward Wake might well have succeeded, but for a joyous exposé by the new *West Highland Free Press*.)

As the Lewis Estate moved to secure these commercial properties at Grimersta and Morsgail, the Bernera crofters were given imperious notice: their grazings on the Uig mainland were now denied them.

They were offered, instead, the farm of Earshader, right across the narrows; what was more, Donald Munro told them grandly, they were – as an absolute condition of this generous concession – to build a dyke, at their own time and expense, right round it: a dry-stone wall over very rough, rugged country and over 7 miles long, confining their cattle to the appointed native reservation.

This was not, of course, for the benefit of Bernera folk at all, but to keep their beasts out of the Morsgail deer forest. The Earshader lands afforded in any event much less grazing – and that markedly inferior – to the big country they had hitherto enjoyed for centuries. And they were granted neither reductions of rent, nor payment for their labour in erecting the wall. 'These grazings were not considered as good as the old ones,' relates MacPhail, but, without security of tenure and well aware of the character of the Chamberlain, the families of Bernera were in no position to demur. And so, at 'a meeting with the *maor* or ground-officer, the crofters agreed to accept the Factor's proposal and also to build a dyke between themselves and the deer forest of Scaliscro.'

But the Bernera folk – and this must seriously have rattled Munro – had self-esteem enough to table an unprecedented condition, as Joni Buchanan advises. They would only accept these terms, and commit themselves to raising that wall, if they were granted a formal lease for these new lands. Until that was agreed, they would not lay stone upon stone, and would continue implacably to use the grazings they had.

Munro decided not to make a stand against this condition; in his eyes, anything agreed on paper with mere tenants-at-will meant nothing anyway. So, in due time, the ground officer brought with him a paper read aloud to tenants and according to which the new grazings would be theirs as long as they held their crofts in Bernera. Most of them could only sign it by making their marks. It occurred to no one to ask for a copy, and it is most unlikely any would have been granted.

Anyone who has ever built a dry-stone wall or, say, a building of the black-house type will be well aware of the effort involved. In a wry Highland saying, you calculate carefully all the rock you think you will need – and then multiply it by ten. The people of Bernera had no modern equipment, no wheeled vehicles – and, in any event, were working in roadless terrain. It took months, in all weathers, to put up these seven miles of detested, confining, punitive wall, up hill and down dale, complete with culverts, the great stones at its base the weight and size of a steamer-trunk and the constant, relentless search for yet more stone, of the right size and shape – months and labour diverted from the tilling of their land and the harvest of the sea. And through all this time, and until the dyke was complete and cattle-proof, they were not allowed to graze a single beast on the Earshader land – though they had lost the rest of their grazings in an instant. The wall was duly completed, late in 1872; it stands to this day, and a more sobering, powerful monument on Lewis to the dignity of a people in the face of absolutism we do not know.

But tyranny is one thing; caprice quite another. Eighteen months later, the Lewis Estate – which is to say Donald Munro – almost casually, and with majestic arrogance, changed its mind. It was worse than callous: there was more than a hint of gloating, by a factor long convinced he was master of all. And even the ground officer, James MacRae – summoned by the Chamberlain of the Lews to be given the latest marching orders – could scarcely believe his ears; he, from Miavaig in Uig, was almost local. But back to Bernera MacRae trudged and, ill at ease and in trepidation, in the early spring of 1874, he called the crofters and told them – looking about shiftily – they were not, after all, and after all that murderous work, to have the farm of Earshader as their grazing ground. They were instead to be granted the still smaller, still poorer farm of Haclete, in Bernera itself. They were to be confined now entirely to their island and on no account to take their beasts to summer pasture on the mainland of Uig.

'The Bernera folk were furious,' writes Dr MacDonald of Gisla, 'and even the ground-officer thought it was a raw deal they had got, and so they refused to accept, especially as they had built such a long wall. Haclete was a grassy arable farm, but there was no wintering for stock.' There was no violence; and no personal abuse or jostling of James MacRae himself, whose humiliation and shame was manifest – but the men of Bernera were adamant. There had been a deal. They had honoured it, at great sacrifice and trouble. They had already – and twice, within 30 years – been forced to accept reduced, inferior grazings. They would not a third time yield. And they would not – they made very plain – co-operate with these new and outrageous arrangements. They knew perfectly well the Estate's real agenda, and that of Munro: to deny Bernera people any legitimate excuse for being near deer at Morsgail or salmon at Grimersta.

MacRae, the ground-officer, duly reported to his master. Donald Munro, Chamberlain of the Lews, was not now accustomed to dissent. He was no doubt puzzled; perhaps angry, perhaps felt just the first stirrings of relish. Some accounts – including MacPhail's – assert Munro now himself visited the area to harangue the Bernera people. But the mass of evidence suggests this was at a later point in the drama. And drama there now indeed was. On 19 March 1874, Donald Munro, Chamberlain of the Lews, procurator fiscal, issued summonses of eviction against 58 Bernera crofters.

For all the subsequent claims of Munro, Ross and their lackeys, the people of this little island throughout what history remembers, less than justly, as the 'Bernera Riot', bore themselves in these days and weeks with extraordinary restraint. This was not just in the teeth of considerable provocation. There is little doubt that Munro and his minions tried to infuriate the Bernera tenants into the sort of conduct that would merit criminal charges. This would not only serve to the advantage of the Chamberlain of the Lews – his 'polyonymous omnipotence', as Professor William Blackie would later, if opaquely, damn Donald Munro – in due subjection of islanders to his will. It would besides vaunt his reputation on a wider stage, as the great man of Lewis who alone could keep the entire populace from rising in mayhem. And all the summonses and papers and court-work involved would be besides a most lucrative business for Munro and Ross.

In his matchless arrogance, Donald Munro was laying a scheme that would win him, at last, only ruinous publicity, and explore the gross abuse of power on Lewis and the manifestly unjust combination of two immensely powerful offices, factor and procurator fiscal.

So intoxicated with authority had Munro become that, by his own later admission, he did not bother to tell Sir James Matheson himself of the wholesale evictions with which he now threatened Bernera. Munro afterwards could not even himself remember exactly how many summonses he had decreed or how many crofters were to be booted from their land. (In fact, as MacPhail determined in 1989 from a surviving April 1874 police report, there were 58 tenants on the list; and, as Grant wrote in 1992, there were 11 summonses. 'Nine of them bore six names each. The tenth had three names. One favoured individual got a summons all to himself.')

Grant may be correct that Munro never meant actually to enforce the removals; it was all but a ridiculous *coup de théâtre* to enforce obedience to his common-grazings decree. As it never came to it, thanks to the yawning hole the chamberlain managed to dig for himself, we will never know. But it is not the view of MacPhail, Dr MacDonald or (to this day) that of the Bernera people themselves. He was wholly capable of throwing out crofters on such a scale, and nothing in the record of Sir James Matheson suggests he would have intervened – or, indeed, even noticed. What is certain is that the summonses were served on the islanders, quite deliberately, with studied melodrama and a determination at every turn to goad and to humiliate.

The gleeful expedition to Bernera was entrusted to Colin MacLennan. He was from Duirinish, in Lochalsh; he may, in 1874, have been the serving sheriff officer of Stornoway, though Joni Buchanan suggests this had been in fact his previous post, and he had been hired back from Lochalsh for this one mission. And MacLennan was a thug – a 'despicable bully', says James Shaw Grant.

As the unpleasant sheriff officer made for Bernera on 24 March, he was accompanied by James MacRae; for all his earlier qualms, he too seems to have relished the occasion. And – as luck would have it – the Uig ferry had also to convey that day the local customs officer, Peter Bain, who had – it was later alleged, though never demonstrated – unrelated business of his own in the district. It would be claimed Bain was now pressed to join them on Bernera, if only to boost their numbers and add to the general grandiloquence. It seems much more likely the Revenue man's presence had been agreed in advance, as an extra witness for legal purposes; if so, the plan would backfire devastatingly.

On the island itself, MacLennan, MacRae and Bain were to be joined by Malcolm MacAulay, the constable of Haclete farm and scarcely a popular local worthy. And imperious word was sent an hour or two ahead. The crofters were ordered to assemble at certain points in each township (as decreed precisely by James MacRae) and hear the pleasure of the Chamberlain of the Lews. Word fast spread anyway that something bad was afoot, and something akin to panic gripped the Bernera townships; but it was just enough notice for quiet, urgent talk: there must be restraint, and discipline must hold.

So, in their vast self-importance, MacLennan and MacRae landed at Bernera, with Bain in their trail looking quiet and grave, and MacAulay awaiting them dutifully. They strutted to their first point of muster: the village of Tobson. The crofters were indeed mulishly assembled. However, they were not quite at the spot MacRae had officiously decreed. He flushed; he was losing face before his important companions. He took the other officials crossly to the hillock he had determined – perhaps a hundred yards from where the men of Tobson actually stood – and then commanded the tenants, as so many dogs, to move over and take heed.

The crofters were loath to shift in so servile a manner. 'If it were for any good to us,' someone snapped in acrid Gaelic, 'you would not have called us here like this.' But shuffle towards these nabobs, after some minutes of pointed inertia, they duly did. MacRae ranted the command anew. They were to give up the Earshader hill grazings and take instead the coarse pastures at Haclete. The men of Tobson demurred. They made their own position plain. The land offered now was too small. They had already been moved, just three years before. And the Estate had besides forced them – at their own expense – to put up that wretched wall. It was not, they pointed out angrily, even for the protection of their stock or for any way to their own benefit. It was to keep their cattle out of the deer forest the Estate had taken away from them. And they had been explicitly promised – in writing – that they would enjoy that new shieling ground at Earshader, unmolested, as long as they paid their rents and worked their crofts. There was not, it was besides added, even any reduction of rent now proposed or compensation of any sort now offered for all that pointless dyking labour and the loss of the Earshader lands.

MacRae blustered and lectured, immovable, implacable, and finally yielded the stage to Colin MacLennan, the sheriff officer. He now grandly called each crofter forward, like a disgraced schoolboy to a teacher's desk, and thrust papers of eviction at him – and not from the grazings of Earshader, but from every foot of land the man had and everything he had built. This was on hard legal paper, whatever the verbal assurances of James MacRae – and, as was now evident, such promises were not worth the air in which they were spoken.

The assorted grandees then marched from Tobson to another village and to another village after that before hostile stares and seething women and staring children, and the atmosphere tightened remorselessly. They served writs of eviction on dwelling after dwelling, save at three houses where the tenant happened to be away for the day or at the fishing: but still, nothing untoward happened, until all was nearly done and the twilight was falling, and Mac-Lennan was leading his footsore posse over the boggy ground between Tobson and Valasay. At this point, and in the dusk, they came under determined fire – a hail of 'plocs', or damp little chunks of sod, garnered up by furious older children, both boys and girls, who were now but elusive, hissing shadows in the gloom.

A criminal incident! To be sure, none of the men was hurt – not a cut, nor a bruise – but Colin MacLennan was thrilled. He turned to MacAulay, the farm constable, and demanded the names of their assailants. MacAulay declared he had not a clue; it was dark, he had not seen their faces.

'If I'd a gun,' rasped MacLennan loudly, 'there'd be Bernera women lamenting their sons the night.' MacAulay flinched, for still folk moved in the shadows, and MacLennan's voice carried far. 'Lucky for you you haven't,' he declared. 'If you did, you'd be a dead man yourself.'

But MacLennan was in no mood to be rebuked. He kept chundering on noisily about a gun. They visited more houses, served more papers, and still the sheriff officer snarled about those louts, and if only he had his rifle, and what he would have done with it. MacRae, MacAulay and Bain grew increasingly embarrassed and angry. 'Watch what you're saying,' they growled, but it made no difference, and crofter upon crofter, woman upon woman heard his threats. The party hunkered down uneasily for the night at Haclete, no doubt in the tenant-farmer's home, and whether he wanted them or not. There were still three summonses to be delivered, and it was dark, and they were tired and apprehensive.

Word meanwhile went round an incensed Bernera that a sheriff officer from town was threatening to shoot their children. Several men of Tobson who, after the earlier harangue from the high ones of town, had gone off to tend sheep at a fank, had returned home after dusk to this news. They included one Angus MacDonald, then in his thirties, skipper of a fishing boat and engaged with his crew to Kenneth Smith, 'California', the Stornoway curer and sturdy foe of lairdly designs on its harbour. This Angus, according to his fondly remembering son Norman in a 1974 interview with Anne Whitaker, was 'a big strong man and a wild man, in those days anyway'. He and some mates were incensed. It was quickly agreed that MacLennan should be confronted before he left the island. The sun was barely up, the following day, before a grim little squad had made for Breaclete, to see if they could recruit more bodies. According to Norman MacDonald – who was born 11 years after all this, in 1885 – the people of Breaclete were dubious. ' "Well," said the Tobson men, "we'll toss a sixpence and if the Queen's head comes up we will go, and if not, we won't go." They tossed, the Queen's head came up and off they went. And they decided that anyone who would not put a hand in the struggle would get quite as much trouble as the Sheriff's Officer.'

When the squad rose the following day and made for the shore and the ferry back to Callanish – they were to board at Riosay, at the back of Breaclete – they found a deputation – 13 or 14 quiet, angry fishermen. What exactly, they demanded of Colin MacLennan, had he said about using a gun? The sheriff officer scowled, said nothing, and tried to get to the boat. One man – Angus MacDonald of Tobson – clutched at his jacket, according to most accounts, insisting he wait and answer the question. There was momentary struggle, and as MacLennan pulled wildly away the fabric tore; another hand seized his waterproof overcoat, folded loose over one arm, and that too ripped slightly, for MacLennan grabbed it and refused to let go. 'We're not going to hurt you, not at all,' the man grappling with the sheriff officer was pleading.

Another version – as related by Angus MacDonald's son Norman, in that 1974 interview to Anne Whitaker – is much more dramatic:

> He took a hold of Maclennan and put him under his knee, while everyone else pushed and shoved around him. Then my father asked him, 'Do you promise me that you won't come here any more as long as you live for the reason you came today?'
> 'Yes,' replied MacLennan.
> 'Nor,' said my father, 'to any other place?'
> 'Oh well, man,' said the other, 'I must be somewhere.'

But this strains credulity; such a business would indubitably have been assault, would have visibly bruised the sheriff officer and been abundantly attested in court. It was not. It sounds very much like a tall tale in later years from a kindly father, all the more diverting when told to a small, wide-eyed boy before an audience of people who had witnessed the real incident for themselves.

Alarmed, the other officials bundled about MacLennan, pushed him on, as a crofter shouted urgently, 'Don't hurt him.' MacAulay, the Haclete farm constable, pressed them to disband, to go home; but the men were adamant – their business was not with him, but with this sheriff officer. Had he threatened to shoot their sons? Why would he not answer the question? The assorted men from town fought to get through; MacAulay continued to remonstrate. The crowd parted with marked reluctance. (Dr MacDonald of Gisla asserts besides they finally secured a promise from MacLennan that he would not return with yet more summonses of ejection, but this seems highly improbable, especially given MacLennan's character and in front of Stornoway witnesses.) The party at last made their boat; oars dug into the water, and they were safely away.

Colin MacLennan looked neither frightened nor chastened. He was chortling. Before Bain's puzzled gaze, he actually seized his oilskin and pulled at the rent, till it was even worse. He was happy; he had got the trouble he wanted, and something for which he could now land these people – or some of them – in court. By the time they scrambled ashore on the Lewis mainland, Grant relates, MacLennan's exultation was such that he grabbed Peter Bain's bagpipes and, all the way to Garynahine, struck up this jolly tune and that. When he gave the jigs and marches a break, he banged on loudly about how, in the course of enforcing the law, he had every right to use a gun if people dared interfere with him.

In time, they were all back at Stornoway, and there MacLennan at once reported to Donald Munro and William Ross in luscious, no doubt richly embroidered detail. He named names. The joint procurators fiscal listened enthused. Formal warrants were quickly drawn up for the arrest of three Bernera men: Angus MacDonald of Tobson, Norman MacAulay of Tobson and John MacLeod of Breaclete. They were 'charged on indictment, before a jury, with assaulting an officer of the law, "in revenge for having executed his duty, and to the injury of his person . . . a crime of a heinous nature and severely punishable".'

Shortly afterwards, Donald Munro himself now visited Bernera – or almost; he went only as far as Earshader, travelling first by stately brougham, by Leurbost and Achmore and Garynahine to Callanish, and then – no doubt wrapped up warm – by the Uig ferry. Donald Munro flatly refused to land on Bernera itself, though it would have been no more inconvenient for him. He may have been genuinely apprehensive; more probably, it suited his purposes to behave as if the place were now in such lawlessness even he could not safely visit. And he no doubt enjoyed summoning the men of Bernera over the narrows, and took pleasure too in beholding their assembly on the shore and the resentful launching of boats.

Fifty men duly marshalled before him, seething, but studiously polite. Donald Munro harangued them like children. They should be more grateful. The farm of Haclete was better than the farm of Earshader, for all their land would then be on Bernera itself. They would no longer have to swim their stock, twice a year, over the straits. It was dangerous. What was now decreed was safer for them, their cattle, their women, their children, declared the factor, looking about him coldly. (No one asked aloud why, were Munro indeed so concerned for the safety of Bernera folk on these yards of briny deep, he had just ordered so many men to brave them.)

And he had another token of the Estate's generosity besides: he was going to have the rents and 'soumings' (the quota of stock permitted per tenant) for the new grazings fixed by three arbitrators. These, he announced (with no apparent sense of absurdity) would be chosen by himself; and he named them – all biddable tenant-farmers. If the tenants did not trust any of them, they could have a fourth arbitrator – which he would also choose.

Munro was evidently struck by the lack of unbounded Bernera joy, for his tone changed. Moreover, he now declared, if the people of Bernera ever again dared to try and take their cows over the sound, he would bring the Volunteers from Stornoway to stop them. Now the men were murmuring, their gaze more furious than ever. And besides, barked Munro – though he knew perfectly well not a single household on Bernera was in arrears of rent – he would have them all evicted from their crofts if they continued in this obduracy.

Even now, the nerve and patience of the Bernera tenants held. They neither stormed him nor would they yield. Munro, seething with fury, dismissed them, and brooded on the position as he schemed with James MacRae, his weaselly ground officer. The chamberlain's bluff had been firmly called. He would now hit those people hard – very hard indeed, with the most ferocious sanction in his power; then, when they were terrified, and biddable, and shaken into obedience, he would (as James Shaw Grant puts it) 'present his commands as if they were concessions'.

His immediate business on Uig now was much darker – and wholly illegal. For, in his coat pocket, Munro carried the 'precognition' – the sworn witness-statement – William Ross had taken down, as joint procurator fiscal, from Colin MacLennan. And, as Grant puts it, 'combining Court business with Estate business, or perhaps even combining business with pleasure, an hour or two later Munro covertly went over the Sheriff Officer's precognition with James MacRae'. It was unlawful enough even to discuss the testimony of one potential witness with another. But Munro went further. He doctored MacLennan's statement so that in every detail it would match the recollections of the Uig ground officer. When this case came to court, Munro would make sure his performing monkeys were thoroughly coached. There remained, now, only the happy business of the arrests – and the full terrors of the law. His law.

On 7 April still another Stornoway grandee embarked on the long, slow journey to Bernera. William Ross (in his capacity as joint procurator fiscal, though one could never be quite sure) trundled, like everyone else, to Callanish, and accompanying him dutifully was Superintendent Donald Cameron.

The police do not generally emerge well in these gloomy pages of Highland history, but Cameron – in command of all officers on Lewis – is a notable exception, and was an interesting man. Despite his surname (one, to this day, associated generally with Lochaber) he hailed from Wester Ross; Donald Cameron was only a little boy when his family were evicted from their own croft at Inverlael, by Little Lochbroom. He was well known on Lewis, greatly liked, had vast common sense and was a fluent, native Gaelic speaker. Cameron took his job seriously – he executed his duty with unfaltering diligence and had all respect for lawful authority, due process, chains of command – but he had a keen sense of what, in modern policing, is known as 'discretion'. It is a sensible dislike of unnecessary scenes and strifes; a keen awareness that bad coppering can foment disorder instead of deterring it.

It was Cameron's job today, under Ross's oversight, to arrest the three named Bernera crofters. At Callanish, though, they were told Bernera was in such a state – the people so furious – it would be imprudent to proceed. (Donald Munro had no doubt said as much noisily on his way back home.) Superintendent Cameron took this with some scepticism (Lewis then, as now, is a place of joyous rumour) and would not think of abandoning the journey. Ross, however, the dainty townee, started to have visions of his head on a spike. He stayed firmly behind, probably over a pint or two at Callanish Inn.

Donald Cameron, as he had all the while expected, met with a reception on Bernera that was not just civil but genial. Quite a few people knew him, and his name was widely respected. He explained regretfully what he was about, this day, and they understood it was his job, and that there was no malice in it. (There was besides the confidence, for those who had witnessed the momentary scuffle a fortnight before, that the three accused had done nothing wrong; besides, with everyone under threat of eviction anyway, things could scarcely become worse.) The superintendent took himself first to John MacLeod's house at Breaclete. His target was away from home, he was told, but would be back that night. Cameron then inquired of the Tobson men, and learned there was to be a midweek prayer meeting there this same evening and that both Angus MacDonald and Norman MacAulay were regular attenders.

According to James Shaw Grant, Donald Cameron then went to see the minister, 'Rev. Mr Campbell'. This raises an eyebrow: John Campbell, minister of Uig Free Church since 1846, was now in his mid sixties and his manse was at Uigen; it is possible he was on Bernera that day (though this in a huge parish with literally dozens of midweek meetings), or that Cameron took a boat across the loch to visit him, but either seems most unlikely. It would have made much more sense for Cameron to write to the Uig minister a day or two before his mission, of which he probably had reasonable notice – and even more probable it was a local elder or 'missionary', a modestly salaried lay-preacher, he consulted on Bernera. Whoever it was, the superintendent explained he would attend the meeting himself (his bearing generally suggests he was himself a Christian and a communicant) and sought help in explaining the position to the people, to avoid any upset.

But only Norman MacAulay, in the event, turned up. Angus MacDonald had made for town that morning on business, MacAulay told Superintendent Cameron after the service, and he was not yet back. The meeting had evidently gone serenely, and the discussion between MacAulay and Cameron was quite amicable. The crofter had not the least difficulty giving himself up, he explained, but he would really rather wait till the other two joined him. Cameron fully understood and was happy to accept MacAulay's word that he and the others, on the due date, would present themselves at Stornoway Sheriff Court.

And the policeman was no doubt in tranquil trim as the boat took him back to Callanish – only to find, on his arrival, that William Ross had left hours earlier, hastening back to town and in evident excitement. What was more, he had left lofty orders behind: the policeman was to stay in Callanish and await, in good time, his instructions. It took Cameron but moments to realise that Ross must have learned of Angus MacDonald's jaunt that day to Stornoway. Well aware of the sort of regime Ross and Munro ran – and their exultation in dramatics and trouble – the superintendent had immediately a very bad feeling. And he felt wryly in his pocket. He had all the relevant warrants – and MacDonald could not legally be arrested, far less detained, without one. This, Cameron knew full well, was the sort of nicety neither Ross nor Munro took too seriously.

Superintendent Cameron ignored the joint procurator lordly orders. He left Callanish at once, making for Stornoway as quickly as possible.

Angus MacDonald, according to his son, had recently finished a season for Kenneth Smith, and had gone to town that April morning to collect his hard-earned wages. He had no reason, at this stage, to fear such proximity to authority; no idea, probably, he was in any trouble at all. According to James Shaw Grant, William Ross had got back to town with a speed remarkable in the age of the pony and trap, for he promptly told Colin MacLennan their quarry was in town, and sent him out on the prowl; MacLennan duly found him – though by then MacDonald must have been in Stornoway for hours, enough time to collect any amount of pay, and would surely have begun the journey back to Callanish, even allowing for some satisfied liquid refreshment in an alluring howff. Norman MacDonald's own account is more believable: by pure mischance, his father was walking contentedly along a street when espied by his own Bernera ground officer, James MacRae. Within minutes – and, ironically, right outside William Ross's stately house on Kenneth Street – Angus MacDonald found himself inexplicably seized by assorted cocky policemen.

He was undoubtedly shocked, and if he had celebrated that season's payment in customary fashion he was no doubt at least a little fortified; but MacDonald had the wits about him to demand what was going on, and perhaps besides to demand production of a warrant: it may be that his English was poor, and that the policemen wrestling with him had worse or non-existent Gaelic, but within a minute there was a violent struggle. The young fisherman stoutly resisted and, as the flustered officers quickly lost control of the situation, passers-by dashed to his aid, and then in turn his own friends, as word reached the harbour. Munro and Ross themselves now appeared, with all the clerks in their offices less than willingly in their train. MacDonald protested furiously that he was quite prepared to turn up at court on any date he was told, but the policemen would not listen – and the joint procurators fiscal certainly would not – and he fought then all the harder, and still more bodies piled into the melee, and more appalled policemen. His son would tell Anne Whitaker – all but bouncing excitedly up and down in his chair – that a

big crowd of men started to gather. And who came when he heard but a man from Valtos, Uig, named John Smith. He made his way through the crowd and the first policeman he caught, he took hold of him by the scruff of his neck and the seat of his trousers, lifted him right up and banged him down on the street. That policeman was walking the street with no bottom in his pants . . .

It was only a hundred yards from the spot where Angus MacDonald was grabbed to Stornoway police station. It took them four hours to get him there, and Joni Buchanan's account suggests a complicated and near-comic ballet indeed, for the police first

lured Angus into a close in the centre of town and four policemen tried to hold him down. The fisherman managed, however, to break free and raced up Francis Street with the policemen at his heels. One of the constables managed to undo MacDonald's braces; his trousers fell down and tripped him up . . .

The capture, enthused the *Highlander*, a new, radical and pro-crofter paper, 'was more easily resolved than done; the policemen found it almost impossible to apprehend the man, and the lookers-on declined to render any assistance. The Fiscal was sent for, the Sheriff-Clerk, and the Sheriff himself . . . and altogether they lodged the terrible man from Bernera in jail.' For – in wild overreaction – someone was sent puffing for Sheriff Spittal himself, who seems immediately to have feared bloody revolution, for he was shortly along in all his splendour to read the Riot Act. Passed at the height of Jacobite panic in the reign of George I, it allowed local authority – on pretty well any pretext it chose – to order the dispersal of any group of a dozen or more people who were 'unlawfully, riotously and tumultuously assembled together', and they had one hour to do so (on pain, potentially, of death) once a Justice of the Peace, or mayor, or provost, or whoever, had read aloud, to the last syllable, this melodramatic formula:

> Our Sovereign Lady the Queen chargeth and commandeth all persons, being assembled, immediately to disperse themselves, and peaceably to depart to their habitations, or to their lawful business, upon the pains contained in the act made in the first year of King George, for preventing tumults and riotous assemblies. God Save the Queen!

This pantomime measure would endure on the statute book until 1973; and probably only died off then in the context of bloody trouble in Northern Ireland. But the ferocious sanctions the Act laid down for disobedience, once the rubric had been read, were for long intimidating. Very slowly, Angus MacDonald's new allies let go, peeled off, slunk away. In fact, one independent witness, according to Grant – in later lines to the *Inverness Courier* – asserted that the actual affray lasted barely half an hour; thereafter there was only a protracted, obstinate, shoving stand-off, as reinforcements were sent for and legalities gone through. Spittal pointedly called on some of the men – he recognised the odd face – to help the police. By the time the shaken fisherman was dragged into the cells – most of the clothing torn from his body, bruised and scraped and cut – he was already past further struggle. He was nevertheless bound hand and foot, and in that trussed condition dumped on the hard cold floor.

Colin MacLennan moved in, his eyes glittering. He wore heavy boots, and he started to kick the man from Bernera, and no doubt aimed at especially tender parts of his body; and Colin MacLennan went on kicking for a long time. People stood about, watching. Pipes were lit.

It dawned belatedly on the officers – and the fiscals – that they had not even a warrant for this man's arrest. Ross and Munro snorted at this trivial concern, and scrawled out some sort of duplicate; they also made sure the battered MacDonald was questioned and committed for trial that same night. But the policemen knew enough of the law to grow seriously worried, and Sheriff Spittal besides began to ask incredulous questions.

The more he learned, the more the irregularities of all this became evident, the more alarmed the sheriff substitute became. He turned to the one man he felt worthy of trust and, quite forgetting his dignity, hastened personally to the home of Superintendent Cameron – who, of course, still floundering across Lewis and blazing against the foolish William Ross, was not at home. Spittal's heart sank when he found Cameron absent. He left firm word with Mrs Cameron: the superintendent was to see him as early as possible the following day.

Meanwhile – and it took them a good few hours – men sped as fast as they could over the moors to Callanish, and thence to Bernera, and thus the news began fast to seep around the island. 'When they reached Tobson,' Norman MacDonald related, 'the people asked them what news there was. "Great news," they said, "Great news indeed. Angus MacDonald is in prison."'

The very next morning they sent a boat to Uig; they said what had happened, told them about my father being in prison, and asked the people of Uig to meet them in Garynahine at twelve o'clock the next day. A messenger went through every village in Uig. They sent another boat to Carloway, and sent messengers from Carloway to Shawbost, and from Shawbost to Bragar and from Bragar to Arnol and around Brue and Barvas and Shader and Borve and as far as Ness. They were all to meet in the Square in Stornoway in the evening.

On the next day when the Bernera people got to Garynahine there was no sign of the Uig people; but in an hour or two the regiment came in sight with a piper leading them.

The Valtos miller, Donald MacRitchie ('An Irish') had rallied crofters there; Donald MacDonald of Bosta, 'Dan', had roused most of Bernera to the cause. The piper – evidently a rather good one – was a Donald MacLennan, from Kneep. The men were armed with everything they could think of – spades, peat-irons, pitchforks and so on – and – desperate as the situation now was – they planned to march on Stornoway and, if necessary, tear the prison down to bring Angus MacDonald out. For now, they quickly snacked on salt meat and bread (probably oat- and barley-cake) and a little welcome whisky, for the stark march facing them. But word ran ahead – the speed with which news ran around Lewis, even in those days before the telephone, never fails to impress – and the authorities heard reports that the terrible men of Bernera were even planning to seize the mast of a ship, and with that to batter down the prison door.

It is unlikely Superintendent Donald Cameron had enjoyed much sleep. It was scarcely after dawn when he coolly reported to the sheriff and, quietly and in every detail, told him everything he knew. Word was already filtering into town of serious trouble from Bernera. Cameron's advice to Spittal was blunt: Angus

MacDonald should be freed immediately. The charges laid against him did not remotely justify his remand in custody; the superintendent was entirely satisfied he and the other Bernera accused would show up for due process without unseemly coercion and – more pragmatically, but still more urgently – the superintendent refused to answer for the consequences if the fisherman was still in jail when the men of Bernera reached Stornoway. Cameron was now certain that – and he was not, deep down, that sure he could blame them – should MacDonald still be immured in chokey, after everything they had endured from Munro and Ross, his compatriots would tear it to pieces.

Sheriff Spittal swallowed hard, and accepted this counsel. Telegram messages were coming in now; there were sensational reports already circling Inverness, and what was reaching Inverness would surely be fast in the ears of Sheriff Principal Fordyce and – worse – of the authorities in Edinburgh. (Later that day, one Inverness paper would go to print with a wholly unfounded report that Fordyce had asked Edinburgh to marshall troops for urgent despatch to Lewis, 'usually one of the most peaceably disposed parts of Her Majesty's dominions', ran the column excitedly.) And – left to the tender mercies of Munro and Ross – or had Spittal not acceded to Cameron's wisdom – it might well have come to lethal military force.

Seldom, if ever, can an accused man have been arrested so messily, imprisoned so brutally and then released with such speed, generosity and distinct alarm. Superintendent Cameron explained, soothed, made sympathetic non-committal noises, allowed the odd vague grunt of horror. Angus Mac-Donald was washed, his cuts and scrapes dressed. He was handsomely fed. He was besides, kitted out quickly with a whole set of new clothes (and one suspects the superintendent made sure they were good clothes at that). He levelled quietly with the fisherman; he explained the danger to property, life and limb – and the cause of Bernera itself – if he did not make quickly on the way to the place and meet his compatriots before they reached town. Angus MacDonald trusted Cameron, and wholeheartedly agreed. He certainly did not want Stornoway laid to waste, or violent confrontation. But, he thought quietly to himself, it would be a shame for the men to come all that way, only to turn back meekly like shushed children . . .

The force from the west tramped on, by track and dale, along the rough road to Leurbost, and then Stornoway. (The 'Pentland Road', with its spur over Beinn a Bhuna to Achmore, would not materialise until the twentieth century.) How many men there were remains unclear; it seems in the event that few, if any at all, at last rallied at Garynhine from any townships north of Uig and Loch Roag. At most, there were 300; probably something between 150 and 200, and for the most part young enough for the hike and old enough to be canny.

And they had just reached Achmore itself, according to Mor MacLeod in 2010, at the heart and almost the summit of north Lewis, with its splendid panorama south, east, west of lochs and hills and mountains – when a familiar if slightly limping, bruised figure loomed before them in smart new clothes.

Angus MacDonald said his words; but if they included the advice to turn round and make for home, one suspects there was little heart behind them. 'Dan', from Bosta, held firm. They need not now think of war, force and masts, he declared; nor brace for a fight – but they would proceed more or less as planned, in might and dignity. They would behave studiously well and, in the morning, they would march in good order to Lews Castle itself. They had seen quite enough of Donald Munro. They would lay their whole case before Sir James Matheson.

MacLennan, from Kneep – probably of past Army service – was a grand piper indeed. He regaled them with 'The Campbells are Coming', with other airs of steady, buoyant, marching beat. Cheered and no doubt rather smug at Angus MacDonald's liberation, the men of Bernera and Uig advanced all the more briskly, down the moors of Lochs, smelling the thickening reek of Stornoway fires. And they mustered for the night at Marybank, on a great park then part of Manor Farm and where cattle and their handlers from the west had always rested at the end of the annual drove, before rallying in the morning to the market itself; and that field is still there, hard behind the house where I write.

For the last and distinctly forlorn time, mighty men in black showed up in the dusk, asserts Joni Buchanan, and beseeched them to go home – the sheriff clerk, and a not greatly abashed William Ross the joint procurator fiscal, and Superintendent Cameron. The men of Bernera were pleasant, straightforward – and unyielding. James Shaw Grant mentions no such encounter until the following day, when the superintendent heard they were in town and, after a night's Marybank rest, moved round to the open land at Goathill. He alone turned up, according to Grant, and such was the welcome that, if he had feared any possibility of disorder, he was fast reassured. Everyone was affable and Cameron was offered a whisky, which he was pleased to accept. They turned joyously on MacLennan, and called on 'an appropriate tune complimentary to me', Cameron would later report. He did not record what it was – perhaps, for all we know, the police boss was tone-deaf – one suspects, though, it was that stomper of the soldiers of Inverness-shire, 'The March of the Cameron Men'.

> There's many a man of the Cameron clan
> That has followed his chief to the field
> He has sworn to support him or die by his side
> For a Cameron never can yield.

I hear the pibroch sounding, sounding
Deep o'er the mountain and glen
While light springing footsteps
Are trampling the heath.

'Tis the march of the Cameron men.
'Tis the march, 'tis the march
'Tis the march of the Cameron men.

Oh, proudly they walk, but each Cameron knows
He may tread on the heather no more
But boldly he follows his chief to the field
Where his laurels were gathered before.

The moon has arisen, it shines on the path
Now trod by the gallant and true
High, high are their hopes, for their chieftain has said
That whatever men dare, they can do.

'Tis the march of the Cameron men
'Tis the march, 'tis the march
'Tis the march of the Cameron men . . .

The fun over, Cameron turned to his duty. He was well aware of a greater danger than Bernera mayhem – panicked, local overreaction to their presence, with cudgels and implements and all. The best way to reassure the sheriff, he explained, was to let the three Bernera accused report for 'judicial examination' by Spittal at the courthouse. The superintendent was not greatly surprised when, to a man, the contingent refused even to think of such a course; were not Angus MacDonald's injuries reason enough? Cameron instead sent for Spittal, who had the good sense and character to come instead to the field of encampment. There, the sheriff substitute met quietly, in turn, with a clerk or two present, with MacDonald, and MacAulay, and MacLeod, and each declaration was soon recorded for the due diet.

Now their great adventure was to hand. The Bernera battalion elected one Angus MacArthur as their speaker, probably because he was deemed to have the best command of English. It was also accepted, without the superintendent demanding it, that it would all the more soothe the gentry of the castle if Cameron accompanied them. The various, conflicting accounts cannot agree either whether all the Bernera force marched up to the castle, or just a select deputation. (Cameron also sent a quiet order back to the station: every policeman in town was to stay indoors, out of sight, until the Bernera brigade was over the horizon and making for home.)

But – first – this sturdy band wanted a little time of just a little quiet triumph, and were not greatly concerned (rather, enchanted) how mysteriously their ranks had swollen, as word went about Stornoway of the delicacies of the sheriff and the affability of the policeman and that there was no prospect of violence or arrests. So MacLennan fixed his pipes again, and they marched proudly, once, in a circuit of Stornoway, the men of Bernera and Uig and with around a thousand people behind them, to the air – as Norman MacDonald would recall in 1974 – of *'Gabhaidh mise 'n Rathad Mor. Olc no maith le cach e'. . .'*

> I will take my own great way
> Whatever the people think of me
> I will take my own great way . . .

And then, and by Porter's Lodge itself and as true gentry, they paraded up that stately drive and by the maturing trees to the very *porte cochère* of Lews Castle, where the Mathesons were waiting for them and, no doubt, with the odd maid peeping wildly from the corners of high windows.

It was stately; it was dignified; and – while harsh and fair things have been here recorded of Sir James Matheson – the drug baron was now a frail old man of 78, and he handled his last important scene to perfection. He was courtly and courteous, immaculately dressed, oozing friendliness. And he listened, as MacArthur related – in clear, slow, beautiful English – and as the scale of what had been done to the Bernera people dawned on him, the proprietor visibly struggled to hide his astonishment. He declared he knew nothing at all – nothing of any of it; this might have been less than credible 20 years before but, despite the sneers of one or two writers, there is no reason to disbelieve the baronet. Munro, he said, had not consulted him, or told him any of this. He was still enough of the potentate to watch his promises. As long as they all returned in Bernera – now, or at least shortly, in peace – Sir James gave his word he would thoroughly look into their grievances. And he would start by sending valuators into Bernera to assess matters on the spot.

Norman MacDonald describes the final Matheson deliverance engagingly in 1974. ' "Oh, well, I'm very sorry," said the landlord. "I didn't hear or know anything about that at all. But I can guarantee that nobody can touch you in your homes or in your crofts." '

The audience was over; Sir James evaporated back into the grand Castle apartments like any emperor, after pleasantly directing his visitors to the great new conservatory. It must have been an overwhelming sight for those used to the humble thatched homes of Bernera – all the glass and light and steamy warmth; the unseasonal flowers; the exotics and succulents; the stately, improbable tree-ferns. Lady Matheson floated in with them, and Superintendent Cameron. Servants hurried with trays, pots. There was fine wheaten bread, and hot coffee – a great novelty – and jugs of milk, and salvers piled high with fine, thinly sliced cold beef.

Her ladyship was pleasant, a little twittery, a little anxious. She kept asking for one assurance: that on no account would the men go back into town. She was probably more worried about their boasting than any potential atrocities – there were, after all, highly respectable families in town who had never been allowed inside this grandiloquent greenhouse – but the Bernera and Uig men were in an awkward position. They were not often in Stornoway, especially in such jolly number. They had still to pay for that whisky; there were things they could buy while here, friends they could see. Cameron sensed the tension and assured the chatelaine of Lews Castle he would take personal responsibility for their conduct. 'Again, his faith was justified,' James Shaw Grant records. 'The men marched into town, spent an hour or two there, and left again in good order, without molesting anyone.'

Cameron apart, policemen everywhere slunk as commanded, glowering, behind doors made fast.

Superintendent Donald Cameron must have been exhausted. He was also furious. Behind a firmly maintained front of serenity, patience and wisdom, he knew how close Stornoway had been brought to mayhem.

A few days later he completed a careful report to his chief constable in Dingwall. And the superintendent was not unduly dainty with his words, or always immaculate in his English grammar. The 'riot' – and he made plain that, in his view, it scarcely merited that description, 'was created by the Fiscal, who ought to be the last official to raise such . . . I have no doubt whatever in my own mind the Sheriff Officer was put up to say something to aggravate the people when serving the writs, in order to get them to commit an offence, which the Fiscal would make a handle for to cause the police to interfere, in order to strike terror into the people so that they will submit to the Factor's arrangements.'

With a trial now looming, Cameron was both furious – and shocked – by the continued antics of Munro and Ross, now trying frantically to cover their tracks as all town buzzed with word of the melee on Kenneth Street, the abuse of a prisoner, the courage and bearing of the Bernera men, the stately reception at Lews Castle, the sweet nothings of Sir James himself – and the incandescent coverage, now, not just in the Highland papers, but in journals far further afield. William Ross, complained Cameron to his superior, was already trying to question police officers in Stornoway about their past service, with obvious intent – to lay suspicions that their inexperience, not his own incompetence, had triggered the fracas in truth begotten by Donald Munro and himself.

Only on Sabbath morning, making for the Free Church on Kenneth Street and past Ross's house, continued Superintendent Cameron, he had been acutely embarrassed when the solicitor and joint procurator fiscal suddenly bustled forth to waylay him, obviously anxious to suborn the senior policeman into some scheme of cover-up or other. Cameron had quite properly told him that he never discussed business on the Lord's Day.

As his commander in Dingwall read on – and he would read Cameron's letter aloud, later, to Sheriff Principal Fordyce himself – additional reason for the superintendent's wariness of any cosy conversation with Ross was soon evident.

Donald Cameron now made two stark predictions. For one, after all that official mishandling, the perceived Bernera triumph – whatever might become of the accused in court – had established a dangerous precedent; from now on, anyone thought unjustly imprisoned in the community would probably be rescued by physical force. (He was right; the folk memory endures, and as recently as the 1990s, in a much more squalid day, a raging mob of island youths of a Saturday night actually stormed the modern Stornoway police station, after friends had been 'lifted'.) And, for another, said Cameron – and perhaps with a degree of grim satisfaction – if that charge against the Bernera trio did come to trial, Donald Munro would sink in a 'bog of his own creating'.

The police on Lewis could get on perfectly well with her people, and without any difficulty maintain excellent order in town and country, Cameron now made very plain, were it not for the fact that the procurator fiscal was also the factor. And, as long as Donald Munro and his partner continued constantly to interfere with their duties, the position of the police on Lewis would remain untenable.

Sheriff Principal Fordyce, a day or two later, listened in silence as Cameron's letter was read aloud to him. 'Well,' he said, 'Spittal's report was expressed in much stronger language.'

That same day – after over 32 years – Donald Munro, by the express decree of the sheriff in Dingwall, was suspended from all the powers and functions of procurator fiscal.

11

Court: The trial of the 'Bernera Three'
– and Donald Munro . . .

Even now – startled, angry, reeling – Donald Munro quite failed to grasp how near the edge of the crater he stood.

He was, after all, still procurator fiscal in title (and no doubt harboured fantasies he would yet regain its powers, and besides remain Chamberlain of the Lews). Despite the frightful publicity – Lewis crofters were 'in a state of virtual slavery', thundered another new and then radical paper, the *Oban Times*, '. . . in conditions which in other lands would foster a state of revolution' – Sir James Matheson remained plainly reluctant to get rid of him.

That was partly the proprietor's own lofty pride; he was of a generation of self-assured men, all talent and entitlement, disinclined to buckle to the press, far less mere tenants and the lower orders. But it was also Matheson's own calculating, amoral self-interest. Monstrous as he was, in the strict job (and executed without scruple) of screwing as much money out of Lewis as possible, Donald Munro had long proved masterly; and if there was anything at all in which Sir James Matheson excelled, it was in reading a balance sheet and enjoying serene contemplation of the gold in his counting-house. By 1874, as reliably assessed in the valuation roll of Ross County, the annual rental of Lewis was £23,804 13s 4d – a nice little earner on an island bought 30 years earlier for £190,000 and on which significant Estate expenditure had long since ceased, save for immediate Matheson indulgence.

And, despite his smooth words to the Bernera men in his porch, Sir James did not lift a finger for them once they were safely away – nothing was ever in fact done to address their concerns, save that the oppressive grazings scheme was quietly allowed to founder. They retained Earshader after all, and in fact a hamlet was soon established there. Sir James Matheson besides, to all inquiries and in the teeth of storming newspaper reports and flaming correspondence columns, stuck stoutly by his chamberlain, in firm and honeyed terms: he would be retained as long as he lived. The words proved at last of no more value than a modern premier's assurance of some beleaguered colleague that his position was 'unassailable'.

Munro's final, terminal mistake was, even after all that had passed, to push the case of those arraigned for the 'Bernera Riot' on to determined trial. Though no longer fiscal himself, he could certainly have had the whole thing quietly dropped by William Ross. That, to their incredulity, Colin MacLennan was unexpectedly charged – for the vile assault on Angus MacDonald – may have coloured their judgement in this. But Munro's judgement had all but gone anyway; unsupervised and unchecked for so long, blithely altering legal records, unmarried and close emotionally to no one, and almost laughably lacking in self-awareness, he was an increasingly delusional figure.

And there was, besides, treachery very near to hand. It is a very fine point indeed as to which – William Ross or Donald Munro – was the more evil man. But Ross was a good deal smarter, and much more coldly grounded. Munro was at bottom a pompous ass; Ross was sleekit, feline, cutting a neat smooth figure in Stornoway parlours. Now, as a consequence of his partner's folly and the erosion of his public standing, he enjoyed solitary eminence as fiscal. He would have not have been human – and certainly not William Ross – had he not pondered what else might drift his way by offices, income and standing, were his cousin and partner's authority diminished still more. And cowardice besides – the need to preserve his own fortunes from any smut of unfolding Munro disgrace – was no doubt an element too.

And there is ground to believe – not least in Ross's curious carriage in the trial to come – that he deliberately stepped back and allowed the Chamberlain of the Lews to fashion as fat a noose for his own neck, poised over as long a drop, as his blinkered arrogance was prepared to take him.

Both, though, must have assumed that the three West Side rustics would have no legal agent – or, at worst, only the compromised Napier Campbell. But a larger hand was firmly at work. Once of the ablest courtroom-lawyers of his day – and certainly the best in the Highlands – suddenly surfaced as defence counsel for the Bernera men. Charles Innes was no radical, and could not credibly 'be called a friend of the crofters', notes I.M.M. MacPhail – certainly, as we shall see, Innes spoke generally of ordinary Lewis people as if they were engaging, somewhat dim children. But he would later be the Conservative agent for Inverness-shire and may have had thoughts of a Parliamentary career in the Tory interest. As late Liberal MP for Ross and Cromarty – a seat bequeathed with no difficulty, and in the same colours, to his nephew – Sir James Matheson offered a tempting target. Anything that brought his island affairs into disrepute suited the Innes agenda.

But Innes did not come cheap. Nor – almost within days of the trial – did an immaculately printed, deliciously detailed Edinburgh pamphlet, *Report of the Trial of the So-Called 'Bernera Rioters'*, snapped up deliriously by the thousand throughout the Highlands. It was been suggested – even by James Shaw Grant, who insists it was a widespread Lewis tradition – that Matheson himself funded the defence, but that is preposterous; he could easily have quashed the case, simply by leaning hard on his own Stornoway lawyers, and the publicity from court did the proprietor enormous damage. Uneasily aware of the fatuity here, Grant then suggests Kenneth Smith the curer as *deus ex machina*; after all, it was in his immediate economic interest that these three men continue to catch his herrings, rather than languish in prison. But he offers no proof of the agency of 'California', and nothing we know of Kenneth Smith suggests quite the skills, the knowledge or the elegantly turned phrase of that glorious pamphlet.

Who, then, paid the clever lawyer from Inverness and wrote and financed this damning publication? One man, asserts MacPhail, who had both the interest and the means

was Daniel MacKinlay, a native of Lewis who had become a wealthy merchant in Calcutta and had taken a lease of the shootings at Gress in Lewis in 1874, not long after the Bernera riot. MacKinlay himself in 1878 produced a pamphlet containing scathing criticism of the whole Matheson regime . . . In it he denounced the removal of whole townships to create sporting estates and the transfer of the people to already-overcrowded townships, the neglect of fisheries, the failure to improve housing conditions and crofting conditions generally. In this respect Sir James was unfavourably compared with his nephew, Alexander Matheson, also a wealthy magnate, who had made his fortune in the East but had transformed his estates of Ardross and Strathcarron. Sir James was said to have spent half a million pounds on Lewis with little return, but MacKinlay, in a detailed analysis of the expenditure, proved that the paternalism or despotism of the Matheson regime had been far from a benevolent one and of little benefit to the crofters. It is as well to add, however, that one should discount some of the stories of Lewismen living in misery in their squalid hovels. The best-known song about Lewis in the nineteenth century, *Eilean an Fhraoich* ('Isle of Heather'), composed in the 1860s by Murdo MacLeod, an exile in Glasgow, made the island seem to be almost heaven on earth; and the description of Lewis life which appeared in the *Glasgow Herald* in the 1870s from the pen of W. Anderson Smith revealed a happy, contented, hardworking people.

MacPhail is almost certainly correct in his identification. And that last is an important point; whatever the outrages and abuses we have noted, and despite the paean of woes recorded a decade later by Lord Napier and company, this was not generally a miserable island. Those of us just old enough to remember the generation born in the last 20 years of the nineteenth century – the men and women who would live (if they were fortunate enough) through two world wars, the *Iolaire* disaster, the destitution and mass emigration of the 1920s and 1930s and the cloud of prevalent tuberculosis to modern comforts and an assured welfare state – can attest to their vigour, their wisdom, their character and extraordinary capacity for happiness that is in contrast to the prevalent bitterness on Lewis today and the stumbling ignobility of its public life. It was also a community – and in some districts till very recently indeed – moulded daily by widespread, sincere, personal religion. The remarkable discipline of the Bernera men in 1874 was conditioned, not least, by the daily family worship, held morning and evening, in practically every island home; many of the men on that march were of character, spirituality and secret prayer.

In his engaging study of the castles of Stornoway, Peter Cunningham too points to the world captured in the early 1870s by W. Anderson Smith (the articles, no doubt to capitalise on all the Bernera publicity, appeared as his book *Lewisiana* in 1875) and cites his 'spirited description of a likable people in a hostile environment and under an oppressive regime', which 'arouses admiration of a resilient and resourceful breed'. And Smith observed neatly that

> We are told that at one time the cottars were offered leases with *only* fifty-four rules attached, the transgression of one cancelling the right of the lessee. One old man, at Ness, laughed heartily at the document; sagely remarking that he could not keep ten commandments for a mansion in the sky, much less fifty-four for a blackhouse in the Lews . . .

And it was against that background that the Chamberlain of the Lews walked the last complacent mile to his destruction. Dozens – if not hundreds – piled into Stornoway Sheriff Court on Friday 17 July 1874, and (as anyone could have foreseen, and as James Shaw Grant duly puts it) the 'trial of the Bernera Three . . . was transformed into the trial of Donald Munro'.

Sheriff Spittal presided. William Ross was in charge of the prosecution and 'Mr Charles Innes, solicitor, Inverness, acted as agent for the accused.' John Ross, the sheriff clerk depute and known to all as 'Little Ross', no relation to the local solicitors and by every account a decent man, served as clerk of court and read – in verbose and majestic Scots form – the long and very detailed charge or 'libel' against Angus MacDonald, Norman MacAulay and John MacLeod; and averred (amidst a great many other words) – 'YET TRUE IT IS AND OF VERITY' – that they did on the

25th day of March 1874, or on one or the other of the days of that month, or of February immediately proceeding, or of April immediately following, in the island of Bernera aforesaid, and at a part thereof situated about half way between the township of Breaclete aforesaid, and the march of the farm of Kirkibost, in the said island of Bernera, wickedly and feloniously attack and assault the said Colin MacLennan, and did surround him in a violent and excited manner, and seize hold of him by the breast or collar, or other part of parts of his person, and did pull and jostle him, and threaten to kill him, and did seize hold of his top-coat, waterproof coat, and leggings, and did maliciously tear and destroy and render the same useless, and by all which the said Colin MacLennan was put in a state of great terror and alarm, and was injured in his person; and all this they the said Angus MacDonald (Norman's son), Norman MacAulay, and John MacLeod, or one or more of them, did, well knowing, or having good reason to believe, that he the said Colin MacLennan was an officer of the law, and on account of, or in revenge for, his having executed his duty as such in manner foresaid . . .

Put simply, the three young fishermen were charged with 'aggravated assault', the aggravation being that it had allegedly been wrought upon an officer of the law. They were now called on to plead; and each voice declared, 'Not Guilty'. Then a jury or 'assize' was balloted for: fifteen men (the usual Scots quota), all but two – Donald MacIver, the miller at Breasclete, north of Callanish, and the present tacksman at Gress, Peter Liddle – being from Stornoway itself or immediately adjacent villages like Sandwick. There were two fish-curers, Alexander Morrison (junior) and Alexander MacKenzie; two shoemakers, Malcolm Matheson and Kenneth MacLean; a tailor, Malcolm MacLeod; a baker, Donald MacRae of Point Street; a joiner, Roderick MacRae; a salmon-fisher, James Young, of Sandwick; a 'spirit-dealer', Malcolm MacLeod; a 'druggist', Alexander MacPherson; a farmer, George Watt of Mossend; a mere 'tenant', John MacLennan of Mill Glen, near Stornoway; and a merchant, Charles Morrison. His is the only name that would mean much to most in Lewis today, for the much-loved chandlery and hardware shop he established in 1864 endured, under the original name and at the same premises and with its original character to the end, until 2002: and good hempen coil is known yet on the island as *sioman Thearlaich*, 'Charlie Morrison's rope'.

One might have expected the Crown to launch its case by calling the central witness for the prosecution, Colin MacLennan himself. But the very first man William Ross presented was someone, one would have thought, he had no need to field at all: the Chamberlain of the Lews, Donald Munro. And partner and cousin duly put his partner and cousin through an oddly brisk 'examination-in-chief'.

'I am a solicitor in Stornoway,' Munro confirmed. 'I am law agent, as also factor or chamberlain, for Sir James Matheson, the proprietor of the Lews. I know Colin MacLennan, sheriff officer. I was in the habit of employing him in my capacity of solicitor; I employed him in March last to serve summonses of removing against the Bernera crofters.'

'I show you the summons founded on in libel,' murmured Ross, procurator fiscal, 'and ask if it was one of those the serving of which you entrusted to MacLennan?'

'It was,' said Donald Munro.

The Crown rested.

Charles Innes stood up. He smiled, looked down at his notes, looked up again, adjusted spectacles, glanced down once more. Then he looked at Donald Munro.

'I should like his lordship and the gentleman of the jury to know exactly who you are, Mr Munro. You have told us that you are Chamberlain of the Lews and a solicitor in Stornoway. Are you anything else, or do you hold any appointment in this island other than that of chamberlain?'

Munro frowned, wondered. 'Do you want to know all the appointments I hold?'

'Yes,' said Innes, 'all.'

'I am chairman of the Parochial Boards of the four parishes, chairman of the four school boards, vice-chairman of the Harbour Trustees.'

'Yes . . .' purred Charles Innes. 'Anything more?'

'I can't remember.'

'Allow me to assist your memory,' said Innes. 'Have you anything to do with the Stornoway Gas Company?'

'Yes, I am a director.'

'The water company?'

'Yes, I am a director of that company.'

'Are you connected with the road trust?'

'Yes,' mumbled Munro. 'I believe I am deputy-chairman.'

By now, most present were hugely enjoying themselves.

'Are you collector of poor rates?'

'No,' said Munro, in momentary triumph.

Innes pretended to look puzzled. 'Are not these rates collected by someone in your office?'

'I believe one of my clerks collects some of them,' allowed the Chamberlain of the Lews.

'Are you law agent for the four parochial boards?'

'No,' said Munro, before proceeding calamitously, 'I am not; I am merely law adviser. I make no charge, to save expenses.'

'Are you the Chief Magistrate of Stornoway?' pressed Innes.

'I was until lately,' mumbled the factor, 'but now I am only a commissioner.'

'Are you a Justice of the Peace?' demanded Charles Innes, 'and are you in the habit of acting in the various courts held in Stornoway in which Justices usually sit?'

'Yes,' said Munro.

'Are you a Commissioner of Supply and a Commissioner under the Income Tax?'

'Perhaps I am,' said the factor, starting just a little to fray round the edges, 'but they are unpaid offices, and I don't care about them, and don't often act.'

'Are you a notary public?' inquired the defence agent.

'Yes.'

'Are you baron baillie of Lewis?'

'I don't know,' said Donald Munro. 'I may be, but I don't hold courts.'

'You surely know whether the appointment is included in your commission,' said Charles Innes reproachfully. 'I see by the Scottish law-list you are so described, and I presume you must have given the editor the information.'

'I may have done so,' snapped Munro, wondering wherever all this was going. 'I don't remember.'

'Very well,' soothed Innes, 'we'll say nothing more about the baron-baillie-ship just now. Are you commanding officer of the 1st Company of Ross-shire Artillery Volunteers?'

'No,' allowed the chamberlain, 'but I was for a good many years.'

'I see by the law-list,' said Innes, 'you are still entered therein as Command-ing Officer, and a very odd place, too, to record such an appointment. I don't suppose it has occurred to any other law agent in Scotland to include such an office in the law-list?'

'Perhaps it hasn't been revised for some years,' said Donald Munro, and continued, 'I get a clerk to attend such matters.'

'Oh!' gasped Charles Innes, stepping back a little, in theatrical surprise. 'By the way, I was almost forgetting a very important appointment. Are you Procurator Fiscal of this district?'

Donald Munro was well aware of Sheriff Spittal on the bench.

'I was,' grated Munro.

'You were,' sighed Innes, in some show of horror and sympathy. 'Have you ceased to act?'

'I have.'

'Did you resign?'

'No.'

'Were you removed from the office?' pushed Innes.

'Sheriff Fordyce,' said the factor, very carefully, 'from whom I derived the appointment, withdrew my commission.'

'Did he give any reason?'

'None satisfactory to me.'

'That I don't wonder at,' said Charles Innes. 'I doubt if he could have given a reason which would have been satisfactory to you. Tell us the reason which was not satisfactory. Had it any connection with the case which has brought us all here today? Did *your* removal take place after the Bernera crofters received *their* summonses of removal?'

'I ceased to act after the summonses were served,' said Donald Munro heavily. 'The Sheriff stated he considered I should not hold the two offices of Factor and Fiscal, but I know there are other factors in the county who act as fiscals.'

On the bench, Spittal's eyebrows arched a little. He did not intervene.

'Will you kindly tell us who they are?' invited Innes.

'I can't recall their names at present,' said Donald Munro.

'If you cannot give any names,' said Innes, 'you should not make such positive statements.'

'There is a factor in your own county, at any rate,' flared the chamberlain, 'who is also a fiscal.'

'And who, pray, is he?'

'The fiscal at Inverness,' floundered Munro.

'For whom does he act as factor?'

'I can't say.'

'Really,' said Innes, in quiet triumph, 'I must beg you will not make rash statements. I take it the difference between you and the gentleman to whom you have referred is this. You have ceased to be a fiscal, while he has ceased to be a factor.'

There were the faintest, stifled, half-gurgled sounds from the public gallery.

William Ross could have risen to object at several points by now. He had not done so. Munro's long, ruinous racking by the defence counsel continued, his credibility draining remorselessly away with every other exchange.

Charles Innes now pushed Munro hard on the orders to MacLennan and party for Bernera, not five months earlier.

'I don't know how many summonses of removing I gave to MacLennan,' declared the Chamberlain of the Lews. 'Possibly fifty-six, but I don't remember. The summonses proceeded on the narrative that each crofter should be removed from the' – and here, presumably, Munro consulted notes, or perhaps looked at the Summons, if Ross had left it with him – 'the "acres, gardens, grass, and houses situated in the several parts of Bernera, together with his share, held in common, of the moor, grazings, and pertinents thereto attached; and his share of the summer grazings or shieling-ground on the farm of Earshader in the parish of Uig." That description includes all the crofters possessed, both in Bernera, where their houses and crofts are situated, and in Lewis at Earshader, where their shielings were. I did not, however, intend to remove them from their possessions in Bernera, but merely from their shielings or summer grazings on the mainland – that is, in Lewis. I thought it right in point of form, to include in the summonses the crofts and houses in Bernera . . .'

Munro had had enough. He now swivelled, called on Sheriff Spittal, protested at the questions. They had nothing to do with the case, he asserted angrily – 'I have merely been cited as a witness in a case I understood was of the nature of a criminal charge.'

Spittal told him calmly that the agent for the accused, Mr Innes, had not divulged his line of defence, that he was not bound to do so, and that, as far as he had already gone, the questions might yet have an important bearing on the case. Especially, said Sheriff Substitute Charles Grey Spittal, when you looked at the fact that one of these very summonses was founded on the libel and a production – the sample summons, produced in evidence – and just identified by Mr Munro himself. 'So,' intoned Spittal, 'you had better answer the question.'

By appealing to His Lordship at all, Munro had made himself look desperate, cornered. Now, slapped down so emphatically, he looked ignorant. And beaten.

William Ross had still not risen to his succour.

'My chief reason for including in the summonses all the crofters' possessions,' the factor waded on, 'was because the shielings were merely pertinent of the other possessions.'

Charles Innes smiled faintly. 'Did you in the summonses describe the shielings as "mere pertinents"?'

'The document will speak for itself,' growled Donald Munro.

'Yes,' said Charles Innes, 'I *know* that, but I want you to tell the gentlemen of the jury what it says, as they can't be expected to read it.' And he cast a kindly, man-to-man glance in their direction.

'The document speaks for itself,' repeated the chamberlain.

'To save the time of the Court,' declared Charles Innes, now – but for Munro – everyone's friend, 'I will read the description in the summons produced. "And his share of the summer grazings or shieling ground on the farm of Earshader in said parish." There is no statement to the effect that these grazings were mere pertinents of the crofts, and there is nothing to show that it was at all necessary to include the crofts and houses in the summons if it was not intended to remove the people from all their possessions.'

He was painting Munro deftly into a corner of entire, ruthless, tyrannical rapacity, with – at best – little grasp of legal detail and, at worst, of scant regard for truth in any context. But Donald Munro mistook it, instead, as some aspersion on his own authority as factor, and ploughed humourlessly into his worst blunder yet.

'I obtained decree on the summonses of removing,' snapped the chamberlain, 'and, if I wished it, I could have removed all the tenants from their crofts and houses in Bernera, as well as from their summer grazings in Lewis, because the decrees gave me power to do so. I did not consult Sir James Matheson about removing the people' – now, Munro had evidently decided, was a good moment to invoke the name of the Most High, with just a hint that they were practically equals – 'and I issued all the summonses of removing against them without receiving instructions from him to do so. I am not in the habit of consulting Sir James about every little detail connected with the management of the Estate.'

There were audible gasps.

Charles Innes beamed, beamed broadly, beamed as the spider to the fly.

'Oh!' he said. 'Then you considered the removing of fifty-six crofters and their families too small a matter to trouble Sir James about?'

'I did,' said Donald Munro.

'Did you ever, on any former occasion, attempt to remove so many families without consulting Sir James or receiving his instructions?'

'No,' said Donald Munro.

'And I venture to say,' said Charles Innes, 'you will not dare to do so again.'

Munro must have grasped, by now, that things were going badly for him, but he continued remorselessly to dig further, deeper, the hole in which he already stood. 'The crofters had the Earshader grazings for about three years, I think; before then they had the grazings of Cualein-hill, and part of Scaliscro. They held the latter grazings for several years, probably as long as I have been in the island – that is, since 1841 – and possibly for a longer period, for all I know. I know I removed them' – Munro might have been talking of household furniture – 'but I don't know if I informed the proprietor of my intention or consulted him about the matter. They were not summoned. I can't say if the people complained about being removed from Cualein-hill to Earshader, but I have no doubt they grumbled. People sometimes grumble when removed to a better place.'

'That is, a better place in your opinion – not theirs,' announced Charles Innes.

'It is a difficult matter to please them,' said Munro. 'I can't say if the Earshader grazings were better than those from which the people were removed. I can't swear there was an understanding between the people and me that they were to be allowed to retain Earshader as long as they held their crofts in Bernera. I don't remember my giving the people to understand that they would be allowed to remain in their crofts, as long as they paid their rents with punctuality and behaved themselves with propriety.'

'Did you prepare a document embodying such an understanding?'

'I don't remember,' said Donald Munro.

'Was such a document prepared in your office, and sent to the ground officer in order that he might read it to the crofters and get them to sign it?'

'I don't remember,' repeated Donald Munro.

'Was not such a document signed by the crofters and returned to you by the ground officer?' demanded Charles Innes, some crafted anger seasoning his voice.

'I don't remember,' said Donald Munro, sounding less believable with each repetition. 'I can't swear that there was such a document, and I won't swear either that I had or hadn't it. I have been told such a document was lodged with me. I can't remember' – the leaden phrase again – 'if I ever saw it. I looked for it, but I have not found it. I can't say if there was or was not an understanding come to with the crofters when they were removed to Earshader. After they were removed to the latter grazings, I believe they built a dyke between them and the deer-forest.' (They certainly had, at his express command.) 'I can't state the length of it, or whether it is seven miles long. I haven't seen much of it, but suppose it is of considerable length. I have seen a part of it from the road, but I never went specially to look at it. I have more important things to attend to. You must remember there are over twenty-two thousand people in the Lews, and that I have the management of all. The crofters built the dyke at their own expense – at least,' said Munro, foolishly qualifying that, 'they gave their labour.'

Innes plunged on that slip like a buzzard on a rabbit.

'Am I then to understand,' he said smoothly, 'that in the Lews the labour of these poor people counts for nothing?'

'It is not worth much,' declared Donald Munro. There was a faint, faint rumble, from the public seats; a hardening of faces. 'I can't say if I promised to pay them for the dyke before they were summoned to remove. My impression is that I told the people they would be paid for the dyke, but I can't tell when or where they were so told. I think I told them myself or by my ground officer, but

I can't swear whether I said it to them or not. I went to Earshader after the summonses were served in the latter end of March. I had arranged a meeting with the people, and about fifty of them attended. I am not sure of the exact day on which the meeting was held. I don't keep a diary. I think I had written some of the people previously; in my letter I think I mentioned about the dyke; when we met we talked about that, and what they were to receive in exchange for Earshader.'

'Did you mention that in your letter?' asked the defence agent.

'I can't remember,' said Donald Munro. It sounded sillier every time.

'Have you a copy of the letter?' sighed Charles Innes.

'I think it is in my letter-book,' allowed the Chamberlain of the Lews.

'Well,' said Innes, in cool tones, 'send for your letter-book.'

'I am not sure it is in the letter-book,' Munro flailed, 'and I don't see that its being sent for will do any good.'

'Will you swear that you wrote to any of the Bernera tenants promising them compensation for the dyke, or that you wrote to them at all before they were served with the summonses of removal, and before what has been called' – a heavy, ironic Innes note now – 'the *riot* took place there?'

'I can't swear. I don't remember. At my meeting with the tenants at Earshader I don't remember that they grumbled at the change I proposed. I thought they were well pleased. I swear that I cannot recollect that the people complained of faith being broken with them. I proposed to take away Earshader, and confine the crofters for the future to the island of Bernera. I proposed to give them Haclete and some other lands. But they were not content with that, but wanted Strome in addition. I had summoned the tenant of Haclete to remove, and I was intending to give him Earshader. I considered the confining of the crofters to the island of Bernera was safer for them, their families and cattle, because they would not have to cross the ferry, which in my opinion was dangerous. I was long of this opinion, but I did not think of changing the arrangement until this year. I did not consult Sir James; and did not think it necessary to do so. At our meeting the people did not appear to be much annoyed. In fact, they were jocular.'

'Indeed!' exclaimed Charles Innes, in dramatic shock. 'Did any of them dare to be jocular with you? Perhaps you will be good enough to favour us with some of the jokes, so that we may enjoy them too.'

There were again weak, throttled noises in the packed courtroom.

'I can't remember any particular joke,' breathed Munro. 'I told them that they would not be allowed to put their cattle across the ferry to the mainland after Whitsunday 1874. I threatened to bring the Volunteers from Stornoway to prevent them if they ventured to do so. That was my joke,' he stumbled on, as lips parted and everyone stared, 'and I thought the people took it as a joke. I am not captain of the Volunteers now; but, as you know, I have had that unpaid honour.'

Innes looked at him. 'Did you not think that by threatening these simple-minded, ignorant people with the Volunteers you would have got them to agree to your terms?'

'Perhaps I did,' said the Chamberlain of the Lews, only sounding as if he endorsed the lawyer's sarcastic description of the Bernera folk. 'At a meeting the people were in a mass, the most of them talking to me at the same time.'

'What!' said Innes, in mock-horror once more. 'The whole fifty? Did they dare to behave in such a manner to you, the great Chamberlain?'

'Yes, they did,' said Munro fatuously; perhaps a little gratified by the description. 'They were excited, I suppose. I can't say if the lands I proposed to give the crofters in exchange for Earshader could carry the same amount of stock. I don't remember telling the people that they would have to reduce their stock on their removal. On the proposed change the rent might be increased' – there were more muffled gasps – 'and the stock might be reduced. Some of the crofters agreed to the proposed arrangement, and I received a letter or paper signed by some of the people. But, I admit, it stipulated that the lands of Strome should be given to them with the other lands, and Strome was not included in my proposal. I thought the lands I proposed to give in exchange for Earshader were more valuable, though they were not nearly as extensive as the latter, and I certainly expected an increase in the rental. I proposed that we should refer the whole matter as to the rent and the stock to three arbiters, who were to act for all parties. I had a document written out to that effect for the tenants' signature. I named all the arbiters, but I told the tenants that if they objected to one of them I would name a fourth. The crofters did not agree to the parties named by me as referees, and the reference has never gone on. When I went to Earshader, I had with me an execution of deforcement of the Sheriff Officer who executed the summonses of removal.'

Innes could not believe his luck: this was a wholly unforced, ruinous admission by the blundering factor. Most in court could not believe their ears.

'An execution of deforcement!' boomed the defence counsel. 'Well, this is something new. Was the officer deforced?'

Sheriff Spittal interrupted, before the chamberlain could answer. 'Wasn't it a precognition?' he inquired sharply of the witness.

Donald Munro sensed trouble. 'I mean I had a precognition of the Sheriff Officer. I made a mistake in saying an execution of deforcement. The precognition was given to me either by Mr Ross, the Joint Fiscal, or by my clerk. It was given to me as I was going to see the people, and also to meet

MacRae, the ground officer, who was with the Sheriff Officer when the summonses were served.

'I did not myself precognosce the Sheriff Officer,' the chamberlain rambled on, 'but I may have had some words to him about what took place on Bernera. So far as I remember, I did not go over the precognition with him, but I went over it with MacRae, the ground officer. I made alterations on the precognition, but I don't now remember what the alterations were. I never before,' he said, 'altered a signed precognition. Although I did so in this case, I am not in the habit of altering a signed precognition when I haven't myself examined the witness.'

Charles Innes smiled again: a tight smile. 'Did you alter the precognition as Fiscal or Factor?' he asked innocently.

'I thought I was doing it in the two capacities,' pronounced Munro. 'I went to Earshader chiefly as Factor; but I took the precognition with me as Fiscal. Mr Ross, I suppose, knowing I was going to Earshader, gave me the precognition, so that I might precognosce the ground officer. I did not precognosce him, but I went over the Sheriff Officer's precognition with him. I suppose I did that in my capacity as Fiscal. I have been Chamberlain of Lewis for about twenty years. I have been in the island since 1841, when I came here as Fiscal. I have not often been in Bernera. The people come to me,' he concluded defiantly, 'I don't go to them.'

'What is the character of the Bernera people?' asked Innes. 'Are they, as a rule, decent, quiet, and well behaved?'

'I decline to answer the question. I am here to give evidence as a witness in what I believe to be a criminal charge. I have nothing to do with the people's character.'

'My Lord,' said Charles Innes, 'I submit I am entitled to ask the witness questions as to the character of the Bernera people in general, and as to the accused in particular.'

'I think the question quite competent,' pronounced Sheriff Substitute Spittal, gazing gravely at Munro.

Innes had to ask the question again before Munro would answer.

'I can't say as to the character of the people,' said the Chamberlain of the Lews.

'I hope you never have to go to Bernera for a character,' riposted Innes.

'They may be like the generality of the Lewis people,' conceded Munro now, 'and, looking at the matter in a Christian spirit, I may say they are decent, but I cannot say if they are quiet.'

There were barely audible titters.

'You almost persuade me to bow to such a representative Christian,' said

Charles Innes. 'But come – sir! – you must know more about these people. Have any Bernera men ever been, during your Fiscalship, accused of committing any crime?'

'I suppose there would be charges against the Bernera people as against others,' said Munro, 'but I can't recollect. I can't speak particularly as to them. I believe that some hundreds of people emigrated from the Lews last year, that some left this year, and that others are intending to leave. They have been assisted by Sir James Matheson, but I decline to tell the amount or kind of assistance. I can't remember the amount.'

'Did you make any bargain with the Sheriff Officer when you employed him to serve the summonses of removing?'

'The only arrangement I made with him,' insisted Donald Munro, 'was that he was not to receive his full fees, as there were so many summonses. The ground officer was to act as his witness, I know; but so far as I remember, I did not instruct either officer to send round messengers to the different townships commanding them to come to different places in the island to be served with the summonses. I certainly arranged that the ground officer should assist and accompany the Sheriff Officer. When the Bernera crofters fall into arrear, I am in the habit of taking the crofts from them.'

'Are you in the habit,' demanded Charles Innes, 'of making the successors of the crofters so parted [evicted] with pay on entry the accumulation of arrears?'

'I decline to answer that question, and appeal to His Lordship whether it is a competent one.'

On this occasion, Spittal decided to give Munro the benefit of the doubt. The continued, extraordinary failure of William Ross at any point to intervene had no doubt by now struck him.

'You need only answer the question if you think it proper,' said Sheriff Substitute Spittal.

'It is quite immaterial,' said Innes, in his most regal tone, 'whether the witness answers the question or not, but if he does not answer it I tell him I shall infer that the iniquitous practice alluded to in the question is carried out in this island.' So, Innes knew full well, would the jury.

'I decline to answer that question,' muttered Donald Munro.

'Very good, Mr Munro. Were the Cualein-hill grazings, after the eviction of the Bernera crofters, converted into a deer-forest?'

Donald Munro again resisted giving reply to this. Spittal, this time, ruled with Innes. The chamberlain admitted that the grazings were indeed now used and occupied for sporting purposes. 'I cannot say if I have been in the habit of fining the crofters whose sheep or cattle trespassed in the forest. The ground officer may have exacted fines, but I am not aware that the people were ever fined, or that I ever sanctioned fines of two shillings sixpence to three shillings a head. I can't say if I ever got such fines. I decline to say that if the crofters allow their sheep or cattle to trespass in the forest they will not be fined.'

Charles Innes had exacted everything he had wanted – and more – from the Crown's witness.

He thanked the Chamberlain of the Lews. Munro lurched from the witness box with such dignity as he could still muster.

William Ross had not intervened at all.

The case for the prosecution never recovered. Colin MacLennan gave a very pretty, hard-rehearsed account of all that fear and alarm; but was then lured by Innes into declaring he had not turned round when pelted with bits of turf – and could not then explain how he was so sure he had been assailed by adults, not children. He admitted, at least, having declared he would return to Bernera with a gun; by the time the defence agent was done with MacLennan, he sounded evasive, shifty and villainous. James MacRae, the ground officer, struggled too to remember what lies he had told – and confirmed, disastrously for the Crown, that he had heard a Bernera man declare, 'Whatever you do, do not injure the man,' and that the men had merely said to MacLennan, 'Are you the party who threatened to shoot us?' MacRae besides made clear MacLennan's waterproof (hanging loose over his arm) would not have been ripped had he simply let go of it; and spoke of the lively tunes MacLennan had played on the pipes back to Garynahine.

Malcolm MacAulay, the Haclete township constable, asked to be examined in Gaelic, by means of an interpreter, and spoke in great detail of MacLennan's repeated imprecations about a gun and how they had tried to quiet him – 'he said he didn't care, as he would throw the contents of the revolver at the people if he had it . . .' He testified, too, to the burden of that great Earshader dyke on them all, which 'we were compelled to build, at our own sole expense . . .'

Ironically, Peter Bain – it was never explained what business 'in the employment of the Excise department of the Inland Revenue' had taken him to Bernera on that day; and he certainly conducted none – had probably been recruited as a professional witness to the Estate's lark. For his evidence proved ruinous. Bain was an honest, respectable man. He described James MacRae's manner at Tobson that morning as 'very offensive, and not calculated to soothe them . . . His language and manner were calculated to provoke their anger.' And, several times 'that night and the following morning, MacLennan repeated the threats regarding the rifle. I believe, from the way he spoke, he was earnest in his threats, as he spoke very determinedly.' Angus MacDonald, Bain asserted, he had 'distinctly heard' assure MacLennan by the ferry he would not be struck or hurt. The sheriff officer's waterproof would not have been torn had MacLennan himself let go and not pulled it. His own had been grabbed, said Bain, 'but I let go my hold, and got it back safe and sound . . . on our way to the boat MacLennan said to me, "Why didn't you stick to your waterproof as I did?" He also said that, if I had done that, we would have a right case against them.'

Murdo MacDonald, another township constable – from Breaclete – examined MacLennan's torn coat and was adamant that it had been only slightly damaged 'when I saw it in Bernera – the tear was then not more than two inches long, and now I see it is half a yard.' He also confirmed the young men had only pressed MacLennan about the gun threats; that they had repeatedly assured their visitors they would not be hurt; and that MacLennan's waterproof was only damaged because he had refused to let it go.

And these were all the witnesses for the *prosecution*. The procurator fiscal had closed his case; Charles Innes led evidence of his own. He had lined up a succession of Bernera fishermen to attest to MacLennan's conduct and what had really happened by the ferry, but only the second had been called when the foreman of the jury made known they 'thought it was not necessary that the agent for the defence should call any further witnesses to prove what had occurred at the meeting with the officer and his party near Breaclete.' Innes graciously acknowledged this observation – it was well into the evening now – but called two more to confirm the sheriff officer's repeated menaces about guns.

After the last witness for the defence had been heard, William Ross, procurator fiscal, addressed the jury. At that late hour of the evening, he said – it was now ten o'clock at night – 'he did not intend to trouble them with any remarks, but would simply rest his case on the evidence adduced, craving at their hands a verdict of guilty as libelled . . .'

Charles Innes now rose. Despite the late hour, he said regretfully, 'I feel compelled to trouble you with, I fear, not a few, but a great many remarks . . .' It was a long address, righteous in tone and florid of rhetoric, larded with patronising references to the 'simple' and 'manly' and 'honest' crofters; and in pitiless detail (for Charles Innes had already demolished the Crown case to a heap of bricks in cross-examination) he now danced and danced on the ruins.

But all was founded 'on the treatment the crofters have received at the hands of the Chamberlain'; and Charles Innes devoted a few minutes to the character and conduct of Donald Munro that laid his reputation to waste and for always. And it did little, either, for the reputation of Sir James Matheson. In commercial life, said Innes quietly,

It very often happens that the manager or secretary of a company absolutely directs and orders the affairs of that company, though he may not have a single share in the concern. In like manner, in the management of large landed properties, it often happens that such properties are absolutely managed not by the proprietors, but by their *doers*. The proprietor of this and the neighbouring islands might be a little king. He lives and entertains, I hear, in princely style, but it appears to me he has, so far as the management of his realm is concerned, absolutely abdicated in favour of the great man we had before us today. The latter told you himself (with my assistance, being modest, as great men always are) the number and the nature of the various appointments – between twenty and thirty in all – held by him; and as they were detailed, it occurred to me, when the long list was closed, that Mr Donald Munro was vested with the whole power, both civil and military, if not entirely of the state, at any rate of the estate of Lewis, and of all its principal officers (except that of His Lordship on the bench), centring, as they do, in his own individual person.

In this court, said the counsel for the defence, 'looking to the nature of his multifarious offices, I can almost fancy it possible for him to appear at one and the same time in the capacity of prosecutor, judge and jury. It is, in point of fact, a matter of great difficulty, if not impossibility, to think in the singular of so great a pluralist. Today and here he has appeared in a new capacity – one in which it is doubtful if he ever appeared before, namely, that of a witness. Many people go about the world sighing for a new sensation – perhaps the Chamberlain is one of them' –

if, then, I have been able to gratify him to any extent, I am sure I am delighted. I can't understand how any human brain could for so many years have stood the wear and tear of such innumerable offices: why, to fulfil all aright, one would require to possess the wisdom of Solomon, and at least a dash of the patience of Job. From the way in which the Chamberlain conducted himself here today, I feel sure you must have observed the extent to which he possesses these distinguishing characteristics; but you must also have observed how frequently Mr Munro, in answer to my questions – especially when they were calculated to tell to the favour of my clients – simply replied, 'I don't remember'; 'I can't remember'. From this it would appear that even his brain and his memory have at last begun to be affected.

'Had this island never been united to the neighbouring islands of Great Britain and Ireland,' continued Charles Innes, 'and had Mr Munro been king *de jure*, he really would not be the great man he is, occupying, as he does, the position merely *de facto*. Then he would have Houses of Parliament and Cabinet Ministers to control him, but now there is no man to say him nay; his power seems to be absolute; his word seems to be law; the people seem to quake and tremble at his approach: his very nod conveys a meaning neither you nor I could convey in a sentence. As the sun is said to rule the day, and the moon the night, so with equal truth it may now be said, Chamberlain Munro rules Lewis and Bernera.

'About this time last year a great potentate visited Great Britain, and for a time took up his quarters in a city therein, called and known by the name of London, and at or near a part thereof named Buckingham Palace. At that time one could hardly turn a corner in a street of that city without being asked by some pert little boy the question, "Have you seen the Shah?" Now it has occurred to me that if the little boys of your town were only half appreciative and sensible enough, they would make a point of asking every stranger, as he landed on your shores, "Have you seen the Baron-Baillie?"

'I, gentlemen, have seen both of them, and I can assure you that your Baron-Baillie is a very much more considerable person than the Shah. However tempting the subject is, as one on which to dilate, I must not at this time say more. I have said enough, however, gentlemen, to enable you, if you did not do so before, to understand the power which the Chamberlain Baron-Baillie possesses. You can fancy how helpless the men of Bernera are in dealing with such a person armed with so much power.

'Oppressed as they have been, I as a stranger cannot but admire them. Had Mr Munro, instead of being Chamberlain of Lewis, been an agent in either Connaught or Munster, he would long ago have licked the dust he has for years made the poor men of this island swallow; but he has reason to thank God he lives on the island of Lewis and not in Ireland; and you have reason to be proud of your countrymen inasmuch as they have, notwithstanding great provocation, not lifted up even their hand against their oppressor . . .'

Charles Innes addressed the jury further and for a long time as the local audience hung eagerly on his every word; as reporters' pencils whizzed in joyous shorthand. Among much else, he pointed out that Munro, even when pressed, 'could not give one single instance in which anyone from Bernera was accused, during the last twenty years, of having committed any crime'. Yet to this peaceful and law-abiding place this party of officials had come, in deliberate intent to provoke and to humiliate; for instance, at Tobson, 'the names of all the tenants in the township were called out, and at the mention of his name each crofter stepped forward, and a summons of removal was put into his hand – insult being thus added to injury by the mode adopted for serving the people.' Innes, long later, at last assured the 15 jurors that with 'confidence I leave the issue in your hands, feeling satisfied that in arriving at your decision you will not in any way be influenced by thoughts as to what may be pleasing or not pleasing to "the powers that be" and rule in this island, but by considerations dictated alone by your own good consciences.'

Sheriff Substitute Spittal then summed up, explaining quietly to the jury the matters of fact in dispute, and the points of law to be considered; but one or two of his own carefully weighed observations still more reinforced the defence, so witless was the Crown prosecution and so hopeless the evidence and the testimony on which it had led.

The jury did not long retire. Indeed, they did not retire at all, and would have struggled to leave their box, such was the press of people in Stornoway Sheriff Court. They conferred, in low murmurs, for but a minute or two. 'After a short interval, the Foreman (Mr MacPherson) rose, and addressing the Bench, said, "My Lord, the jury unanimously find the panels NOT GUILTY." The verdict having been recorded, the accused were at once dismissed from the bar.'

The disaster for Munro and Ross and Sir James Matheson was all but complete. And it was still worse the following day, Saturday morning. John Smith, that Stornoway baker from Valtos, was briskly tried for 'violently resisting and obstructing two police officers while they were conveying Angus MacDonald (Norman's son) . . . along Kenneth Street, Stornoway, to the police office there; also, for assaulting one of said officers, and for committing a breach of the peace. Smith, who was defended by Mr Innes, pled not guilty, and evidence having been led at considerable length both for the prosecution and defence, the new jury unanimously found the charges not proven . . .' This is a curious and very Scottish verdict, which notionally acquits on the basis merely that the Crown has failed to prove its case: cynics suggests 'Not Proven' really means, 'Go away and don't do it again.'

Thereafter, Colin MacLennan himself, the loutish sheriff officer, was tried on the charge of 'having wickedly and feloniously assaulted' Angus MacDonald, while the Bernera fisherman was trussed up helplessly and in police custody. MacLennan, defended by the fatuous Napier Campbell, nevertheless pled not guilty. But this third jury, by a majority refused to agree, and found him guilty, though they 'at the same time, unanimously recommended him to the leniency of the court'. There were probably family circumstances, known to them, that bore on this; and everyone knew MacLennan would never again be employed in any legal capacity. Sheriff Spittal fined him 20 shillings, with the alternative of 10 days' imprisonment.

Colin MacLennan paid the fine on the spot.

12

Dust: The final fall of an evil man . . .

Donald Munro was all but ruined: his reputation shredded, his authority quite gone, held in relieved, open derision on Lewis and, as the newspapers raged and even distant London journals exclaimed, nationally and at once an ogre and a joke. To one superior, he was now an entire embarrassment. Only a month after the acquittal of the Bernera Three, Sheriff Principal Fordyce dispensed with him utterly. Days later, 'Little Ross' – at the open book of Stornoway Sheriff Court, and with what emotion we do not know, minuted the fall:

> Edinburgh 18th August 1874. The Sheriff with reference to his suspension of the appointment of Mr D. Munro as Joint Procurator Fiscal of the Lews, in April last, now cancels the said appointment & directs this Order to be engrossed in the Books of Court.
> (Signed) Geo Dingwall Fordyce
> Sheriff of Ross, Cromarty and Sutherland.

But the chamberlain was not yet utterly destroyed. Still, Sir James Matheson hung by his grand vizier, as a new threat boiled up from a wholly new direction.

Daniel MacKinlay had the Gress shootings again, this summer of 1874; and even as he prepared to encompass the chamberlain's exposure at Stornoway Sheriff Court, he heard word from Ness and murmurings in town. That Disaster Fund built so generously after the Great Drowning of 1862 had not been well administered. Most of the money was still in the bank – worse, he was told, in Munro's own account. He heard besides of the farce on Ness rent-days – how widows were not even allowed to get their hands on the coin, but had to watch it slung as their rent straight into the coffers of the Lewis Estate, even as they could scarcely clothe their children, heat their homes or be sure from whence tomorrow's meal might come, or if there would be food the morrow at all.

MacKinlay had been at school with William Donald Ryrie, who had done so well in London and had done so much to raise money for the widows and orphans of Ness. He sent word now to his old classmate: Ryrie should start making inquiries about the Disaster Fund immediately.

Ryrie did. He found there was still nearly £600 sitting smugly in a Stornoway bank; that it was indeed in Munro's name; that it was drawn on under his sole signature; that it accrued interest – presumably for Munro – and that there had never been an audit. He wrote Donald Munro; then he wrote him again. He also contacted Kenneth Smith, the prominent curer in town, and other men of influence in town. Stornoway, writes James Shaw Grant

was buzzing with rumours that something was afoot. Munro took action to protect himself. After the Bernera Riot, he did not wish another public exposure. He also had to protect his master. The 'honour' of Sir James would be impugned, if it came to public notice that a fund, gathered under his chairmanship, to relieve the distress of widows and orphans, had been used, in effect, to guarantee his own rents. The members of the two Committees were also in a delicate situation. They had been less than vigilant, in leaving so much to the discretion of the factor, although, in fairness to them, it must be said that they began to ask questions, in a desultory sort of way, long before Ryrie raised the matter in public. At a meeting of the Central Committee in 1871 – the first for five years – they ordered Munro to submit his accounts, for audit, to John Ross, the Sheriff Clerk Depute. The audit, however, never took place. Munro ignored the Committee's instructions, and called no further meetings.

But a bare audit would simply have confirmed funds had indeed been regularly paid out. It is most unlikely the Central Committee would have grasped the extent to which it had been perverted; that the money was in truth underwriting chunks of Matheson's Lewis Estate. And, by September 1874 – only days after the calamitous trial of the Bernera fishermen – Munro was in serious trouble.

For one, Ryrie had now thoroughly buried his teeth in the Disaster Fund irregularities – and the Committees were growing restive. For another, if still in office, the authority of the Chamberlain of the Lews was now collapsing, on every front, with each succeeding day. The people were not afraid of him now and, on an unrelated front in Ness, the crofters of Swainbost – whom Munro had recently stripped of their summer grazings – had seen the Bernera example, and taken note.

The factor's judgement was fast fraying. He now, on his own initiative and without consulting anyone, gathered the Disaster Fund accounts and gave them to Walter Rose for audit. He seems to have been evidently startled when the men of the Central Committee expostulated. Rose was his own employee, yet another clerk at the Estate Office, they snapped – worse, he was one of Donald

Munro's nephews and, to cap everything, he 'was clerk to the very fund he was being asked to audit'.

Rose's report, of course, showed all to be in perfect order; the Central Committee, quite properly, refused to accept it. Munro now desperately ordered another, from one R.G. MacKenzie – who was not qualified in any way as an accountant; he was described as a 'shipbroker' and produced only the thinnest of reports. It concluded besides with a glowing tribute to the chamberlain himself – all the more improbable by this autumn of 1874 – reminding everyone that Donald Munro had toiled long on this Disaster Fund and in the interests of all those Ness widows and orphans, quite unpaid, 'for which the widows and all concerned ought to be grateful'.

Committee surprise at this paean of praise evaporated in an instant when they learned Munro had paid (without their authority) the fat fee of six guineas, out of the Fund, to MacKenzie for his auditing. (Munro had besides paid three guineas, without consulting them and again out of the Fund, to his young kinsman Walter Rose.) And the factor had further shelled out – again, from the Fund, and without consultation – the sum of £5 9s 6d for an 'Opinion of Counsel as to division of Funds among proper parties.' (Munro had good grounds to fear about the legality of a Disaster Fund policy he had decreed, that any widow who remarried was at once and for the rest of her life denied any benefit from it; this was much resented in Ness, and Ryrie was already probing it.) And the chamberlain had suppressed the Opinion for good reason – all the signs are that the Edinburgh advocate had pronounced the rule unlawful.

As wrath boiled around him, and the menace to his own position increased, Donald Munro won cross Central Committee approval to distribute all the remaining money now, in one glorious act of bounty and in equal shares to widows remarried or no. But, of course, there had to be due and careful process to identify whom precisely still lived and qualified for a share, and where they were, and William Donald Ryrie wanted besides to secure the approval of all Disaster Fund subscribers for this resolution – and to pile on the pressure against the Chamberlain of the Lews. On 30 November, after due advertisement in *The Times*, he convened a meeting in London. (It would speedily pass two resolutions – first, one demanding full and properly audited accounts, with explicit detail as to 'the authority under which drafts' were made, and a list of all those originally recorded as widows, orphans and dependants entitled to benefit; and a list of all who remained. The second was still more robust, authorising Ryrie both to send the first, in writing, to both Central and Local Committees and personally to every member; and to continue his investigation and finally and in full to publish his findings.)

Meanwhile, word that same day, 30 November, reached the chamberlain's office at Carn House: the crofters of Swainbost were marching to Stornoway, demanding an audience of Sir James Matheson and return of their forfeited grazings. Munro knew of the London meeting; he could not now wait for the certain outcome. Though, in the event, the men of Swainbost did not that day head for Stornoway, Munro could not know that. The factor now panicked.

He sent word to Ness – to both ministers, Revds Donald MacRae of the Free Church and Donald MacKay of the derisory Established congregation; and to the local Free Church catechist: he wanted them as witnesses. Then Munro drew every last penny of the Disaster Fund out of the bank, and hurried back to his office with the bulging bags, where his manservant was ready with the horse and gig. It was already snowing – hard – but the factor thought of those terrible, perhaps dangerous crofters from Ness, perhaps tramping already, from the opposite direction, and perhaps armed, all set to collide with him on the road. He turned to his office and rooted in cupboards. And when they finally set off for Ness, the Chamberlain of the Lews bore besides two loaded revolvers, one in each pocket. This was a man now wandering the far shores of paranoia.

And thus, as Grant puts it, the story of the Ness Disaster Fund 'which began in tragedy, ended in farce'. It takes a long time to reach Ness by horse-drawn vehicle: my great-grandfather took that slow, desperate trundle from Stornoway as recently as 1926, summoned home from the fishing to his second's wife's funeral; which he only made when a man in Laxdale saw him bleakly walking out towards the Barvas road, straight off the boat, and promptly put himself and horse and cart at his disposal when he learned the circumstances. (They made it just in time; the elder had just lifted the Bible, declaring, 'Well, we will not see big Angus today,' as the cart came in sight over the Habost brae.)

It took Munro, probably, and not least with swirling snow and drifts on the roads, a full 12 hours; and likely he just put in for the night – perhaps at the parish manse, or with a less than thrilled tenant-farmer – before going forth in the morn as Father Christmas. The ministers and the catechist were in dutiful attendance, the widows and other dependants were summoned – and, before their astonished eyes, at once delighted and suspicious, wealth hitherto undreamed of, in hard coin, was bestowed on them. The sums ranged from £4 10s to a giddying £26; and most of the endowments were on the high end of the scale, for they were to people who had not in many years received a penny.

Then, to the discomfiture of the churchmen and the bemusement of the people – and at the chamberlain's insistence – a curious rite took place. A resolution was solemnly moved, seconded and passed, and signed (or at least marked) by the nouveaux riches: 22 'widows' (though over half had remarried) and 15 other dependants. The two ministers and catechists stood as witnesses, and signed too. And, when the Central Committee met in Stornoway to receive

Donald Munro's final report and resolve all, they were expected to believe – as the chamberlain insisted – that a gathering of poor folk in northern Lewis, most women, most uneducated, a good number quite illiterate, and most with command only of Gaelic, had spontaneously declared that in

> taking payment of our final division of the Ness Widows Fund . . . we heartily tender our best thanks to Sir James Matheson, for the great kindness and liberality evinced by him in being the mainspring of securing a large Fund for our benefit; and we also beg to offer our best thanks to the chamberlain for his great trouble, without fee or reward, over a period of twelve years; and to the Central and Local Committees for the aid and great interest taken by them on our behalf; and finally, we approve of all past actings and of the Treasurer's intromissions.

It must remain a mystery, as Grant points out dryly, 'how thirty-seven people, few of whom could read, write or speak a word of English, were able to compose, between them, so elegant a testimonial, and set it down in proper form.' It is unlikely any on the Central Committee believed in the slightest ageing ladies in Ness knew words like 'intromissions'. Ryrie had not the least doubt: it had, of course, been composed by Donald Munro himself. But the preposterous excursion to Ness, and the beautifully turned tribute to the proprietor by a humble tenantry was just enough – for the winter – to save Munro himself.

Sir James relaxed in the chair; glowed a little. Men eyed one another nervously. Sweet reason oozed from the chairman, the laird, as this or that sceptic demurred. The Central Committee (and one suspects many members wanted to hold their noses, or at least cross their fingers) dutifully passed the accounts. They besides passed a resolution endorsing Munro's 'whole acting and intromissions', and thanking him 'for his long and gratuitous services'. Only two men had the character to dissent in the face of this repugnant whitewash: the Reverend Donald MacRae of Ness, and Norman MacIver, a local shipowner and bank-owner. There was not sufficient information before them, they insisted; they had been denied any sight of the detailed papers. No one supported them.

Munro was besides foolish enough, afterwards, to write to Ryrie in London, with a copy of the minutes and some highly satisfied remarks. Though no one had done more than William Donald Ryrie to raise money after the Ness disaster, he was now mocked by this disgraced panjandrum of the Hebrides for his failure 'to look into the administration of the funds for upwards of eleven years. Surely there is some culpability here, if you had any *locus standi* in the business? . . . I feel satisfied,' closed the complacent Munro, 'that all manner of justice has been done to parties concerned.'

But the Chamberlain of the Lews, early in 1875, crowed too soon. He could quiet the indolent Central Committee, but not the multitude. He could bully clerks and underlings, but not a press that continued to seethe – and the journals in London that were now causing such delicious clucking among high-born, nobly born, friends of the Mathesons, and who had always and ever so delicately looked down on them as but self-made parvenues.

Munro certainly could not intimidate William Donald Ryrie, nor Kenneth 'California' Smith nor Daniel MacKinlay, whose sensational pamphlet on the trial, recounting everything in pitiless detail, was selling by the parcelful all over the delighted Highlands and eagerly devoured on Lewis itself. MacKinlay was already at work on another, scrupulously researched and in righteous wrath, about the entire Matheson administration of Lewis: it would only appear, so sensational was it, once Sir James himself was safely dead. And the great factor was no longer a dreaded, all-commanding figure on Lewis; nor, even as 1875 stretched on, did the clamour for his head and widespread scorn for his name and his works greatly recede on a wider stage. The case of the *Arrow*, for instance, aroused renewed indignation in March 1875, when Munro and Ross were attacked in the court for their neglect of what was now a worthless vessel; and Catherine Stephen's death, that June, renewed shocked talk of her dead infants – but by then, for Donald Munro, it was thank you and goodnight.

The chamberlain thought he had quite squared his employer. Sir James Matheson yet needed him; certainly, Sir James owed him. Nor was the Lewis laird a man of natural democratic instincts, inclined to bow to the dictate of a newspaper or the rumble of a mob. But Munro, according decades later to one distinguished son of Ness, the Reverend Norman C. MacFarlane, had quite failed to cultivate – or even to think of – the one force the proprietor of the Lews could not evade and mildly feared.

Lady Matheson cared greatly for their good name, their hard-won social standing. She fretted more and more, in gatherings of Highland gentry, and at stately Lews Castle house parties of important visitors alighting from elegant yachts, and through their annual sojourn at Menton on the Riviera, where the Mathesons liked to refresh themselves anew for the service of their tenantry, especially in the winter months.

She cringed besides at London salons in their Stornoway House lair – it would later be home to Lord Beaverbrook – as great ladies asked needled little questions about Lewis affairs, and glanced at her as they talked, whispering, behind immaculately manicured hands. And, soon, her plaints and murmurs at table, and wherever her mannered, ageing husband found her, were no longer of kipper houses, and herring smells, and hairy fishers doing noisome chores at the bottom of her garden. They were all of the entire liability to their reputation that was now Donald Munro.

Sir James Matheson said nothing at all to his lieutenant, and kept up every appearance of affability and confidence, until the last, when it was done in an instant. On 18 May 1875, Donald Munro was sacked as factor, dismissed as Chamberlain of the Lews.

The shock apart, the deed was daintily done. Indeed, Sir James effected it simply – and in very complicated legal form – by appointing someone else. His Edinburgh agents, Stewart and Cheyne, drew up a long and detailed 'commission' for Hugh MacKay Matheson as Baron Baillie, Factor and Commissioner for the proprietor of Lewis. When it arrived at Stornoway for Sir James's attention, he signed the order briskly, with his butler and his valet as dutiful witnesses. The new appointment was made, the commission unblushingly declared, 'considering that Donald Munro Esq . . . who has for a considerable period past acted as my Chamberlain, Factor and Baron Baillie . . . has resigned, or is about to resign, the said office.' It came as entire news to Donald Munro.

There were but two hints of mercy; one for the people, one for the fired henchman. For one, the administration of the whole Estate was heavily recast; Hugh MacKay Matheson would hold more responsibility than actual executive power. The position and duties of 'Factor and local Manager' were expressly conferred on the man now promoted from the chamberlain's deputy, William MacKay, who was a kinsman of Matheson himself. Neither he nor Hugh MacKay Matheson (also, it would seem, a relative) would enjoy, as individuals, the total power long wielded by Munro.

And the discarded ex-chamberlain himself – who was stripped besides of every other position Matheson had given him – was given some weeks for final disentanglement, and a degree of legal immunity, for on 8 July 1875, the Sheriff Court Minute Book further records that, final accounting being done, Sir James Matheson had agreed to 'exoner, acquit and discharge' the said Donald Munro and his 'heirs, executors and representatives of his actings as Factor, Chamberlain and Baron Baillie'. The final accounting was not done, of course, for Munro's comfort. It was done lest, as the laird no doubt feared (and as was almost universally suspected), the factor had been robbing him blind for years. In fact, the books and records were in perfect order. Munro was many things, and his wickedness we have attested in detail and in many aspects, but he was no thief. It is the lack of greed or criminal self-enrichment that, in large measure, makes his malignity so baffling.

Munro was enough of the lawyer to insist on that. It is unlikely there was much of a severance payment, if any at all; there is certainly no evidence of a pension. He was already 64 – old by the standards of his day – and had been deprived of every salaried position. He was now wholly dependent on what he could earn as a solicitor; and in only one capacity would there yet be Matheson gold, for Munro and Ross – as a joint concern – retained the Estate business; though Munro himself was expressly forbidden to handle it.

The lives of the rest in this story went on, though not long for Sir James Matheson himself. On 31 December 1878, he died at Menton; and in due course he was laid to rest not on Lewis, but his native parish of Lairg. The estate was entailed on his nephew, Donald Matheson, the high-minded Christian who had quit the family empire rather than taint his hands with the profits of opium. He instead went on to a distinguished legal career, becoming an advocate and at last Sheriff of the County of Edinburgh. And he would be 77 years old before he could to enjoy his Hebridean inheritance, for Sir James had left his widow the life-rent.

Lady Matheson lived remorselessly until 19 March 1896, spending less and less time on Lewis every year while causing as much trouble as possible. She besides foolishly made her will with English lawyers and by English law, so that when she died – leaving much Scottish estate – there was no end of trouble. Sheriff Donald Matheson proved 'the most self-effacing of landlords,' writes Peter Cunningham, 'and seems to have entered little into the life of the community.' He is remembered, if at all, only for opening the new Lewis Hospital, at Goathill, in August 1896 – it would be superseded, or perhaps relocated, to vast new premises, as Ospadal nan Eilean, late in 1992; and the original buildings have been replaced by modern housing, or adapted to it. Donald Matheson also gifted an adjoining field, the 'Goathill Parks', to the 'youth of the town for recreation'; and it is still the top football ground on Lewis, where cup finals in the Lewis and Harris League are played. He held the estate for only three years before signing it over to his son, Major Duncan Matheson, who by 1899 was 51. This last of the line is still remembered as an upright man, who supposedly cared greatly for Lewis and did much for its welfare – and yet he would fight to the very end of his rule, with lots of Edinburgh lawyers, for as few new crofts as possible to be carved from his precious sporting grounds.

It was Duncan Matheson's honour to entertain the king and queen at Lews Castle, on a celebrated official visit to Lewis in August 1902, shortly before the coronation postponed from June after Edward VII's near-fatal appendicitis. It is said that some excited, elderly Stornoway ladies took to the harbour in a rowing boat, splashed about the moored royal yacht, peeked boldly through a porthole and beheld their sovereign, quite naked, in his bath. It is not recalled if he saw them.

Major Matheson built a family tomb – an enclosure or *cabail* – at Aignish itself, by the ancient sepulchre of assorted MacLeod chiefs and a solitary Earl of Seaforth. But it would never be occupied and stands empty to this day, for the laird never recovered from the death of a beloved son down south, and elected to be buried beside him. That was not until 1930, long after – burdened, short of money – he had sold his Lewis estate, in 1918, to William Hesketh Lever – ennobled the previous year as Lord Leverhulme, an old man in a hurry and the last individual to own all Lewis.

There were two widely publicised crofting disturbances in the later Matheson years. Ironically, both followed soon after the Crofters Holdings (Scotland) Act of 1886, built on the Napier Commission's findings of 1882–83 and which finally conferred security of tenure and other basic rights.

The Act, however, did nothing to create new crofts, or otherwise greatly limit the powers of the landed gentry: it would be the present century before meaningful land reform was enacted in Scotland. The Park Deer Raid of November 1887 was triggered by local fury, in the grossly crowded townships of South Lochs, at the bland insistence of Lady Matheson in converting the former Park sheep farm to a sporting estate rather than resettling it with crofters. She felt too important even to acknowledge two very polite letters requesting such use of the land in a district where there was serious hardship. Weeks later, early in 1889, the long debated land of Aignish farm really did become theatre to a riot – or a widely leaked, ineptly executed land raid that became one, though the landing on Lewis of a large contingent of Marines in anticipation scarcely cooled the popular mood. Only the tact – and a timely joke – of a new sheriff substitute, Donald Fraser, averted bloodshed and probable loss of life.

Both events seem much more celebrated today than the Bernera Riot of 1874 – partly because huge, determinedly modernist monuments in stone now mark their spots, and are on main tourist routes through Lewis; and because they fit much more neatly into the 1880s, Skye-dominated, narrative of the 'Crofters' War'. The Park men, by the way, were acquitted of mobbing, rioting and trespass by an Edinburgh jury; the raiders of the sheep runs at Aignish and Melbost were not, on a deliberately vaguer charge of 'forming part of a riotous mob'; all 13 spent up to 15 months in prison, with no provision for their families. Only one lived to finally win a croft in Aignish, when the hated farm was at last broken into them in 1905.

Yet the Bernera stand was far more significant than either, and, unlike either Park or Aignish, it ended in triumph, achieving everything the community had wanted to accomplish and ridding Lewis of a hated despot. There were, after all, no evictions in 1874. Nor were the people deprived of the Earshader grazings. And 'some concessions were made to the Bernera people by the Estate,' Joni Buchanan records. 'For example, they acceded to a request for more land by the villagers of Bosta. Five years after the Riot, the Bosta people were given Kirkibost and in the winter of 1879 they carried the roofs of the old dwellings to their new villages. Without the Riot, these people would have been off on emigrant ships.

However the sense of injustice, based on land hunger when so much of their surroundings lay empty and idle, survived. The last attempt on Bernera to take more land into crofting was in 1901, when six Tobson crofters took possession of Croir, which had been leased to Malcolm MacDonald in 1880, but had previously been in crofting tenure. The raiders wrote to the Congested Districts Board: 'There are 43 souls of us. Surely our lives are of more account than that of one man, or of 100 sheep.' It was a long struggle before they finally obtained legal access to the land.

Angus MacDonald attained a respectable age, dying in 1918 and known, to the last, as *Aonghas a' Phriosan*: 'Angus of the Prison'.

The Small Landholders (Scotland) Act of 1911 established clear government powers in the determined – though unsteady – bid at last to create more crofts in the most overpopulated corners of the Highlands and Islands. Yet every detailed proposal was fought at every turn and in every county by the lairds, and it was 1914 before hard plans for Lewis were agreed between the Estate and the Board of Agriculture. Carnish and Ardroil in Uig, Galson on the west side, and – not before time – Steimreway and Orinsay in Park, all emptied over 60 years before, were to be resettled with families on new crofts, as were the Gress and Tolsta farms. It is still widely believed on Lewis that only the outbreak of the Great War delayed most of these schemes; in fact, it was Major Matheson, taking cynical advantage of the fact that so many Lewismen were off the island and fighting for their country. (It is only fair to point out that he himself also served throughout the War, while keeping in close contact with his Edinburgh solicitors.)

That August, though, there were suddenly more important things to think about; and when the guns at last fell silent, there was Lord Leverhulme, who wrung reluctant assurance from the Scottish Office that – for the time being – there would be no resettlement until he had accomplished his promised economic miracle. It is small wonder, after decades of fair words and minimal action, that angry young war veterans in the overcrowded Back district promptly launched land raids, though they were almost universally condemned in wider Lewis.

When Leverhulme broke his word – laying off workers and halting assorted schemes amidst a temporary cash-flow problem – Edinburgh, for once, very properly abandoned the deal and proceeded with resettlement. Leverhulme's will and patience failed: he flounced out of Lewis and transferred his vision to Harris, where all ended overnight with his sudden death in 1925. The new townships, and others – such as Dalmore – were duly born; and, save for Steimreway, they support communities to this day.

William Ross, who had so neatly – and with determined lack of scruple – kept himself just enough apart from Munro's disgrace, and besides perhaps given fate a helping hand in the process, was never shamed himself. He was never liked either, nor greatly trusted, and was scarcely less skilled a juggler of hats than Munro. Yet Ross gave himself to that power-grabbing, wealth-amassing wickedness of the bland, fair-faced, Matheson variety; apt to grow rich and elude any assault on its privileges. Such men seldom slip.

If not greatly – or at all – his cousin's moral superior, Ross carried himself more carefully in the community and was decidedly the cleverer. He was fortunate in other respects too. He is still absurdly credited, in local folk-memory as 'the man who built the Lewis schools' – though not a penny of his own money went towards them, whatever his oversight and responsibilities in the project – and many of the bad things he did, or was party to, were instead blamed exclusively on Donald Munro.

William Ross died, still in office as procurator fiscal, in 1894; and the position was inherited without the least trouble by his son John, who survived him by only two years. It would fall, for most of the succeeding century, through the successive talents of a far more honoured dynasty, the Mac-Kenzies; and the last of this line in the post, Colin Scott MacKenzie, is the proud if wry owner of Donald Munro's infamous chair, which, it seems, he was not allowed to remove from the fiscal's office.

The late chamberlain, Grant sighs,

> was seen as an unmitigated target. Ross was seen rather as an honest man doing his, at times, unpleasant duty. Even those who suffered at his hands do not seem to have borne so deep a grudge as they did against Munro. According to the record, Ross was much more active than Munro in the legal harassment of my mother's family, but I have only once heard his name mentioned in that connection. The fact that Munro was factor, and had much more direct contact with his 'victims', and had dealings with almost everyone in the island, accounts in part for the distinction drawn. I do not think it is the whole story. The hatred with which Donald Munro is regarded, a hundred years after his death, is due less to the fact of what he

did, than the style in which he did it. As Benjamin Franklin has pointed out, many men are capable of forgiving an injury, but no one ever forgave contempt.

Donald Munro, remarkably, never left Lewis, which, in these circumstances, one might have expected. Perhaps he was foolish enough to dream of a comeback. But his last years are still remembered and spoken of by our oldest people with quiet horror.

Island believers often talk, with the Apostle Paul, of those 'given over' to sin – some, such as those destroyed by the bottle, to the merciless consequence of a particular vice; but some (and you could still find one or two instances in most little communities, in a Lewis township or anywhere else) simply to sin itself. Munro declined steadily in standing, in prosperity, in abilities, in judgement, in faculties and in health; but his character, such as it had ever been, fell finally into some inchoate void, until there was just this diminished, broken figure, shuffling along Stornoway streets in what had once been smart and new clothing fitted to a far fuller figure, a wreck of an old man entirely consumed in defiance, and despair, and hate – and from whom you could only avert your eyes, inexplicably repelled.

For the first few years in the new, solitary role of a town solicitor and senior partner of Munro and Ross, he was sustained by quiet arrangement between them. Until it was exposed in evidence given to the Napier Commission, Munro and Ross frequently appeared on opposite sides in the same case; the first such curious outing was only a month after his dismissal by Sir James. When John Ross, William's son, returned to Stornoway, assorted Ross and Munro combinations made the town's courtroom or litigious life still more complicated.

For various reasons – vainglory, and perhaps an abiding fury at Matheson and the Estate (for which it is hard, in all conscience, entirely to blame him) and because, of course, he needed the money – Munro on several occasions became gamekeeper turned poacher, appearing in court on behalf of this or that crofter, or group of crofters, against the laird and his lackeys. In his prime, we should not forget that Donald Munro had been a competent enough lawyer, and in his early island career he had represented clients (such as that woman impregnated, abandoned and defamed by the frightful Dr MacAulay) against spectacular injustice, and with some success. But his prime was long gone by 1875 and, with repeated blunders and an increasing disdain for due process, established authority and at times reality itself, he became something of a liability to the business.

Grant records, in oppressive detail, the case of Seaforth's Well, in July 1877, when the new factor sought an interdict against certain tenants in Tong to stop then using a popular shortcut – the tide on the Cockle Ebb permitting – through Goathill Farm. 'MacKenzie's Well,' as Grant calls it, affords a cold and refreshing drink by the wayside, and may once have been prized for healing properties, though Dr Finlay MacLeod affords it no mention in his engaging little book on the island's averred tonic waters. As Grant records, the Tong crofters 'did not resist the interdict. In fact, some of those involved didn't even know they were being interdicted, although summonses were delivered to their homes by a Sheriff Officer.' They were, of course, in English. Then Munro suddenly hired a gig – he had no longer the means to retain one – and turned up at Tong, on the side of the angels. He was still lordly enough not actually to leave his transport, but to send the driver into this and that cottage to invite the potential client out; and by this means he won a number of signatures and marks to his apparent authority to act for them in court. (But at least one old man, a former soldier called Malcolm MacLeod, subsequently admitted he had not the least idea what he was signing, though he was adamant the paper had been quite blank.)

Whether Munro had a mandate from MacLeod, or not, MacLeod had soon an order from Munro: he was sent obediently round Tong houses to fetch all those summonses. Grant gives much diverting detail of the wary crofters, innocent old ladies and frail little widows in Tong who were gulled – or refused to be gulled – into any court case got up by Donald Munro, not least the sturdy fellow who, when assured that Munro only wanted to regain him 'the privilege of going to MacKenzie's Well', told him straight that he could do without the well, and did not want Munro to go to any trouble on his behalf.

Things fell apart when Munro loomed up at Stornoway Sheriff Court, brandishing a mandate and advising he now represented the crofters in question. Sheriff Spittal agreed to reopen the case; but, when it duly came on the agenda, he was startled to receive on the bench a new document – this a declaration signed, or at least marked, by some of Munro's claimed clients, adamant that they had never authorised the ex-chamberlain to represent them. (Apart from the embarrassing association, many recalled George Stephen's fate after he was prevailed upon to engage Munro and Ross in the recovery of an essentially trivial debt.)

As the five Tong folk were already in court, Spittal rallied from this surprise and announced he would now examine them on this matter: had they indeed given authority to Munro to act? At this point, Donald Munro rose and walked out. Spittal told him to wait. Munro said he could not wait. Spittal said he must return within 15 minutes. Munro told him it was not convenient – and so left, as the sheriff substitute turned a distinct purple.

Spittal waited half an hour. Then he closely examined, and took statements, from the five. When – later in the day's rounds of cases – Munro sauntered back in, Spittal commanded him – in open court – to be present at noon the next day. The ex-factor did not appear, nor was any reason supplied.

Munro no doubt knew – or had strong suspicion – of Spittal's part in his dismissal as procurator fiscal, to say nothing of his experience at the Bernera trial. There was no love lost here. Munro blankly defied a messenger sent to his offices at once to call him to court. He ignored another order to return the 'Interdict Process', still in his hands and essential for any lawyer who was to represent these Tong people. He was asked to tender proof of his mandate from them – and could not. Munro then announced he was dropping the case. But Spittal was firmly in this fight now, and subsequent 'interlocutors' to Edinburgh attest to the sheriff substitute's fury, with a faint tinge of bewilderment: statements that were 'glaringly and obviously false', 'not only unprofessional but thoroughly disgraceful'. Munro had strolled from court, against specific command, in 'grave contempt'. And Spittal therefore suspended him from appearing, at all, in Stornoway Sheriff Court, for a year.

He was brave and he was right. And Sheriff Principal Fordyce, in Dingwall, did refuse to hear any appeal from Munro – at least one presented by Munro himself: he had, Fordyce properly pointed out, been quite suspended as a solicitor, and was not allowed to act in court. Fordyce hoped there would be no further Munro attempt to regain 'the functions of a procurator as long as he is judicially disbarred from exercising them'.

But higher authorities would not support Spittal's stand. Munro still had one reliable ferret up his sleeve: William Ross Skinner, in Edinburgh, who lodged an appeal at the Court of Session. They, incredibly, sided with Munro and against Sheriff Substitute Spittal, not because of the merits of the case (they deemed any 'critical survey' of the details to be 'undesirable') but because 'the circumstances were not such as to justify the Interlocutor of the Sheriff-Substitute'. One suspects these amounted to that grand old Edinburgh attitude: this was in the Outer Hebrides, and no one really cared.

So Donald Munro waddled on. There was a similar, subsequent tussle with the sheriff substitute, when Munro again claimed to represent a party in an action – a group of Lochs fishermen – and the evidence of his authority was again dubious; in an interesting detail, their boat was being sold for debt incurred to that Stornoway chandler, Charles Morrison, a juror in the trial of the Bernera Three. Again, Munro could not explain how he had come by the 'doubles' – the signed documents of his mandate – but Fordyce would not support Spittal in this dispute either, and the fishermen in any event soon dispensed with the ex-chamberlain's services, assuming they had ever commissioned him in the first place.

There are final murky stories. In a cynical alliance, Munro and Ross combined with Napier Campbell in a bid to prevent the young John Norrie Anderson from hanging out his shingle as a new solicitor in town; they did hold off the enterprise for a while, but Anderson's qualifications and right to practise were finally recognised by the Sheriff Court. Though whisky finally did for him what the intrigue of these three squalid characters could not, the firm he founded – Anderson, MacArthur and Co., Solicitors and Estate Agents – is in Stornoway business to this day.

And, after a very involved row over the administration of an Edinburgh trust fund – to the benefit of a Thomasina Munro, daughter of a first cousin of both Ross and the increasingly derelict ex-chamberlain – the old family threesome, including Skinner, were forced to hand over direct control of that money to the young lady, being now of age, and forgo its associated fees and goodies. A year or two later, around 1878 and in a still more obscure case, Munro and Skinner fell out entirely; the latter even setting Napier Campbell on his old mentor. 'After thirty years together,' Grant observes, 'the "mafia" was falling apart.' Munro and Ross were still in business, at least, when the Napier Commission hit Lewis – to judge by the maledictions against them from local crofters – but the old man by that point was probably past any useful work, and after this final embarrassment it can have been little more than a paper arrangement.

Munro may, around the mid 1880s, have sustained a stroke; or perhaps a degree of dementia now started to erode his thinking. The last two or three years leave us only anecdotal glimpses of a man little more than a derelict, living on capital, his gait reduced to a pathetic shuffle in worn-out shoes, snarling and mumbling as taunting boys danced about him, chanting again and again, without pity and without mercy, 'Cuir mi as an fhearan thu! Cuir mi as an fhearan thu! I'll have the land from you! I'll have the land from you!'

Mostly, what had been the Chamberlain of the Lews ignored it; now and again he wheeled on them, his stick lashing, his eyes in terrible fire, and he would bark at them in his raw strange Gaelic, 'Put your feet in a bag and walk . . .' – perhaps a tormented reference to his own mounting disability, as his heart failed and his chest glugged, and death fingered the more firmly his collar.

There was only Dr Charles MacRae there at the last, it would seem, a thick and creepy summer night, assuming he was there at all in time and that Munro did not die with no sound but his own breath in his ears and flickers on the wall for company, gurgling to eternity by 'pulmonary congestion', congestive heart failure, which amounts to a slow, agonised drowning. But the maid had appeared, now with the soap and Lysol, the hot water and the towel; and Dr MacRae arose from almost the last duty concerning Donald Munro, this 12th of August 1890.

The cause of death would finally be certified by the other Stornoway practitioner, Dr Donald MacDonald, a native of Garrabost who had begun his working life as a joiner: he was never a well man and rather difficult to get on with. It may be that, as a matter of good practice, Dr MacRae and Dr MacDonald routinely certified the demise of one another's patients, or that MacRae was simply unavailable when an old foe turned up demanding some doctor's line for the registrar.

There was, to widespread surprise, no significant estate either – days later when what had to be done had been done, and the affairs could be checked – indeed, none at all.

The one mystery is the house at 24 Lewis Street, which is still there, and little changed, and now half of a local accountancy business; for Munro's sister Eliza duly came to live in it, and was finally buried beside him in 1909 – and found the necessary, too, to erect a smart headstone, in pink granite, recording both their names in due time and his only as 'Donald Munro, Solicitor'. It is probable that at some point he had put the house in her name, and that he kept all the money he owned in cash and close to hand, and that his sister had her hands on it and the chest of gold safely away before any lawyer had a whiff of it. If there was a will, it was never found, and quiet concealment of a pot of money was a reasonable precaution – William Ross being near kin to Munro and from what we know of his character. Perhaps Munro set up some other wheeze; perhaps Ross found the loot (and any will) before Eliza did. Even today, there are still very old island people who loathe lawyers and loathe banks even more, and who die with prodigious sums of cash in a trunk or up a chimney or under the bed – there have been instances in my own family, and there was a sensational one in Harris as recently as July 1995. Thus, even in death, Donald Munro could somehow confuse, trouble and defile.

A day or two later, someone appeared before the local registrar to record the demise – an old man himself, a hard face that had once been blankly handsome, a powerful fellow about Stornoway. He had little to say. He supplied each detail as it was sought; he handed over the slip from Dr MacDonald, the certificate of death. Only when he was asked how he should be described as the 'Informant' did William Ross – near relative of Donald Munro, his protégé, and for decades his partner – momentarily hesitate.

'Neighbour,' said William Ross, after cold calculation.

He did not attend the funeral. No one came to the funeral of Donald Munro, save the men paid to convoy the remains to the Sandwick burial ground, and without ceremony to bury them. It is said that they bantered as they attended to the final business, shovels of soil and gravel thudding on to the cheap deal box – 'Pile it on, lads, for many a clod he piled on others . . .'

Weeks and months passed; the earth settled; below, boards softened and gave way. And the worms and the crevice-creatures moved in, for they had things to do.

Maps

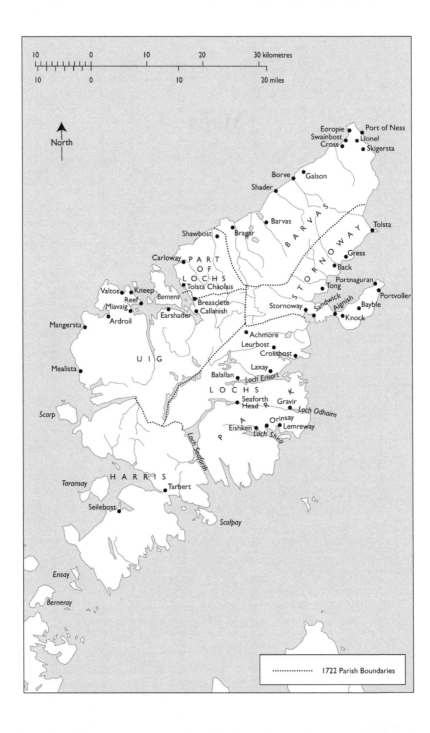

North

10   0   10   20   30 kilometres

10   0   10   20 miles

Eoropie   Port of Ness
Swainbost   Lionel
Cross   Skigersta

Borve   Galson
Shader

BARVAS

Barvas   Tolsta

Shawbost   Bragar   STORNOWAY

Carloway   PART   Gress
OF   Back
LOCHS
Tolsta Chaolais   Tong   Portnaguran
Valtos   Kneep   Stornoway   Sandwick   Portvoller
Reef   Bernera   Aignish   Bayble
Miavaig   Breasclete   Knock
Ardroil   Earshader   Callanish

Mangersta

UIG   Achmore
Leurbost
Crossbost

Mealista   Laxay
Balallan   Loch Erisort

LOCHS   K
Seaforth   Gravir
Head   R   Loch Odhairn
Scarp   A   Orinsay
P   Eishken   Lemreway
Loch Shell

Loch Seaforth

HARRIS
Taransay

Tarbert
Seilebost

Scalpay

Ensay

Berneray

.... 1722 Parish Boundaries

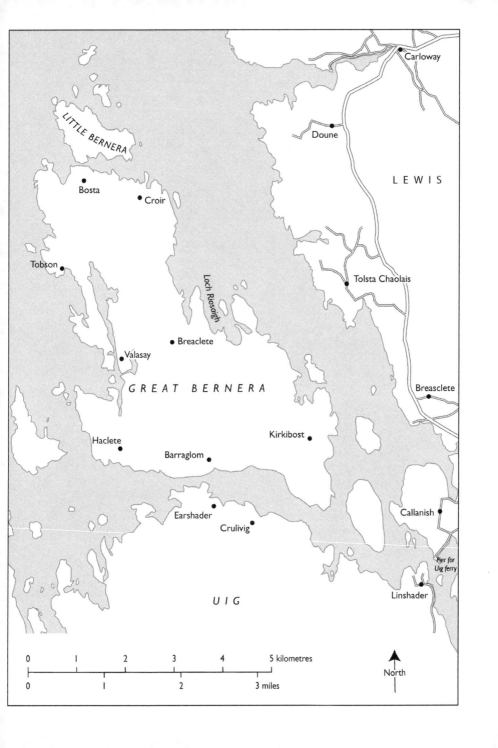

Sources

The fullest account to date of Donald Munro's dark overlordship of Lewis is James Shaw Grant's 1992 study, *A Shilling For Your Scowl: The History of a Scottish Legal Mafia*. Unfortunately it is far from Grant's best book; born in 1910, he was already in his eighties, and it has a meandering, scatter-brained character with at times chaotic organisation. It would have been readily improved by some firm editing, a better, more interesting cover and far less misleading subtitle. It has a strong emotional edge which is only explained in the last pages. The dearest friend of Grant's boyhood, his cousin Stephen M. MacLean, a gifted young lawyer, was a great-grandson of George and Catherine Stephen, and first proposed a book about the man who had ruined his forebears on the eve of his death, still only 36, shortly after the Second World War – yet another victim of the tuberculosis that then so blighted Lewis. In stark irony, the MacLean family home was then 24 Lewis Street – formerly Donald Munro's home – and Stephen MacLean not only died in the same house as the loathed chamberlain, but almost certainly in the same room.

Grant, whose father William founded the *Stornoway Gazette* in 1917 and who suddenly inherited the concern when still a very young man, owned and edited the paper for many years and served besides in some important public positions. He was a gifted storyteller and capable of far better work than *A Shilling For Your Scowl*; his best book may be his 1977 study of his region and its people, *Highland Villages*. He also wrote engaging plays and short stories. Early outings in the regular 'In Search of Lewis' column he wrote for the *Stornoway Gazette* were collated in four successive, privately published anthologies; and these have also been an important source here: oddly, they contain, here and there, some striking material on Donald Munro which does not feature in his 1992 history.

Grant apart, the other significant examinations of Donald Munro and his fall have been by I.M.M. MacPhail in *The Crofters' War* (1989) and Joni Buchanan, in her 1996 book *The Lewis Land Struggle – Na Gaisgich*, the first bravely to challenge the prevailing view of general Matheson benevolence.

There is still no really good one-volume history of the Isle of Lewis: Donald MacDonald's 1978 book, *Lewis: A History of the Island* is engaging and important, but the organisation is thematic rather than chronological and the Tolsta-born headmaster was no stylist. Frank Thompson's *Harris and Lewis*, which has appeared in several editions, remains a very clear and accessible outline of the landscape, character and economy of the Long Island. The best book ever written about the Hebrides generally remains W.H. Murray's 1973 study, *The Islands of Western Scotland*. On the wider history of crofting and the Highland land-struggle, James Hunter is now the acknowledged authority and *The Making of the Crofting Community* is the standard work, though more popular and beautifully illustrated Hunter works for Mainstream Ltd. in Edinburgh have been widely read and of great influence.

The original Stornoway Town Hall – which also housed the town's library and all the records of the Lewis Estate – was destroyed in a catastrophic 1918 fire while occupied by the Admiralty, fortunately without loss of life. Apart from the anguish of historians, the destruction of an irreplaceable archive and the loss, for instance, of all croft-boundary records still complicates island life today, as any Stornoway solicitor can attest. James Shaw Grant amassed a considerable collection of old papers and information, and these were bequeathed at his death in 1999 to Stornoway Public Library; but they fill entire suitcases and have not yet been catalogued or made publicly available – a sad reflection on an important but ill-resourced facility shamefully neglected by the local authority. The Angus MacLeod Archive – amassed privately, over the years, by that remarkable son of Calbost – has by contrast been meticulously organised and is available to scholars and the general public at the Ravenspoint Centre, Kershader; it is an especially important source for the history and culture of Park, that tract of Lewis most blighted by her lairds.

While the authorship of that anonymous 1874 pamphlet about the trial of the 'Bernera Three' cannot now be definitively established, I have followed the modern consensus and attributed it to Daniel Lewis MacKinlay.

Donald Munro's home at 24 Lewis Street is now occupied as offices by a local accountancy and financial-consultancy concern, and is not open to the public. The site where the offices of Munro and Ross stood was cleared for a new art deco cinema, The Playhouse, in 1934; but it did not long survive the advent of colour television and closed finally in 1979. It now serves as the clubhouse of the Royal British Legion. Carn House, where the chamberlain's offices were to be found, was demolished over half a century ago. A plaque mounted in the adjacent Town Hall gable (where the line of the Carn House gable can still just be discerned) commemorates the birthplace of Colin MacKenzie, Surveyor-General of India; a similar tablet on the Francis Street elevation of the Martin's Memorial Church of Scotland (formerly 'Stornoway Free English') marks the nativity of Alexander MacKenzie the explorer.

The Bernera triumph and the fall of Donald Munro inspired much Gaelic verse; Joni Buchanan includes several examples. The outstanding piece is *Spiorad a' Charthannais*, 'Spirit of Charity', by the Earshader bard Iain Mac a' Ghobhainn, John Smith (1846–81). He was the illegitimate son of the local tacksman, a gifted bard and a highly educated man; only ill-health – he was long stalked by tuberculosis – precluded completion of medical studies at the University of Edinburgh. The technical excellence of *Spiorad a' Charthannais* is undoubted, and the stanzas I have quoted dealing directly with Donald Munro still solemnise, but the poem is extremely long and its religious reflections (the Free Church was then trying both to engineer a contentious marriage with the United Presbyterians and, absurdly, prevent the final abolition of patronage) have a self-righteous, huggy-kissy air that did not reflect general Lewis sentiment at the time. Buchanan's book apart, the standard text is that found in *Bardachd Leodhais*, reissued as an attractive Acair Ltd paperback in 1998.

Donald Munro's infamous chair passed through successive procurators fiscal – latterly a succession of MacKenzies – and is now owned proudly by Colin Scott MacKenzie, retired in Stornoway and who has had a discreet plaque attached beneath the seat to outline its provenance. The chair was, alas, overzealously restored by a supposed professional some years ago, quite losing its antique patina.

A Short History of Scotland, P. Hume Brown, new revised edition by H.W. Meikle, Oliver and Boyd Ltd, Edinburgh, 1955. The first edition of what for many years was the standard Scottish history text in our schools was published in 1908.

The Lewis Land Struggle – Na Gaisgich, Joni Buchanan, Acair Ltd, Stornoway, 1996. A most readable, passionate and angry account, 'written unashamedly from the crofters' point of view'. A daughter of Uig, Isle of Lewis, Ms Buchanan is the wife of Brian Wilson, founder of the *West Highland Free Press* and a noted Labour politician whose contribution to modern Highland affairs has been incalculable.

Land for the People? – The British Government and the Scottish Highlands, c.1880–1925, Ewen A. Cameron, Tuckwell Press Ltd, East Linton, 1996. A 'Scottish Historical Review' monograph, though covering a later period than the terrain of this book.

Skye, Derek Cooper, Queen Anne Press/MacDonald & Co. (Publishers) Ltd, London, 1989. The most recent edition of this 1970 classic gazetteer: Cooper, raised in England of Skye and Lewis parentage, is best known as a highly influential writer and broadcaster on food.

The Glens of Silence – Landscapes of the Highland Clearances, David Craig and David Paterson, Birlinn Ltd, Edinburgh, 2004. There are still those who deny the scale or even the fact of the Clearances. Craig's text and Paterson's sobering photographs of ruined, deserted community upon ruined deserted community are ample rebuke.

The Castles of the Lews, Peter Cunningham, Acair Ltd, Stornoway, 2008. A beautifully produced, amply illustrated volume about the castles of Stornoway. Born in 1918 and an early pupil of Jordanhill College School – half a century before myself – W.A.J. 'Peter' Cunningham is one of its most distinguished former pupils. He settled in Stornoway as a customs officer after the Second World War, married a Carloway girl and has been a pillar of the community ever since, universally respected for his beautiful manners, lightly borne intellect and quiet Christian carriage. In his tenth decade he is still the globally recognised authority on the bird-life of the Outer Hebrides and an active lecturer and public figure, and no one knows more about the flora and fauna of these islands. Mr Cunningham's love and knowledge of the Lews Castle policies (which remind me, too, of the Jordanhill woods) can excuse his somewhat lenient treatment of Sir James Matheson, who planted them.

The Church in Victorian Scotland 1843–1874, Andrew L. Drummond and James Bulloch, The Saint Andrew Press, Edinburgh, 1975. The second of an authoritative, masterly trilogy on the history of Scottish faith since 1689, this book is particularly important for its study of poor relief and education after the Disruption and reflects the keen, intelligent social conscience of both authors, who were distinguished parish ministers.

West Highland Steamers, C.L.D. Duckworth and G.E. Langmuir; Brown, Son & Ferguson Ltd, Glasgow, 1987. The fourth edition of a classic work, which first appeared in 1935.

Royal Dukes, Roger Fulford, William Collins Sons & Co. Ltd, London, 1973. A new and revised edition of Fulford's 1933 work – still the most delicious study of the seven well-meaning but generally ridiculous sons of George III who survived to adulthood.

Highland Villages, James Shaw Grant, Robert Hale Ltd, London, 1977. An engaging, detailed account of his country and probably Grant's finest book.

The Hub of my Universe (1982), *Surprise Island* (1983), *The Gaelic Vikings* (1984), *Stornoway and the Lews* (1985) – James Shaw Grant, James Thin Ltd, Edinburgh, in collaboration with the author. These collections of Grant columns from the *Stornoway Gazette* are rich in anecdote and colour, and their gentle conversational style is most engaging. Grant maintained his 'In Search of Lewis' column, more and more infrequently, till the year of his death – the last, in January 1999, was about the Harris casualties of the *Iolaire* disaster – but the glory had departed.

Discovering Lewis and Harris, James Shaw Grant, John Donald Publishers Ltd, Edinburgh, 1987. A first-class guide to his native island for the intelligent visitor, disciplined, well illustrated and most informative.

A Shilling For Your Scowl, James Shaw Grant, Acair Ltd, Stornoway, 1992. An important but woefully mispublished book, at a time when Acair Ltd were not nearly as well led or resourced as they are now.

Mightier than a Lord – The Highland Crofters' Struggle for the Land, Iain Fraser Grigor, Acair Ltd, Stornoway, 1979. A tight and accessible study, early and influential.

'Back to the Wind, Front to the Sun' – The Traditional Croft House, Caroline Hirst (based on the collections of the late Angus MacLeod of Calbost), The Islands Books Trust, Isle of Lewis, 2005. The best study to date of the tradition Hebridean black-house, and the economy it exemplified.

The Making of the Crofting Community, James Hunter, John Donald Ltd, Edinburgh, 1976. The standard work.

Skye – The Island, James Hunter and Cailean MacLean, Mainstream Publishing Company (Edinburgh) Ltd, 1986. An elegant but important coffee-table book; Hunter's reflections and MacLean's photographs are a mighty combination. Mac-Lean, incidentally, is a nephew of Sorley MacLean, and no mean writer on his own account.

Scottish Highlanders – A People and their Place, James Hunter and Cailean MacLean, Mainstream Publishing Company (Edinburgh) Ltd, 1992.

The Soap Man – Lewis, Harris and Lord Leverhulme, Roger Hutchinson, Birlinn Ltd, Edinburgh, 2003. I know of no better account of Lewis history for the decades following this book, and Hutchinson is a sparkling wordsmith whose commitment to working-class politics adds a strong moral edge. It is a useful corrective to Nigel Nicolson's 1960 study, below, though Hutchinson would be the first to acknowledge his debt to the substantial scholarship on West Highland and land-struggle history since Nicolson's work.

St Columba's Church at Aignish (The Church of the Ui) – A Lewis Church in its Historical Setting, Bill Lawson, Bill Lawson Publications, Northton, Isle of Harris, 1991. An early, brilliant outing in a succession of deceptively thin little books, packed with information and dripping with authority and the gentle Lawson humour.

Harris in History and Legend, Bill Lawson, Birlinn Ltd, Edinburgh, 2002. The best book about Harris I know, written cleverly as a ramble around her townships and anchoring this authoritative history firmly in her landscape. The material about the Harris Clearances has not lost its power to shock. Lawson uses the Gaelic place names, as standard, in all his books.

The Clearances in Lewis – Truth or Myth?, Bill Lawson, The Islands Books Trust, 2006. Delivered originally as the third Angus MacLeod Memorial Lecture at Pairc School, Gravir, in October 2006, Lawson's reflections caused quite a storm and much fizzing correspondence. Unfortunately, the Lawson analysis is dispassionate, the documentation meticulous and the logic impeccable.

Lewis – The West Coast – in History and Legend, Bill Lawson, Birlinn Ltd, Edinburgh, 2008. 'It always surprises me,' writes Lawson, 'that so little is made of the action of the

Bearnaraigh men, which achieved its aim, compared with the Pairc Deer Raid, Aignis Riot etc., which had little practical effect at the time, however much they may have influenced public opinion in the longer term.'

The Prince in the Heather – The Story of Bonnie Prince Charlie's Escape, Eric Linklater, Hodder & Stoughton Ltd, London, 1965. A classic work, if something of a pot-boiler for a celebrated Scots novelist in the evening of his career, and under a curious commercial restraint – the book was sponsored by the Drambuie liqueur company, and Linklater (one can imagine the quiet shudder) had solemnly to reinforce their claim that Charles Edward Stuart found time to hand over the recipe while on the run for his life.

Aspects of the Religious History of Lewis up to the Disruption of 1843, Murdo Macaulay, Stornoway Gazette Ltd, 1985. An important, much underestimated book by perhaps the island's most influential post-war minister. Unfortunately only a few hundred copies were printed.

Tales and Traditions of the Lews – Collected by Dr MacDonald of Gisla, Donald MacDonald, Birlinn Ltd, Edinburgh, 2004. This is a modern paperback edition of a privately and indeed posthumously published work, assembled from assorted notes and essays by the Lewis GP's widow after his death in 1961. Born in Stornoway in 1891, of Uig and Shawbost stock, 'Dolly Doctor' had the great good fortune in 1923 to win the hand of Lord Leverhulme's niece in marriage. The last laird of all Lewis made a present of the Uig estate to the happy couple. As you do. These articles are engaging and interesting, though few could be dignified as scholarship and some – 'Dr MacDonald's Speech on Opening a Sale of Work in Aid of St Peter's Church Funds', which sounds less like a chapter heading than an obscure Pre-Raphaelite painting – are simply silly.

Dolly Doctor – Pictures of Bygone Island Life, photographs by Dr Donald MacDonald, foreword by John Randall, biographical introduction by Peter Cunningham, The Islands Books Trust, 2010. Peter Cunningham long accompanied Dr MacDonald as his projectionist on a protracted fund-raising tour for a proposed museum of island folklore, and many of the images in this engaging little volume are important social documentary. (And, well into his nineties, Mr Cunningham is still driving the length and breadth of Lewis and still projecting them, these days by far more amenable technology.) That said, Randall's warning that Dr MacDonald 'was not a particularly gifted photographer' is in many instances evidently the understatement of 2010.

Lewis: A History of the Island, Donald MacDonald, Gordon Wright Publishing Ltd, Edinburgh, 1978. There has been a recent edition by Acair Ltd, Stornoway. Born in North Tolsta in 1904, MacDonald – who should not be confused with the Uig physician above – had a distinguished career, but never again made permanent home on his native island. A subsequent, 1984, history of his own community, *The Tolsta Townships* – which clamours for a reprint – is perhaps a still more important book.

It Must Be Stornoway – The Story of Stornoway Pier and Harbour Commission 1865 to 2004, Catherine Mackay, Argyll Publishing, Glendaruel, 2008. An immaculately researched and magnificently illustrated book, compromised only by the dreary title. There is a deliciously fly foreword by Alexander Matheson.

The Prophecies of the Brahan Seer, Alexander MacKenzie, The Sutherland Press, Golspie, third revised edition with footnotes, maps, illustrations and a foreword by Terence Robertson Hart, 1976. This reheated 1970s' paperback of MacKenzie's original 1877 work is a pleasant serving of spooky, fireside Highland tosh. No serious historian believes the 'Brahan Seer' ever existed.

Diary 1851, – John Munro MacKenzie, Chamberlain of the Lews, John Munro Mac-Kenzie, with foreword and biographical introduction by James Shaw Grant, Acair Ltd, Stornoway, 1994. The discipline of Grant's essay here – it is in striking contrast to his book about Donald Munro and chums – is impressive. When read in its entirety, Munro's predecessor emerges as a sympathetic figure in a near-impossible position.

Report of the Trial of the So-Called Bernera Rioters At Stornoway, On The 17th and 18th July 1874, With Address To The Jury By The Agent For The Defence And Charge By The Sheriff; anonymous; attrib. Daniel Lewis MacKinlay; William Blackwood & Sons, Edinburgh, 1874. A lending-copy – more accurately, a photocopy – is available from Stornoway Public Library. An original pamphlet is on display at Museum nan Eilean, Francis Street, Stornoway.

A MacDonald for the Prince, Alasdair MacLean, Acair Ltd, Stornoway, 1982; revised edition 1990. This is an excellent account of Charles Edward Stuart's flight through the Hebrides, if compromised by the dire cover and quite misleading blurb typical of too many Acair books in the period. Dr MacLean, general practitioner in South Uist, was yet another of that talented family from Osgaig, Raasay: his three brothers were John, headmaster of Oban High School, Sorley – who needs no introduction – and Calum, the much-loved folklorist for the School of Scottish Studies, who died a relatively young man.

An Leabhar Mor – The Great Book of Gaelic, edited by Malcolm MacLean and Theo Dorgan, 2002 (Canongate Books, Edinburgh), slightly revised edition by The O'Brien Press Ltd, Dublin, 2008. A desperately worthy slab of a tome, notionally of Scottish and Irish Gaelic verse against much contemporary art, but heavily front-loaded to the last half-century. (After all, the editors regularly meet those folk at parties.) I have drawn on its translated excerpt of John Smith's glorious diatribe, 'Spiorad a Charthannais', though with a little tweaking of my own, on the cheerful basis that the more translations the merrier.

The Norse Mills of Lewis, Finlay MacLeod, with drawings by John Love, Acair Ltd, Stornoway, 2009. An identical Gaelic edition was also published. Though notorious for his abrasive views on Highland Presbyterianism, Dr MacLeod is a distinguished writer and scholar: this is a first-class study, and extraordinarily accessible, both for children and adults.

Togail Tir – Marking Time – The Maps of the Western Isles, edited by Finlay MacLeod, Acair Ltd and An Lanntair Gallery, Stornoway, 1989. A very fine book.

Banner In The West – A Spiritual History of Lewis and Harris, John MacLeod, Birlinn Ltd, Edinburgh, 2008.

Highlanders – A History of the Gaels, John MacLeod, Hodder & Stoughton Ltd, London, 1996.

A Brief Record of the Church in Uig (Lewis) Up to the Union of 1929, John MacLeod OBE DL MA, 2001. A posthumously published work by an eminent Lewis educationist, though with the clunking title that too often marks island outings in church history and very little reference to Bernera. John MacLeod (1928–1998) would no doubt have addressed these issues had he been spared. His scholarship, though, is meticulous.

Charles Edward Stuart – A Tragedy In Many Acts, Frank McLynn, Routledge, London, 1988. There have been many, many biographies of the 'Bonnie Prince'; McLynn's sober, scholarly and splendidly written life will never be equalled.

The Crofter's War, I.M.M. MacPhail, Acair Ltd, Stornoway, 1989. As Bill Lawson has observed, this book has been inexplicably undervalued: it is one of the outstanding texts, with MacPhail's characteristic discipline and concision. Brought up in Dumbarton, both of his parents were natives of Lewis. Of a generation when our finest minds were as apt as not to go in for schoolteaching, MacPhail's interests and aptitudes – notably his facility with languages – were formidable. He also had a distinguished and very brave war, volunteering for the nerve-shredding duties of bomb disposal. He crowned his career as Principal Teacher of History in Clydebank High School, and died in 1990. *The Clydebank Blitz* (1974) remains MacPhail's best-known work.

The Islands of Western Scotland – The Inner and Outer Hebrides, W.H. Murray, Eyre Methuen, London, 1973. Part of Eyre Methuen's 'Regions of Britain' series, this outstanding book reflects the interests and authority of a man best remembered as a great Scottish mountaineer.

Lord of the Isles, Nigel Nicolson, Weidenfeld and Nicolson, London, 1960; paperback edition by Acair Ltd, Stornoway, 2000. Nicolson's study of Lord Leverhulme's ill-fated endeavours on the Long Island is sometimes (and unjustly) mocked as unduly sympathetic; but it is important to have varied perspectives, and he conducted much research – notably face-to-face interviews on the ground with men who knew Leverhulme well; and in some instances had fought him – that could not be done now. The Acair edition is cheapened by another ghastly cover.

Glimpses of Stornoway – A light covering of history in words and pictures from Viking times to the 1950s, edited and compiled by Fred Silver, Intermedia Services, 2009, with financial support by the Stornoway Trust and the Stornoway Amenity Trust and a foreword by Alexander Matheson, Lord Lieutenant of the Western Isles. A magnificent book.

Memorial Inscriptions in Old Sandwick Cemetery, Stornoway, Stornoway Historical Society Publications, Stornoway, 1997, two volumes. A remarkably addictive read.

Restoration of the Matheson Monument – Stornoway – Outer Hebrides, Stornoway Amenity Trust and Stornoway Trust, no author, photographs by Fred Silver, Tony Robson and John MacQueen, Intermedia Services, 2005. I am sorry the Stornoway Trust and Stornoway Amenity Trust did not dynamite the memorial. I would have.

Ravens and Black Rain – The Story of Highland Second Sight, Elizabeth Sutherland, Constable and Company Ltd, London, 1985. This includes a comprehensive outline of MacKenzie history, the 'Fall of the House of Seaforth' and entire demolition of the 'Brahan Seer' myth.

An Introduction to Gaelic Poetry, Derick Thomson, Victor Gollancz Ltd, London, 1977. One of our greatest Gaelic poets himself, Professor Thomson's discussion of John Smith and *Spiroad a' Charthannais* is well worth reading.

Harris and Lewis – Outer Hebrides, Francis Thompson, David & Charles Ltd, Newton Abbott, 1968; revised paperback edition 1973; revised hardback edition, 1987.

Our Holy Redeemer – Ar Fear-Saoraidh Naomh – Stornoway, Francis Thompson, 2007. A pleasant little booklet, well illustrated, to mark the dedication of a new building for the town's Roman Catholic congregation; but the portrait of Sheriff Substitute Andrew Lothian MacDonald is far too lenient.

'Toss Of A Coin Led To Bernera Riot', Anne M. Whitaker, *Eilean An Fhraoich* (the *Stornoway Gazette* annual magazine, 1974.) Whitaker's interview with the 89-year-old Norman MacDonald, a son of *Aonghas a' Phriosan*, is enjoyable and diverting, though Mr MacDonald's account should be treated with caution.

Index

1st Company, Ross-shire Artillery Volunteers, commanded by Donald Munro 150, 153, 218, 236, 241–242
72nd Highland Regiment (Seaforth Highlanders) 35, 40, 44
78th Regiment (Seaforth's) 117
1745 Jacobite Rising 13, 20 *et seq*, 48, 55

A' Bheinn Mhor (Shawbost) 44
Aberdeen 31, 146, 200; Gaelic and Highland societies, 207; Aberdeenshire, 165
Achanalt 35
Achany estate 101
Achmore 6, 217, 224, 225
agricultural failure on Lewis in 1830s 102
Aignish 63; Mary Carn MacKenzie funeral at, 67–69; 129, 151, 198; Major Duncan Matheson erects family tomb, 258
Aignish Riot, 1889 258
Alberta 137
Alexander, James, tenant-farmer at Aignish 129, 198
Alexandra, Queen, visit to Stornoway, 1902 257
Aline 192, 210
Am Bathadh Mor 153–154
Amity, harbour hulk 181, 191
Amity House 34
America, United States of 60, 61, 114, 206
Amhuinnsuidhe 210
Anderson, Alexander, procurator fiscal 51
Anderson, John Norrie 90, 198; wins right to practise law in Stornoway, 264
Anderson, MacArthur & Co. 264
Anderson, William 199
apartheid 128
Applecross 149
Arbroath 146
Ardhasaig 210
Ardmeanish 88
Ardroil 51, 191, 259
Ardross 232
Ardrossan 112
Argyll, Marquis of 34
Arisaig 22, 28
Arnish 25–27, 54, 59, 178, 183
Arnol 8, 223
Arrow, schooner, and legal case 198–200; 255
Ashburton constituency 101
Assaye, battle of (1803) 117
Assynt 19
Auldearn, battle of (1645), heavy Lewis losses in 31; 106

Australia 63, 166, 203, 204, 206
Avoch 61
Ayr 34; Ayrshire constituency, 190

Back 57, 79, 82, 150–151; hounding of fishermen after MacIver bankruptcy, 161–165; overcrowding after Great War, 259
Bagh Ciarach 30
Bain, Peter, customs officer 213, 215, 216; evidence at trial of 'Bernera Three', 245–246
Ballalan 79
Ballantrushal 6
'Balmoralism' 206
Balnacille 35, 38
Baltic Sea 199
banknotes issue in Stornoway 43
Bannatyne Manuscript 37
Barbados 36, 38, 91
Baremsevay 93
Barkin Islands 39
Barlow, emigrant ship 136
Barra 66, 104, 133–134, 149
Barra Head 65
Barraglom 209
Barret, James 34
Barvas 1, 7, 8, 29, 41, 51, 79, 111, 113, 223
Barvas (Saskatchewan) 136
Bayble 56, 129
Bayhead 65; clearance of for Manor Farm 108; 130, 178
Beaton, John, crofter near Goathill 197–198
Beaverbrook, Max Aitken, 1st Baron Begnigary 64
Beinn a' Bhuna 224
Beinn a' Chualein ('Cualein-hill') 209, 239, 243
Belfast 59
Benbecula, Isle of 22
Bernadotte, Marshall 61
Bernera, Great 1, 51, 82, 138; confrontation with Donald Munro, 206, 208 *et seq*; description of, 208–209; and Beinn a' Chualein grazings, 209; and stripped of Earshader grazings, 211–212; summonses of eviction, 212–213; visit of sheriff officer and party, 213–217; of Donald Munro, 217–218; of Superintendent Cameron, 218–220; march of Bernera men on Stornoway, 223–228; Matheson's broken promises, 230; piety and discipline of, 233; 237; happy ending for, 258–259
Bernera, Little 161, 208
'Bernera Riot' 5, 212; description of, 220–222; 228, 251, 258

None Dare Oppose